Joyce's Modernist Allegory

Joyce's Modernist Allegory
U*LYSSES* AND THE H*ISTORY OF THE* N*OVEL*

Stephen Sicari

University of South Carolina Press

UNIVERSITY OF SOUTH CAROLINA *BICENTENNIAL*

© 2001 University of South Carolina

Published in Columbia, South Carolina, by the
University of South Carolina Press

Manufactured in the United States of America

05 04 03 02 01 5 4 3 2 1

Library of Congress Cataloging-in-Publication Data

Sicari, Stephen.
   Joyce's modernist allegory : Ulysses and the history of the novel / Stephen Sicari.
   p. cm.
   Includes bibliographical references (p.) and index.
   ISBN 1-57003-383-8 (cloth : alk. paper)
   1. Joyce, James, 1882–1941. Ulysses. 2. Joyce, James, 1882–1941—
Knowledge—Literature. 3. Fiction—History and criticism—Theory, etc.
4. Dante Alighieri, 1265–1321—Influence. 5. English fiction—
Italian influences. 6. Modernism (Literature)—Ireland. 7. Allegory. I. Title.
PR6019.O9 U698 2001
823'.912—dc21
                                                           00-012029

To Mae, who is always there for us;
to Mark and Anna, who continue to grow in charm and virtue;
and, this time, especially to Sarah and Rebekah,
the newest delights in our life

Contents

Preface ix
"O, rocks! Tell us in plain words"

List of Abbreviations xvii

Introduction
Rereading *Ulysses* 1
Naturalistic Novel Becomes Modernist Allegory

Chapter One
The Novel as Death 30
The Limits of Naturalism

Chapter Two
The Novel as Humanist 64
From Naturalism to Abstraction

Chapter Three
The Novel as Truth 96
The Problem of Languge in *Ulysses*

Chapter Four
The Novel as *Nostos* 142
Family Romance Becomes Epic

Chapter Five
The Novel as Allegory 165
Bloom as Christian Hero

Conclusion
Allegory and High Modernism 193

Notes 223

Works Cited 241

Index 245

Preface
"O, rocks! Tell us in plain words"

In *The Myth of the Modern,* Perry Meisel asks an important question: "If *Ulysses,* as Eliot claims, is a mythic replication of *The Odyssey,* why, then, is the book not called *Odysseus*?" (Meisel, 145). We are so used to calling this novel by its name that we are hard-pressed to imagine anything else ever sounding right to our ears, but questioning the reason for the choice of the Latin name rather than the Greek one might yield some fruit. For Meisel, it is Joyce's way of indicating his distance from the original story, a gap between modernity and the lost origin that Joyce thus indicates as unpassable. Christine van Boheemen similarly argues that the Latin name emphasizes distance: "The title as sign functions as an epitaph, marking the last remains of the *Odyssey.* In giving his novel the title *Ulysses,* Joyce incorporated Homer into his fiction as the paradoxical presence of a defunct absence" (van Boheemen, 145). John S. Rickard considers the Latin title Joyce's way of suggesting that his "book is a palimpsest . . . in which we read an ambiguous modern ending inscribed over layers of older, 'closed' texts" (Rickard, 170). These three critics understand Joyce's title to indicate a distance and difference both from the original text and from the origin itself, a way of suggesting that the modern epic will not take seriously the prospects of a return home but instead will celebrate an openness toward life and experience. They see the title as Joyce's way of distancing himself from the nostalgia that keeps us locked in a backward-looking stance, mourning over a lost origin that is not to be recuperated.

But Joyce's choice of the Latin might indicate instead the persistence of the attempt to return home in and through writing and his decision to work within the revered tradition of what W. B. Stanford calls "the Ulysses theme." The title may not announce his ironic modernity but instead may establish the permanence of the theme of return. As Wallace Stevens, who as we shall see shares certain sympathies and aims with Joyce, says in *Notes toward a Supreme Fiction,* "From this the poem springs: that we live in a place / That is not our own and, much more, not ourselves / And hard it is in spite of blazoned days" (Stevens, 383). For Stevens, all great poetry is inspired by our alienation from the planet on which we have our being. The "Supreme Fiction" is that we belong on this earth and that it is our home. Every age writes the story anew, and *Ulysses* is Joyce's attempt to write such a fiction. It is not a distance from the original story but the persistence of the original theme of writing that inspires Joyce's choice. It is not abandonment of the theme but its renewal that interests Joyce.

I especially appreciate Meisel's point and agree that Joyce is keenly aware of his belatedness in relation to his original. Joyce knows he is late on the stage of literary history and that there have been many other efforts to write the story of return. But that awareness does not have to end, as Meisel argues, in burlesque of the attempt to recuperate origins. What Joyce learns in his review of the many efforts to recuperate origins and return to a lost home is that these efforts no longer suffice, if they ever did suffice in the first place. Aware of his belated status, Joyce has become profoundly mistrustful of any lofty rhetoric or literary language that is used to present the theme in the modern era. There is undoubtedly plenty of burlesque and parody in *Ulysses*, but the novel is an attempt to find the right language for the return home that Meisel seems to despair of. *Ulysses* is not all burlesque, or constant burlesque, or aimlessly repeated burlesque of the writing that seeks to recuperate origins. The book is a series of stylistic experiments designed to try out, and discard, various kinds of literary language until the right one is found, until the language capable of presenting the way home is finally discovered.

Because Joyce is a keen student of Dante, it may not seem strained at all to wonder if the Latin name of this hero is meant to lead us to a serious consideration of Dante's Ulysses from canto 26 of *Inferno*. Such is my contention. At first this might suggest that Meisel is correct, that Joyce wants to warn us from becoming nostalgic and confined to a backward-looking regret toward a lost home, for Dante's hero refuses to go back to Ithaca but instead seeks new experience in a brave and reckless way. But Joyce is pointing us to Dante's Ulysses in the same way Dante himself kept coming back to that figure. Joyce's *Ulysses* is a sustained and profound meditation on the very same problem Dante presents in canto 26 of *Inferno* and meditates upon throughout the *Divina Commedia:* the potential for language to be used fraudulently and the extraordinary difficulty of finding the right language to complete the journey homeward, the journey toward a fundamental truth on which we can base our lives.

Both Joyce and Dante are chiefly concerned with seeking a language with which to indicate something true, and Ulysses is the figure who causes Dante great anxiety because he uses language to mislead his audience into sin. In fact, Dante frequently makes note of Ulysses and his fate throughout the *Divina Commedia,* beginning in the opening canto when Dante looks back to the wood as one "who with labouring breath has escaped from the deep shore turns to the perilous waters" from which he had just escaped, unlike Ulysses who dies in a shipwreck in a storm at sea. In canto 8 of *Inferno* when the fallen angels who guard the city of Dis seek to separate Dante from his guide, they say to Virgil about Dante, "Let him return alone on his mad way and see if he knows it"— the "mad way" (*la folle strada*) being an anticipatory rhyme with Ulysses' own "mad flight" (*al folle volo*) as he sails beyond the pillars of Hercules. Most directly, in canto 27 of *Paradiso,* toward the end of his journey upward through the various spheres of heaven, Dante looks back upon Earth as a little threshing floor and notes "beyond Cadiz, the mad track of Ulysses." Ulysses is in a sense the frequent measure of Dante's own journey, a standard of sorts against which he can suggest the success of his poem as true speech against the failure of Ulysses' rhetoric as fraudulent counsel.

As Dante begins his approach to the eighth *bolgia* of the ninth circle of hell in canto 26 of *Inferno,* the pouch of simple fraud where the false counselors are punished, Dante explains his poetic approach to the subject of fraud: "I grieved then and grieve now anew when I turn my mind to what I saw, and more than I am wont I curb my powers lest they run where virtue does not guide them" (lines 19–22). He is careful to inform his reader that he will not use all his powers of speech as he describes Ulysses, because he wants to make sure that he does not commit the same sin in his great poem that Ulysses committed when he moved his hearers to follow him beyond "the narrow outlet where Hercules set up his landmarks so that men should not pass beyond" (lines 107–9). Dante will curb his poetic powers as he describes a man who does not place limits on his rhetorical powers, as a way for us to make a crucial distinction between a man who wants to lead us safely to truth and a man who wants to inspire in us a desire for experience that will end in our ruin. Both Ulysses and Dante, then, are poets, but the successful poet is the one who takes care not to mislead his reader. Dante is the poet we can trust because, in short, he is willing to suspend his rhetorical powers in the service of truth.

From the start Dante is careful to articulate the importance of poetry to this journey that ends with beatitude, especially in his choice of Virgil as guide through hell and up Mount Purgatory. When Dante expresses doubts and fears about the journey Virgil has invited him to begin, Virgil tells a story about three ladies in heaven, especially about Beatrice, who is the one who bade Virgil help Dante and the one who is promised to meet Dante at the summit of Purgatory. When Virgil finishes the narration,

Dante responds in a way that emphasizes the role of language in inspiring the dangerous journey: "O she compassionate that succoured me, and thou who of thy courtesy wast quick to obey the true words she spoke to thee! Thou hast so disposed my heart with desire for the journey by thy words that I have returned to my first intent" (*Inferno*, canto 2, lines 133–38). Virgil, as poet, was able to hear Beatrice's words as "true words" and was so able to relate those words to his listener that Dante now desires to begin the journey. Ulysses' false words inspire his hearers with desire too, but somehow the true poet is able to distinguish the true from the false and to relate that distinction so that a reader is inspired only by the true and not the fraudulent.

The *Divina Commedia* is in large part a sustained meditation upon language, especially upon poetic language, as one learns to make this crucial distinction between fraud and truth. Not only are the two chief protagonists of the first two canticles poets, but Dante comes in contact with many poets throughout his journey, in *Inferno* and especially in *Purgatorio* but, perhaps surprisingly and quite instructively, not in *Paradiso*. When he enters Limbo in canto 4 of *Inferno,* he meets Homer, Ovid, Horace, and Lucan, and along with Virgil, Dante is welcomed by them and made one of their company—which is quite an honor, to be sure, and a sign of Dante's confident evaluation of his own place in literary history. But such a welcoming is also a danger, for these five classical poets are, after all, condemned to hell, albeit a circle of hell that is pastoral, noble, and filled with learning and dignified conversation. Dante moves beyond these poets (while still accompanied by one of them), and in that moving past we see that poetry itself is not enough to ensure salvation.

There are not many poets in hell, and the most powerful speaker in all of hell, maybe in all of the *Divina Commedia,* may well be Ulysses. Poetry is found primarily in Limbo and in Purgatory—that is, in places not quite hellish and yet not yet filled with the truth and grace of heaven. Dante is brought along to the entrance of Purgatory by Sordello, and then for the last three terraces of the mountain he and Virgil are accompanied by Statius. Dante needs several poets, apparently, to guide him through Purgatory, which is where poetry is actually discussed, in detail and at length, on the terraces that purge gluttony and lust. It is as if to say that poetry, at its best, can bring one near the condition of purity from which one is accounted worthy of ascent to paradise but not fully back to that Edenic state. Poetry can bring you close, but it will get you stuck in gluttony or lust, where the delights sung about in poetry can become goals that distract and obtrude. As Dante meets and passes beyond the great poets of antiquity, so too he meets and surpasses the sensual poets that make up his immediate heritage, Guinicelli and Arnaut Daniel. Daniel may be the better craftsman, but Dante is on his way to see God! (You may bet that T. S. Eliot was aware of just such an irony in his tribute to Ezra Pound.) Poetry can guide you up as it instills a desire for things of beauty and joy, and it can be purged of its excess until it brings one through the flames of lust and into Eden.

So Dante does respect poetry and its powers but offers a powerful appraisal of its dangers as well as its strengths, especially its inadequacies. At the opening of *Purgatorio,* Dante invokes Calliope and asks for poetry to be raised from the dead, an analogous resurrection for poetic language to his own rebirth from the horrors of hell. We rise through Purgatory with the aid of great poetry, epic poetry, but we will not need poets in heaven. Those truths call for a different kind of language. Joyce learns from Dante that language, and especially poetic language, must be chastened and purged and ultimately rejected if one is to reach highest truths.

I wish to suggest that Joyce's *Ulysses* is a profound meditation on the role of language in laying out propositions that can be considered true, in a permanent and stable sense. And the underlying irony of Joyce's novel is that Joyce, master of poetic language though he be, will not trust poetry, or lofty rhetoric, to present these truths. The quotation from Dante that gives this preface its title is spoken by Cato, the guardian of the island of Purgatory, as he responds to a long and lofty request from Virgil that he help the two pilgrims begin their ascent up the mountain of Purgatory: "But if a lady from heaven moves and directs thee, as thou sayest, there is no need of fair words; let it suffice thee to ask me for her sake" (*Purgatorio,* canto 1, lines 91–93). This is a mild but pointed rebuke aimed at the oratory of Virgil, who speaks for over thirty lines and invokes Cato's wife Marcia as a sufficient reason for his aid to the pilgrims. Cato tells him to save his breath; the simple and plain statement that a lady from heaven favors the two would have sufficed, without the "fair words" that cost so much effort from the poet. Singleton translates the Italian differently: what Sinclair gives as "fair words" Singleton translates as "flattery," and the difference is great and instructive. Putting the two together, we move to the center of Joyce's novel, in which we must face the proposition that the fair words of poetry may indeed be nothing more than flatteries, and flattery is one of the first sins in the eighth circle of hell where the various types of simple fraud are delineated. The fundamental irony of Joyce's *Ulysses* is that it will be teaching us that language, especially poetic language, is inherently fraudulent and that to present a reader with something called truth will first require a thorough investigation of the various kinds of language that have often been used for such portrayal. Hence the different styles of *Ulysses,* and hence the novel's many parodies.

The progression of styles in *Ulysses* can be thought of as a series of lessons about language's failure to present truth, until we come to "Ithaca," until we return home. Nothing could be less poetic than "Ithaca," written in the plainest style imaginable. And it will be in this episode that Joyce presents his truth, which is that Bloom is an incarnation of Christian love, in a style that has very little to commend it as beautiful or lofty. Molly gives the clue to the novel's deepest intentions: "O rocks! Tell us in plain words" (4.343). It is on the rocky island of Ithaca that Joyce will tell us, in the plainest style he could invent using the plainest words one could use, that Bloom is "the traditional figure of hypostasis."

In this study I will try to demonstrate how Joyce initiates a new kind of writing that I will call "modernist allegory," a kind of writing designed to present truth in plain words. *Ulysses* is a text largely about its ability to move toward and achieve this kind of writing. It begins as a critique of the novel, suggesting its inadequacy as a genre capable of providing an appropriate sense of nobility and heroism; and, as has been noted since its publication, it slowly builds into another kind of writing, what we have traditionally called "epic." What has not been yet fully appreciated is that the epic genre is, to Joyce's way of thinking at any rate, also not adequate to the deepest purposes he has set for himself. The epic too is presented only to be superseded by another kind of writing, the allegory.

This view of *Ulysses* can be grounded in an understanding of Dante's fundamental division of his *Divina Commedia* into three kinds of writing that just so happen to coincide with the three places he visits. *Inferno* is the most graphically realistic and "low" kind of writing in the poem, the one most like the novel genre as Joyce understands it in its commitment to the depiction of people confined to a set of behaviors and attitudes that are sinful and a punishment in themselves. Joyce describes the style of *Dubliners* as a "scrupulous meanness," and such a style is required to represent people whose moral state is best described as "paralysis." Dante regrets, as he reaches the bottom of hell, that he lacks the "harsh and grating rhymes" fit for such dismal fates, a regret indicating that a certain style must be pursued for writing about souls stuck in hellish patterns of incontinence, violence, and fraud. At the opening of *Purgatorio* he calls for poetry to be raised from the dead and for Calliope, the muse of epic poetry, to attend his writing of the second canticle. Joyce ends his "hellish" section of *Ulysses* with "Hades" as the last episode to be written purely in the initial style of rigorous naturalism, after which he too works for his writing to be raised from the dead. Purgatory is the place for the epic to be renewed because it is where souls purge themselves of the stains of being in history and achieve an original purity associated with the Garden of Eden. In other words, the individual rises above the conditions of history, and that is what the epic has traditionally been about—a great man who transcends his time and place and makes his mark upon his culture by the strength of his transcendent personality. Each soul, upon completion of the purgative process, achieves a kind of heroism Dante wishes to associate with the epic poem. And in *Paradiso*, Dante is finally able to meet the souls of the blessed who, having moved beyond space and time fully yet still being in some profound way connected to humanity, approach truths that are akin to the central mystery of Christianity, the incarnation, in which mystery the person of Christ is understood as being both God and man. Medieval allegory, coming from Pauline allegory, is based on the notion that the central event in human history is the incarnation. In *Paradiso*, Dante writes allegory, having passed from the novelistic and the epic to the place where eternity and time intersect.

That is the structure of *Ulysses*, the movement from naturalistic novel, to epic, to modernist allegory. Joyce's great work is about its own attempt to present the truth of our lives in a form that reaches beyond any sort of relativity. The effort to say the most simple thing, as Joyce himself said about *Ulysses*, does indeed require the most complex means.

Abbreviations

EC	Eliot, "East Coker" in *Four Quartets*
DS	Eliot, "The Dry Salvages" in *Four Quartets*
LG	Eliot, "Little Gidding" in *Four Quartets*
CW	Joyce, *Critical Writings*
AP	Joyce, *A Portrait of the Artist as a Young Man*
SH	Joyce, *Stephen Hero*
NA	Stevens, *The Necessary Angel*

Joyce's Modernist Allegory

Introduction

Rereading *Ulysses*
Naturalistic Novel Becomes Modernist Allegory

Representing the Ideal

The purpose of this study of *Ulysses* is to demonstrate how James Joyce comes to fashion what I call modernist allegory as his response to an urgent need to find a way to represent the ideal in writing. Having chosen to work in a genre devoted to what can be called realism, Joyce discovers that the history of the novel has led to a certain reductionism, a deflation of the ideal or the permanently valuable to something lower, more time-bound, and so more tied to the body and to history than the ideal can suffer without degenerating into the realm of the naive and merely wistful. For Joyce, the history of the novel as reductionist mirrors the history of the culture in which the novel emerges, and so Joyce's critique of the novel is at the same time a critique of the culture in which he lived. He came to the conviction that the novel is inadequate as a means for representing what his culture needed, the representation of a genuine ideal not susceptible to various reductive forces at work in the culture. As a result, he came to write what begins as a novel and becomes, slowly and deliberately, an allegory. *Ulysses* is a novel that includes a devastating critique of the novel, a critique that exposes its limitations in regard to the representation of the ideal. Karen Lawrence and Daniel Schwarz have already made the claim that in *Ulysses*, Joyce brings the reader on an "odyssey of styles."[1] However, I want to show that this readerly journey is one that brings us from the genre of the novel, which is best suited to a representation of our life in the body and so in history, to the genre of allegory, as understood by the early Christian exegetes of the Bible and by Dante in his *Divina Commedia*. This study, then, brings the work of such readers of Joyce to a new level, watching more carefully exactly how Joyce teaches us to read his novel (and the novel) and how he brings us to an appreciation of the ideal through his renewal of ancient and medieval allegory.

Joyce is enacting a literary and cultural critique in *Ulysses* as he tries to find a way to represent something ideal, permanent, and absolute in writing. His critique of both literary and cultural history is tied to a keen and penetrating understanding of language and its relation to something called reality, an understanding that has more recently been given powerful philosophical expression in the thinking that we place under the heading "poststructuralism." Dennis Brown notes Anthony Easthope's placement of poststructuralism in relation to literary modernism as "later 'philosophical' understanding of what was first encountered in art" and then asks an important question: "But does this mean that we must necessarily construe Modernism in specifically Poststructuralist terms?" (Brown, 7). Brown understands that the modernists performed in their art what later theorists were able to abstract into principle and law but that the aims and ambitions of the modernists may not be identical with the aims and ambitions of the later theorists. My claim is that Joyce understands the workings of language in the same fundamental way that poststructuralism understands them but that his art uses that understanding to pursue aims and ambitions that most poststructuralists wish to deny—namely, the representation of the ideal in writing. His book is a series of investigations into the way language is used to represent reality, especially the way language is used fraudulently to represent higher things. He debunks most versions of idealism as fraudulent, implying that language is not a fit vehicle for the representation of ideals. In this way he seems to share with the poststructuralists a radical skepticism regarding ideals and all things not material, and many recent critics have used Joyce's writing to indicate in modernism the lurking presence of what we now call postmodernism. But this misses Joyce's ultimate ambition, that after showing various kinds of literary language to be incapable of representing the ideal, he goes beyond skepticism and fashions a style fit for such representation. My sense of Joyce is that he is disgusted by the fraudulent use of language to mislead people into a too easy belief in false ideals but that he is an idealist—a secret and subtle idealist—who works with extraordinary care and ingenuity to bring readers to an apperception of something ideal. Joyce is a skeptical writer, even to the point of being skeptical of his own skepticism, and in this movement beyond skepticism he finds a way to cling to a belief in something outside language that can serve as the ground on which we can erect meaning for our lives. His critique of writing is thus a critique of our culture, as he analyzes various styles and techniques of writing in order to teach us how to read for something we may still wish to call "truth."

Joyce is in no way naive in his understanding of what is at stake in his effort to represent an ideal in *Ulysses*. He is in fact so aware of the problems associated with idealism that he feels compelled to organize his text as a series of lessons designed to educate and empower the reader: first, not to be fooled by fraudulent language misleading us about the ideal; and second, to be capable of reading beyond such skepticism and still discover the ideal. Joyce is no sentimentalist regarding this possibility; in fact, no thorough reader of *Ulysses* can be unaware of Joyce's own discomfort in the presence of any sentimental gushing about the ideal or the ethereal. He creates the character of Buck Mulligan out of his own desire to debunk what has become the merely conventional and to deflate the stances of those who utter what has become hardened into dogma. We are meant to delight in Buck's mockery of the ideal when it presents itself in such forms, and many readers have been led (misled, I am tempted to say, deliberately and intentionally) by his brilliance and wit to confuse Buck and his creator. This is an error, for Joyce considers the easy and mindless debunking of the ideal as sentimental as its easy and mindless assertion. Recall the telegram Stephen sends Buck and that Buck reads aloud in "Scylla and Charybdis": "*The sentimentalist is he who would enjoy without incurring the immense debtorship for a thing done*" (9.550–51). It takes work to assert the ideal, and the sentimentalist is not willing either to work hard or acknowledge a debt to those who do. Joyce recognizes that his culture has become both cynical and sentimental (to Joyce, these are intimately bound) and requires a series of difficult and complex lessons about the problems and possibilities of idealism. *Ulysses* is Joyce's attempt to create a reader who can read beyond the skepticism of his culture and still discover, and maintain a belief in, an ideal form of behavior.

I want to make essential to my argument that Joyce sees himself as a benefactor of something called culture by giving to it the potential to find within itself a permanent set of values upon which we can assign meaning and identity to ourselves and our culture. There is in Joyce an acute awareness of language and its limitations, but never is he so overwhelmed by the failure of language to present truths that he loses the conviction that the literary imagination is the agency of the human mind that can gain access to, and represent in language, a set of values or a kind of belief that can be called permanent, stable, unchanging, absolute. Yet he is hardly naive in this conviction nor ignorant of the various attacks on just this possibility by the modern sensibility born in the Enlightenment, a sensibility that was attempting to find universals but wound up giving way to a series of relativizing theories in the nineteenth century, the most famous and important of which are those of Karl Marx, Charles Darwin, Friedrich Nietzsche and Sigmund Freud. As it looked for signs of stability and universal truth, the mind became increasingly aware of change as its most vital principle. Marx sought to identify the iron laws of history and found that change and development were at the heart of those laws; Darwin sought laws of natural development and found a principle of change in the law of natural selection; Freud sought a model for the human mind and made transformation its principle; Nietzsche most self-consciously of all denies all claims for the absolute. It is ironic that this pattern is precisely the pattern described by Jacques Derrida in "Structure, Sign, and Play in the Discourse of the Human Sciences," about the result of structuralism: that in seeking to discover the structure for the various human sciences, structuralism brought about the acute and sudden awareness that structures themselves are not innocent but constructed in time and by power. In these parallel developments what was meant to locate the stable and universal gives way quickly and suddenly to a consciousness of change and human power.[2] Both discoveries lead to skepticism, if not cynicism, about the possibility of stability and permanence in anything related to something once called humanity. Joyce is aware of the former of these events and the consequent loss of values, and he reacts against it; I am aware of the later of these events, and I want to react against it. I would like to think that we can make a successful defense against the sweeping cynicism of recent critical theories by watching how Joyce worked against the reductionism that was dominant in his time.

How different from our own critical situation is Joyce's artistic challenge? We are still living within a culture of critical attitudes in which one is not to look for something permanent in literary art, but rather to discover the historical basis for what the author may have believed was permanent. I do not say that this approach has been wrongheaded in its entirety, for it has exposed as partial and relative what was often uncritically accepted as transcendent and absolute; but I do wish to argue that this approach, applied uncritically, leads to a critical blindness that denies out of hand the possibility for art to transcend its culture and reach a level of reality that may indeed be permanent and absolute.

I want to invoke the positions of three literary theorists whose work has tended to move beyond the dogmatic skepticism of poststructuralism and to open up the possibilities of reading for the ideal once again. Tobin Siebers, in *Cold War Criticism and the Politics of Skepticism,* advances the position that modern skepticism has become as dogmatic as the totalitarian dogmatists it set out to oppose. We must learn, according to Siebers, to think against skepticism, an effort that would "reveal the dogmatic side of the most skeptical positions and . . . locate perspectives that skeptics have opposed not because they have thoughtfully rejected them but because these perspectives would threaten their own personal skepticism" (Siebers,

4–5). Siebers goes on to argue that among these other perspectives is the possibility of belief in a transcendent ideal. Charles Altieri argues strenuously that the various poststructuralist methodologies, especially the new historicism, can only teach us "negative ideals" and leave us blind to "the reconstructive powers available in literary traditions" (Altieri, 9). Altieri warns us to be suspicious of the "hermeneutics of suspicion" (22) and to read through rather than against a text in order to note the author's struggles to construct meaning and value. Even Paul de Man, in "Criticism and Crisis," warns critics to be wary of being so quick to demystify texts that we never allow the literary artists to approach the realm of mystery. He uses a pithy phrase: "When modern critics think they are demystifying literature, they are in fact being demystified by it" (de Man,18). With these three critics establishing a way to move beyond the often valuable but severely limited insights of poststructuralist analysis, we can turn to Joyce. In Joyce we have an author who self-consciously makes the ability of language to present truth the major theme of his novel, and so we must watch more carefully how this author may work to achieve a method of writing capable of indicating, if not presenting, this truth.

While in my conclusion I will examine briefly the work of other "high modernists," it is my contention that Joyce's *Ulysses* is the central modernist document in this regard, for it takes as its purpose the exposure of the novel's inability to depict ideals and values, an inability that is not at all accidental but part of its very nature. Joyce makes his novel enact the history of the novel, showing how its tendency toward naturalism and irony render it unable to do the work Joyce is aiming at, the presentation of a good man as a model for behavior. By watching how Joyce first exposes the limits of the novel and then supplements it with a kind of writing meant to be the modernist version of a particular kind of ancient and medieval allegory, we will be in a position to read Ezra Pound's *Pisan Cantos*, T. S. Eliot's *Four Quartets*, and Wallace Stevens's *Notes toward a Supreme Fiction* as modernist allegory in just the way Joyce first presented. Modernist allegory will be the solution to a nagging problem facing these artists: the need to find a way to present ideals and values in a way rendered immune from the reductionist assaults of their intellectual culture. The large aim of this book is to describe this aspect of literary or high modernism.

I want to turn briefly to some of Joyce's critical writings, especially what we have of his famous lecture on William Blake delivered in Trieste in March 1912, just two years before he was about to start work on *Ulysses*, because in this and some other comments from even earlier writings we get a glimpse of Joyce the idealist. Joyce relates how Blake took care of his brother Robert: "During his long sickness, he spoke to him of the eternal world and comforted him. For many days before his death, he watched over his sickbed without interruption, and at the supreme moment he saw the beloved soul break loose from the lifeless body and rise toward heaven clapping its hands for joy" (*CW,* 216). William Blake "died singing in a strong, resounding voice that made the rafters sing. He was singing, as always, of the ideal world, of truth, the intellect and the divinity of the imagination" (219–20). Joyce admires this idealism in Blake and seems to think it is the ultimate purpose of great art: "If we must accuse of madness every great genius who does not believe in the hurried materialism now in vogue with the happy fatuousness of a recent college graduate in the exact sciences, little remains for art and universal philosophy" (220). It is as idealist that Joyce seems to prize Blake: "The same idealism that possessed and sustained Blake when he hurled his lightning against human evil and misery prevented him from being cruel to the body even of a sinner, the frail curtain of flesh" (216). Joyce places Blake in company of Emanuel Swedenborg, St. Augustine of Hippo, Dante, and St. John of the Cross, the last of whom Joyce calls "one of the few idealist artists worthy to stand with Blake" (221). We can see from this sampling of citations that Joyce is interested in an art that is idealist, visionary, and concerned with the order of things we call eternal, permanent, absolute.

That this lecture on Blake was coupled with one on Daniel Defoe, who occupies the opposite pole in the spectrum of idealism/materialism, does not lessen the value Joyce places on idealism but rather sheds light on what will be seen as Blake's "excess" in "Nestor": that he has no patience with the things of this world and flies after the absolute in an art that is at times almost wholly unintelligible. In an essay on James Clarence Mangan written in 1902, Joyce criticizes the romantic school for just such excess, a criticism he extends and puts in the mouth of Stephen Dedalus in *Stephen Hero*:

> A classical style, he said, is the syllogism of art, the only legitimate process from one world to another. Classicism is not the manner of any fixed age or of any fixed country: it is a constant state of the artistic mind. It is a temper of security and satisfaction and patience. The romantic temper, so often and so grievously misinterpreted and not more by others than by its own, is an insecure, unsatisfied, impatient temper which sees no fit abode here for its ideals and chooses therefore to behold them under insensible figures. As a result of this choice it comes to disregard certain limitations. Its figures are blown to wild adventures, lacking the gravity of solid bodies, and the mind that has conceived them ends by disowning them. The classical temper on the other hand, ever mindful of limitations, chooses rather to bend upon these present things and so to work

upon them and fashion them that the quick intelligence may go beyond them to their meaning which is still unuttered. (*SH*, 78)

Though written early, these may be the most important words Joyce ever wrote about the intentions of *Ulysses*. For he is careful not to negate the value of ideals but to insist on a method that is capable of representing the ideal in such a way that it can be beheld in "these present things"[3] that then suggest the unutterable meaning of the ideal itself. Those writers of the romantic temper, such as Blake, are not wrong for being idealists but for lacking the patience to search for a writing that can be "fit abode for its ideals." Their efforts are the ones Joyce will parody in *Ulysses*, but if these early words still apply ten years after they were written, Joyce's parodies and mockeries are never aimed at the intention of seeking out and representing the ideal but rather at the inadequate and often fraudulent efforts to manifest the ideal in writing. Joyce respects the skeptical thinking that the novel as a genre reflects, the kind of thinking that insists on the body and on the material world and on history, the kind of thinking that the romantic temper often avoids in its impatience and excess. He will work explicitly with the notion of gravity in *Ulysses*, making us aware of the solid body of his hero who nonetheless will become the embodiment of a cultural ideal, of a permanent and eternal ideal. In an even earlier essay called "Drama and Life," Joyce notes the need to revive romance in the ordinary:

> Life indeed nowadays is often a sad bore. Many feel like the Frenchman that they have born too late in a world too old, and their wan hope and nerveless unheroism point on ever sternly to a last nothing, a vast futility and meanwhile—a bearing of fardels. Epic savagery is rendered impossible by vigilant policing, chivalry has been killed by fashion oracles of the boulevards. There is no clank of mail, no halo about gallantry, no hat-sweeping, no roystering! The traditions of romance are upheld only in Bohemia. Still I think out of the dreary sameness of existence, a measure of dramatic life may be drawn. Even the most commonplace, the deadest among the living, may play a part in a great drama. (*CW*, 44–45)

Joyce expresses the desire for romance, as long as it is depicted in a way that is realistic and plausible. He wants ideals, but only as long as they are in solid bodies obeying the laws of gravity. He wants to oppose the ennui of a modern world of decadent sensibility by enacting a revival of heroism and idealism in the genre of the novel, for that genre is defined by its emphasis on the plausible and the realistic. This will be Joyce's challenge, to make a genre increasingly dedicated to the exposure of human limitation capable also of representing the ideal.

In all these comments Joyce expresses on the one hand admiration for the romantic temper and on the other hand concern for its fate in the modern age, and by "modern age" I am willing to let the phrase stand for the post-Enlightenment sensibility that values scientific rationality and intellect above all else, as so well documented by Stephen Toulmin.[4] Blake, then, is the great example of the romantic temper responding to the narrowing of human life by the increasing powers of rationality and its technological achievements. Joyce is worried about the fate of romance, which needs a classical artist to embody in something so well grounded that it cannot be debunked by reason and intellectual wit. Joyce wants an idealism that is rendered safe from the reductions of the enlightened mind, safe from the skepticism of the mocking spirit of the modern age. That is why *Ulysses* begins with a medical student—a man of enlightened and humane science—who happens to be the greatest mocker in all literature; for the goal of *Ulysses* is to rise above the mocking culture of enlightened rationality and to find a fit abode for Joyce's ideals.

Allegory and the Novel

It is my contention that Joyce employs, as the organizing principle for his novel, the kind of allegory Saint Paul instituted and medieval exegetes of the Bible perfected in understanding the relation of the Old Testament to the New. This approach allows us to establish the relation of the later episodes of *Ulysses,* so wildly experimental in nature, to the earlier naturalistic episodes as analogous to the way the New Testament is taken to "reread" certain features from the Old. What is gained is an understanding of the later experimental episodes as "rereadings" of the earlier episodes, as they allow the naturalistic novel to remain valid and ongoing while at the same time isolating and focusing upon an aspect of reality we can refer to as the eternal, the permanent, the ideal. After a process of abstraction from the naturalistic representation, it is in "Ithaca" that Joyce establishes a way of writing that locates a fixed point capable of governing the meaning of the rest of the novel.

Perhaps the thorniest problem facing the last two decades of scholarship on *Ulysses* has been to find ways to account for the decision to begin the novel with such lucid depiction of sights and sounds and smells, as well as the extraordinary presentation of the thoughts of fictional characters in the interior monologue for which the opening episodes are so famous, only to abandon such "realism" in favor of the innovations of the later episodes. Jeffrey Perl writes succinctly that "the whole history of the European novel, from Cervantes to Fielding to Tolstoy to James, can be read as one long story about the dialectical battle between various kinds of realism and various kinds of idealization" (Perl, 174). My thesis allows us to say that Joyce is not abandoning such "realism" but instead has followed nineteenth-century naturalism to its limit, exhausting its resources and needing new ones if he is to be able to present in Bloom what he wishes for us to find, which is that in this unassuming ordinary man lies, hidden from the naturalistic narrator's eyes, a dimension that can be called a "Christ dimension." Joyce is acutely aware of having come quite late in the tradition of the novel, sharing what Perry Meisel calls the precondition for modernism, a feeling of belatedness (Meisel, 5). As a result of this awareness, he decides that he must end the novel as a genre and move beyond it to allegory. Traditional models of narrative technique having proven inadequate to his purpose, Joyce is compelled to experiment boldly in order to expand Bloom's significance without denying the validity of what naturalism can present. To present in Bloom what another high modernist, Eliot, in "The Dry Salvages," calls "the intersection of the timeless with time," Joyce returns to the central mystery of Christianity, the Incarnation, and the model of reading that was able to comprehend that mystery, the allegory of theologians.

I am acutely aware that this thesis will meet with some resistance because it is still somewhat unfashionable to assert that any work of literature, no less a work as complex and heteroclite as *Ulysses*, can be approached as having established a fixed center, a transcendental signified that governs its meaning. There has been some fruitful and intelligent criticism in recent years that seeks to make Joyce into a postmodernist who delights in the aimless display of brilliant language and the chaos of various perspectives thrown together in planned randomness to frustrate our efforts to find a center that controls the meaning. One such effort, by Kevin Dettmar, has the instructive title *The Illicit Joyce of Postmodernism*, as if this aspect of Joyce's text is under some sort of ban by an orthodox scholarly community. Rather, as Siebers helps us see, the orthodox position in the present critical climate may just be that Joyce's text is best approached in a way that foregrounds play and openness. This postmodern or poststructuralist emphasis has produced much fruit but at some cost, leading us to ignore Joyce's carefully inscribed intention to discover a language and a style fit for idealism. My position is that Joyce's retrieval of ancient and medieval allegory for his modern purpose allows him the free play that recent theories wish to emphasize and at the same time the closure required to establish order and value. Inherent in my argument, then, is the contention that Joyce's allegory is a hallmark of high modernism in its attempt to defy reductionist accounts of ideals as the result of mere human construction and to point to an event outside the web of language that can ground our idealism. Outside of language is the Christ event; outside of words is the Word.

As Jeffrey Perl notes, "*Ulysses*, beginning with its extraordinary title, implies a history or theory of the novel" (Perl, 148). My study takes very seriously that *Ulysses* is largely about the history of the novel, as Joyce works carefully to indicate the strengths and limitations of the genre he has chosen to work in, ultimately coming to the conclusion that the novel cannot sustain his larger ambitions, which are to present an ideal for his culture to recognize and embrace as a standard for its behavior. The novel, as Joyce understands it and exposes it in *Ulysses*, must be supplemented by other kinds of writing that can allow this ideal to be indicated clearly and surely, if also secretly and obliquely. Joyce is not like the Henry Fielding whom Perl describes as he tries to understand the relation of the novel as a genre and the epic; once again according to Perl, who follows Ian Watt in this, Fielding begins the "novel/epic theory," but Fielding's intentions are in one important respect quite the opposite from Joyce's: "Fielding's novel [*Joseph Andrews*] exposes what masquerade as heroism and epic style in order to extol and embody a more authentic classicism and a less idealized, more Homeric human race" (147). Joyce too is interested in the exposure of the false and the sham, but not to embody a less idealized race. Perhaps Fielding, coming at the beginning of the novel as a genre, was compelled to use the new freedom to get rid of as much trash from our literary conceptions of the ideal man and his behavior as possible, but Joyce is interested in the novel being able to bear the full weight of the epic ambition, namely to present a hero capable of giving a symbolic identity to its culture. In *Ulysses*, Joyce will demonstrate that the novel is not capable of such ambition, and he will work carefully toward the establishment of a new kind of writing, what we will be calling modernist allegory.

One of the most important events in the history of biblical exegesis occurs within the Bible, when Saint Paul explains how a Christian is to read certain events in Hebrew scriptures. As Robert Hollander explains, "it is in Galatians 4:22–26 that we find the first explicit Christian use of the word 'allegory'" (Hollander, 58). This passage reads as follows: "For it is written that Abraham had two sons, one by a slave and one by a freewoman. But the son of the slave was born according to the flesh, the son of the free woman through promise. Now this is an allegory: these women are two covenants. One is from Mount Sinai, bearing children for slavery; she is Hagar. Now Hagar is Mount Sinai in Arabia; she corresponds to the resent Jerusalem, for she is in slavery with her children. But the Jerusalem above is free, and she is our mother."

Paul's "spiritual" reading of the Old Testament does not deny the historical validity of the story: Abraham had his two sons by the two women in just the way Genesis describes. But for Saint Paul there is a level of signification at work in this story that does not cancel out the validity of

Genesis, that can only be read after the Christ event, and that "fulfills" the letter with the spiritual truth. The Old Testament story is "reread" from the privileged position of one living after the Christ event.

It is my argument that Joyce uses just this kind of allegory in writing *Ulysses,* and he devises a passage in "Ithaca" that instructs us about how to read this episode in a way strikingly similar to Saint Paul's instruction to the Galatians. In this pivotal late episode, the episode in which the hero returns home, we are asked to reconsider the meaning of an earlier event, and in so doing we will be enlarging our sense of Bloom's character. The passage in question concerns "the previous intimations of the result" of the Gold Cup that Bloom had throughout the day before reading the *Evening Telegraph* in the cabman's shelter:

> In Bernard Kiernan's licensed premised 8, 9, and 10 Little Britain Street; in David Byrne's licensed premises, 14 Duke Street: in O'Connell street lower, outside Graham lemon's when a dark man had placed in his hands a throwaway (subsequently thrown away), advertising Elijah, restorer of the Church in Zion; in Lincoln place outside the premises of F. W. Sweny and Co (limited), dispensing chemists, when, when Frederick M. (Bantam) Lyons had rapidly and successively requested, perused, and restituted the copy of the current issue of the *Freeman's Journal and National Press* which he had been about to throw away (subsequently thrown away), he had proceeded towards the edifice of the Turkish and warm baths, 11 Leinster street, with the light of inspiration shining in his countenance and bearing in his arms the secret of the race, graven in the language of prediction. (17.329–41)

In this passage the "Ithaca" narrator reflects on earlier moments in Bloom's day and "rereads" them. An event that we would have been likely to have dismissed as pure and meaningless coincidence—that is, an event that as readers we would have with great ease and confidence "thrown away"—is brought back to our attention and made significant in a new and unexpected way. What exactly is the relation of the version of this event as recounted in "Ithaca" to earlier versions, especially to the one described at the end of "Lotus Eaters," when Bloom performed the act of inadvertently giving Bantam Lyons the tip about Throwaway, the dark horse who wins the Gold Cup? Unknowingly and accidentally Bloom predicted the winner, and he is amused and perhaps bewildered at this coincidence. The "Ithaca" narrator, however, is not confused but understands it in a way that Bloom, a character in a realistic novel, does not, for the last lines quoted above depict Bloom walking away from Lyons in a very different way than was described at the end of "Lotus Eaters." There, "Mr. Bloom folded the sheets again to a neat square and lodged the soap in it, smiling. . . . He walked cheerfully towards the mosque of the baths" (5.543–44, 549); in "Ithaca" he is seen "with the light of inspiration shining in his countenance and bearing in his arms the secret of the race, graven in the language of prediction." The narrator in "Ithaca" sees more and differently than the narrator in "Lotus Eaters." The earlier narrator can only see the "realistic" content of the event, what actually happened in what we can call the "literal dimension of reality." The "Ithaca" narrator is responding to and recording a different dimension of reality, what we can call the "allegorical dimension of reality." Both are equally valid and truthful, and they do not cancel each other or stand opposed to one another. As "Lotus Eaters" has it, Bloom "walked cheerfully" to the baths; this is what occurs in the literal dimension of reality, and Bloom's interior monologue—a device shaped and limited by the constraints of a rigorous naturalism—betrays no sign of the solemn and awesome powers ascribed to him by the later narrator. Yet what "Ithaca" presents is equally valid and does not efface the limited truth of the early version; the significance of that early event can only be felt now—in the penultimate episode—is only understood now, can only be expressed now. The "Ithaca" narrator can see, in the Bloom of ten o'clock in the morning, "the light of inspiration shining in his countenance." It was there, at that time, when Bloom walked to the baths; but only the later narrator, who is in the position to reread the event, can see it.

This passage from "Ithaca" is Joyce's way of giving his readers the exegetical clue about how to read his novel. We must reread the earlier events from the privileged position of the later episodes, especially "Ithaca," which contains a "Christ event" of its own when Stephen sees in Bloom "the traditional figure of hypostasis" (17.783). When we look back at this strange coincidence about the horse named Throwaway, what looked like accident to a naturalistic narrator looks like prophecy to a narrator capable of seeing allegory. The phrase used by the "Ithaca" narrator—"the light of inspiration shining in his countenance and bearing in his arms the secret of the race, graven in the language of prediction"—was part of the oratorical display of "Aeolus" and in that episode referred to Moses bringing the law to the Jews in the desert. So the "Ithaca" narrator sees Bloom in the company of Moses and leads us to reconsider who Bloom is and what he means. There is also the pun about the "secret of the race"—for it is at one and the same time a reference to the Gold Cup of which Bloom "knows" the secret and a reference to the secret of the Hebrew race, the secret that the Messiah would be born to them and would even be a secret to many of them, who would miss it. The narrator of "Lotus Eaters" is like the authors of the Old Testament, offering precise accounts of actual "historical" or "literal" events; also like them, this narrator is blocked from a full understanding of what he narrates. They are blocked from the secret; the train of events, mainly coincidences and accidents, that began with the inadvertent tip is fulfilled when we hear that Bloom is an "advertising Elijah," an ad canvasser with prophetic powers.

It is difficult to determine exactly how Joyce came to write *Ulysses* in this manner, but the way he establishes his allegory in "Ithaca" suggests that Dante's example is crucial. Joyce presents Bloom's and Stephen's exit from 7 Eccles street with the background music of the 113th Psalm, the very psalm Dante uses to describe his method of writing allegory in his famous letter to Can Grande. Charles Singleton effected a revolution in Dante studies when he advanced as a rigorous principle for interpretation the poet's own distinction between two kinds of allegory, what Dante calls the "allegory of poets" and the "allegory of theologians," arguing that he wrote the *Divina Commedia* using the latter:

> The radical difference lies in the nature of the literal sense in the one and in the other. The "allegory of poets," which is that of fable, of parable (and hence also to be found in the Scriptures), is a mode in which the first literal sense is one devised, fashioned (*fictio* in its original meaning) in order to conceal, and in concealing to convey, a truth. Not so in the other mode, as we may see from the example cited [by Dante in his letter to Can Grande]. There the first sense is historical, as Dante says it is, and not "fiction." The children of Israel did depart from Egypt in the time of Moses. Whatever the other sense may be, this first sense abides, stands quite on its own, is not devised "for the sake of." Indeed it was generally recognized that in Holy Scripture the historical sense might at times be the only sense there. These things have been so; so they have happened in time. This is the record of them. (Singleton, 62)

The "allegory of theologians" allows Dante to write about his spiritual journey in such a way that his own itinerary is taken as true while at the same time occasionally signifying on other levels of meaning (the allegorical, the moral, and the anagogic levels, as he specifies them in the letter to Can Grande). The "allegory of poets" (the one usually meant when literary critics use the term "allegory") is based on an entirely different conception of the "letter," of the literal sense. The letter is devised to suggest some other meaning, the one standing for the other and having no validity in itself, on its own, for itself. When critics object to having *Ulysses* called an allegory, it must be the "allegory of poets" that they have in mind, and it seems to me that these objections are absolutely correct and necessary. The critics who want to emphasize the "naturalistic" aspect of the early episodes at the expense of the more "symbolic" aspects of the later ones do not understand why Joyce would expend such energy and skill at representing nature (that is, character, scene, plot) only to dissolve it. The "literal" or the "historical" or the "naturalistic" sense of *Ulysses* is designed to be accepted as real and not merely devised to be effaced by some symbolic "truth." But the "allegory of theologians" allows Joyce, as it allowed Dante, to work on the literal level of meaning in such a way as to enlarge its significance, to expand its meaning, to find within the literal another, equally valid, level of meaning. Bloom is always a realistic character and becomes in the later episodes, also and at one and the same time, a moral exemplum of Christian charity. Those critics who have followed Edmund Wilson and S. L. Goldberg have been right in insisting on the importance of plot and character established by the early episodes but wrong to regret the "ornamental complications" (Wilson's phrase) of the later ones. The early episodes do not stand in relation to the later ones as the literal stands to the symbolic meanings in the "allegory of poets" but as the literal stands to the symbolic in the "allegory of theologians." The later episodes are a "rereading" of the earlier ones, establishing another level of significance within the literal events, a level that does not replace the earlier meaning or cancel it out with a better meaning, but coexists with it. Having inherited a novelistic tradition that was fundamentally defined by its emphasis on the realistic and the plausible and that had become increasingly determined by an extreme version of realism best called naturalism, Joyce apparently feels compelled on the one hand to continue that tradition in his own brand of prose fiction (*Dubliners* is a wonderful example of naturalism), even if on the other hand his larger and ultimate ambition is to find room within that tradition for a representation of a set of ideals. A naturalism not effaced by ideals, an idealism not unloosed from or reduced by but rather firmly grounded in naturalism—that's the accomplishment made possible by the allegory of theologians for a modernist allegory.

Joyce has chosen to work in a genre that has come to be increasingly naturalistic in its emphasis on human characters operating within a naturalistic context with laws that determine and limit the characters' actions and destinies. Gillian Beer and George Levine have shown the tremendous influence Darwinian theory had on the development of the novel in the later nineteenth century, and Joyce's history of the novel emphasizes this movement toward Darwinian naturalism. Levine describes Darwin's impact on nineteenth-century narrative: "The patient, ostensibly detached registration of human character and behavior is an aspect of the Darwinian ethos central to the experience of the Victorian novel; it is part of a movement describing a new place for man in nature and tends to imply a material explanation for human behavior" (Levine, 14). Joyce's discovery of what I am calling modernist allegory, based as it is on Pauline allegory, allows him never to relinquish the naturalistic worldview while at the same time sanctioning his effort to elevate his hero to an ideal level of existence. Bloom has a material body and lives squarely in a lucidly depicted material world, and all natural laws apply to that body in that natural environment. Any astute reader of *Ulysses* knows that Joyce delights in the depiction of Bloom's and Dublin's physicality. But his modernist allegory permits him to find other levels of significance within the naturalistic that do not cancel the body and nature as ineluctable features of human existence. Bloom's elevation to an ideal height, his ascension if you will, is with body intact, like Christ's Ascension.

There is one further feature of the "allegory of theologians" that is essential to it, that certain literal events of the Old Testament are found to have their fulfillment only in the Christ event. It is not just any kind of symbolic significance found within the literal in this mode of allegory, but a level of meaning based on the Incarnation, which is the Christian mystery that resolves the tension between God and man, between the divine and the human, between the spirit and the flesh, between the timeless and time, between the ideal and the natural. Christ was both human and divine, bound to the laws of time and space, fully contained within both history and natural law yet beyond these as God is beyond them. Joyce's intention to reconcile the natural and the ideal is met in the very essence of the allegory of theologians.

To write in this manner is to write the way God writes. For while God did not literally write the Bible, according to medieval theology he orchestrated certain events that are recounted by human authors in what we now call the Old Testament, events that suddenly and surprisingly become meaningful in a symbolic way once the Christ event occurs. In just this way, Dante invents the fiction of his spiritual journey that becomes increasingly—and, to the character named Dante, quite unexpectedly—suggestive of the Christ event. Following Saint Paul, whom Hollander calls "the first great theologian of the Incarnation" (Hollander, 59), Dante makes the Incarnation the ground that governs the meaning of his entire poem: "With its first meaning as an historical meaning, the allegory of the *Divine Comedy* is grounded in the mystery of the Incarnation" (Singleton, 74). John Freccero advances Singleton's analysis and emphasizes the way in which Dante's own itinerary is based upon the Christ event and must be understood from the perspective of the Incarnation: "This retrospective illumination is the very essence of biblical allegory, what Dante called the 'allegory of theologians.' The Christ event was the end term of an historical process, the 'fullness of time,' from the perspective of which the history of the world might be read and judged according to a meaning which perhaps even the participants in that history could not perceive" (Freccero, 132–33).

All events, whether public and political or private and personal, are to be judged in "retrospective illumination," from the privileged point of view of the Incarnation, the event that is within time and so subject to change yet stable and permanent because it partakes of the divine and timeless as well as the human and temporal. As Dante the pilgrim, the character in the poem, discovers in the unique facts of his own private experience the pattern of the Christ event, he becomes increasingly aware that he must interpret his own history and that of the world from the fixed perspective of the Incarnation. Freccero goes so far as to say that Dante's poetry "*is* the allegory of theologians in his own life" (Freccero, 134). So it is not, to repeat, just any set of ideals that Joyce must present if we are to call his method "modernist allegory." No other set of ideals exists both in the temporal and the timeless realms, in the flesh and spirit, in the human and divine worlds. So we must learn to see how "Ithaca" contains an analogous "Christ event" and so functions as the fixed perspective from which the rest of the novel may be read and understood, in the same way that the Christ event organizes and gives meaning to Dante's itinerary and as the Incarnation functions as the fixed point from which to review Hebrew scriptures. *Ulysses* is "reread" from the privileged vantage point of "Ithaca."

It is, I hope, clear that the passage from "Ithaca" analyzed above is Joyce's way of giving us the exegetical clue about how to read his novel. I want to go so far as to say that Joyce is teaching us how to read *Ulysses* within the novel itself, in many smaller ways prior to this passage that is, in my opinion at any rate, the most explicit and far-reaching of all his lessons. I have already said that the "Ithaca" narrator is writing from a more privileged position than the "Lotus Eaters" narrator, being able to see all that the earlier narrator saw but also the full "truth" of the event. The "Lotus Eaters" narrator is like the authors of the various books of the Old Testament, offering precise and accurate accounts of actual historical events but blocked from the full and final understanding of the events so clearly but so partially seen. The "Lotus Eaters" narrator is a naturalistic narrator, able to see only within the limited frame of natural law and realistic expectation. He is completely unaware of the prophetic moment taking place before his very eyes, eyes that see the physical details but miss what the "Ithaca" narrator sees. In between "Lotus Eaters" and "Ithaca," this event—Bloom's accidental tip about the dark horse Throwaway—is made to expand in significance as it moves toward its fulfillment in "Ithaca." In "Lestrygonians," Bloom is given a "throwaway" announcing the coming of Elijah in the person of Dr. Alexander J. Dowie, which he promptly "throws away." At first, however, Bloom thought that the piece of paper was about himself: "Bloo . . . Me? No" (8.124). The proposed identification of Bloom with the great Hebrew prophet is so silly that we must throw it away. But in "Wandering Rocks" the crumpled piece of paper bearing Elijah's name keeps coming back, making a journey of its own on the Liffey and taking a place among the various characters the episode follows. As silly as the identification may be, it keeps being proposed. In "Cyclops" the earlier inadvertent tip comes back to haunt him, as the patrons of Barney Kiernan's pub are led to believe that Bloom has won a handsome sum of money on Throwaway. The throwaway that he threw away (both in "Lotus Eaters" when he is about to throw the newspaper away and in "Lestrygonians" when he throws away Dowie's throwaway) comes back and fuels the citizen's venom against Bloom. The ending of this episode is presented by one of the parodic narrators whose absurdly inflated rhetoric we cannot take seriously, and in this kind of discourse the identification of Bloom with Elijah is tried once again, only to be deflated at the end by a devastatingly mocking voice. It takes the "Ithaca" narrator to see the full significance of the coincidence about this "Throwaway" and describe it in a way not susceptible to rational skepticism or mocking cynicism. Only this late narrator has found the way to present Bloom in his fullest significance, as an "advertising Elijah" and "the traditional figure of hypostasis." I will explore the various styles of *Ulysses* as they move toward "Ithaca," the pivotal episode of the novel that governs the meaning of the whole.

Allegory, Memory, and the Empowered Reader

Let us begin with a statement that is both obvious and contentious: *Ulysses* is first and foremost a piece of literary art organized by a skillful shaper for certain ends, even if those ends are so complex and so oblique that they often defy the simpler expositions of unity favored by the New Criticism. And when the shaper of this work of art takes pains to give the reader exegetical clues about how we are to read the novel, we must avoid the trap of ignoring the author, or declaring him dead. One of the cardinal points of my study is that Joyce is making his relation to the reader an important part of the text itself, as the author struggles to present certain lessons about reading this novel, and all novels, to a reader who is increasingly empowered to become the constructor of the novel's epic and allegorical climaxes. My approach will seem anachronistic, no doubt, to the practitioners of what Charles Altieri has labeled "various hermeneutics of suspicion" because I intend to assert the primacy of the shaper's hand and intention as he points us to the "allegory of theologians" as our interpretive guide. I think that Altieri's argument for the reader's renewed respect for authors and their intentions is important and well founded. He argues that we "better fit the ideals about reading developed by those writers whom we take the time to read if we imagine ourselves as reading *through* the text," not "against the text," as critics such as Geoffrey Hartman advise, who see reading as inaugurating skepticism and disbelief. Altieri calls for a reader to grant "provisional authority" to the text in order for us to "construct the best possible case for the text as a window on possible values in experience. This approach saves us from a rather vulnerable smugness; it forces us to extend our imaginations; and it keeps authority within an imaginative dialogue with great minds, rather than placing it in some contemporary interpretative practice" (Altieri, 45). With Joyce and for *Ulysses,* this counsel is especially apt, for he organizes the text as a series of lessons about how to read for the ideal, a series of lessons designed to construct a reader who can make it to "Ithaca" and its representation of the ideal in Bloom. Joyce works to earn the reader's confidence that he is indeed an authority capable of inscribing an ideal in his text.

Altieri is careful not to sound naive or anachronistic in his call for the reader's renewed respect for the author and his "provisional" cultural authority. He values the radical doubt of poststructuralism but laments its inability to teach anything but negative lessons, lessons about how not to be fooled by language, about how not to be mystified by language's seeming ability to present truths. Without giving up the strengths poststructural methodologies have gained for our reading, we must learn to do more than note what the author is blind to but seek to ascertain what the author actually sees and can show us. Altieri asks us to value once again what he calls "authorial struggles" (Altieri, 13) to present a set of values emanating from the author, through the text, to a reader. We ought not limit ourselves to debunking and demystifying because that greatly limits the scope of what literature can be said to present as valuable. We ought to allow the possibility for the author to be a controlling presence leading the reader to a positive lesson about values and ideals. With Joyce this model of reading works especially well, for this author is hardly naive about the nature of language, especially literary language, and its capacity to mislead a reader to easy assent to a false ideal merely by the power and beauty of style and technique. Altieri's model fits Joyce's text well because Joyce is teaching his reader all the negative lessons about mystification on the way to a discovery of a language that can be trusted to represent the ideal in writing.

It is fitting, therefore, that Joyce pattern his novel upon the allegory of theologians, which is a way of reading as much as it is a way of writing. Perhaps it is best to say that it is a way of writing that is about reading, for what Saint Paul inaugurates is a way of reading beyond the intentions of the human authors of the various books of the Old Testament to the intention of their true and ultimate author, God. Saint Paul refuses to read merely for the literal meaning but finds, after the Christ event, a way of reading beyond the veil to the spiritual truth of the texts. Analogously, Joyce devises narrators whose capacities are too limited and whose intentions too narrow, and he places enough exegetical clues in the episodes that we become aware of these limitations and begin reading beyond what the narrator of any episode knows and depicts. *Ulysses* is about learning to read beyond its own narrators, and Joyce writes this book to be about certain parts of it being read, or reread from a later privileged point of view. Episode after episode presents the reader with a lesson on how to read this particular text, until we are so empowered as readers that we know how to create the conclusion of the novel ourselves. The allegory of theologians and, in turn, Joyce's modernist allegory are a kind of writing that is based on a kind of reading, a kind of writing that includes its own lessons about how to read itself.

This liberation of the reader from the naturalistic or literal levels of signification and the empowerment to become a spiritual reader are precisely what the allegory of theologians accomplishes. According to Paul, those who read the Old Testament only for the letter are kept from its truth: "Since we have such a hope, we are very bold, not like Moses, who put a veil over his face so that the Israelites might not see the end of his fading splendor. But their minds were hardened; for to this day, when they read the old covenant, that same veil remains unlifted, because only through Christ is it taken away. Yes, to this day whenever Moses is read a veil lies over their minds; but when a man turns to the Lord the veil is removed" (2 Cor. 3:12–16).

Joyce in his turn has fashioned a level of significance analogous to the old covenant, a level of meaning presented in terms of the naturalistic novel that sees the literal or historical truth of our lives. But those who can read the novel from the point of view of Joyce's "Christ event" presented through Stephen's recognition of Bloom as a version of Christ in "Ithaca" are the ones who can lift the veil of the naturalistic novel and reread *Ulysses* as modernist allegory. The "Lotus Eaters" narrator cannot lift the veil from Bloom's face and so cannot see "the light of inspiration shining in his countenance" that the "Ithaca" narrator sees so clearly, after the fact and so upon retrospection. Some of us are bound to read as the Mulligans of the world read, with a cynical eye that deflates the ideal and drains life from the world; but some of us can read with an eye trained in the allegory of theologians and lift the veil of naturalism, piercing beneath its cover to see in Bloom something that was always there but kept hidden from our sight. Freccero comments on Paul's second letter to the Corinthians in a way that is useful to this study of *Ulysses:* "The significance of the letter is in its final term, Christ, who was present all along, but revealed as the spirit only at the end, the conversion of the Old Testament to the New. Understanding the truth is not then a question of critical intelligence applied here and there, but rather a retrospective illumination by faith from the standpoint of the ending, a conversion" (Freccero, 122). Understanding *Ulysses,* then, is a question of learning to reread it from the privileged position of Stephen's recognition of Bloom as a version of Christ in "Ithaca"—that is, near the very end of the novel. The meaning of the naturalistic novel suddenly undergoes a transformation—a conversion, to use Freccero's language and to continue the analogy—as we must review the plot and the characters after the revelation. The naturalistic novel is converted to modernist allegory.

The "allegory of theologians" and Joyce's modernist allegory are then firmly bound to the operations of memory, as the reader must "remember" or "reread" earlier events in light of later ones. At this point I want to emphasize a phrase of Freccero's that reminds me of a phrase from *Ulysses.* His "retrospective illumination" reminds me of Tom Kernan's phrase "retrospective arrangement," which is first introduced in "Hades" by Mr. Power as he and the others in the funeral carriage make fun of Kernan's propensity for lofty phrases and fancy words. The phrase is picked up by later narrators: in "Oxen of the Sun," as Bloom recalls his youth (14.1043); in "Circe," as Bloom invites Mrs. Breen to recall earlier days (15.443); and in "Eumaus," as the narrator reflects upon failed homecomings as Bloom is leading Stephen back to 7 Eccles street (16.1401). Beginning as a joke at Tom Kernan's expense, the phrase gains in potential significance through the repetitions; in fact, to read this book we must learn that what begins comically in *Ulysses* often becomes quite serious—what is at first mocked often later becomes sacred. This phrase is Joyce's clue to the reader that the novel must be approached as a "book of memory," as one whose meaning unfolds only upon the retrospective arrangement of material permitted and encouraged by memory.

John S. Rickard has written an impressive study in which he details the various sources for Joyce's understanding and use of memory in *Ulysses.* Rickard relies on a distinction between two kinds of memory described by Edward Casey, a passivist and an activist model of memory. The first sees memory as a storehouse of fixed or dead images that have been collected and can be retrieved when the mind so desires (Rickard, 9). The activist model of memory posits a more complex agency in which what is stored is not only retrievable but open to the operations of interpretation and imagination (10). Rickard sees both kinds of memory operating in *Ulysses* and in fact sees the novel not as "an odyssey of styles," as Karen Lawrence sees it, but as an "odyssey through memory" (13) where the characters try to use memory to resolve their personal problems. I do not wish to follow Rickard as he watches how the characters use one or the other form of memory as much as to watch how the text, at different points, relies on one and then the other form. In the earlier naturalistic episodes the passivist model rules, and as the novel develops the activist model becomes increasingly relevant. Obviously, the allegory of theologians relies on an activist memory, which can shape and reassess earlier events and not merely retrieve fixed images. The reassessment in "Ithaca" of Bloom's tip, which he inadvertently gave back in "Lotus Eaters," is a wonderful example of memory as activist. The reader becomes empowered to move from the relative paralysis of the passivist model to the freedom and fulfillment of the activist.

The source for Joyce's understanding of memory, never mentioned by Rickard, is ultimately Dante, who calls *Vita Nuova* "my Book of Memory" in which he struggles to understand the full significance of his lifelong relation to Beatrice, who has become, in the retrospective illumination of memory's operation, "the *now* glorious lady of my mind" (*Vita Nuova*, 3, my emphasis). By the time the book is finished, Beatrice has become almost identified with Christ, as the one who bears salvation for Dante and the one who brings him the vision that becomes the *Divina Commedia*. Dante's epic is also written "in retrospective arrangement," for the poet has already experienced the journey and writes it as he remembers it. The distance between the pilgrim in the story and the poet who writes it is large at first but slowly narrows until they are one, in the upper heavens seeing God. The poet remembers what he was like before the experience and writes about how the pilgrim became the man who can write the poem.

Joyce's writing is closely tied to the laws and operations of memory. For both Joyce and Dante, memory is central to the kind of writing they employ to present their visions. Rickard cites Saint Augustine, who in his *Confessions* makes the claim that we have access to knowledge of God in and through the agency of memory (Rickard, 101). Rickard cites as a classic study of memory, which contains spiritual light and truths, Frances Yates's *The Art of Memory*, in which Yates demonstrates how for medieval theologians, memory was an activist agency that worked upon images until they shone with the light of God. Joyce's interest in Giordano Bruno is relevant in indicating his "medieval" understanding of the powers of memory. Joyce in fact organizes his text to move from one kind of memory to the other, from the passivist mode that can only retrieve fixed images to the activist mode that can transform those images into spiritual truths. The text holds onto earlier images and plays with them until they are finally understood, as the identification of Bloom with Elijah and Christ is advanced and debunked, only to keep on being advanced until it can be maintained. The reader indeed goes on "an odyssey of memory," journeying through the various lessons of the text until he can understand what Joyce is presenting to him in "Ithaca." It is no accident that the final image of the text, the last words of "Penelope," are Molly's memory of an event that occurred sixteen years ago but that has been made to grow in significance as the ringing affirmative that ends the book. The reader has learned to reread, or remember, earlier events until he is empowered to witness the revelation of Bloom as the "traditional figure of hypostasis."

The challenge is to present this revelation in a way that is not susceptible to mockery.[5] That mockery is a central problem of *Ulysses* is made evident on the opening page, where the greatest mocker in all literature presides over a mock-Eucharist. The manner of communication of the ideal in *Ulysses* is, then, by careful design, oblique and secretive, almost defying the reader to discover the key to the novel's hidden meaning. The allegorical dimension of Bloom's character must be kept secret from those who know only how to read the letter, from those adept at mockery and ironic reduction of the ideal to its lowest possible existence. To simplify for the moment, we can say that Joyce's experiments with style and technique have as their goal the simultaneous depiction and concealment of Bloom's allegorical identity. It is to be presented, but so obliquely that it is kept safe from easy discernment; in a word, it must be protected from mockers. Frank Kermode makes secrecy a principle fundamental to all narrative in *The Genesis of Secrecy*, as he argues that all tellings have an inside and an outside, spiritual readers who can read for truth and carnal readers who are blocked from the spirit and can only read the letter.[6] *Ulysses* is written so obliquely largely to produce a reader who can see what Stephen sees in "Ithaca," who can penetrate to the inside, who can read for spiritual truth. The empowered reader constructed by the narrative experiments of *Ulysses* approaches the truth this text wishes to indicate and from this position creates the order and meaning of the novel.

Modernist Allegory and Postmodernism

Ulysses, in its dazzling array of perspectives and seemingly inconclusive nature, offers critics a wonderful opportunity for celebrating what Umberto Eco calls the "open work." Ihab Hassan makes openness a hallmark feature of "the postmodern turn," and he cites a Joyce critic, Robert Adams, as he defines open form as "a structure of meanings that 'include a major unresolved conflict with the intent of displaying its unresolvedness'" (Hassan, 13). Eco is an especially important critic for my argument, for he appreciates both the ordered cosmos of the medieval world that was able to create allegory with its ordered levels of meaning and the "open" work that, because it lacks the "key to [its] symbolism," is inexhaustible in significance (see "The Poetics of the Open Work" in *The Open Work*, especially pages 5–9). If *Ulysses* has no center, no revelation that is outside the play of language, then it is best approached as an example of the open work, or what Eco calls in another work specifically on Joyce, a "chaosmos," a pleasure-giving version of chaos, without order, without goal: the medieval world of Dante without the transcendent center, without which the extraordinary amount of perspectives and observations collapse into chaosmos. And without doubt such approaches have borne much fruit in illuminating aspects of this and other modernist texts that were ignored, or at least pushed into the background, by approaches that searched for unity and wholeness. *Ulysses* shares many of the characteristics of what we now call postmodernism, and critics such as Eco have been extremely instructive in helping us enjoy the playfulness and ambiguities of Joyce's text. But in refusing, out of principle, to look for a fixed perspective from which to view the novel as a unified and cohesive whole, we have allowed a powerful critical trend to transform *Ulysses* into something it is not, a "postmodernist" work that eludes any attempt to find its master narrative, that gladly slides from perspective to perspective and so avoids the fixity that postmodern language theory never can permit as a possibility. It is time to make a definition of modernism that insists on the achievement of unity in the face of the immense challenge of chaos and diffusion.

As the better critics of postmodernism have always insisted, "postmodernism" as a critical term is not meant to refer to a specific time period (the era after modernism) but a kind of writing and a kind of reading that can retrospectively be applied to any text from whatever historical period. But the kind of writing that we celebrate as postmodern may indeed be the writing produced in the years after World War II and during the cold war when fears of ruthless totalitarian order were still active; writers living with the fresh memory of the horrors of totalitarian rule tended to avoid closure in their works and refused all gestures toward grand unity and order. Up until quite recently we were still living in this climate of suspicion so well described by Tobin Siebers in *Cold War Criticism and the Politics of Skepticism*, and criticism of Joyce's text has been highly influenced by this kind of skepticism. It appears quite plainly that recent, maybe even current, critical trends, when they confront a text such as *Ulysses*, shy away from imposing any fixed perspective or final meaning to the text, as if doing so were totalitarian and ruthless. The skepticism that opened criticism up to new insights has, in true totalitarian fashion, closed off the possibility of closure and finitude, even if the text plainly was making efforts to reach such. There is a tendency to see any effort to find unity and cohesion as fascistic, as playing out a desire for order that is in some sinister way brutal and aggressive. I hope to show that the kind of order made possible by Joyce's modernist allegory is gentle and loving and more capable of providing joy and kindness than the kind of openness so blindly celebrated. The critical skepticism Siebers describes may be well attuned to the ambitions of many writers of the cold war era, but it fails to do justice to the high modernist texts of the pre–World War II era, which were intended to react against skepticism and present ideals in an oblique and almost secretive way, rendered safe from the mocking cynicism of a Buck Mulligan. By following Joyce's efforts to present an ideal form of behavior, we can once again learn to appreciate modernism in its most subtle and supple manifestation.

With this much said, I want to admit that there is much in *Ulysses* that encourages what we can call a postmodernist approach and that the insights of postmodern critics have opened up Joyce scholarship in important ways. In fact, I want to go so far as to say that, up to a point, the postmodern critics see Joyce's book more clearly and more keenly than the earlier critics who may have assumed closure and unity uncritically. *Ulysses* is best approached as a playful book of multiple perspectives creating bliss and joy in our reading, but only up to a point, for the allegory of theologians allows for a positing of a center that is not ruthless and totalitarian, a governing principle that does not insist on every detail coming under its powerful sway but instead allows for free play of most details while only gathering a strand into full significance. Joyce's modernist allegory allows for an order that comforts and a free play that gives joy.

I want to look briefly at some "postmodern" critics of Joyce's book to establish my own sense of the grand solution to these problems that Joyce carried out with his "modernist allegory." In *The Myth of the Modern*, Perry Meisel argues how T. S. Eliot's reading of *Ulysses*, in its emphasis on unity and order, had more to do with his own efforts in *The Waste Land* than it does to Joyce's text, and that Richard Aldington's claim—that *Ulysses* is "an invitation to chaos"—is more apt. For Meisel, Joyce values more than order and unity "the free play of language" that puts in question the mythical archetypes "by which the Homeric analogue seems to give a fixed order to what is otherwise a porous and pleasurable chaos" (Meisel, 143). The order and unity are only apparent, the use of Homeric parallel "an ironic gesture toward the kind of mythic replication erected by Eliot as the novel's ultimate organizing device. Any reading of *Ulysses* is, to use Hugh Kenner's phrase, one of "so many trial alignments," or, to use Fritz Senn's terms, reading *Ulysses* is a "polytropic endeavor" based upon any of a variety of "serial approaches" (Meisel, 144). There is no key to the book that unlocks its secrets and masters its apparently discrete details, only various efforts to understand aspects of the book that, when valid at all, are ultimately partial and local, not total or universal. In a powerful critique of nostalgia, Meisel argues that Joyce turns away all efforts to recuperate origins in a witty refusal to become backward-looking and mournful, and instead he turns forward to a series of styles and techniques meant only to give pleasure. What Meisel wants to emphasize is the irony and burlesque in *Ulysses,* the great joy in parody and the delight in moments of apparently free play. Valuing these seems to require a relinquishing of any key to the book and any center to ground and govern meaning. The reader is given an ultimatum.

The most useful study of the postmodern aspects of *Ulysses* for my purposes is Kevin Dettmar's *The Illicit Joyce of Postmodernism,* for his intention is to construct a postmodern paradigm that he can apply to Joyce's book; his study shows the many strengths and the severe limitation of such an approach, a limitation that modernist allegory addresses and corrects. He is particularly indebted to the writing of Jean-François Lyotard and Roland Barthes, and as I review Dettmar's book I will indicate how my own approach relies on such postmodern critiques of language and seeks to adjust to an idealist agenda. Citing Lyotard's formulation that grand or master narratives have lost their credibility (Lyotard, 37), Dettmar argues that "the postmodern moment . . . is the point at which we see these narratives of containment breaking down, failing to account for the wildness we feel in our reading experience" (Dettmar, 8). The wildness of reading Joyce's text occurs, I presume, when the various narratives he constructs fail to hold up and the detail, dazzling and discrete, explodes before us in its playful bliss. Like Meisel, Dettmar seems to assume that to return to the joy of Joyce's text one must surrender the grand narrative and high modernist purpose: "Postmodern stylistics, I argue, values textual play over high artistic purpose, respects mystery over the writer's desire for mastery, and renounces global narrative structures in favor of small, local, often capricious textual strategies, celebrating the ineluctably heterogeneous, participatory, and excessive character of all texts" (Dettmar, 10). It seems to me that Joyce has found a way to have it both ways, celebrating the excess while still providing a master narrative of global significance.

Dettmar turns to Barthes's discussion of bliss to explain Joyce's postmodern sense of language: "Modernism remains wedded to the project of ever more faithfully representing the signified; but the pleasure of the text,

Barthes claims, derives from 'value shifted to the sumptuous rank of the signifier'" (Dettmar, 21). Joyce does indeed have this awareness of language, which allows him to bring the reader on a journey through various styles and techniques where each literary language deployed is not able to represent anything like truth. We watch a series of stylistic experiments that seem to have no interest in anything outside language, no interest in the signified, but instead celebrate the signifier. How else to explain the fun of reading episodes such as "Sirens" and "Oxen of the Sun," where the language is almost opaque and the interest in representation seems minimal at best? Dettmar wants us to abandon a search for the author's message and instead merely delight in the language, to abandon a concern for the author's ends and instead focus on the means (24). I want to affirm that this approach does indeed capture the Joycean spirit of play, yet abandons the possibility that Joyce, in his playfulness, may still have a message and still believe that there is a truth to indicate in his writing. Dettmar quotes Barthes effectively: "When I reread . . . it is invariably for a ludic advantage: to multiply signifiers, not to reach some ultimate signified" (26). Again, Dettmar points us directly to the gist of the problem: no text is more playful than *Ulysses,* and no author desires our joy in our reading more; yet rereading Joyce's book does eventually, after multiplying signifiers, point us to an ultimate signified.

When Dettmar cites Barthes to the effect that language is never neutral and transparent but instead is a "discursive space, heavy with the odor of previous usages and incapable, unwilling to serve as the instrument for the search for Truth" (Dettmar, 39), I want to counter that Joyce senses this very problem with language but has not given up on truth, nor on his ability to indicate it in and through writing. When Dettmar cites Lyotard that "language has become a self-conscious critic of its own ability to transcend its inherent materiality" (39), I again want to exclaim that Joyce had already seen this and in *Ulysses* works to bring us toward a moment of such transcendence. I agree with Dettmar that the "stylistic pyrotechnics" of the later episodes "serve not to 'express' the episodes' events more clearly, but rather by calling attention to the writing itself to elevate style to the level of an event, and to call attention to the intrinsically artificial nature of all discourse" (Dettmar, 142). In *The Postmodern Condition,* Lyotard makes the point that the artist, and the critic, must give up the search for "truth" and instead look for the rules one must accept to play the game of significance (Lyotard, 39). When these rules are found, the artist must question them, and when questioned the rules soon appear to be a means not to find truth but to deceive. My study is based on this very awareness that Joyce makes central to *Ulysses,* and my claim is that Joyce differs from these postmodern critiques of language only in and simply by not abandoning the search for a language capable of representing truth. Joyce includes the postmodern critique of language in his book and works to overcome its challenges and its stated limitations to artistic possibilities.

Dettmar makes a claim that I have no quarrel with and in fact would like to make central to my own study: "Joyce, all his life long, harbored within himself these two contradictory spirits: the high modernist purpose and the low postmodern play, a belief in the work as creation of the artist as God, and an awareness of the Text as the construction of the Artist as *bricoleur*—the co-creation of a Text and its readers" (Dettmar, 108). My quarrel with Dettmar and the general effort to make *Ulysses* into a postmodern text is that such critics make the ideological choice of abandoning the high purpose for the low play, a choice Joyce does not make because his modernist allegory reconciles the two.

To indicate how Joyce's method of allegory may indeed reconcile these apparently contradictory spirits, I want to return to an apparently small point made by Singleton in the course of his groundbreaking analysis of Dante's use of the allegory of theologians: "Indeed it was generally recognized in Holy Scripture the historical sense might at times be the only sense there. These things have been so; so they have happened in time. This is the record of them" (Singleton, 62). The allegory of theologians does not call for every detail on the literal level or in the historical sense to become part of the pattern on the allegorical level of meaning; not every event must be reread from the privileged point of view of the Christ event as having anticipated that cardinal event. Only a strand of details must be gathered up in this rereading and made part of the allegorical pattern, allowing other details to remain discrete, open, free. The allegory of theologians, and by extension Joyce's modernist allegory, permits closure on the highest level of meaning while still allowing free play on the lowest. High modernist purpose and low postmodern play are indeed reconciled in this mode of writing.

Joyce has discovered a kind of order based on love that does not close off the possibility of free play and indeterminacy of meaning for much of its details. Not every detail must become part of a totalizing unity; it is an order that is not ruthless and total, that gathers up some details into a noble ideal while allowing the life of the body and materiality and history to move on in its random and indeterminate way. Joyce's modernist allegory provides a satisfying order while still allowing free play.

This kind of writing can answer the problems that postmodern critics leave hanging in their analyses. Phillip Herring, for instance, has written a study of Joyce called *Joyce's Uncertainty Principle* in which he claims that

Joyce carefully leaves out essential evidence in order for unsolvable problems to remain in his texts (Herring, ix–x). Herring boldly claims that the information we need for full identity and closure to exist in *Ulysses* simply does not exist and that every effort to find such closure is doomed to failure (xii). He advances two examples of such missing information, Stephen's unsolvable riddle in "Nestor" and the man in the mackintosh who first appears in "Hades." I agree that the second of these especially is unsolvable and that there is nothing in the text that can be used to make a clear and certain identification of this enigmatic figure. But Joyce's allegorical mode of writing allows for such indeterminacy to exist on the literal level; not every mystery need be cleared up, not every riddle answered. But Joyce's writing allows for some closure, and it is enough if we can see what Stephen sees in Bloom—that he is a figure of Christ. Bloom's identity is not indeterminate, but the modernist allegory can allow M'Intosh's to be so. The need for order is not total or totalizing in Joyce; not everything and everyone need be mastered. Just certain details need to be made allegorically meaningful, and that pattern of Christian love is enough.

Joyce has found a mode of writing that allows this reconciliation of apparently contradictory needs, the need for closure and the need for openness, the need for an ideal pattern and the need for random play. And the mode of writing that accomplishes this is profoundly Christian, requiring a vision of Christ to function as the center of this loving and playful order. Robert Boyle has studied Joyce's relation to Catholicism and testifies to Joyce's distaste for organized religion but his profound need for faith and mystery (Boyle, 8). Boyle even notes how Joyce sees great works of literature as analogous to inspired Scripture (9) and that Joyce's aesthetic may be based on the Incarnation (47). But this Catholic critic does not quite grasp just how thoroughly and how precisely Joyce devises a kind of writing based on Scriptural allegory. An earlier Catholic literary critic, William Lynch, who is not thinking about Joyce's writing, actually comes closer to describing what I am calling modernist allegory when he discusses what he calls "the Christian imagination." He calls for a literature that works to universalize while at the same time remaining concretely particular, and this is "Christian" because it is in the Incarnation that we have a model for a being who is both timeless and bound to time, universal and unique, ideal yet fleshly (Lynch, 187ff.). Even in the Resurrection narratives, where he is revealed as fully divine, there is an emphasis on Christ's material body.[7] Joyce's modernist allegory places a vision of Christ at the center as Bloom, very much a man of flesh and blood, is raised to allegorical significance in and through Joyce's writing. In this way Joyce exhibits the fullest Christian imagination since Dante.

The study of *Ulysses* that follows is by and large a careful reconstruction of Joyce's attitude toward the genre in which he chose to write, following the development of this text as it offers a series of critiques of the novel as a genre and its inability to accomplish the larger purposes Joyce has in mind. The first chapter examines the opening six episodes of *Ulysses*, demonstrating that Joyce's skills in naturalistic depiction are intended to show the limits of the naturalism and to reject its tendency toward deflation and death. The second chapter shows how Joyce begins to take liberties from the traditional novelistic mode of representation, beginning a process of abstraction similar to the abstraction of modernist painting as understood by T. E. Hulme. The third chapter examines Joyce's self-consciousness about various kinds of rhetorical devices and about language itself, as the reader is being led to look outside language for something permanent and stable. In the fourth and fifth chapters I show how the reader has become so empowered by these critiques that he can see traces of another story in *Ulysses* beyond the novelistic story, the story of an epic return home in chapter 4 and of an allegorical climax in chapter 5. Stage by stage *Ulysses* instructs its reader about itself until we can see the allegory that is its secret goal.

Once we can follow the way Joyce writes modernist allegory, we will be able to see how Eliot, Pound, and Stevens all enact the same kind of writing in what critics have long seen as their greatest works— *Four Quartets, The Pisan Cantos,* and *Notes toward a Supreme Fiction,* all written about the same time and under the extraordinary pressure of World War II. With the violence of that war making the claims of history and of reality impossible to dismiss with the flight of imagination, these modernists are led to a reevaluation of their understanding of the imagination's role in responding to history. Like Joyce, they find a way to reconcile the demands of history with the needs of the imagination, the realistic appraisal of human life as violent and fragmented balanced by a respect for the imagination's ability to find order and unity. As I will argue in the conclusion, allegory's very special quality is that it can provide the unity of an ideal without the oppressive control of a totalizing force. Modernist allegory provides a solution to the dilemma that became our central poetic and critical concern in the 1950s to the present, how to balance our need for order and our fear of oppression. Joyce wrote the earliest, and fullest, modernist allegory, and his example allowed for the flourishing of great writing by his fellow modernists when their poetic lives were most challenged.

Chapter One

The Novel as Death
The Limits of Naturalism

The significance of the early episodes of *Ulysses* can only be fully grasped upon a rereading of the novel, and even then only if one is reading from the moment in "Ithaca" when Stephen sees in Bloom "the traditional figure of hypostasis." It would be disingenuous, it seems to me, to pretend that any serious and helpful account of *Ulysses* can be the product of anyone's first reading, and it seems equally disingenuous to tailor an account of the novel's unfolding "as if" it were one's first time through it. All readings of *Ulysses*, then—and of any novel, for that matter—have already been "rereadings," so what makes the present study different? I think the difference is that I will be examining the episodes before and the episode after "Ithaca" as they take on meaning in relation to a privileged point of view. The novel is designed to take on its fullest meaning only once this moment is confronted and understood. So when analyzing the opening six episodes, I will be asking questions that are prompted by having already experienced the moment of hypostasis.

If I am correct about Joyce's use of the "allegory of theologians," *Ulysses* is constructed according to a model of writing that is based on the Incarnation. This throws new weight on the opening of the novel, in which Buck Mulligan playfully performs a mock-Eucharist. In "Proteus," Stephen uses the word "hypostasis" to refer to the eternal presence of Christ in the Eucharist, whereas the term is meant to refer to the union of God and man in Christ. This "error" may be of the kind that in "Scylla and Charybdis" Stephen calls "a portal of discovery," for we are invited to see how Joyce is using the Eucharist to suggest and stand for the Incarnation. In fact, Robert Boyle contends that "Stephen is considering, as Occam did, that the hypostatic union effected in the Incarnation is the basis for the multilocation effected in the Eucharist" (in Kain, 51). Boyle's clarification allows us to see that Stephen is pondering how the artist as priest can take the singular event of the Incarnation—it happened just once and for all time, in the person of Jesus—and make it, through the power of ritualistic words, occur in many places at the same time; that is, the artist can repeat the Incarnation in the Eucharist. What Buck mocks so gaily in the opening scene is the possibility of a ritual—religious or artistic—bringing the divine into the world. About *Dubliners,* according to Ellmann, Joyce made this comment to his brother: "Don't you think that there is a certain resemblance between the mystery of the mass and what I am trying to do? I mean that I am trying . . . to give people some kind of intellectual pleasure or spiritual enjoyment by converting the bread of everyday life into something that has a permanent artistic life of its own . . . for their mental, moral, and spiritual uplift" (Ellmann, *James Joyce,* 103–4). This statement carries the exuberance of youthful bravado, yet it is interesting that Joyce has recourse to the ritual of the Catholic Mass in which ordinary bread and wine are transubstantiated into the body and blood of Christ as he tries to describe what he is trying to do in and by his writing. Note how "the bread of everyday life" is to be transformed into "something that has a permanent artistic life," the transient becoming permanent. Ellmann notes that Joyce uses the word "eucharistic" to describe the intent and effect of his youthful epiphanies, and a scene occurs in *Stephen Hero* where Stephen melodramatically reflects that he "spent days and nights hammering noisily as he built a house of silence for himself wherein he might await his Eucharist" (*SH,* 30). This last image is quite instructive, for it depicts the artist working feverishly to build a church wherein the Eucharistic event—the repetition of the Incarnation—can take place. "Ithaca" will present such a place and such an event.

Yet he opens the novel with the voice and sensibility of a glib and witty mocker who is always prepared to deny and reject the kind of elevation to heroic or ideal height that Joyce intends to perform with Bloom. Robert Bell sees Buck's role well: "Buck persistently burlesques everything abstract, ethereal, or idealistic. Nothing is left unchallenged; everything is open to travesty, parody, mockery. The tug downward is insistent in *Ulysses,* and Buck Mulligan is the apostle of gravity" (Bell, 14). The opening episode, indeed the first six episodes, can be said to be written in the style of the mocker, the style of naturalistic fiction that reduces all ideals to some lower, more vulgar, and for some reason more "realistic" motives, usually sex and money, and sets the individual within the narrow constraints of various kinds of environmental determinants.[1] But Bell is wrong to say that "the text eventually approaches Buck's view" (21); in fact, just the opposite is true. But Buck Mulligan dominates the opening episode of *Ulysses* to present the challenge the novel must confront, to overcome the ironic reduction of the cynical mocker whose sophistication and wit are turned against ideals. While Joyce intends elevation, he begins his novel with the voice of reductive and deflating mockery. If Bloom is to rise, it will be against the strenuous pull downward of "the apostle of gravity."

In some important ways it will also be against the strenuous downward pull of the novel, as a genre, itself. One of the main features of my argument about *Ulysses* is that it is enacting the history of the novel, and for the most part concluding that the genre is a dead end, that it is not able to perform the acts Joyce wants to perform upon Bloom. We do not need to look beyond the pioneering work of Ian Watt to be convinced that the novel as a genre has as its essential criterion the principle of plausibility, and to make events seem plausible novelists will often reject ideals as motivations and will tend to make characters seem realistic by attributing to them motivations that are low, common, vulgar. The tradition of the novel that sees itself as most realistic tends to present characters as caught within a web of circumstance that defines their identities and determines their options, which are quite severely limited. Of course, this is only a tendency, but it is one that deserves to be considered a dominant tendency and one that becomes increasingly powerful in the nineteenth century—in England in the novels of George Eliot and Thomas Hardy, in America in the novels of William Dean Howells and Stephen Crane, and, for Joyce, most importantly in France in the works of Gustave Flaubert and Emile Zola. This tradition of realism in the novel comes to its most extreme expression in what we call naturalism, and Joyce begins his own career as a fiction writer by producing some of the finest stories in the naturalistic mode.

I define "naturalism" as a way of regarding human existence from a strictly naturalistic point of view, a way of evaluating and understanding humanity that restricts itself solely to explanations based on natural laws and principles. Such a definition depends on a Darwinian understanding of nature and our place in it. For Darwin, even the aspects of our lives that are most usually understood as outside or above mere nature—intellect, artistic performance, morality—are understood within a purely naturalistic context as developments increasing our ability to survive in a brutal and competitive natural world—as developments best understood through the concept of "natural selection." Gillian Beer and George Levine study the impact of Darwinian thinking upon the novel in the mid to late Victorian era, and their studies underlie my own sense of the genre as Joyce inherits it and chooses to understand it. Levine argues that the attempt at scrupulous realism in this period was encouraged and even conditioned by the scientific discourse initiated by Darwin (Levine, 12). While the novelist in the Victorian era still found design in our lives that becomes the basis for plot, Darwinian thinking emphasizes randomness and mere sequence of events that only end with death (16–18). Joyce's naturalism is this radical kind of naturalism: the only shape the naturalistic novelist can find is paralysis, which I understand as the repetition of attempts to escape the human condition that fail, and death. The only telos in the naturalist's worldview is decay and death.

Joyce in *Dubliners,* and in the opening episodes of *Ulysses,* is a writer of prose who studies human subjects from a strictly naturalistic perspective. What Joyce does by writing these is to provide himself with an important lesson about the realistic or naturalistic style, that what it does best is present failure, limit, confinement, death. Each of the stories in *Dubliners* presents a character struggling to break free from the paralysis of Dublin, only unable to make the movement away that would be a sign of hope, if not outright success. Joyce manages to present a variety of characters all suffering from the same disease, a variety marked by different degrees of self-consciousness about their confinement and different responses to it. There is the slight self-awareness of an Eveline or a Maria and the more acute and refined consciousness of a James Duffy or a Little Chandler, but intellect is no advantage in successfully coping with the situation. Each and every story is about failure and loss, as if that is all such a style can render, as if that is all naturalism is capable of presenting.

There is the possible exception of "The Dead," in which Gabriel Conroy at least manages a moment of sympathy with his wife and for whom we might entertain some degree of hope. But we can also choose to emphasize the coldness of the ending, the hint of his own passing away as the only solution to his predicament, the covering of all Ireland with the coldness of death as Gabriel manages his moment of self-conscious longing; after all, the story is called "The Dead," and death is what all naturalistic tales might ultimately be about.

As Joyce was writing these stories, he was also busy at work on *Stephen Hero,* which by its very title indicates the dissatisfaction Joyce was feeling with the mode of *Dubliners;* he needed to find a style in which to write about heroism, and that is the modernist problem, as Wallace Stevens announced forty years later in "The Noble Rider and the Sound of Words."[2] Since Joyce tried to burn the manuscript for *Stephen Hero,* we are offered a dramatic image of just how inadequate the traditional style of the novel was proving itself for the ends Joyce was moving toward. He was able to transform a story about a young artist as hero into *A Portrait of the Artist as a Young Man,* an ironic rendering of what he had thought of as heroism, a detached portrait of that young man struggling for heroism but not necessarily succeeding. What I want to suggest is that the reason for the existence of *A Portrait* in its present form is Joyce's inability as yet to find a style capable of presenting the noble, the heroic, the ideal. This is not to say that *A Portrait* is simply a longer story that could fit into *Dubliners*; instead, we ought to see in it an advance from naturalism toward something we might want to call ironic realism. For Joyce is trying to present a young man trying to break free from the paralysis of Dublin and failing, only to try again, and again, and again; when *Ulysses* opens, we are used to a young man who is not given to accepting defeat. The structure of *A Portrait* is ironic: each episode ends with what looks to the youthful protagonist as a triumph, as an act of heroism, only for that act to be punctured by some event or some set of events in the very next episode. That is the structure of ironic realism, for the young Stephen to continue to come to the realization that his escape is not as easy as he had been expecting. If *A Portrait* is Joyce's version of the growth of a soul, that growth is not marked by some steady movement toward fullness but by fits and starts, as the young man achieves what he hopes is some moment of greatness only to learn that he has failed. These moments of ironic self-awareness are perhaps the moments of growth, as the young man learns that escape from Dublin is not simple or easy and that it will require some extraordinary act of which he is not yet aware. Rather than seeing *A Portrait* as a version of a *Dubliners* story, it is more instructive to see how this protagonist is never successful in his effort to escape but also never defeated.

A brief description of *A Portrait*'s structure will be useful to set up my argument about Stephen's role in *Ulysses*. The first chapter ends with a very young Stephen being accorded a hero's welcome by his fellow classmates after he returned from the rector's office having informed Father Conmee of Father Dolan's unjust treatment of himself. The boys saw this as a bit of plucky courage, and Stephen is quite smug in his cool reception of the boys' cheers. The episode ends with this act of triumph, only for it to be taken away by a casual remark by his father in the next chapter. Having by chance encountered Father Conmee somewhere in town, Simon recounts the priest's version of Stephen's triumphant moment, which ends with the two priests laughing over Stephen's courage and Simon's own laughter in telling it all to the family. We are not brought into Stephen's mind at this point, but we are invited to see what effect this would have on the sensitive child: his act of heroism only provided the adults with a comic story! This is how Joyce chooses to have Stephen grow, with sudden moments of self-awareness about his own failures at achieving his heroic status. The second chapter ends with another moment in which Stephen feels triumphant, as he enters a prostitute's vulgar room but sees instead romance and wonder. His freedom from Dublin morality, which is what his sexual awakening means to him, is abruptly taken away in the next chapter by the sermon he hears on hell at the school's retreat. The third episode ends with Stephen's heroic conversion to piety, as he becomes holy and chaste in the manner of great saints, only for that to be taken away by his recognition of the emptiness of the priest's words when he talks to Stephen about a vocation. Stephen heroically chooses the wandering, erring life of the artist, and we are not sure whether or not this decision is taken back by the long last chapter. Perhaps we have watched the artist grow to self-conscious maturity; for while the rhetoric at the end of the fourth chapter is excessive and to be distrusted, in the last chapter he is able to articulate the rudiments of an aesthetic theory and to begin his own writing. Perhaps he has grown enough that we are not pessimistic about his prospects abroad in Paris, when he literally at least escapes Dublin.

It is important to note that Stephen is a writer at the end of *A Portrait*, for the novel ends with Stephen's own written entries into a diary he is keeping that chronicles his growth. One entry indicates Stephen's growing awareness of the dangers of language. He dismisses the mental games Cranly plays with a grandiloquent phrase: "This mentality, Lepidus would say, is indeed bred out of your mud by the operation of your sun. And mine? Is it not too? Then into Nilemud with it!" (*AP*, 250). He reflects on this passage two days later: "Disapprove of this last phrase." While prone to flights of melodramatic rhetoric ("Then into Nilemud with it!"), he is become wary of such flights and can, upon reflection at least, see that this kind of language is not appropriate to his artistic purposes. Another entry gives us even greater cause to hope that Stephen has achieved an artist's soul: "Turned off that valve at once and opened the spiritual-heroic refrigerating apparatus, invented and patented in all countries by Dante Alighieri. Talked rapidly of myself and my plans. In the midst of it unluckily I made a sudden gesture of a revolutionary nature. I must have looked like a fellow throwing a handful of peas into the air. People began to look at us" (*AP*, 252). I find this a moment of great promise, not because he thinks he has achieved greatness but because he has achieved a certain distance on himself and is able to write about himself in clear and accurate prose. Not only is he aware of his acting coolly heroic in a borrowed mode ("the spiritual-heroic refrigerating apparatus" learned from Dante), but he is able to capture his excited gesture in the street: "I must have looked like a fellow throwing a handful of peas into the air." He is not so caught up with himself that he fails to see his own foolish, adolescent posturing, which he sees clearly and, more than that, can present quite powerfully. He has learned irony and distance as he leaves Dublin for Paris, and we have some hopes for him that he may not fail.

When *Ulysses* opens, Stephen is back in Dublin, and no matter what else we learn about him in the opening pages, this fact is enough perhaps to deflate any hopes we may have been entertaining as *A Portrait* ends. On the opening pages of *Ulysses*, Stephen is in the company of the arch ironist Buck Mulligan, whose warm and witty voice dominates the opening scene. The young man who struggled to learn irony is in the company of the great mocker: that is the dynamics of the opening scene. It is appropriate that the model for Buck Mulligan just happened to be in 1904 a medical student, for the perspective on life of a physician would tend to reduce most considerations to a material, physical level—"And what is death, he asked, your mother's or yours or my own? You saw only your mother die. I see them pop off every day in the Mater and Richmond and cut up into tripes in the dissecting room. It's a beastly thing and nothing else. It simply doesn't matter" (1.204–7).

Such a view is earned by hard experience and is valid, as far as it goes. "It's a beastly thing" is a fine and sincere assessment of death from a physician's point of view, but we may (and I think ought) to balk at "and nothing else. It simply doesn't matter." Death is indeed a "beastly thing" in that it is an aspect of our existence in nature that we share with the beasts. Buck's "naturalistic" view is valid but partial, severely limited to and by the material world and its concerns. To apply Tobin Siebers's thesis once again, this kind of skepticism doubts everything but its own doubting; Stephen is being given exposure to the most extreme kind of irony, that of the mocker. We, along with Stephen, must learn to doubt the doubter's ability to see the truth, to see beyond his limited perspective, to "mock the mocker," as William Butler Yeats sings in *Nineteen Hundred and Nineteen*.[3] We already know Stephen, and we are watching Buck perform through the artist's "displeased and sleepy" eyes. Stephen, and not Buck Mulligan as Robert Bell would have it, is our standard through whom we are to measure the irony and mockery of naturalistic prose.

It is Buck's tendency to reduce most concerns to a low level through his charming banter and mockery. His favorite target, at least on the morning we are privileged to hear him, is Christianity. "The Ballad of Joking Jesus" is prominent, I imagine, in most impressions of "Telemachus" for its skillful wit and happy blasphemy. Most tellingly, what Mulligan is mocking is the Incarnation, the Christ event:

—I'm the queerest young fellow that ever you heard.
My mother's a jew, my father's a bird.
With Joseph the joiner I cannot agree,
So here's to disciples and Calvary.

(1.584–87)

The mystery of the Incarnation is mocked in what seems a merry drinking song. One of my cardinal points about Joyce's method in *Ulysses* is that he will mock, through one of his characters, the very things he will be taking seriously. Mockery of things spiritual or idealistic is central to the design of this novel, for mockery—extreme naturalism in its wittiest and most engaging form—is the danger to be overcome. Mulligan's song concludes with mockery of Christ's ascension:

> —Goodbye, now goodbye! Write down all I said
> And tell Tom, Dick and Harry I rose from the dead.
> What's bred in the bone cannot fail me to fly
> And Olivet's breezy—Goodbye, now, goodbye!
> (1.596–99)

The ascension of Christ is a particularly important motif for *Ulysses*, for it establishes the possibility of a man of flesh and blood overcoming the downward pull of gravity and rising heavenward. When in "Ithaca" we are told of Bloom's weight—eleven stone and four pounds—we are also told that he last weighed himself on the last feast of the Ascension. Bloom's weight—the measure of the force of the earth's gravitational pull on matter—is what the early episodes are limited to describing and what the later episodes attempt to overcome as he rises to the heavens and becomes one with "the stars at which [he and Stephen] gaze." This last phrase comes from a famous letter to Frank Budgen in which Joyce describes the purpose of the style of "Ithaca," a letter I will be referring to quite regularly (*Letters* 1, 160). The point here is that Joyce uses Mulligan on the opening pages to mock the very things—the Eucharist, the Incarnation, the Ascension—that Stephen will be taking seriously and that the novel is designed to make real in Bloom.

Opposed to the reductive irony of science is Stephen's poetic sensibility. When the old woman delivers the milk for their morning tea, Mulligan treats her with contempt (mocking her religiosity, his favorite target), while Stephen attempts to elevate her significance through his imaginative powers, "Old and secret she had entered from a morning world, maybe a messenger. She praised the goodness of the milk, pouring it out. Crouching by a patient cow at daybreak in the lush field, a witch on her toadstool, her wrinkled fingers quick at the squirting dugs. They lowed about her whom they knew, dewsilky cattle. Silk of the kine and poor old woman, names given her in old times. A wandering crone, lowly form of an immortal serving her conqueror and her gay betrayer, their common cuckquean, a messenger from the secret morning" (1.399–406).

While David Hayman calls her "an allegory of Ireland" (Hayman, 36), I want to call this a failed allegory, a sign of Stephen's desire to invest the old woman with higher significance and his inability (thus far, at any rate) to do so in a way that can still satisfy the strenuous demands of the generic criterion of realism. Here is where the distinction between the kinds of allegory becomes textually indicated and useful to my argument. In Stephen's musings the old woman is a figure in the "allegory of poets"; her concrete particularity is effaced as Stephen tries to make her something more than what she is. Stephen rather desperately and, I think, lamely labors to create an alternate world in which higher and ethereal things can be registered; his figure of the old woman owes much to the Celtic twilight and decadent symbolism that Stephen, in other moods, knows he must reject. We have with Mulligan and Stephen the two poles that the "allegory of theologians" attempts to bridge, the reductive irony of naturalism and the elevated significance of "symbolisme."

Stephen feels slighted by the old woman's response to Mulligan: "She bows her old head to a voice that speaks to her loudly, her bonesetter, her medicineman: me she slights" (1.418–19). That the old woman ignores Stephen and fawns over Mulligan is enough to explain the last word of the episode, "usurper." The naturalism of a Mulligan has triumphed over the symbolism of the 1890s; the sensibility that attends only to the material and physical has usurped the place once accorded to poets and people of imaginative power. Stephen feels that his rightful place in his culture has been usurped by a sensibility that deflates and reduces; imaginative power has been replaced by mockery. The purpose of this novel, then, is to bring the imagination back to its place of prominence in western culture, which is why the thinking of William Blake is so important to *Ulysses*.

My point thus far is that the opening six episodes of the novel, written in a uniform style, establish what Karen Lawrence calls "a narrative norm" (Lawrence, 35) of hard, lucid naturalistic prose against which the later episodes will work in their expansive efforts. The first six episodes of *Ulysses* are a high point of naturalistic fiction, but we miss their place in the novel if we fail to see that Buck Mulligan—the "gay betrayer"—is the presiding spirit of the opening, the high priest of naturalism, a designation we are invited to assign to him by his imitation of the Mass on the opening page. As interesting, funny, touching, and incredibly lucid as these opening episodes are, they are inadequate to carry on Joyce's larger purpose, which is to present an ideal of behavior in Bloom, a purpose Mulligan and what he represents have betrayed in their merry mockery. The Darwinian naturalism that Beer and Levine describe has left no place for a kind of prose writing capable of representing the ideal without its being debunked. But there is only so much debunking that one can do. Ricardo Quinones makes useful commentary on this aspect of modernism, as a response to the triumph of mechanistic science in the nineteenth century: "what had been a highly effective and inspiring code had reached a state of exhaustion by the end of the nineteenth century" (Quinones, 65). The sensibility of the medical Mulligan, which fails to see anything beyond the material, provides the narrative norm for *Ulysses* and is used to suggest the exhausted state of the novel as a genre, the dead end that naturalism has brought the novel to face. Citing Nietzsche, Jeffrey Perl makes a point about modern drama that I wish to transpose to the history of the novel: Nietzsche entertains the "wish that science—or the theoretical *Weltanschauung*—be 'at last pushed to its limits and, faced with those limits [be] forced to renounce its claim to universal validity.' In the new drama, science and symbolism will embrace with the fierceness of enemies who have fallen in love" (Perl, 119). Science and symbolism, naturalism and romance—these will be made to embrace in the kind of writing I am calling modernist allegory. Naturalism is valid but not universally so; it explains and diagnoses aspects of the human condition that need explanation and cure. But it is incapable of building up and sustaining positive ideals that form the basis of a healthy culture. No one will disagree that the opening six episodes of *Ulysses* are naturalism "pushed to its limits"— that is, they are an epitome of naturalistic prose. Such prose is exhausted and must be challenged. It has done what it could do and exposed what needs to be exposed, and now it needs to be confronted with the demands of symbolism.

Naturalism in prose can be associated with death, in that it can only deal with the material and time-bound world that ends ultimately in death. The logical end of any naturalistic account of human life must be death. And thoughts of death abound in the early episodes: Stephen, playing Hamlet, is still mourning his mother's death and confronts some rather ghastly thoughts of her deathbed; Bloom is dressing for a funeral, which, when he attends it in "Hades," is the source of an extended meditation on our mortality; and we are frequently reminded of their mourning clothes, which suggest loss and mourning and death in an almost constant basal manner. Death is the limit of our existence and also the final limit of naturalism, for as long as one is committed to scientific naturalism one cannot move beyond death and entertain concepts that counter it, such as the Resurrection. Naturalism must lead to a focus on death because naturalism must attend to our life in time and space: that is the basis of Joyce's rejection of naturalism as an adequate and competent narrative method—time in its movement toward decay and death.

One cannot overstate how wrong Wyndham Lewis is in *Time and Western Man* when he calls *Ulysses* a "time-book" and Joyce "dedicated to Time" (Lewis, 84). Lewis places Joyce among other modernists who fall under the sway of a Bergsonian "Time-philosophy" (see pages 90ff.) that emphasizes the representation of human life in a realistically depicted flux of time. Lewis draws interesting conclusions about such philosophy as ultimately mechanistic and dead, and I think his points are important ones for understanding Joyce, because Joyce shares with Lewis his distaste for this Time-philosophy and tries to show its limitations in the early episodes about *Ulysses*. Lewis's comments about this book only apply to the opening episodes that are indeed about the "flow of time" and the "stream of consciousness," and so he fails to see that his own objections to this way of looking at human life are shared by Joyce and that Joyce, even more than Lewis, has exposed the limitations of this kind of naturalism as a way to write about humanity.

"Nestor" is crucial in establishing the theme of time in *Ulysses*, for it is the episode about history. While teaching a history lesson, Stephen silently muses upon the poet who had least regard for history and for nature, "Fabled by the daughters of memory. And yet it was in some way if not as memory fabled it. A phrase, then, of impatience, thud of Blake's wings of excess. I hear the ruin of all space, shattered glass and toppling masonry, and time one livid final flame. What's left us then?" (2.7–10). Blake imagines the destruction of history in the ruin of space and the combustion of time. It is worth noting that Stephen is rejecting the impatience and the excess attending Blake's understanding of poetry, but not necessarily its larger goals and ambitions. Teaching a history lesson seems to bring Stephen to a reluctant realization of the very real limits that space and time are for our existence: "What's left us then?" He would like to escape from history as Blake suggests is quite possible, but the demands of the naturalistic view are not that easily defied. We recall the famous phrase later in "Nestor," "History . . . is a nightmare from which I am trying to awake," but we seldom remember that in his mind he follows this pithy rejoinder to Deasy with a more sober thought: "What if that nightmare gave you a back kick" (2.377, 379). History is dangerous and powerful. If you try to ignore history and devise Blakean allegories, it will come back to haunt you. The demands of history, and thus of naturalism, must be met, and Blake is guilty of impatience and excess.

It is worth pausing over Blake's rejection of nature and history, for we know that he exercised a considerable influence over Joyce's thinking. As we learn from reading his annotations to Wordsworth's poems, Blake calls for an utter rejection of nature. The true poet does not seek inspiration from the natural world: "Natural Objects always did & now do Weaken deaden & obliterate Imagination in Me" (Blake, 654–55). Nature is opposed to the spiritual for Blake: "I see in Wordsworth the Natural Man rising up against the Spiritual Man. . . . There is no such Thing as Natural Piety Because The Natural Man is at Enmity with God." A poet expressing such sentiments will not attend closely to the demands of the world of nature and history, nor would he seek a style capable of rendering clear and scrupulous descriptions of nature. The true poet deals not with nature but with inner vision. Commenting on Wordsworth's call for "observation and description," Blake responds, "One Power alone makes a Poet.—Imagination The Divine Vision." Imagination is for Blake completely distinct from nature: "Imagination has nothing to do with memory." Blake is brought into the text of *Ulysses* to register the poet's complaint about the state of the Imagination in the modern world, as the novel and its description/observation becomes increasingly the criterion of literary art, even in a poet as great as Wordsworth. Blake is brought into Joyce's novel to bring the boldest claims about the Imagination to the reader as he deals with the naturalism of *Ulysses*. Like Stephen we may sympathize with Blake but also like Stephen we must regard his views as impatient and excessive—"Blake's wings of excess."

However, Blake is not brought into our field of attention to be rejected but to be corrected. It is worth citing some of the passage from *Stephen Hero* I used in the introduction where a younger Stephen makes the distinction between the romantic and classical tempers:

> A classical style, he said, is the syllogism of art, the only legitimate process from one world to another. . . . It is a temper of security and satisfaction and patience. The romantic temper . . . is an insecure, unsatisfied, impatient temper which sees no fit abode here for its ideals and chooses rather to behold them under insensible figures. As a result of this choice it comes to disregard certain limitations. Its figures are blown to wild adventures, lacking the gravity of solid bodies, and the mind that has conceived them ends by disowning them. The classical mind on the other hand, ever mindful of limitations, chooses rather to bend upon these present things and so to work upon them and fashion them that the quick intelligence may go beyond them to their meaning which is still unuttered. (*SH*, 78)

Joyce must have had this passage, or at least these seminal definitions, still in mind when he wrote the "Nestor" passages about Blake. For Blake lacks the "patience" that the young Stephen so rightly prizes among characteristics of genuine art, the patience to find a "legitimate process from one world to another," from the world of naturalism to the world of symbolism. The romantic temper disregards limitations—those of space and time—and runs wildly after insensible figures with which to present his ideals. We catch a glimpse of the way the young Joyce—the Joyce still writing the exquisite naturalism of *Dubliners*—sees the purpose of art: to fashion an abode fit for high ideals. We can speculate about the young artist's struggle as he is writing those stories: schooling himself in a lucid naturalistic style, he is learning about the limitations that the romantic temper wants to ignore, respecting the conditions of space and time, the conditions of history but not—this must be emphasized—capitulating to them. He is mindful of limitations but is seeking to find that "legitimate process" from naturalism to symbolism, from history to ideals. Ideals must be found within history, which, when it is not respected, can give a powerful back kick. Blake is the poet with the most extreme ambition for the imagination, to present its ideals, but is ultimately rejected for his excess and impatience.

As Stephen's history lesson loses its focus, one of the boys in the class asks him for a ghost story. In response, Stephen turns to "Lycidas," which is indeed a ghost story, as it describes the death of Edward King and the poet's conviction that his friend will rise "Through the dear might of Him that walked the waves." The placement of "Lycidas" after Stephen's meditation on Blake and history is telling. First, it suggests that the forces of nature that end in death can be overcome, as death is overcome by the power of Christ and the Resurrection. As such, it may at first seem to lend support to Blake's views, that nature is a limit that can be safely ignored. But in "Lycidas" nature is overcome by Christ, who took on human form in the Incarnation and conquered it through the power of God in the Resurrection. The figure of Christ is Joyce's answer to Blake and the romantic temper he represents, for we can find "the only legitimate process from one world to another" in the Incarnation alone. Christ is the figure that solves more than a theological need; he is the figure, as William Lynch argues at the end of his book in a chapter called "The Christian Imagination," that can be used to solve a nagging aesthetic problem. For Joyce finds in the Christ event the solution to the aesthetic question of how to produce an art capable of being, like Christ, both time-bound and eternal, temporal and permanent, based in the world of history and still ideal.

Stephen's role in *Ulysses* will be as the artist capable of seeing the Incarnation, so it is important to note that he takes seriously the effect of Christ on human history: "Of him that walked the waves. Here also over these craven hearts his shadow lies and on the scoffer's heart and lips and on mine. It lies upon their eager faces who offered him a coin of the tribute. To Caesar what is Caesar's, to God what is God's (2.83–86). The shadow of Christ was brought into the world of *Ulysses* ironically by the scoffer Mulligan and is brought in again here by Stephen. Buck is associated with those who set out to trap Christ, those who by asking whether Jews ought to pay taxes to Caesar or not are seeking to confine the Incarnation within the parameters of the material world. Either answer, they assumed, would land Jesus in trouble with someone: either the Jews, if he answered that taxes ought to be paid to the Romans; or the Romans, if he answered that the Jews were exempt from such obligation. Christ's answer allows him to elude their trap; more pointedly for our purposes, in the context of "Nestor" and its theme of history, this answer establishes the twin claims of history and the spirit. One has obligations both to Caesar and to God; you cannot do away with one for the other. Both history and its demands and the spirit and its demands must be confronted and met. One may be of less importance and thus subordinate to the other, but history cannot be ignored for the spirit, nor can the spirit be denied in favor of a naturalistic worldview that only respects the material world of history. Once again, Blake's flight from history is countered in Stephen's mind with the person and example of Christ.

Yet Blake's work still represents one of the most important attempts in western literature to do what Joyce wants to do, to "sing . . . of the ideal world, of truth, of the intellect and the divinity of the imagination," as Joyce describes Blake's ambitions in his lecture on Blake delivered in 1912 in Trieste (see *Critical Writings,* 220). While "Nestor" is teaching us that history cannot be denied, it also makes sure that we are not too quick to reject altogether such idealistic flights by making the chief exponent of history, in this episode and for the novel, a man excessively committed to history, Mr. Deasy. The old schoolmaster's association with history is underscored by his preoccupation with money. "Money is power," he lectures Stephen, who feels that each time he is paid by Deasy another noose has been placed around his neck. Deasy respects the claims of Caesar only. That he makes fundamental mistakes about facts and expresses anti-Semitic views renders him suspect; yet Stephen is deferential to him, silently thinks of him as a "good man," and agrees to help him in his fight against foot-and-mouth disease. This last item is important: without being to some extent committed to history, one would never be able to do good for others, and eliminating or controlling the spread of foot-and-mouth is worth doing. What makes Deasy most suspect is his total commitment to history, an excess that matches Blake's opposite extravagance: "All human history moves towards one great goal, the manifestation of God" (2.380–81). This is to value history too highly and make it the ultimate good itself, in that its telos is the gradual manifestation of the divine within a human framework. Quinones sees this faith in history as the legacy of the Renaissance against which many modern writers react: "The idea of perfectibility was removed from a vertical hierarchy, leading to the religious, and instead placed lengthwise at the end of a temporal process of development. In short, existence became progressive and divinity was lodged in history" (Quinones, 145). Deasy represents the culmination of such a view in the Victorian belief in progress. Stephen's rejoinder to Deasy, that God is "a shout in the street," takes issue with such confidence in history and progress. God reveals himself suddenly, Stephen implies; he enters the human dimensions of space and time not in a gradual unfolding of himself as nineteenth-century Hegelian philosophy would have it, but all at once, as a surprise, as sudden as an unexpected shout in the street. Stephen counters Deasy's faith in amelioration with a Christian belief in the Incarnation, God's radical eruption into history.

So Blake and Deasy are at opposite poles on this issue, and Stephen must negotiate successfully between their respective excesses. In fact, one of the central characteristics of Stephen's struggles, in both *A Portrait* and *Ulysses*, is to steer a middle course between extremes, as the Daedalus myth suggests and as critics have long recognized in "Scylla and Charybdis." The Incarnation is historical in that it is prepared for in history (that is, the history of Israel) and it occurs in history (in the person of Jesus Christ). But—and this is a crucial difference—it is not the result of the historical process; it is not the goal at the end of a gradual unfolding of events in history. The Incarnation is the sudden entrance of the divine into the human world bound by space and time. But Stephen too has made an error, for his "shout in the street" misses a central feature of the Incarnation. God's entry into history is sudden, but it is also quiet. Stephen is misquoting Isaiah, who says that God's chosen "will not cry or lift up his voice, or make it heard in the street; a bruised reed he will not break, and a dimly burning wick he will not quench" (Isa. 42.2–3). Part of the plot of *Ulysses*, the part that pertains to Stephen and his role as artist, is to watch if he can recognize the Incarnation in the unassuming, apparently ordinary and humble Leopold Bloom.

Deasy's anti-Semitism is thematically relevant, for it is the result of his excessive commitment to history. To endow history with the grand plot of manifesting God as its goal is to totalize, to make the apparently disparate and fragmented world of human events join together in a meaningful order that, when fully realized, would explain all. As we will see in my fifth chapter, allegory does not insist on all events in history being reread according to a later goal; only certain earlier events of history are to be reread and given meaning by the later Christ event, which is used to redesign history but not in a totalizing way. Deasy's more Hegelian view is a totalizing myth of history in which all events are moving the world closer to the manifestation of God. As Hannah Arendt has taught us, when history is viewed as a field of action that can be shaped toward a unifying goal, one result is to posit an enemy that is thwarting the movement toward such unity and order.[4] Deasy believes that the Jews are working against this movement of history: "England is in the hands of the jews. In all the highest places: her finance, her press. . . . As sure as we are standing here the jew merchants are already at their work of destruction. Old

England is dying" (2.346–51). To believe in history in this absolute way is to bring one to the kind of paranoia that makes history the nightmare from which Stephen wants to awake.

It is here that Joyce's text makes its contribution to our understanding of how high modernism can counter the postmodern critiques to which it is susceptible. Lyotard sees in nineteenth-century Hegelian philosophy the beginnings of the tendency for western thought to totalize, to seek for first principles that can become the ground on which a unifying and totalizing narrative of human history can be erected. In *The Postmodern Condition* he argues that nineteenth-century philosophy sought to unify knowledge and sent western thinkers on a "project of totalization" (Lyotard 29–30), a project that we in the latter half of the twentieth century have seen deteriorate into sinister designs and brutal policies. Joyce seems to have anticipated this aspect of totalizing theories, and as we reject Mr. Deasy's views we are rejecting totalizing myths of history. Stephen's attitude toward history is much more "postmodern" in its emphasis on eruption and surprise, and Lyotard calls this the "catastrophe model" for causative explanation of events (59). But Joyce is not a prophet of post–World War II postmodernism but actually a keen critic of Darwinian thinking. For there is a line of Darwinian thought much neglected in the nineteenth century that more recent—let us say postmodern—students of Darwin, such as Stephen Jay Gould, have emphasized and that places "catastrophe" at the center of all change and development. Levine also identifies a "catastrophist" element in Darwin's thinking that complicates his legacy to the Victorian era: on the one hand there is "uniformitarianism," which holds that all events in nature can be explained by causes now in operation; and on the other hand there is "catastrophist" thinking that sees sudden eruptions of wholly new events leading to unexpected developments (Levine, 15, 54–55). The first can lead to Deasy's view that change is best explained by the gradual unfolding of a design controlled by a Creator, while the latter looks for random and unexpected changes—catastrophes—that inaugurate new lines of development. The first is actually a misreading of Darwin and the second a more accurate view that "postmodern" critics have seen and emphasized. In the naturalist worldview of the nineteenth century there is room for this emphasis on the discontinuous, the random, the discrete, the eruption or disruption of smooth linear development—a "shout in the street," if you will. Joyce counters Deasy's totalizing and unifying worldview with what seems a quite postmodern view of change as surprise, a "postmodern" view with roots in nineteenth-century natural science.

The attitude to history of a Mr. Deasy is a view forced upon us by one strand of strict naturalism, for with a severely naturalist context we are always bound by space and time and so must try to find our hopes entirely within the confines of history. No wonder, then, that Joyce begins *Dubliners* with a line that may now resonate more loudly, "There was no hope for him this time." There seems to be no hope for characters bound within a naturalistic style and bound to history, unless it is the kind of hope that Deasy holds out, the hope for totalizing forces that can tame the forces of evil—that is, the nightmare of history that Joyce so presciently foresees. While Blake just wants to burst through space and time to escape history and reach the ideal, Stephen knows that a more patient aesthetic is required to reconcile the claims of both history and the ideal, of time and the timeless, of the temporal and the permanent. He already intuits that the Christ event offers the only possible solution, for the Incarnation is at one and the same time an event prepared for in history and yet a surprise eruption disturbing the smooth linear development of history; and "Nestor" is the episode that establishes this awareness on Stephen's part.

Naturalism forces on us either a sense of random occurrences without any shape whatsoever or a desire to find unifying principles that explain every aspect of our lives in nature: either chaos or totalizing myths. Joyce opts for a naturalism that leads to chaos, and "Proteus" presents the constant flux of time as manifested in human consciousness without almost any order or design. Levine identifies as Darwinian thinking the notion of development without telos (Levine, 16). Jeffrey Perl offers a fine analysis of this episode and then reaches the following conclusion, with which I partly agree: "The protean process is sometimes creative, sometimes destructive, but in no case can it ever lead anywhere. We are not permitted even the small comfort of a telos" (Perl, 194). Ignoring why a telos is only a small comfort, I agree that the purpose of "Proteus" is to present flux without telos, time without the purposefulness that could give it shape or form. But the episode does seem to lead to death thoughts, so while the episode may lack a telos, it does imply that time's movement is toward decay and death. Richard Ellmann has noted that "Proteus" is taken up with thoughts about corruption: "mortality suffuses [Stephen's] every thought. . . . Stephen sees all created things in process of decay, everyday dying a little, as if death were a concurrent process" (Ellmann, *Liffey*, 24). The flux of time simply moves inexorably toward decay and death. Even the hope of resurrection, suggested in "Nestor" by "Lycidas," is undercut by the placement of an allusion to the poem in a new context: "A corpse rising saltwhite from the undertow, bobbing a pace a pace a porpoise landward. There he is. Hook it quick. Pull. Sunk though he be beneath the watery floor. We have him. Easy now" (3.472–75). The rising from the dead promised in "Lycidas" and hoped for in "Nestor" becomes the rising of a drowned body to the surface of the water, the result of natural laws and expected sometime this day. The Incarnation is mocked as the episode comes to an end, Stephen needing no Buck Mulligan to perform this duty of deflation: "God becomes man becomes fish becomes barnacle goose becomes featherbed mountain" (3.477–79). Our life in time moves only toward death, and God's becoming man leads only to the transformation of the food cycle.

But the episode ends in a way that must be acknowledged as a problem. As Stephen looks over his shoulder, he sees "Moving through the air high spars of a threemaster, her sails brailed up on the crosstrees, homing, upstream, silently moving, a silent ship" (3.503–5). A ship with its sails brailed up should not be able to move upstream, yet this one does. An episode entirely given over to the naturalistic depiction of "the stream of consciousness" ends with a ship moving against that stream in a way that defies nature. Naturalism has its limits, in that it cannot account for the sudden introduction of the divine into the human dimension. Naturalism cannot account for miracles, such as this ship, or even for the man we are to meet when we turn the page, Leopold Bloom.

Before turning to Bloom's unexpected entry into the novel—after all, shifting from Stephen to Bloom so abruptly and turning the clock back three hours to start the day again are little disruptions of the plausible, little miracles if you will—it is worth noting that Stephen rouses himself to get up and continue his walking with words that call up the figure of Christ on the cross: "Come. I thirst" (3.485). Of course, Stephen is being flippant, using Christ's words on the cross to state to himself that he wants to begin his drinking binge. But the placing of these words so near the sighting of the "threemaster," with her "crosstrees,"[5] is to suggest that Stephen's flippancy may have a significance further than any he imagines. This episode, so filled with death thoughts, ends with this ironic suggestion of Christ's death and with the image of the silent ship, which suggests something miraculous, such as the Resurrection. It is easy to dismiss such a slight reference as this as no more weighty than anything else in the episode; the same can be said about any such reference, such as those I have been accumulating from the opening scenes. Only upon rereading the novel, with "Ithaca" as the fulcrum, do the moments I have isolated stand out as more worthy of attention and capable of larger significance than others. The narrator of the opening episodes does not know that these are indeed references that later episodes will transform; only the reader who has followed Stephen through to "Ithaca" will be able to provide a full rendering of the opening scenes, just as only the person who has experienced the Christ event can read the Old Testament properly.

This is a crucial element of any reading of a novel as complex as *Ulysses*, to find a way to justify the prominence of one set of allusions over and above the rest. It is my contention that the "allegory of theologians" allows us the comforting confidence to elevate certain moments as the pivot on which the rest of the novel turns, as the Old Testament is made to signify in its proleptic and unconscious anticipation of the Christ event. Joyce fashions the novel so that it moves to Stephen's recognition of an analogous Christ event in Bloom, and that moment is the center from which this "Christian" reading, this allegorical reading of *Ulysses* emanates. That there are moments of the novel not brought into the design of this Christian reading is actually one of the features of this kind of allegory—that only certain events are to be made part of the Christian design. This allows other readings of *Ulysses* still to be true and interesting and fruitful, while this reading remains the central and fullest rendering of meaning.[6]

The first three episodes given over to Bloom's day go over the same hours of the day as the first three episodes of Stephen's and are written in much the same naturalistic style. That Bloom's adventures begin with "Calypso" suggests that Bloom is captive as his day begins. The Homeric parallel suggests that Bloom is a prisoner of Molly as Odysseus is bound to remain on Calypso's island until she agrees to free him. The parallel allows us to see Bloom as a Dubliner, as someone unable to extricate himself from the confines of an island, a prisoner bound to serve the whims of a powerful female. Almost the first thing we see Bloom doing is serve Molly breakfast in bed, an action suggestive of servitude and submission. But to press this way of understanding the Blooms is to overestimate Molly's power and underestimate Bloom's strength. It is more fruitful to consider Bloom held captive more by the style of the episode than by Molly; he is caught within a narrative that can only see the literal level of human existence and can offer no imaginative escape from time and space. Even more forcefully, we ought to consider ourselves, as readers of the novel, as the captives, held bound by the narrative style to seeing only what Bloom sees, hearing only what he hears, thinking only what he thinks. The novel is about the reader's ability to understand Bloom, and we will watch how various narrative styles try to bring us to see aspects of his character that this style is incapable of presenting. We will watch Joyce try out various styles, only to find them inadequate. It will be the episode most without style, "Ithaca," that will bring us closest to the fullest significance of Bloom's character and behavior.

Bloom tends toward gloominess this morning, as is only natural on a day on which he is to attend a funeral and confront, internally at any rate, the prospect of Molly's infidelity. And as he tries to escape from time and place by constructing fantasies (about the Near East especially), it is his own gravity that punctures the illusions he has set up as comforts: "Probably not a bit like it really" (4.99). After a brief indulgence in a fantasy of idleness in "the garden of the world," Bloom remembers the formula for the law of falling bodies: "Thirtytwo feet per second per second. Law of falling bodies: per second per second. They all fall to the ground. The earth" (5.44–46). Bloom needs no Buck Mulligan, "the apostle of gravity," to puncture easy and indulgent flights of fancy. As long as the reader is confined to a view of things dominated by Bloom's consciousness, we will not rise above the limits of naturalism. It has become somewhat of a cliché in Joyce criticism to gush about how "human" Bloom is, and the early episodes do indeed establish his "humanity" in perhaps the most fully realized depiction of a character in all literature. Yet that is the problem: Joyce wants to move beyond the human. Naturalism and humanism might go hand in hand. Held within a naturalistic depiction of human consciousness, the reader—and Bloom as well—have no hope for escape and must remain prisoners of time and space. Nothing will be able to get off the ground and stay there as long as this kind of narrative is in place. Let us recall again the famous letter about "Ithaca": "not only will the reader know everything and know it in the baldest coldest way, but Bloom and Stephen thereby become heavenly bodies, wanderers like the stars at which they gaze" (*Letters*, 1, 159–60). What enables them to defy gravity is the way the reader learns about events. Style is the key to this elevation.

All this is not to deny the importance of the opening episodes, for they establish the illusion that Bloom is a three-dimensional character with a full range of personality traits, some admirable and some not so admirable, a realistic presentation of a full man. We are reading the establishment of the historical letter, or the literal level, of *Ulysses* that the later episodes will be rereading, relying on as a solid ground on which to enlarge and heighten. With "Ithaca" in mind, it seems appropriate that Joyce's first words about this hero tell us about the food "Mr Leopold Bloom ate with relish." The illusion Joyce manages to create with nothing more than words is that of a real man, of flesh and blood, a man with a body that is brought to earth by the force of the earth's gravitational pull. That is the strength of naturalism, to depict the body in time and space. We begin with the body that is weighed down by food, and we will end with the body that defies gravity and wanders the heavens like the stars. "Calypso" begins with food prepared, eaten, and digested and ends with food excreted, as Joyce is eager to present the body that is the object of the naturalistic narrator's scrupulous art.

The day chosen for the action of the novel is not a typical day in the life of this man, for not every day does he attend a funeral (though this is not a unique occurrence in the life of a man); nor does one have to confront the prospect of a wife's first marital infidelity every day. This last item marks 16 June 1904 as an absolutely unique day for Bloom, and we are given the privilege of watching how he responds to this most challenging experience. It seems worth noting in passing that Joyce was a most jealous man, obsessed with his own wife and almost pathologically suspicious of her fidelity, a theme he tried to work out in his play *Exiles*.[7] In my reading of *Ulysses* the main plot of the novel, as far as it concerns Bloom, is his ability to allow his wife the freedom to pursue her own desires and needs and still maintain a relationship with her based on love. In "Calypso," Molly is the captivating witch who holds Bloom prisoner; in "Penelope" she is the wife who welcomes him home. What happens in between the episodes—thematically and stylistically—transforms her from the one into the other.

One of Bloom's chief attributes, first seen in "Calypso" and developed throughout the novel, is his passivity regarding her approaching infidelity. Thinking about her rendezvous with Blazes Boylan this afternoon, Bloom already has made the decision in "Calypso" to do nothing: "Will happen, yes. Prevent. Useless: can't move" (4.447–48). That is an expression of paralysis fit for a *Dubliners* story! In "Aeolus" he confronts the issue again: "I could go home still: tram: something I forgot. Just to see before dressing. No. Here. No" (7.230–31). This rather strange reflection—expressing the wish to see how Molly is dressing for her affair—moves beyond mere passivity as paralysis and into the theme of perversion. Christine Froula studies Bloom's passivity from a psychoanalytic perspective, arguing that Bloom desires Molly's infidelity and derives pleasure from it. She advances a powerful argument describing Bloom's desire as perversion, but when she cites Louise Kaplan on perversion as a mask for violence and as hatemaking (Froula, 185–86), I think she goes astray. In his passivity, which I see as motivated by love, Bloom is allowing freedom, and rather than deriving joy from the infidelity, he tolerates it and derives joy instead from his love for Molly notwithstanding. In "Lestrygonians," the affair now less than three hours away, he confirms his decision to be passive: "Useless to go back. Had to be. Tell me all" (8.633). While this last moment develops the theme of perversity—now he would like to hear all about it from Molly later that night, a prospect that at the same time holds out the possibility that his relationship to Molly is still to be based on an odd form of intimacy—what I would like to emphasize here is the word "useless" as perhaps the key to understanding this aspect of Bloom; after all, "useless" and "Ulysses" are almost anagrams, a Joycean way of suggesting the importance of the one to the character of the other.[8] It seems useless for Bloom to protest to Molly or confront Boylan, though many a different man might disagree. Such utter passivity, such complete surrender to the inevitable (though it may not be inevitable at all, if only he would do something!), hardly seems heroic; in fact, it may seem to most of us weak-willed and cowardly, and for Froula it is a sure sign of perversity. Bloom begins his day looking more like a character from *Dubliners* than he does a hero in a modern epic, for he apparently shares with the figures in Joyce's naturalistic series of short stories the trait central to modern man, paralysis. Like Mr. James Duffy, or Little Chandler, or Eveline, Bloom seems paralyzed, unable to take action; he goes so far as to pretend that the affair is inevitable, though to a neutral observer such pretense only seems an excuse to remain passive.

In *Dubliners*, Bloom would be another victim, another failed man, because naturalism can only see failure and victimhood; but in *Ulysses* this sense of the uselessness of action is part of the heroic character of this modern Ulysses. The marvel that Joyce intends is that this seemingly ignoble trait will be elevated to noble heights and be made to seem the epitome of Christian virtue; to present it in this way is the purpose of the stylistic innovations of the later episodes. Unlike other novelists, who might decide to trace the gradual changes in their characters from some ignoble mode of behavior toward some admirable action by the end, Joyce will keep Bloom the same all day long; what will change will be our perception and understanding of his character and his mode of behavior. The reader, and not the fictional character, will change, gradually learning to see in Bloom's passivity not weakness but strength, not weak-willed paralysis but vigorous action that is Joyce's version of an *Imitatione Christi*, a way of being a hero whose passive acceptance of his changeable but necessary fate is an act of courage and a way of personal redemption.

So what seems a flaw or weakness from the naturalistic narrator's perspective will be worked upon by various styles until it becomes an achievement of epic proportions. But the Bloom of the early episodes is not to be dismissed as an entirely, or even a mainly, negative portrait; far from it. He manifests constantly the resilience needed to maintain his equanimity despite his troubles that will be central to his ability later to be elevated to the stars. His first three episodes are structured by a rhythmic movement down and up, up and down; gravity is the operative force, though Bloom is able to keep from falling flat on his face because of his resilience and equanimity. We already noted how he allows himself momentary relief from depressing reality by indulging in fantasies of the East, fantasies he himself punctures. Here is an instructive moment from "Calypso":

> No, not like that. A barren land, bare waste. Vulcanic lake, the dead sea: no fish, weedless, sunk deep in the earth. . . . Dead: an old woman's: the grey sunken cunt of the world.
> Desolation.
> Grey horror seared his flesh. Folding the page into his pocket he turned into Eccles street, hurrying homeward. . . . To smell the gentle smoke of tea, fume of the pan, sizzling butter. Be near her ample bedwarmed flesh. Yes, yes.
> Quick warm sunlight came running from Berkeley road, swiftly, in slim sandals, along the brightening footpath. Runs, she runs to meet me, a girl with gold hair on the wind. (4.219–42)

He had been indulging in a fantasy of the exotic Near East, puncturing the image he conjures with a set of "naturalistic" details: barren land, dead waste, vulcanic lake, no fish, weedless. He is plunged by this reflection on the "reality" of the land of fantasy (a skewed reality, to be sure, focusing on the worst features in order to puncture the ideal) into a despair he seldom feels this strongly in the course of the day. He is able to lift his emotions from this downward plunge and against the pull of gravity by indulging in realistic domestic images, ones drawn from Homer's hero who had been wishing only to see the smoke from his chimney before he dies. In fact, this is an anticipation of the end of the novel, when Bloom will return to her "ample bedwarmed flesh" in much the same way that Odysseus returns to his bed in book 23 of *The Odyssey*. He recuperates his emotional state with images that the reader can recognize as part of the heroic subtext of the novel. What renders Bloom's capacity to solace himself with images of domestic warmth extraordinary is that he already suspects her infidelity. Despite this, he is able, for a moment at any rate, to rouse himself from "grey horror" and construct a happy little allegory (of the lesser kind) about the approach of the sunlight.

If we continue reading from where I left off, we see how difficult Bloom's day is going to be: "Two letters and a card lay on the hallfloor. He stooped and gathered them. Mrs Marion Bloom. His quickened heart slowed at once. Bold hand. Mrs Marion" (4.243–45). He gets his heart pumping vigorously, excited by the prospect of a return home, only to be confronted with a sign of Molly's adulterous designs. "His quickened heart slowed at once": Joyce is masterful at bringing our attention to the physical, bodily responses to psychic events. This naturalistic narrator brings the body to our attention. Bloom had fought vigorously to turn his mood upward, only to be forced downward again. The way the episode ends enforces an important lesson on the reader:

> In the bright light, lightened and cooled in limb, he eyed carefully his black trousers: the ends, the knees, the houghs of the knees.

> What time is the funeral? Better find out in the paper.
> A creak and a dark whirr in the air high up. The bells of George's church. They tolled the hour: loud dark iron.
> *Heigho! Heigho!*
> *Heigho! Heigho!*
> *Heigho! Heigho!*
> Quarter to. There again: the overtone following through the air.
> A third.
> Poor Dignam! (4.541–50)

Despite his efforts to recuperate his emotional state, despite his already demonstrated and perhaps overrated resiliency, the episode ends with Bloom in a somber, even depressed mood—ostensibly about "poor Dignam" but more pointedly about Molly and his marriage. We note his pathetic attempt to make the tolling of the "loud dark iron" bells of the nearby church sound happy and carefree: "*Heigho! Heigho!*"; but he cannot fool himself nor raise his mood against the persistent downward pull of gravity. Joyce chooses to end Bloom's first episode with an expression of sorrow and sadness, and with this choice he implies that Bloom's efforts to rise above circumstance will end in this kind of pathetic failure. As admirable as Bloom is in this episode, and as likable as he has already proven himself to be, the ending of "Calypso" signifies that Bloom is ultimately confined to a level of existence in which one must constantly battle depression, a battle one will occasionally win but ultimately will lose: "Poor Dignam!"

The next episode, "Lotus Eaters," begins Bloom's wanderings through Dublin; and "wanderings" is the proper word for this episode, as he has no clear objective for his movements but is merely killing time until the funeral at eleven. One dominant symbol of the episode is the lotus flower that, in the ninth book of *The Odyssey*, induces a drowsy easiness that causes its victim to forget any thought of returning home. Three of Odysseus's men eat the lotus, and he must drag them forcibly back to the ship, where he warns the rest of his crew, "No one taste the Lotus, or you lose your hope of home" (9.108–9). Odysseus's men may be forgiven their desire for rest and forgetfulness after ten years of war and the prospect of an uncertain sea voyage back to Ithaca; but Odysseus insists, for his men and for himself, that the pain of exile and the hardship of wandering must be accepted if one is ever to return home. Even more pointedly, one must not yield to the desire to forget, which makes life easy, but to remember one's home and keep it as one's desired object, even if that memory is painful. In his analogous trial Bloom must avoid the temptation to partake of false ease and unearned rest offered to him and all Dubliners by several kinds of lotus, the temptation to forget "home" where Molly will be unfaithful and to indulge in a sloggy amnesia. Memory in this episode is not activist but passivist, retrieving a fixed image from the past that causes pain to the subject, a pain that must be embraced if the journey toward home is to be continued.

Among the kinds of lotus Joyce presents in this episode are nicotine and drink, but the most dangerous lotus—and thematically the most powerful temptation to forget—is confronted when Bloom slips into the open back door of All Hallows. In this episode the Mass, especially the Eucharist, is associated with the lotus of *The Odyssey* as a narcotic that lulls and stupefies. This identification brings Bloom's experience into line with Buck Mulligan's in "Telemachus," where he presented a mock-Eucharist. An important distinction between Buck's mockery and Bloom's debunking begins to emerge: the former merely provides glib entertainment from a point of view that can take nothing seriously, while Bloom responds to a precise danger and debunks the power of the Eucharist not in mockery but in an effort to remain safe from its narcotic effect. That Bloom rejects the power of the Eucharist by no means implies that Joyce seeks the reader's rejection; in fact, a Eucharist of sorts is presented in "Ithaca" in a new Church, as I will demonstrate later. This is a principle for reading *Ulysses*, especially the early episodes: what is registered as an important theme is important for that episode but not necessarily to be applied directly to later episodes. Bloom is a vegetarian in "Lestrygonians" for thematic purposes relevant to that episode alone, especially when we consider that Bloom's day begin with a pork kidney and that later he eats liver and bacon. The rejection of the Eucharist here is not the same as Buck's but is purposeful and limited to that thematic purpose.

In fact, Bloom's rejection of the Eucharist is motivated by his determination to forego the false ease of a narcotic and instead to feel the pain of clearheaded memory of home, and in this, the episode implies, he is a true follower of Christ. Thinking about the Eucharist, Bloom says to himself, "Wonder how they explain it to the heathen Chinee. Prefer an ounce of opium. Celestials. Rank heresy for them. Buddha their god lying on his side in the museum. Taking it easy with his hand under his cheek. Josssticks burning. Not like Ecce Homo. Crown of thorns and cross" (5.326–30). Bloom shows himself to be quite perceptive about the central feature of Christianity (though less so about Buddhism) in that he knows that Christ is a suffering God, not one to be pictured taking ease or rest but depicted most frequently in his Passion. The "heathen chinee" prefers his narcotic to the thought of a deity who enjoins his followers to pick up their crosses as the way to salvation. As Odysseus counsels his men to accept their suffering as part of the way back home, Bloom understands that Christianity emphasizes the role of suffering in the process of redemption.

But the rituals of the Church can work in ways not intended by Christ, nor perhaps by the ecclesiastical authorities. Bloom watches the communion service and thinks, "The priest went along by them, murmuring, holding the thing in his hands. He stopped at each, took out a communion, shook a drop or two (are they in water?) off it and put it neatly into her mouth. . . . Shut your eyes and open your mouth. What? *Corpus:* body. Corpse. Good idea the Latin. Stupefies them first. Hospice for the dying. They don't seem to chew it; only swallow it down. Rum idea: eating bits of a corpse. Why the cannibals cotton to it" (5.344–52). One thing this passage establishes is Bloom's unfamiliarity with Catholic ritual and language: he calls the host "the communion" and the ciborium "the thing"; thinks the priest is shaking off water from the host (whereas he is making the sign of the cross); and after correctly translating *corpus* as body, he mistakenly thinks of the host as the corpse—the dead body—of Christ. This last error is most suggestive, for in episodes written in a naturalistic style Christ dies only and remains a corpse; that Christ's living body is in the Eucharist makes no sense to this narrator, nor to Bloom, nor to Mulligan in the opening scene. I will make much of Bloom's ignorance of the finer points of this ritual in a moment. But we must pause to see what he does understand. In his eyes the communicants approach the Eucharist blindly, with eyes closed and mouths open, accepting whatever the priest gives without question. The Latin stupefies the communicant so that she is not fully conscious that she is receiving the body of Christ offered up in the Crucifixion as a sacrifice to her redemption. The Catholics at All Hallows are more like the heathen chinee with his ounce of opium than like Ecce Homo.

Ulysses begins with Mulligan's mockery of the Eucharist and now includes Bloom's more gentle yet more compelling critique of the sacrament. Whereas Mulligan merely mocks it and so rejects it out of hand, Bloom exposes a real and serious misuse of the ritual, that it can function as a narcotic agent rendering life easy and slothful. That the chief opiate in Dublin is the Eucharist is underscored as Bloom continues to watch the ceremony:

> He stood aside watching their blind masks pass down the aisle, one by one, and seek their places. . . . Look at them. Now I bet it makes them feel happy. Lollipop. It does. Yes, bread of angels it's called. There's a big idea behind it, kind of kingdom of God is within you feel. First communicants. Hokeypokey penny a lump. Then feel all like one family party, same in the theatre, all in the same swim.

They do. I'm sure of that. Not so lonely. In our confraternity. Then come out a bit spreeish. Let off steam. Thing is if you really believe in it. Lourdes cure, waters of oblivion, and the Knock apparition, statues bleeding. Old fellow asleep near that confessionbox. Hence those snores. Blind faith. Safe in the arms of kingdom come. Lulls all pain. Wake this time next year. (5.353–54, 359–68)

This is a clear and powerful indictment of the Eucharist as it may actually function in Dublin, serving as a form of lotus that can "lull all pain" and allow its communicants to indulge in the false illusion of safety and community. It will be difficult to undo the force of this passage, and many critics of the novel have felt satisfied with such a passage as expressing the attitude of the author, the attitude of the book. The Eucharist will be prominent in the way the novel comes to its climax, but that climax will be presented so obliquely that, even if it is seen, it pales in comparison to the clarity and force of these early indictments. That is Joyce's way in *Ulysses,* to present a clear naturalistic narration that establishes a certain level of understanding that requires a later adjustment, an adjustment so subtle that it may not seem as powerful as what it is correcting. Bloom's indictment of the Eucharist as a narcotic is something we are meant to accept, and his clear acceptance of pain and suffering is to be admired. But the implicit rejection of the ritual is not necessarily a conclusion we can jump to.

The Homeric parallel encourages us to see the Eucharist as a kind of lotus offering a false ease that must be avoided if one is to continue the journey back home, a journey marked by hardship, deprivations, and suffering. Just a moment later, when Bloom sees the I. H. S. on the back of the priest's garment, he erringly recalls what it means, "I have sinned: or no: I have suffered" (5.373). To refuse to accept the Eucharist as a form of the lotus is to be like Odysseus, but it is also to be like Christ, who presented his passion as a model for our way to salvation. We have long been trained to look for Homeric parallels in *Ulysses,* but we need to recognize that even these parallels are subordinate to the more compelling parallel to Christ. And after Bloom has endured in later episodes the pangs of having accepted his suffering, he will be ready to perform his own version of the Eucharist, not as lotus but as a ritual sharing that forms the basis of a new Church. But that is an idea that these early episodes do not allow us to discuss. We can only see the negative side to the propositions at this point because we, like the characters, are confined to a purely naturalistic view of such things.

Here is a principle of the "allegory of theologians" that applies to *Ulysses:* that there are some moments presented in the early naturalistic episodes (which form an analogue to the literal history of the Old Testament) that are, without this narrator's awareness, to be fulfilled in the later episodes, most especially in "Ithaca," that episode of homecoming in which Stephen recognizes the "traditional figure of hypostasis." Not all the themes or images of the early episodes need to be reread from the vantage point of the Christ event; that is a cardinal principle of biblical exegesis, of Dante criticism since Singleton and, I propose, of *Ulysses*. But certain moments are presented in the early episodes that do actually become "fulfilled" in later scenes. In the example we have been pursuing about "Lotus Eaters," for instance, there is a rest that is dangerous, the rest that comes from the various narcotics available in Dublin; and in this episode we are meant to admire Bloom's ability to avoid these temptations and pursue his painful journey. But there is an ease that is allowed when the journey is done; as "Ithaca" states: "Womb? Weary? He rests. He has travelled" (17.2319–20). This later ease, proper and earned, is hinted at in "Lotus Eaters," presented through an allusion to an episode from Christ's life. As he reads Martha Clifford's letter, he embarks on a train of association that leads him to a scene from Luke's gospel:

> Martha, Mary. I saw that picture somewhere I forget now some old master or faked for money. He is sitting in their house, talking. Mysterious. Also the two sluts in the Coombe would listen.
> *To keep it up.*
> Nice kind of evening feeling. No more wandering about. Just loll there: quiet dusk: let everything rip. Forget. . . . She listens with big dark soft eyes. Tell her: more and more: all. Then a sigh: silence. Long long long rest. (5.289–99)

Bloom recalls a picture of the scene in which Martha complains to Jesus that she is doing all the work while Mary just sits by the Lord's feet and listens. To Martha's surprise, Jesus defends Mary's rest, saying that she has chosen the better portion and it shall not be taken away from her. This is the rest that is allowed, to choose to lie at Jesus' feet and listen to his words. Bloom takes the gospel story and mixes his own life into it, which is easy to do since his secret correspondent is named Martha and his wife's name is a variant of Mary. He actually puts himself in Christ's place by imagining returning home after much wandering and being listened to by Molly as she watches him with "big dark soft eyes." This imagined scene from "Lotus Eaters," presented amid many other scenes and images in the naturalistic manner of the episode, is in a sense prophetic of the ending of "Ithaca," where Bloom speaks to Molly, who lies at his feet and listens to him, after which he has a "long long long rest." The imagined scene comes true, even (as we shall see) the identification of Bloom with Christ.

This kind of ironic identification of Bloom with Christ is Joyce's way of preparing for a more serious identification later in the novel, though it is an identification still fraught with difficulties. "Lotus Eaters" ends with a louder and more emphatic identification, as Bloom anticipates taking a bath: "Enjoy a bath now: clean trough of water, cool enamel, the gentle tepid stream. This is my body" (5.565–66). Recalling how many errors Bloom made as he watched the mass, we are not at all sure if he is conscious that he is repeating Christ's words at the Last Supper, the words inaugurating the Eucharist that the priest, in Latin, repeats during consecration and communion. Aware or not, the identification here is ironic, as naturalism would have it, too easily and too lightly placing Bloom in a Christian paradigm. Yet the identification is presented, and presented just after the unconscious prophecy about "Throwaway." If we have to wait until "Ithaca" for the full revelation of the significance of Bloom's inadvertent tip to Bantam Lyons, it seems quite reasonable in the world of this novel to have to wait until that same episode for the full working out of these ironic identifications of Bloom with Christ. What is inadvertent, accidental, and ironic in "Lotus Eaters" will became meaningful and inevitable by the end of the novel.

"Hades" deserves special attention as the last of the episodes of *Ulysses* given over almost completely to naturalistic depiction of the events of the novel, and as such it is fitting that it revolve around the theme of death, which is the limit of naturalism and so the limit of the novel as genre. As I argued in my account of Stephen's last early episode, scrupulous attention to human life as it exists in space and time must end in death, so "Hades" functions as the counterpart to "Proteus" and as the end—the funeral, if you will—of the purely novelistic part of *Ulysses*. All things caught in space and time are transient and are moving toward death, and Joyce brings Bloom to a funeral so he can confront the thought of death; his response is more complex than has been previously noted.

The episode is littered with small details that make death prominent: Bloom thinks of his father's suicide; of the "ward for incurables" near his house on Eccles street, "Our Lady's Hospice for the dying. Deadhouse handy underneath" (6.376–78); that "tomorrow is killing day" at the slaughterhouse (392); and that there are "funerals all over the world everywhere every minute. Shovelling them under by the cartload doublequick. Thousands every hour. Too many in the world" (514–16). It is quite in keeping with the rigors of naturalism for a character to have such thoughts as he rides along with some companions in a funeral carriage on the way to the cemetery. What we are interested in is the way Bloom responds to these thoughts. First, let us note that he rejects the comforts offered by the central Christian doctrine of the Resurrection. When Tom Kernan quotes the Protestant service he is familiar with, *"I am the resurrec-*

tion and the life. That touches a man's inmost heart," Bloom agrees audibly but thinks to himself, "Your heart perhaps but what price the fellow in the six feet by two with his toes to the daisies? No touching that. Seat of the affections. Broken heart. A pump after all, pumping thousands of gallons of blood every day. One fine day it gets bunged up: and there you are. Lots of them lying around here: lungs, hearts, livers. Old rusty pumps: damn the thing else. The resurrection and the life. Once you are dead you are dead. That last day idea. Knocking them all up out of their graves. Come forth, Lazarus! And he came fifth and lost the job" (6.670–79).

Bloom regards a belief in the Resurrection only as a solace for the living, allowing us to ward off fear of death; but "once you are dead you are dead." His gentle mockery of the Lazarus story indicates as clearly as possible that Bloom is no Christian as far as articles of faith are concerned. He may even remind us of Buck Mulligan in such mockery and also when he regards the heart as a pump and nothing more: no sentimentality for either Mulligan or Bloom as they contemplate death. This raises an interesting problem, for, we may recall, Robert Bell contends that "the text approaches Buck's view," and here Bloom and Mulligan seem quite similar in debunking features of the Christian faith. But Bloom is silent while Mulligan is noisy, Bloom is compassionate while Mulligan is self-absorbed, Bloom is humble while Mulligan is arrogant. The reductive irony that opens the novel through Buck Mulligan's sensibility is too harsh and too general, and the novel moves from this toward Bloom's more gentle and discriminating irony.

But this point must be made: if Bloom is to be presented as an incarnation of Christian charity, it will be despite the fact that he is not a Christian, at least in matters of faith. Brook Thomas has noted that Joyce includes in "Hades" a warning to those who seek a facile identification of Bloom with other figures, especially Christ (Thomas, 121). Thomas refers us to Corny Kelleher's story about Mulcahy from the Coombe, in which two drunks search for the grave of their friend Mulcahy one foggy evening. Upon finding it, one of the pair notes the statue of Christ erected by the widow: "And, after blinking up at the sacred figure, *Not a bloody bit like the man,* says he. *That's not Mulcahy,* says he, *whoever done it*" (6.731–32). I do not want to laugh at the drunk's mistake while ignoring my own possible error as I advance my thesis about a possible identification of Bloom with Christ. In fact, my argument owes quite a bit to Thomas, who provides just the model of skepticism that I think Joyce wants to construct through Mulligan and Bloom. The resemblance between Bloom and Christ is not easy to discern—"not a bloody bit like the man," we might wish to say; yet Stephen will see it, and we will learn to see it through Stephen's eyes. The resemblance will not be in matters of doctrine; in fact, Bloom can indulge in gentle mockery of the faith and yet will become, through Joyce's art, a model of Christian behavior.

While denying the Resurrection, Bloom does find his own way to confront death thoughts. While we do not have access to the other characters' mental processes, it may be safe to assume that because Bloom denies himself the comfort afforded by Christian doctrine, his contemplation of death is more vigorous and sincere (and more naturalistic) than his fellow Dubliners.' Ironically, because he faces his death thoughts more nakedly than his fellows do, he has the opportunity to overcome the fear of death, something their easy acceptance of the Resurrection does not allow. It is by turning to thoughts of Molly that he wards off the gruesome contemplation of death. Of his own death he thinks, "One must go first: alone, under the ground: and lie no more in her warm bed" (6.554–55). The great moment of the episode occurs when he rejects the morbidity that a focus on death will occasion: "There is another world after death named hell. I do not like that other world she wrote. No more do I. Plenty to see and hear and feel yet. Feel live warm beings near you. Let them sleep in their maggoty beds. They are not going to get me this innings. Warm beds: warm fullblooded life" (6.1001–5). I think we are meant to admire Bloom's capacity to rouse himself, by thinking about Molly and her bed, from a morbidity that the other Dubliners are prone to, a morbidity indicated by the description of Martin Cunningham that comes right after Bloom's small triumph: "Martin Cunningham emerged from a sidepath, talking gravely." While Cunningham and the other Dubliners are "grave," Bloom is able to rebound and assert a joyful attitude, captured nicely in the last line of the episode, his ironic comment on John Henry Menton's superciliousness that reflects his own mood: "How grand we are this morning!" We respect this resilience, though we might question whether or not one could continue to overcome death thoughts all day and all life long, whether a triumph of resiliency such as this can be sustained. If we would continue the episode a few moments more, would Bloom get depressed again? Is not this kind of triumph ultimately too exhausting to feel good about? Nonetheless, the naturalistic early episodes of Bloom's day end where the artist chooses to end them, and we are left with a cheerful and satisfied Bloom who has overcome the depression that this day has been trying to force on him, and that this way of telling is trying to force on us. Bloom overcomes depression and, we might want to say, the naturalistic style of the early episodes that will be boldly challenged when we turn the page and see the newspaper headlines of "Aeolus."

There is one final complication. That Molly's body and Molly's bed seem to be the source of his resilience in the face of death thoughts would make perfect sense and be more satisfying if not for the fact that Bloom is also facing the prospect of her infidelity this very day. Infidelity and death are somehow linked: as we saw above, the graves at Glasnevin are "maggoty beds." He had connected Boylan with maggots earlier in the episode: "But they must breed a devil of a lot of maggots. Soil must be simply swirling with them. Your head it simply swurls. Those pretty little seaside gurls" (6.783–85). His own bed back home is also a maggoty bed in that his marriage is being violated today and so in a sense is to die.

It is no accident, then, that Bloom's first of several important encounters with Blazes Boylan occurs early in this episode dominated by death. Just as he thinks to himself, "He's coming in the afternoon," his fellow passengers in the funeral carriage see and greet the man who represents death to Bloom. His response to this close encounter creates some problems for us:

> Mr Bloom reviewed the nails of his left hand, then those of his right hand. The nails, yes. Is there anything more in him than they she sees? Fascination. Worst man in Dublin. That keeps him alive. They sometimes feel what a person is. Instinct. But a type like that. My nails. I am just looking at them: well pared. And after: thinking alone. Body getting a bit softy. I would notice that: from remembering. What causes that? I suppose the skin can't contract quickly enough when the skin falls off. But the shape is there. Shoulders. Hips. Plump. Night of the dance dressing. Shift stuck between the cheeks behind.
>
> He clasped his hands between his knees and, satisfied, sent his vacant glances over their faces. (6.200–210)

Noteworthy here is Bloom's ability to feel "satisfied" so soon after the agitation of the near encounter with Boylan. He stares at his nails to avoid his neighbors' faces and so gain some degree of self-possession. But from what does he derive the satisfaction? From thoughts about Molly; more particularly, from thoughts about her body. His brief meditation begins with the slightly nasty thought that Molly is getting older and her body is "getting a bit softy." Such a thought is most likely a sign of envy. But, he soon realizes, only he would notice this, because only he can remember her younger days and her harder body.[9] Boylan, who would have no basis for comparison, would see what is still quite admirable. And this is the curious thing about Bloom's satisfaction, that it seems to derive from his thoughts about how attractive Molly still is, especially about how she will appear to her new admirer. He recalls a particular image of Molly, as she was dressing for a dance, the bazaar dance Bloom recalled at the end of "Calypso," the dance at which she and Boylan began the flirting that will culminate in their rendezvous later today. He feels satisfied after recalling how attractive she looked on the night we can say her infidelity began.

Are we to say along with Froula that Bloom takes a perverse pleasure in the prospect of his wife's affair, that he derives some satisfaction from the breach of his marriage? There is a certain element of perversion in Bloom's acceptance of pain and suffering and the extraordinary passivity that characterizes his response to Molly's infidelity, a perversion that will come howling out in "Circe" and, I think, be resolved there. There is more to his ability to achieve satisfaction than mere perversion, though in "Hades" it seems more that than anything else. But we do get a hint of this something else at the episode's conclusion. Just after his triumph over death thoughts quoted earlier, he notices John Henry Menton and recalls the source of Menton's dislike of him (which Menton already recalled at 6.695–701): "Solicitor, I think. I know his face. Menton, John Henry, solicitor, commissioner for oaths and affidavits. Dignam used to be in his office, Mat Dillon's long ago. Jolly Mat. Convivial evenings. Cold fowl, cigars, the Tantalus glasses. Heart of gold really. Yes, Menton. Got his rag out that evening on the bowlinggreen because I sailed inside him. Pure fluke of mine: the bias. Why he took such a rooted dislike to me. Hate at first sight. Molly and Floey Dillon linked under the lilactree, laughing. Fellow always like that, mortified if women are by" (6.1007–14). Bloom's train of association comes to focus on a scene that becomes increasingly prominent as the novel unfolds, evenings at Mat Dillon's when Bloom first met and courted Molly. Kenner has made the claim that the image of "Molly and Floey Dillon linked under the lilactree, laughing" "stands for Eden, a fragrant girl-filled garden" (Kenner, *Ulysses*, 77); as such, it functions as an image of Bloom's days before the fall that is about to come to a crashing climax later this afternoon with Molly's affair with a bounder. Bloom can return to Molly as a source of comfort, happiness, and strength even on this day of all days because of his extraordinary powers of imagination—not an imagination unloosed from memory and so from history, as Blake would have it, but an imagination capable of resting in memory as a place of permanent joy and peace. He reaches back beyond Molly's dressing for the dance two weeks ago, all the way back to an Edenic past that is stable and can function as a source of joy despite the present sadness: that is an imagination firmly rooted in memory! We begin to see the potential within memory to resolve some of the novel's complications. Bloom seems to have achieved a triumph over time as this episode—and the first movement of the novel—ends, a triumph over naturalism that would bind us to place and time.

Bloom's continual return to thoughts of Molly's body and Molly's bed ironically reflects Stephen's return to thoughts of his mother's body. For both men, the body of the woman signifies our connection to the past, to history, and to the body that lives in time. After all, in the Incarnation it is a mortal woman who gives flesh to the divine, who brings the timeless and divine into time and history. It is woman who is our concrete tie to a human past, whereas paternity may be just a legal fiction. It is therefore woman who stands for our lives as material creatures in space and time. Both men are bound to thoughts of these powerful women, and even if both would like to free themselves from these thoughts and these women, we have seen in "Nestor" that such escape from history and the body is not possible. That Stephen is depressed by thoughts of his mother and Bloom is able to use thoughts of Molly to elevate himself from depression signals a difference in the two men that shall make the one able to become the father to the other. If Bloom returns to Molly's bed at the end of this long day, he will have brought Stephen home to her house and given him hope for a relation to the body and to history that is not confining but liberating. Bloom returns, in memory here in "Hades" and literally in "Ithaca," to Molly and brings Stephen along the way to give him a new start. One cannot escape from the conditions of naturalism, the conditions of material reality in space and time, but one can find a relation to these conditions that allows for freedom and nobility and truth.

The first six episodes of *Ulysses* have established a style and a focus that we can call a scrupulous naturalism, and we have watched both figures combat the implications of this style as they confront the limit of naturalism, death. Both characters wear black to underscore how they respect the conditions of space and time that lead to death, how they are moving squarely within its confines yet hoping for escape. Stephen with his theory of imagination based on Incarnation and Bloom with his active imagination rooted in memory both seek to find a way beyond death, as the novel will soon be seeking its way beyond naturalism. When we turn the page and confront the newspaper headlines of "Aeolus," we know that something drastic has happened to the novel, that an explosion of sorts has occurred that begins to break the stranglehold the novel and its commitment to realism have placed on its practitioners. Joyce is freeing his novel from naturalism, and so freeing it—and us—from death.

Chapter Two

The Novel as Humanist
From Naturalism to Abstraction

"Aeolus" begins what critics have called the "middle-stage" of *Ulysses*, a second movement of sorts in which Joyce begins to loosen the powerful grip that naturalistic narration has had on character and plot. In this chapter I will offer analyses of the episodes from "Aeolus" through "Wandering Rocks" from the point of view of the following thesis: that by defying the standards of naturalistic prose, Joyce is defying the traditional novelistic concern for representation in a way analogous to the defiance of representation by modern abstract painters.

While there is little to suggest that Joyce was reading T. E. Hulme's work, it would not be surprising if he had, given Joyce's close association with Hulme's champion, Ezra Pound. But I am less interested in tracing a line of influence than in assigning a certain context for Joyce's experiments in abstraction that commence boldly and loudly with the newspaper headlines of "Aeolus." Hulme's writing on modern abstract art provides us with a keen perspective from which to view these middle episodes. In the essay "Humanism," Hulme sees the tendency toward abstraction in art as an effort to break away from the grip of humanism and to establish a higher set of permanent or absolute values: "The disgust with the trivial and accidental characteristics of living shapes, the searching after an austerity, a *perfection* and rigidity which vital things can never have, lead here to the use of forms which can almost be called geometrical. Man is subordinate to certain absolute values: there is no delight in the human form, leading to its *natural* reproduction; it is always distorted to fit into the more abstract forms which convey an intense religious emotion" (Hulme, 53). We must be careful in transposing what Hulme says about abstract visual art to Joyce's novel; for instance, to say that there is a "disgust with the trivial and accidental characteristics of living shapes" and "no delight in the human form" in *Ulysses* is to miss the great joy of reading the early episodes and getting to know Bloom and Stephen "from the inside."[1] But I do want to take from Hulme certain terms and attitudes that can be fruitfully transposed to a study of Joyce's stylistic experiments, for Joyce is reacting against the traditional representations of the "human" and "vital" and "natural" that he provides so lucidly and fully in the opening episodes, distorting these to "fit more abstract forms which convey an intense religious emotion." There is a relationship between naturalism as a style and humanism as an ethic, and Joyce is dissatisfied with both. To glorify the vital forms that humanity can take on in its attempt to adapt to and even master its circumstances is the best naturalism can do; Joyce wants to move beyond the naturalism that serves humanism and find a style capable of presenting something permanent and absolute. The Bloom of the early episodes, an epitome of humanism, is worked upon until he becomes "abstract," standing for values that move beyond a culturally determined context and reach toward the timeless. That is the "religious emotion" *Ulysses* is moving toward.

Michael Levenson documents the development of Hulme's thought, and he sees in "Humanism" and "Modern Art" its emergence beyond the rather narrow confines of the earlier distinction between "Romanticism and Classicism" to a more compelling distinction between naturalism and abstraction, between humanism and antihumanism.[2] It was Hulme's reading of Wilhelm Worringer's *Abstraktion und Einfuhlung* that enabled him to begin his critique of humanism based on Worringer's subtle critique of empathy. According to this critique, there are two tendencies in art, one toward empathy and one toward abstraction. Empathy is the pleasure we take in viewing works of art that are naturalistic or realistic as we find in them "an objectification of our own pleasure in activity, and our own vitality" (Hulme, 85). In geometric art, "there is no delight in nature and no striving after vitality. Its forms are always what can be described as stiff and lifeless." Joyce has Stephen make a similar distinction in *A Portrait of the Artist as a Young Man* between kinetic and static art, the former stimulating its beholder into active emotions (desire or loathing) and the latter aiming at arresting the mind and lifting it above such human emotions (see especially pages 204–8 of *A Portrait*).[3] What Hulme, through Worringer, and Joyce have in common here is the call for an aesthetic that does not seek to arouse its beholder to an admiration of our human state but instead seeks to create a static condition in the beholder where something lifeless may be beheld.

Hulme asks and answers an important question: "What is the condition of mind of the people whose art is governed by [the tendency to abstraction]? It can be described most generally as a feeling of separation in the face of outside nature" (Hulme, 85). Such an art assumes that there is something in "outside nature" that is dangerous and to be opposed, and in terms of what we have been seeing in the first six episodes of *Ulysses*, this something is our body, that part of our human nature subject to time and so moving toward death. Abstract art, according to Hulme, is based not on the desire to celebrate this vital body but instead on the "desire to create a certain abstract geometrical shape, which, being durable and permanent shall be a refuge from the flux and impermanence of outside nature" (86). When Stephen refers to Dante's Beatrice as "the isosceles triangle miss Portinari he fell in love with" (14.886–87), we may note that Stephen grasps what abstraction accomplishes, the movement away from flesh and blood toward something permanent and filled with spiritual power. What Joyce has done in the opening episodes of *Ulysses* is to present a world of flux out of which the rest of the novel seeks to extract something durable and permanent, a world of naturalism that arouses our human responses that will be distorted in order to present a set of values above mere human emotion. To return to the language Joyce used in *Stephen Hero*, in order to make a fit abode for our ideals, the very conditions of our human nature must be distorted and rendered abstract. What Hulme says about abstract geometric art is true of the later episodes of *Ulysses:* "All art of this character turns the organic into something inorganic, it tries to translate the changing and limited into something unlimited and necessary" (Hulme, 106). Joyce writes a novel that is largely about its own development from one kind of art to another, and the episodes of the middle-stage represent a transition from the one to the other.

I have already issued some warning that we apply Hulme's sense of painterly abstraction to Joyce's book in that there is more joy and delight than disgust with the body in *Ulysses,* more delight in depicting vital forms than revulsion or loathing. Joyce does not wish, as Hulme would have it, to abandon the body and material creation as much as to find within nature a higher reality of spiritual truth. Ihab Hassan cites Norman O. Brown, who in turn cites Alfred North Whitehead, in calling abstraction "a denial of the living organ of experience, the living body as a whole" (Hassan, 18). Following Brown, Hassan calls for a return to the vital and the material that modernism, in its intense pursuit of the permanent, lost sight of and respect for. I want to use Hulme's thesis because there is an element of abstraction in *Ulysses* attempting to accomplish just what he says it seeks, "an intense religious emotion," but never at the expense of the body, never entailing a loss of the body. If Bloom rises above nature, he still carries nature with him, just as Christ did in his Resurrection and Ascension.

But Joyce does want to expose the limitations of naturalism, a style he has just employed for six episodes to give us the illusion of reality in Bloom and Stephen. The monologue method that represents the stream of consciousness is Joyce's contribution to naturalism, but it is a limited way of representing his characters. Dorrit Cohn's study of the history of the novel, *Transparent Minds*, provides a useful context for my argument here, for she studies scrupulously the various ways in which novelists have depicted human consciousness in fiction and sees in this presenting of consciousness a hallmark of the novel. She describes the "inward turn" of the novel as "a gradual unfolding of the genre's most distinctive potential, to its full Bloom in the stream-of-consciousness novel and beyond" (Cohn, 8). She cites Schopenhauer: "The more *inner* and the less *outer* life a novel presents, the higher and nobler will be its purpose. . . . Art consists in achieving the maximum of inner motion with the minimum of outer motion: for it is the inner life which is the true object of our interest" (9). Cohn's statement that "modern writers of Joyce's generation themselves thought of the history of the novel in this fashion" (8) allows me to make an important correction: Joyce may well have seen the novel as moving in the direction of providing ever clearer and more intimate access to the inner workings of the human characters depicted, but that is a movement he chooses to question and halt in and through *Ulysses*. For Bloom will be seen from the inside only through the first eleven episodes (with a return in the second half of "Nausicaa," episode 13), but the most important actions of the day will be seen from outside Bloom's consciousness, especially in "Ithaca" where we watch the climax of the novel from the loftiest vantage point imaginable. As I will be saying once we get to "Cyclops," Joyce is moving outside the consciousness of his characters because the truth is not inside the mind but outside it. Hulme's notion of "abstraction," coupled with this application of Cohn's study as it pertains to Joyce, provides the framework for this chapter and indeed the ones to follow. From "Aeolus" onward we will be watching how Joyce is (to use Hulme's language) abstracting Bloom from a naturalistic context, or (to use Cohn's language) how Joyce is exposing the limitations of the "inside view" and is working to find a perspective from which to present the truth of Bloom's character.

The process of abstracting Bloom begins in "Aeolus," sometimes in ways that are obvious (the newspaper headlines) and sometimes in smaller ways (which I will be looking at in a moment). But first something about the process of writing "Aeolus" must be addressed. Through the work of Walton Litz and Michael Groden we have been taught about possible changes in the conception Joyce had of his novel as it progressed and as he was reviewing the earlier episodes in light of the later ones on which he was working. Groden claims that "the last nine of the eighteen episodes transfer concern from character to technique" (Groden, 37), but I think that such a statement places too little emphasis on what should be an obvious point: that there is as much "style" and "technique" in the early naturalistic episodes as there is in the later abstract ones. I do not want to make a casual distinction between character and technique, for I believe that the characters are always as important as, and ultimately inextricable from, the techniques. Brook Thomas has provided a clue for my analysis, noting that Joyce was in an unusual, if not unique, position regarding his text: that he was reading published versions of the early episodes as he was working on the later ones. According to Thomas, "What Groden does not point out . . . is that changes from stage to stage correspond closely to Joyce's own re-reading of his text in preliminary form. A major departure from his initial technique occurred soon after Joyce must have re-read drafts of the early chapters for publication in the *Little Review*. Similarly, Joyce's final revisions, many reflexive in nature, are prompted by his reading of the book in proof before final publication" (Thomas, 281). Thomas has noted what is potentially of monumental importance in studying this novel, that Joyce was writing *Ulysses* in the way that Saint Paul was reading the Bible, making features of his own reading part of the later writing. Paul was offering rereadings of Old Testament events as part of a writing that becomes the climax of the very book he is reading. Joyce is reading published versions of the book he is still writing, and so he is in an unusual relationship to those early episodes: on the one hand they seem part of the text he is still engaged with, and on the other they seem quite different and unusual, something already in print and so already with a life of their own. It is as if he is watching characters established by another author upon whom he is now offering later commentary. His writing is a kind of rereading; the later episodes are the result of how he wants to rewrite the story already in print.

This is to overstate the case, because Joyce did not feel bound not to change the *Little Review* versions as he was bringing the novel to final publication. But he was busy in reviewing those episodes, and as Litz and Groden inform us, the first six episodes received relatively few and primarily small changes. But concerning "Aeolus," Groden makes the following crucial point: "Of all the early episodes, 'Aeolus' exhibits the most pronounced differences between the fair-copy *Little Review* and the final versions" (Groden, 32). Groden's scrupulous scholarship serves to reinforce my conviction that as Joyce begins to reconsider the larger purpose of his novel and the role that the early episodes will play in that purpose, "Aeolus" functions as the pivotal episode. Of all the episodes up to this point in the novel, Joyce reworks this one the most extensively in order to mark the beginning of the end of one kind of novel and to prepare us for the later, more elaborate developments. Groden shares this attitude toward "Aeolus": "The subheads shatter the comfortable uniformity of the early-stage episodes, and they make the later developments much less surprising" (Groden, 32). So as Joyce begins revising earlier episodes in light of this practice of rereading, it is "Aeolus" that occupies his attention and where we will be able best to infer the changing intention of the author.

We ought to ask what exactly it is that Joyce hopes to accomplish as he revises "Aeolus" for final publication, adding the often comic headlines that disrupt the flow of what is, for the most part, still a naturalistic narration. The answer is precisely that the flow is disrupted, that the illusion of this prose to mime a "stream of consciousness" is punctured by these bold and loud headlines that freeze the action. It is as if Bloom's or Stephen's thoughts and the action surrounding them abruptly stop for a moment as we have to read these often absurd headlines. Pressing this point a bit further, we might even say that the headlines, being so odd and unexpected, do more than arrest the action; they may even deflect our attention from the action as we want to enjoy the comedy of the headlines and pause to solve the problem of their sudden appearance. The headlines provide a comic version of Stephen's "stasis." Joyce makes us acutely aware of the artifice of writing, that what we are reading is a book and not life, a book that no longer wishes to be simply a transparent window onto the world. The illusion of transparency that Cohn celebrates and locates especially in the modern novel is, if not shattered, certainly called into question with these headlines. This is the beginning of the abstraction of Bloom and Stephen, of taking them out of the naturalistic context of the early episodes written in the initial style.

It must be pointed out that, while the process of abstraction is begun here, the flow of naturalistic prose continues for the most part without the technical pyrotechnics we will be witnessing starting with "Sirens." "Aeolus" through "Wandering Rocks" occupies a middle ground in my chart of the novel's changes, as a loosening of the grip of the naturalistic style but not its shattering. But Joyce's revisions of "Aeolus" do not end with the headlines. He adds more rhetorical devices to the many already there in the *Little Review* version, and he adds more pure noise to the surroundings and more figurative uses of "wind" as he revises the episode for final publication (Groden, 64). (The same kind of revision is made for the next episode, "Lestrygonians," where Joyce adds as many references to food and digestion as he can to underscore the parallel to Homer's story.) These additions do not, one by one, violate the criteria of naturalism; but as Joyce piles on the references to wind in the one and to food in the other, the sheer amount of such parallels begins to seem absurd and "unrealistic" for a narrator's language. In this small way he begins to bring the reader to an awareness of the existence of what Hayman calls "the arranger," "a significant, felt absence in the text, an unstated but inescapable source of control" (Hayman, 123). Behind the narrator of the naturalistic prose lurks this other narrator, whose job it is, I think, to begin the distorting of naturalism and its attendant humanistic ethic as the text prepares for the movement toward abstraction.

A wonderful example of the work of this arranger in "Aeolus" occurs when Professor MacHugh flosses his teeth:

> He took a reel of dental floss from his waistcoat pocket and, breaking off a piece, twanged it smartly between two and two of his resonant unwashed teeth.
> —Bingbang, bangbang.
> Mr Bloom, seeing the coast clear, made for the inner door. (7.371–75)

In no piece of naturalistic prose could the process of flossing one's teeth produce the sound "Bingbang, bangbang," no matter how resonant one's teeth may be. The combination of scrupulous attention to detail (we watch him remove the floss from his pocket, break off a piece, and "twang it smartly"; we even learn that the teeth are unwashed!) with the absurdity of the noise the process produces is a perfect example of the way Joyce works in these middle episodes, poking fun at the naturalistic narrator, behind his back, as it were.

There are, it seems safe to say, at least two narrators for "Aeolus," one of whom we can call "the naturalistic narrator" or "the naturalist," and the other, following Hayman's happy term, "the arranger." What I will turn to now is an analysis of just what the arranger does to the naturalist's account of the episode's events. By interrupting the flow of the naturalist's narration, the arranger begins to abstract the characters and the events from the confines of space and time, beginning the process of lifting them beyond their narrow historical locus and rendering them more permanent and durable. What I will be arguing is that this playful narrative presence serves to make the reader more aware of certain aspects of the novel's purpose, serves to make the reader more conscious of his own role in making the novel meaningful. *Ulysses* will be about its own reading.

The two main events in the episode are Bloom's efforts to land the renewal of the Keyes advertisement despite the editor's indifference and Stephen's recital of one of his stories to a largely unappreciative audience. These events are quite in keeping with the demands of naturalism, for both are merely following the dictates of the careers they have chosen, Bloom to canvass for ads and Stephen to write stories about Dublin. Yet the arranger's regular interrupting of the naturalist's account has the effect of abstracting what they are doing from the local context in which they are doing. Bloom is not just pursuing his professional obligations; he is seeking to find the key he has left in his other trousers pocket. The keyless citizen is searching for the Keyes he will need to be able to effect a return home: we are moving in the direction of symbolism, encouraged to do so by the loosening of the vicelike grip of naturalism that would reduce Bloom's actions to their "realistic" function alone and would see only a coincidence between the name Keyes and Bloom's forgotten key. Where the naturalist can only understand coincidence as accident, the allegorist sees in coincidence evidence of a larger design that establishes a series of coincidences for later revelations of significance. It is only a coincidence, from within the perspective of the Old Testament historical accounts, that so many younger brothers supplant older ones: Abel supplanting Cain, Isaac supplanting Ishmael, Jacob supplanting Esau, Joseph and David supplanting their older brothers. But this series of accidents is actually part of a careful design revealed only in the New Testament and only seen from its perspective, where the new covenant replaces the old, where the new teaching supplants the old tradition. The arranger occupies a middle role between the naturalist on the one hand and the allegorist on the other, for his playful presence is Joyce's way of beginning the shift from the one to the other. The search for "Keyes" in "Aeolus" smacks of symbolism while still remaining mostly an event in a naturalistic account of Bloom's day. The symbolism of keys is deferred until and fulfilled in "Ithaca," where Bloom and Stephen are called the "keyless couple" (17.81) and Bloom "a competent keyless citizen" (17.1019). While in these early episodes being keyless is an accident, the novel attempts to make it an inevitable accompaniment to Bloom's character, symbolic of being an exile blocked from any easy return home: we may recall Hulme's phrase about the aims of geometric art, that it attempts to translate what is changing and limited into what is necessary and unlimited. Rickard, in his study of memory, makes the point that "memory allows chance to have meaning" (Rickard, 158), and the allegorist rereads earlier chance events from the perspective of destiny and providence. The accidental is to be changed into the necessary, and this process of transformation begins in "Aeolus." We learn (7.430–31) that Alexander Keyes is at Dillon's auction house, and the Dillon who owns the auction house in 1904 Dublin has nothing to do with the Mat Dillon from 1886. The coincidence of the names is an accident that will allow us to say, in the retrospective arrangement permitted by and taken from the perspective of "Ithaca," that Bloom seeks the key that will let him return home to Molly and the evenings at Mat Dillon's when he first met Molly, in that Edenic world of "lilactrees." If the novel is to end triumphantly for Bloom, it will be because he finds that key, not in the realistic order of the naturalist but in the symbolic order of the allegorist. The arranger occupies the middle ground between the two, permitting us to glimpse the symbolic possibilities in the accidents laid out before us by the naturalist.

Stephen dominates the second half of the episode, and the telling of his story, "A Pisgah Sight of Palestine, or the Parable of the Plums," is the telos that renders the episode's emphasis on rhetoric meaningful. What is brought to a climax in Stephen's story is an analogy between the people of Israel in the Exodus story and the people of Ireland in 1904, especially as they are represented in *Dubliners* and *Ulysses*. This parallel is begun when J. J. O'Molloy recites a sentence from a speech of Seymour Bushe in which he refers to the Moses of Michelangelo: "*that stony effigy in frozen music, horned and terrible, of the human form divine, that eternal symbol of wisdom and prophecy which, if aught that the imagination or the hand of sculptor has wrought in marble of soultransfigured and of soultransfiguring deserves to live, deserves to live*" (7.768–71). First, this is offered as an example of high rhetoric with the capacity to move its hearers to assent merely by its power, and Stephen is momentarily won over by it: "Stephen, his blood wooed by grace of language and gesture, blushed" (7.776). In this way begins an important theme of *Ulysses* that I described in the preface, the danger of language to mislead and the quest for a style capable of presenting truth. Lofty rhetoric especially is dangerous in that it can lead us to assent to proposals and propositions that may be dangerous and destructive. Second, it begins the train of association that leads to the recitation of John F. Taylor's speech, which also cites Moses, and ends with Stephen's story, whose title alone tells us that Moses figures as the key to its meaning.

But Bushe's sentence also figures as a clue to Joyce's intentions, in the episode and in the novel as a whole. The statue of Moses is cited as an example of an artist's ability to make out of the recalcitrant material provided by the world something that is "soultransfigured" and "soultransfiguring." It is "frozen music," an image of the "human form divine," an "eternal symbol of wisdom and prophecy." It is, in short, just what Joyce hopes to do with the character he has created in Bloom, to make this man the bearer of such wisdom. Bloom's Jewish heritage makes him more capable than most other Dubliners of an identification with Moses; in fact, in "Scylla and Charybdis," Mulligan mockingly guesses his name to be "Ikey Moses" (9.607), an ironic identification through the mouth of the mocking Malachi.

Rhetoric has become the explicit theme of the episode at this point, and Moses an implicit one. What the arranger's interruptions accomplish is a freezing of the action—"frozen music"—that allows us to pull out of the context in which he has brought up the figure of Moses so we can apply it elsewhere, as I have just briefly done. Now one might wish to point out that such lifting and application occur all the time in our readings of all sorts of literary objects, and of course I would have to agree; but the point is not that we would not do this without the arranger's work, but that we are being made aware of the process of reading, that we are being taught by the book how to read it. Bushe's speech reminds Professor MacHugh of a speech by Taylor precisely because Moses figures prominently in both, and this increases the importance of Moses to the novel, though that is not the intention of the orators at the newspaper office. No one present in the newspaper office would see that Moses is the key to the events occurring around them; the naturalistic narrator would not recognize this himself, Moses being merely the subject of famous speeches and the element that explains a train of association. But the arranger has so much disrupted the context for the flow of events that we, as readers, seem invited by the novel to take similar liberties. We must note carefully just how the headlines operate in the text: not only do they disrupt the flow, but they often emphasize in the narration that follows not its main feature but a trivial detail; the headlines are seldom pointers to the important points to follow but most often a joke highlighting an oddity or a quirk. The work of the arranger is to encourage us to see what other story is being presented alongside the main one, what other emphasis is possible outside what seems to be center stage. Taylor's speech reminds Stephen of his story in which the figure of Moses is only obliquely present; it is not until it is over and has been named that its hearers—and its readers—can trace the train of association that recalled it to Stephen. At that point the naturalist in us is satisfied, and so is the arranger in us, who is willing to see more than coincidence in all these Moses stories and is eager to play with possible meanings for them. The reader is empowered by the arranger's presence.

Taylor's speech does more than just bring Moses increasingly to the reader's attention in a general way; it presents a concrete way of connecting the people of Israel to the Dubliners of 1904—both peoples under the heavy oppression of a foreign power and struggling to maintain their own identities while in captivity and the sense of their superior mission. The arranger has allowed—even encouraged—the reader to begin constructing a parallel narrative alongside the more dominant, naturalistic one, and we feel quite certain that this parallel is far more important to the meaning of *Ulysses* than any of the characters—and, more important, than their narrator—could guess. The history of the people of Israel will become increasingly important to our understanding of the novel, coming to a climax in "Ithaca" where Stephen and Bloom will perform a rite rooted in Hebrew scriptures. The Irish are to be regarded as in some way a people set apart by the author of this novel, the way the people of Israel were set apart by God, to bear the burden of a higher destiny, one they usually fail to understand and maintain. Joyce has found his ingenious manner of providing the reader with thematic motifs hidden from the view of the narrator. While the naturalist can only think that he is providing another example of high rhetoric to the episode about rhetoric, the reader is able to see the slow emergence of another theme alongside the more obvious—and to be frank, the more trivial—plot action of "Aeolus." The reader is quite able to see the beginning of a thematic plot that, from the point of view of "Ithaca," is far more important than Bloom's and Stephen's activities at noon. As we reread the novel from "Ithaca," we will focus on what the naturalist would only see as accidental but that now looks to be part of a necessary design, the parallel between the Jews and the Irish as bearers of an important destiny. The reader will say about "Aeolus" that it prepares us for a later reading in which the Irish, like the Jews, are working out a destiny to be fulfilled in the coming of a Christ event. We will not be able to grasp the full meaning of this parallel until "Ithaca," when Stephen and Bloom perform a ritual "exodus from the house of bondage into the wilderness of inhabitation" (17.1021–22). The phrase "house of bondage," so important to the meaning of "Ithaca," is introduced to the novel in "Aeolus" through Taylor's speech (7.865). In fact, the crucial phrase from 'Ithaca" that first alerted me to Joyce's allegorical method—the one describing Bloom as an "advertising Elijah" "with the light of inspiration shining in his countenance and bearing in his arms the secret of the race, graven in the language of prediction" (17.339–41)—is also first introduced to the reader in "Aeolus" through Taylor's speech, where, with little difference, it describes Moses (7.867–89).

With the Moses theme thrust upon the reader, it seems quite natural to ask whether Bloom is, then, in some way some sort of incarnation of Moses. This is a difficult question to answer at this point, for the novel has done little thus far to make this, or any, identification work. We are still not free from the demands of the naturalist, who would puncture such an identification with a glib joke, nor will we ever be totally free of the naturalist's influence, even in "Ithaca": the allegory of theologians never allows the divorce between naturalism and symbolism, as I indicated in my introduction and as we will see when we finally arrive at "Ithaca." Still under the sway of the naturalist, but aided by the pranks of the arranger, we are at this point only beginning to see the possibility of such identifications. In fact, we will see several identifications attempted in later episodes, most important to Elijah and Christ in "Cyclops," only to see these fall apart. It can be said that I am writing this critical study of *Ulysses* out of sequence by moving through the novel more or less chronologically, for we can only see the place of these speeches in a different configuration of the plot of the novel when we have almost finished the novel, from what I will be calling the fixed perspective of "Ithaca." I try to point us ahead just enough to place these early episodes in a different—and their proper—relation to the novel as a whole than they can possibly take on here, while still deferring full discussion of "Ithaca" to the end of the study. What I want to emphasize here is that the revisions to "Aeolus" constitute the beginning of the process of showing us another way of reading reality, a way of reading that looks for evidence of the permanent under the flow of time and that seeks the meaningful pattern in a narration by a narrator who cannot recognize the pattern himself.

The final and most important contribution to the Moses theme in "Aeolus" is Stephen's story, which, until the title is given us, has no ostensible connection to the speeches that have dominated the pages up to its telling. Stephen begins by saying, "I have a vision too" (7.917), his response to professor MacHugh's comment on Taylor's speech, "It has the prophetic vision" (7.909–10), which is an ironic way of suggesting how prophetic Taylor's speech will eventually prove to be for the novel. Stephen's story is to counter Taylor's speech in ways that are important to my reading of *Ulysses*. While the points of comparison between the Jews and the Irish are explicit in Taylor's high-flown oratory, any such relation is oblique in Stephen's much plainer and more modest story. Anne Kearns and Florence MacCabe, the "two Dublin vestals" in the story, plan and make a day's outing that is to climax in a climb up Nelson's pillar. As they view the city from this lofty vantage point, all they note are the different churches whose tops they can see, and they settle down to "peer . . . up at the statue of the onehandled adulterer." The ending is like the ending of the failed visions of *Dubliners,* as they stop looking around them and eat the plums they brought up with them, "wiping off with their handkerchiefs the plumjuice that dribbles out of their mouths and spitting the plumstones slowly out between the railings" (7.1025–27). Without the title we could see in this story an ironic indictment of the empty goals available to the citizens of Dublin. And that is the story's meaning, though complicated when we learn its title, *A Pisgah Sight of Palestine* or *The Parable of the Plums* (7.1055–56). Moses was allowed a "Pisgah sight of Palestine" as his earthly reward for having led the Jews out of Egypt and through their forty years of desert wandering. If we apply the Moses story to Stephen's, we may conclude that the two old women also have been granted an opportunity to see the promised land, which is all about them, in dear dirty Dublin. Their failure lies in their lack of imagination, in their inability to see the promised land right where they are. There is also an indictment of the church and the state, represented by the various churches that dominate Dublin and the statue of the great English naval hero. Stephen's "I have a vision too" now resonates more loudly as his quiet claim to have the capacity to see something of God's glory in Dublin. Stephen is laying claim to what we may want to call a historical imagination, a kind of imaginative power able to transform the ordinary into the extraordinary. We will be watching to see if he can recognize in Bloom the promise that the two elderly women missed.

This story of Stephen's occupies another crucial place in the novel's unfolding meaning. The plain naturalistic style of Stephen's story is right out of *Dubliners* and yet still claims a visionary capacity. Stephen's plainness contrasts strongly with the high rhetoric that has dominated the episode, the kind of rhetoric Bloom dismisses as "high falutin stuff. Bladderbags" (7.260) and that Stephen braces against ("Noble words coming. Look out" [836]). Both of the novel's protagonists are wary of rhetoric, and so ought we be if we take Stephen's story seriously. For he uses a simple and plain style to depict his story about visionary promise, and the response to his story by Professor MacHugh emphasizes the theme of vision: "Yes, he said, I see them" (961); and three times he says, "I see" (1059, 1061, 1065). There is in this novel a fundamental distrust of language itself, and the plain style of the naturalist is not to be sneered at, for it can make us see better than high rhetoric, which is used to mislead and confuse more than to lead us to truth. After all, the aim of Taylor's powerful speech is to convince its hearers that the Irish ought to cling to their own language and culture, something Joyce never believed at all! We are to distrust high language as much as we are to be wary of the limits of the naturalist. Our hopes are now on Stephen, who combines plainness with visionary promise. Hearing is subordinated to vision, language to sight: we must learn to see what Stephen sees, a vision of the traditional figure of hypostasis, and a plain style will bring us to that vision.

It is worth repeating Groden's central observation about "Aeolus," that "of all the early episodes" it "exhibits the most pronounced differences between the fair-copy *Little Review* and the final versions" (Groden, 32). Only when he had finished the drafts of the entire novel—only, that is, when he knew what he had to make the early episodes lead to, prepare for, set up—did Joyce begin fashioning the bridge between the early naturalistic episodes and the later symbolic ones. He looks back at "Aeolus" and works it up to prepare for the changes to come. "Aeolus" is the loudest and boldest of the middle episodes—in my chart of the novel's development, episodes 7 through 10—in announcing to the reader that the initial style is soon to be abandoned and replaced by styles intended to abstract the permanent from the flux, the eternal from the time-bound. The reader has been empowered to halt the flux and look for evidence of other layers of meaning being laid down for future fulfillment.

The next episode, "Lestrygonians," continues this movement away from naturalism toward abstraction primarily in its excessive use of references to food and the process of digestion. I say "excessive" because they are not at all required by the naturalist to describe the events, and their sheer amount points to Hayman's arranger who accumulates so many of them that part of the fun of the episode is to enjoy the ingenuity that can find so many ways to use descriptions of the digestive process to advance the narrative of Bloom's day. Again, it seems clear to me that these references serve to distract the reader's attention from the flow of the naturalistic narration, which in "Lestrygonians" is still dominant but disrupted enough by the arranger to distance the reader from the immediacy of the action. The ideal of the artist as expressed by Stephen in *A Portrait*—that he, "like the God of creation, remains within or behind or behind or beyond or above his handiwork, invisible, refined by existence, indifferent, paring his fingernails" (*AP*, 215)—is temporarily suspended as Joyce works to make us aware of the process of narration. Made aware of the arranger by "Aeolus," we are prepared to note the liberties taken in this episode; and the more we are aware of the author playing with his narration, the more distance we have on the scenes and characters being depicted. This process will conclude in "Ithaca," where the author writes as if he is God, or at least is writing from a God-like view. Aware of the author as well as the character, we have a double view of these middle episodes.

The references to food and digestion make prominent the body and its needs, that favorite and inevitable focus of naturalism. The effect of the arranger's antics in this episode is to present the body as the theme for analysis. Whereas in "Hades" we were encouraged to think about our mortality, in "Lestrygonians" we are more inclined to think about the body as a coarse and vulgar thing, as a machine that ingests and processes food as the source of its energy. Bloom makes the point when he contrasts the human body with the bodies of mythical beings, "quaffing nectar at mess with gods golden dishes, all ambrosial. Not like a tanner lunch we have, boiled mutton, carrots and turnips, bottle of Allsop. Nectar imagine it drinking electricity: god's food. Lovely forms of women sculped Junonian. Immortal lovely. And we stuffing food in one hole and out behind: food, chyle, blood, dung, earth, food: have to feed it like stoking an engine. They have no. Never looked: I'll look today. Keeper won't see. Bend down let something drop. See if she" (8.925–32). Bloom imagines that goddesses do not take in food merely to stoke the engine, as we must our bodies; he imagines that they do not excrete the food they ingest, nor even have an orifice for the job, which he plans to verify by observing the statues of goddesses in the library museum. It is our lot to "stuff food in one hole and out behind," a rather vulgar lot it seems to Bloom at this point of the day. In fact, everything attached to food and digestion seems vulgar and low to Bloom as the clock approaches two o'clock. This morning the prospect of eating was narrated differently, "with relish," we might be tempted to say; but not so now. We can guess, and the episode bears it out, that the body now seems vulgar because the hour of Molly's infidelity is approaching, when she will fulfill her body's desires by committing adultery.

So the emphasis on food and digestion in "Lestrygonians" can be linked to the theme of infidelity, in that the body seems a vulgar machine directing our behavior and course of action to fulfill its desires and needs. The body is a machine in "Lestrygonians" that demands that certain attention be given its powerful desires. The "abstraction" of this episode, the emphasis given to food and digestion by the arranger, is to place the body in the foreground as an obstacle blocking Bloom's way to equanimity.

So Bloom needs to eat. In fact, we are told quite explicitly that he is depressed at this hour because he is hungry, showing how the body drives the spirit:

> One born every second somewhere. Other dying every second. Since I fed the birds five minutes. Three hundred kicked the bucket. Other three hundred born, washing the blood off, all are washed in the blood of the lamb, bawling maaaaaa.
> Cityful passing away, other cityful coming, passing away too: other coming on, passing on. Houses, lines of houses, streets, miles of pavements, piledup bricks, stones. Changing hands. This owner, that. Landlord never dies, they say. . . .
> No-one is anything.
> This is the very worst hour of the day. Vitality. Dull, gloomy: hate this hour. Feel as if I had been eaten and spewed. (8.480–95)

His body's hunger makes him depressed, feeling that life in time is merely a coming on and a passing on, the sentiments expressed about our lives in *Ecclesiastes*, where all things under the sun are vanity. An awareness of the body's need for food leads Bloom to this awareness of the ultimate futility of the body, always feeding it to replenish its energy only to end in the finality of death. There is no goal toward which the body makes progress, no telos that renders the body's constant call for attention purposeful, nothing but this constant repetition of eating and defecating, being born and dying; thoughts about food lead to this meditation on the vanity of our existence. His hunger—his awareness of the body's need for its energy source—makes him feel we are nothing but bodies: "No-one is anything." His hunger depresses him more than anything else on this day will, with the sole exception of Molly's infidelity, which as we have already noted is connected to this hunger. He hates this hour because it leads to awareness of the body as a constant problem to be overcome.

Disgusted by the coarse, almost animal-like behavior ("See the animals feed," he thinks) at the Burton, Bloom handles this aspect of the body's needs rather easily by going to Davy Byrne's "Moral pub" for a light snack of cheese and wine: nothing had to be killed for this meal, a fact that appeases his suddenly squeamish scruples that accompany him at this hour. It is possible for Bloom to be understood as a scrupulous vegetarian in "Lestrygonians" and as a happy carnivore in "Calypso": the episodes are at one and the same time part of a whole that is called *Ulysses* and individual units with a cohesion and purpose of their own. At this hour it is appropriate for Bloom to refrain from killing, for he is facing both the hunger occasioned by his body's needs and the jealousy occasioned by his wife's: he will not be violent in responding either to his needs or to Molly's. His effort to respond to his jealousy is more complex. He thinks about the night two weeks ago when Molly and Blazes began the relationship that is to climax in about two hours: "She was humming: The young May moon she's beaming, love. He other side of her. Elbow, arm. He. Glowworm's la-amp is gleaming, love. Touch. Fingers. Asking. Answer. Yes" (8.589–91). This memory disturbs Bloom, and he tries to combat its power by conjuring up another, happier image from the past: "I was happier then. Or was that I? Or am I now I? Twenty eight I was. She twenty three. When we left Lombard street west something changed. Could never like it again after Rudy. Can't bring back time. Like holding water in your hand" (8.608–11). This will be a crucial issue for the last episode of the novel and for *Ulysses* as a whole: can one "bring back time" through the power of memory? The answer there will be that memory has that power, but that is possible only after the workings of the rest of the novel, especially "Ithaca." It will be possible in "Penelope" for memory to defy time and bring back an image from the past as the conclusion to the novel, but here in "Lestrygonians," an episode dominated by the body vulgar, the answer is no. For the body, time is irreversible, "like holding water in your hand."

Just a few lines later Bloom thinks, "Useless to go back. Had to be. Tell me all" (8.633), but he is not thinking about memory here; he is thinking that it is useless for him to return home in order to speak to Molly and perhaps prevent the breach in their marriage. It is worth repeating that

"Ulysses" and "useless" are almost anagrams, a Joycean way of suggesting that this hero's greatness will be in accepting the futility of action, in resigning himself to the uselessness of most of our efforts to avoid destiny. It is useless, at least in "Lestrygonians," for him to return home at this point in the day because what is happening today has its roots in the past that cannot be changed, beginning with the death of Rudy. It is useless to go home to Molly now because he cannot go back to Molly then.

Time in "Lestrygonians" is relentless in its movement, stopping for no one or nothing and ending eventually in the cessation of the machine. When Nosey Flynn says about Molly's upcoming concert tour, "Isn't Blazes Boylan mixed up in it?," Bloom's response is to look at the pub clock: "Two. Pub clock five minutes fast. Time going on. Hands moving. Two. Not yet" (8.790–91). The "not yet" means both not yet two and not yet the hour of the rendezvous. Nothing can stop this movement toward the pivotal hour of this day, and Bloom looks forward to a later time in the day: "Then about six o'clock I can. Six. Six. Time will be gone then" (852–53). What he means, of course, is that *the* time will be gone, the dreaded hour of four o'clock will be past. The emphasis on the clock's hands moving may be Joyce's way of indicating that time is as mechanical as the body in this episode, moving inexorably onward in its repetitive efficiency. But are we being given a hint here that in some way time will be over, that something will happen by the end of the novel to suspend time and allow us to witness the revelation of something without time, something permanent and timeless? This is given comic confirmation in "Nausicaa" when Bloom is asked the time and he notes that his watch has stopped measuring the passage of time: "Funny my watch stopped just then. . . . Was that just when he, she?" (13.846–48). Such is the goal of Joyce's artistry, to make time be gone so that we can view Bloom from the aspect of eternity in "Ithaca." And in "Penelope," Molly will do what Bloom here thinks cannot be done: she will defy this kind of mechanical time and bring back the past, specifically the time when she and Bloom first made love on Howth.

But that is for the ending of the novel that is only being set up here in "Lestrygonians," where, because the body vulgar dominates, time is too powerful to be escaped or countermanded and where memory only brings about a sense of gloom and diminishment for Bloom. He becomes depressed when he recalls the first time he made love with Molly:

> Stuck on the pane two flies buzzed, stuck.
> Glowing wine on his palate lingered, swallowed. Crushing in the winepress grapes of Burgundy. Sun's heat it is. Seems to a secret touch telling me memory. Touched his sense moistened remem-

bered. Hidden under the wild ferns on Howth below us bay sleeping: sky. No sound. The sky. . . . Pillowed on my coat she had her hair, earwigs in the heather scrub my hand under her nape, you'll toss me all. O wonder! Coolsoft with ointments her hand touched me, caressed: her eyes upon me did not turn away. Ravished over her I lay, full lips full open, kissed her mouth. Yum. . . . Wildly I lay on her, kissed her: eyes, her lips, her stretched neck beating, woman's breasts full in her blouse of nun's veiling, fat nipples upright. Hot I tongued her. She kissed me. I was kissed. All yielding she tossed my hair. Kissed, she kissed me.
Me. And me now.
Stuck, the flies buzzed. (8.896–918)

The tender scene that is fixed firmly in Bloom's memory is placed in a context drawn from the present scene, a context that controls the significance of the memory for Bloom and the reader at this point in the novel's course. The juxtaposition of the buzzing stuck flies with the vivid memory implies that Bloom only feels loss as he looks back on the scene on Howth, establishing a contrast between the "me then" and the "me now." Not able yet to bring back time, memory serves only to make Bloom aware of his diminishment from a happier past, of his present poverty in comparison to a former wealth. Such is memory as naturalism and the body would have it, a dangerous power of the human mind that can fix us in a backward-looking stance that denies the present of any possibility for joy and fulfillment. Bloom is a victim of the kind of nostalgia that Nietzsche warns us against, and Derrida along with him, a sorrowful looking-back at an irrecoverable past that makes the present seem small and sad.[4] Indeed, the "postmodern" reading of Joyce's book would emphasize such a moment, as Joyce teaches that to be nostalgic for a happy past is self-destructive. The great modern theme of return is rendered suspect by such a scene, and Joyce can be made to look like a postmodern writer characterized by "a relentless refusal to submit to the past" (Meioses, 157). At this point Joyce does seem to be making a case against memory as mere indulging in a futile nostalgia, as a power of the mind capable of making us paralyzed. Like the flies on the tar paper, Bloom is stuck in a present he feels it is useless to try to change. Instead of taking action, as we would expect of a hero in a modern epic, Bloom is stuck in the backward-looking paralysis of nostalgia.

Something will happen between "Lestrygonians" and "Penelope" to transform this memory-image into an affirmation. Something will happen to make nostalgia no longer impotent and sad but active and happy. For Joyce chooses this very same scene on Howth for the image to end the novel, narrated this time by Molly: "and then I asked him with my eyes to ask again yes and then he asked me would I yes to say yes my mountain flower and first I put my arms around him yes and drew him down to me so he could feel my breasts all perfume yes and his heart was going like mad and yes I said yes I will Yes" (18.1605–9). The loading of the last four lines of the novel with eight "yeses" is certainly an affirmation; but affirmation of exactly what? I will be arguing that "Penelope" is an affirmation of memory as an agency of the human mind capable of overcoming the apparently relentless movement of time toward decay and death. It has the power to bring back to present significance a moment thought to have been lost in the seemingly inexorable process of temporal movement. Something happens between episode 8 and episode 18 that permits for the expansion of memory's power so that it can bring Bloom back home to that happier past. Not stuck in a backward-looking nostalgia, he will return home, thanks to memory.[5]

But stuck and impotent he appears in episode 8, and it ends in a way that suggests that he is wholly unqualified to be the hero of a modern epic. He is given the opportunity to do something, in the present, to prevent the breach in his marriage from ever taking place and so make possible a "real" return to that happier past. This opportunity occurs when he spots Blazes Boylan: "Straw hat in the sunlight. Tan shoes. Turnedup trousers. It is. It is" (8.1168). Bloom responds not by confronting Boylan but instead by walking briskly away from him: "His heart quopped softly. To the right. Museum. Goddesses. He swerved to the right" (1169–70). He even thinks that Boylan may be following him, as if the adulterer would go out of his way to meet and taunt the man he is about to cuckold. Bloom wants to duck into the museum, where he can make that experiment he had been planning about the statues of the goddesses; in fact, he thinks that he will feel safe there: "Cold statues: quiet there. Safe in a minute" (1176–77). He wants to avoid any action in the present, preferring to be "safe" with cold statues that are safe precisely because they are cold, devoid of any life. Bloom seems passive to a fault, as we have already noted in "Calypso." Hardly a hero, he seems as paralyzed as any of the pathetic figures Joyce drew with scrupulous meanness in *Dubliners*.

But we might be able to find another way of assessing Bloom's conduct here, one that is more hopeful. When Bloom successfully avoids the encounter with Boylan, he feels "Safe!," which as the last word in the episode has a special status inviting critical attention. What is he safe from? I suggest that he is safe from having to play a role he is sorely tempted to play and that his culture expects him to play, the role of outraged husband who, according to conventional morality, ought to try to prevent his wife's infidelity by standing up to the bounder. Critics beginning with Kenner have taught us to regard Blazes Boylan as a caricature, as little more than a cardboard figure of a cad; Bloom wants to avoid having to play an equally conventional role. His effort today is to allow the affair to occur, despite all the pressure of conventional morality to take action. His work today is to be heroically passive.

Placed in the foreground of our critical horizon by the ending of "Lestrygonians" is Bloom's passivity, which from the naturalist's perspective must seem weak and ignominious. But the reader is being freed from the confines of that perspective in order to be able to glimpse another possibility just beginning to be suggested, that there might be something noble about passivity. The lesson of "Lestrygonians" is that everything we do for the body is ultimately useless in that it must be repeated everyday and brings us no further along the way to something high or noble that is worthy of being called a goal or purpose. So Bloom's decision to do nothing is his way of refusing the body's demands and moving into a realm free of the constraints the body places on our spirit. As the novel continues, we will be invited to see in Bloom's passive nature an incarnation of the humbly passive Christ, who allowed human beings to ridicule his character and to torture his body. But that is not accomplished by "Lestrygonians" and is only established in this episode as a possibility when Bloom decides to deny the body its total control over his life. We are moving away from naturalism and its focus on the body and therefore also moving away from a humanist ethic that wants to find value only in the world of human time and human space. Bloom will always be in the body—that is why he does eat in this episode, a delicate meal of wine and cheese to give the body its due but not to let it control him—but he is beginning to move away from its constraints. Abstraction is moving us away from the body and away from mere humanism.

"Scylla and Charybdis" returns to the sort of loosening of the naturalist's hold on *Ulysses* that we witnessed in "Aeolus," a bolder sort of loosening than that of "Lestrygonians." It seems that Joyce takes more liberties with style when Stephen is present than when Bloom is the focus, perhaps implying that Stephen's role is to become the artist who can break the hold of naturalism upon the novel. When we look ahead to "Nausicaa" and recall that in that late episode, apparently long after naturalism has been abandoned, we return to the presentation of Bloom's inner monologue as in the early episodes, we might speculate that Joyce is implying that Bloom is always the man of gravity and holds more strenuously to "realism" than Stephen as artist is wont to do. Groden speculates that in "Scylla and Charybdis," "inspired perhaps by Stephen's playful mood, perhaps by his own impatience, Joyce experiments with the form of the page to reflect

Stephen's view of the library scene—he introduces musical notation, free verse, and dramatic monologue.... In retrospect, these liberties with the initial-style narrator signal the beginning of the end of the method" (Groden, 32–33). I want to pause over Groden's attribution to Joyce of a certain "impatience" with the initial style, because I think Groden is basically correct in this, and his scrupulous study provides valuable support to my own assumptions. Groden speculates that Joyce began to feel the need to move "beyond Bloom and Stephen to present them from viewpoints other than their own" (34). While it takes until episode 12, "Cyclops," for Bloom to be represented from other perspectives, in these middle episodes we are becoming aware that the perspective offered by what Groden calls the "monologue method" is only one perspective among others. The liberties that Joyce takes with the monologue method in these episodes all function to make the reader acutely conscious of his position as reader, aware of the fact that he is reading a text written by an increasingly playful writer. Somewhat liberated from the grip of the naturalist, the reader is empowered to lift what is prominent in the telling—in "Scylla and Charybdis," Stephen's *Hamlet* theory—out of the context in which it is presented and to apply it in ways beyond the narrator's intention.

I do want to quibble with Groden's expression of "impatience" on Joyce's part, for it is precisely the attitude of impatience that is condemned by Stephen about Blake in "Nestor" and about the romantic temperament in general in *Stephen Hero*. Joyce may have been impatient with the restrictions imposed by the initial style, but he did not "creepycrawl after Blake's buttocks into eternity of which this vegetable world is but a shadow" (9.87–88). Blake's excess is not Joyce's way. He first scrupulously constructs the naturalist's style in the opening six episodes and, while he wants to fly beyond them, must then playfully disrupt the style while beginning that movement into high abstraction. These middle episodes, from "Aeolus" through "Wandering Rocks," are the results of Joyce's classical patience in making a bridge from one world to the other, from naturalism to abstraction.

It is worth repeating that "Scylla and Charybdis" is more like "Aeolus" than it is like "Lestrygonians," in that the liberties with the initial style are often more visual and so more blatant. In both Stephen is doing something artistic: in the first he tells a story; and in the second he delivers an aesthetic theory. Dettmar thinks that *Ulysses* laughs at Stephen (Dettmar, 135–36), but I contend that through his artistic performances he presents the interpretative key to the book in a way of seeing; we are invited by the arranger to take these artistic performances out of the naturalistic context and use them as ways to approach the novel as a whole, beyond any intention the naturalist and Stephen may have in presenting them. The reader is already "beyond the characters' perspectives," as he is able to assess the naturalistic action from a privileged point of view.

In this way I feel authorized to offer my understanding of Stephen's *Hamlet* theory and to show its relevance to the plot that the novel has been establishing mainly through naturalistic narration. But as we will see, Joyce shapes the episode in such a way to encourage just this sort of application, for Bloom will enter the scene almost at the exact center of the episode: he is first mentioned in line 585 and his silhouette seen in line 597 out of a total of 1,225 lines for the episode, allowing us to say that the episode centers on Bloom, is structured around Bloom.

Bloom's passivity, so crucial to "Lestrygonians," is the point of relevance for Stephen's *Hamlet* theory and provides continuity between the two episodes. Stephen's understanding of *Hamlet* emphasizes the theme of vengeance in the play and posits as its inspiration Shakespeare's own deep need for revenge. Bloom's passivity is the opposite of Shakespeare's aggressive need for vengeance. Stephen's argument hinges on the legend that Shakespeare himself played the ghost of Hamlet's father, for he sees in this Shakespeare's calling for a son to take vengeance on his own brothers, Edmund and Richard, who, in Stephen's theory, cuckolded William by sleeping with Anne Hathaway. Shakespeare's son Hamnet died when he was eleven, and so the poet had to create a fictional son in Hamlet to enact the revenge he so desired. Most of Stephen's argument is devoted to making these speculations seem somewhat plausible in light of the few facts and several legends made available by certain late-nineteenth- and early-twentieth-century "biographers" of Shakespeare, George Brandes, Frank Harris, and Sidney Lee. Stephen sees in Hamlet's father and thus in Shakespeare a father who calls on the son to avenge his cuckoldry, a father who demands obedience and calls for aggressive and violent action.

As critics have long recognized, Bloom resembles Stephen's Shakespeare in some interesting ways. First and foremost, Bloom is about to be cuckolded. He too had but now lacks a son to take vengeance on his enemy; while Hamnet Shakespeare died at age eleven years, Rudy Bloom died at age eleven days, and would be eleven years old in 1904 had he lived. The reader might begin to see how Shakespeare's creation of a fictional son might inspire the plot of Joyce's novel, as Bloom attempts to adopt Stephen as a replacement for Rudy; when in "Circe," Bloom and Stephen look in a mirror and see Shakespeare's face, the point is not that together they make a Shakespeare but that Shakespeare is the author of their conjunction.

But the difference between Bloom and Stephen's Shakespeare remains paramount, for Bloom will not take revenge upon either wife or rival. Bloom is to be a passive hero, not an active one; a man who tolerates, not avenges; a man capable of forgiveness and mercy, not mean-spirited spite and bitterness. For while Shakespeare's last gesture toward Anne is to leave her his second-best bed (which Stephen reasonably sees as a slight), Bloom will end this day with his usual good-night kiss and lie peacefully next to his adulterous wife in their bed.

Stephen's theory, centering on vengeance, might blind him to the potential greatness of the passive nature Bloom embodies. Just as Stephen misunderstood Isaiah in "Nestor" and calls God a "shout in the street," so here he might be prone to see as heroic the taking of action, the taking of vengeance. But this episode opens with some pertinent words, as "the quaker librarian" Lyster quotes Goethe on Hamlet, calling him "a hesitating soul taking arms against a sea of troubles" (9.3–4) and "the beautiful ineffectual dreamer who comes to grief against hard facts" (9.9–10). In other words, the episode opens with an emphasis on inaction, on passivity. But Hamlet's passivity is his weakness, while Bloom's will be his greatness. The question that "Scylla and Charybdis" raises is: can Stephen recognize the greatness of Bloom despite his *Hamlet* theory?

It is worth recalling at this point that Stephen is consciously playing at being Hamlet by excessively keeping in mourning for nearly a year after his mother's death, wearing his "Hamlet hat," and melodramatically feeling fatherless despite Simon's very real presence. Despite his theory, might we not be tempted to think that Stephen, who is not a man of action, might be prone to an admiration of the passive nature, of the figure who refuses to take vengeance? Joyce makes a point of Stephen's passivity in the early episodes, as a moment from "Telemachus" makes clear, when Mulligan asks for a loan of Stephen's handkerchief to wipe his razor: "Stephen suffered him to pull out and hold up on show by its corner a dirty crumpled handkerchief" (1.70–71). Stephen makes a somewhat melodramatic display of a passivity of his own that does indeed characterize his relation to Mulligan; after all, he allows him to take the key and decides to let him "Take all. Keep all" (1.279). Might not the *Hamlet* theory be something of a dodge, concealing his own nature? It is, I think, for this reason that he uses the word "lapwing" five times in the course of a single page of "Scylla and Charybdis" to refer to himself: "Lapwing you are. Lapwing be" (9.953). According to Thornton, this bird's "characterizing trait is that it conceals its nest very carefully, and, on anyone's approach, it flutters or makes short, sporadic flights away from its nest, hoping to lead the person away and thereby protecting its brood" (Thornton, 208–9). The *Hamlet* theory he constructs, so filled with aggression and violence, may be Stephen's way of protecting himself, of hiding his passive nature from the view of the others, who might see it as a sign of weakness and mock it. We know that Mulligan barges in on Stephen's theory, and we might be tempted to see the theory—in which Stephen is quick to admit he does not believe—as a way he can shield himself from the cynicism of a mocking world that would trample upon the thing he values.

We see in this episode the motive behind Stephen's contemplation in "Telemachus" of various heresies that have confronted the orthodox Catholic position concerning the nature of the Trinity, most specifically the relation of God the Father to God the Son. It is helpful to his argument for him to find precedent for the expansion of the possibilities and meaning of fatherhood, in that he wants Shakespeare to be "not the father of his own son merely but, being no more a son, he was and felt himself to be the father of all his race, the father of his own grandfather, the father of his unborn grandson" (9.867–69). But we can use his ruminations on fatherhood for a different purpose, one that we as readers see clearly and Stephen does not see at all, at least at this point in the novel: namely, we can use Stephen's theological discourse on divine fatherhood, and the heresies that surrounded this doctrine in the early Church, to advance the case that Bloom can function as Stephen's father. Stephen uses theology to liberate himself from Simon, right after he recalls a phrase Mulligan has just used about Bloom ("he knows your old man," which links the "real" father to the potential one): "Fatherhood, in the sense of conscious begetting, is unknown to man. It is a mystical estate, an apostolic succession, from only begetter to only begotten. On that mystery and not on the madonna which the cunning Italian intellect flung to the mob of Europe the Church is founded and founded irremovably because founded, like the world, macro and microcosm, upon the void. Upon uncertitude, upon unlikelihood. *Amor matris*, subjective and objective genitive, may be the only true thing in life. Paternity may be a legal fiction. Who is the father of any son that any son should love him or he any son?" (9.837–845). These lines are among the most important in all of *Ulysses*. One of the most ingenious aspects of *Ulysses* is how Joyce manages to bring into his novel one of the genre's most important themes, the foundling's discovery of his true heritage and the construction of the family as a legally binding social unit. The rise of the novel in the eighteenth and nineteenth centuries has much to do with the need for a discourse that can secure the place of the family as the paramount legal unit for modern society, and so many novels, both those of great fame and canonical importance and also those not yet and perhaps never to be brought into the canon, have had as their theme the orphan seeking and finding family.[6] Stephen, haunted by mother and displaced with father, is hardly an orphan; but this meditation—in fact, the burden of the entire ninth episode—is to free him from the biological family he now belongs to and so to place him in an orphaned state. His refusal to kneel at his mother's deathbed looms larger now than before: it was a rejection of the one true thing in life, his biological link to his past and to a family he no longer wishes to be a part of. By making fatherhood no more (and, it must be added at once, no less) than a legal fiction, he is opening up the possibility that writing can legitimize a new father and allow him a new identity.

Joyce manages to make *Ulysses* part of the novel tradition that seeks to provide the normalizing and legitimizing discourse for the construction of the family, but he does so in a way that makes the foundation of the family spiritual and not merely human, founded (as Stephen explains) on the mystery of the father and not the biology of the mother. If the mother represents the body and so history, the father is an absence and therefore represents the spirit. The family in *Ulysses* is moving away from its physical foundation—its purely *human* aspect—toward a spiritual foundation, a founding of a unit on the void. Again we see how these middle episodes move us away from a traditional novelistic humanism and toward a spiritual dimension. But Stephen, haunted by mother and so by history, is still too quick to assert a theory that denigrates the mother's place as subordinate to father and as adulterer. Bloom will bring Stephen back to a home where the mistress is master, where the adulterous woman gets the last word. This father will bring the son back to a mother, as truth and history, spirit and flesh, are reconciled.

But Stephen's theory that dominates this episode does focus on the father as the foundation of a Church, and we must use it to understand how Stephen will become Bloom's son. The reader is willing to take this theory out of its context as merely part of Stephen's scaffolding for a *Hamlet* theory he does not even believe in and apply it to the eventual union of Bloom and Stephen as father and son. When they do come together at the end of "Circe" and through "Ithaca," we will be prepared by this speech of Stephen's to call their relation that of mystical father and son, based on the relation of God the Father to God the Son on which the Church is founded. Bloom and Stephen will be forming a "mystical estate," an "apostolic succession," a new Church, in fact, when they come together in Bloom's kitchen at 7 Eccles street. It is more than a coincidence that the name for Bloom's street address, Eccles, which is the name of a real Dublin street whose number seven house was to let on 16 June 1904, contains the root for the Greek word for church, *ecclesia*. This father and son are coming together to provide the morality for a new Church. When we look at "Ithaca," we will be returning to "Scylla and Charybdis" to provide us with the language and theory with which to understood its climax.

Fatherhood is, for Stephen's theory and for the novel as a whole, a legal fiction on which relations are founded, a void on which a Church is founded. And into this scene, almost exactly in its center, walks Bloom, or at least his shadow, for that is all we see of him: "A patient silhouette waited, listening" (9.597). Bloom is a shadow in this episode and as such can be linked to Hamlet's father, a ghost intruding upon the affairs of the living. Bloom will take the place of Hamlet *pere,* a passive father replacing an aggressive one, a forgiving and loving father replacing one who calls for violence and hatred. But more important, we see Bloom's ghostly appearance in the center of the episode as extraordinarily perceptive on Joyce's part about the nature of the kind of construct he is building, a fiction of a new Church founded on a ghostly void, an absence. For is not this just what Derrida so persistently tries to teach us, that at the center of all our structures is an absence that can only be inferred and that can never be present? Especially in "Structure, Sign, and Play in the Discourse of the Human Sciences," Derrida works to make us appreciate this marvel of all our human constructs, how they are poised upon the supposition of a center that is never given, that is never itself, that is never present. For Derrida, this absence at the center is what permits the play of signification; for Joyce, Bloom's ghostly presence at the center at once permits play of meaning but also limits it to a series of relations forming a construct called Church, one different from other human constructs in that it is consciously founded on a fatherhood that is both void and person.[7]

Mulligan's words that introduce Bloom to Stephen are both comic and prophetic, befitting his role as a mocking Malachi: "He knows you. He knows your old fellow. O, I fear me, he is Greeker than the Greeks. His pale Galilean eyes were upon her mesial groove. Venus Kallipge. O, the thunder of those loins. *The god pursuing the maiden hid*" (9.614–17). So Bloom did make that experiment to ascertain if the Greek goddesses had the physical mechanism for excretion; and in such a posture the clown Mulligan meets the hero-to-be! Joyce certainly makes Bloom's elevation to heroic status difficult. But in Mulligan's comic words are some truths for us, the empowered readers, for Bloom *is* "Greeker than the Greeks" in his embodiment of the heroic traits of a modern Odysseus, though that is not what Mulligan is suggesting. And while Bloom does not have "pale Galilean eyes," the phrase from A. C. Swinburne's "Hymn to Proserpine" makes an ironic identification of Bloom with Christ that we will be trying to make stick by the end of the study. It is even more ironic when we recall that Swinburne is lamenting Christ's interference in what he deems a healthier and more glorious Greek and pagan culture. Mulligan uses Swinburne to deplore the effect of the Jew Bloom upon his own Hellenistic ideal, whereas we are ready to see Bloom as the Jew who brings to Greek culture the revelation of the Hebrew God.[8] Mulligan is a comic prophet, but he is like his namesake in a subtle and, we might say, allegorical way. Malachi, the last prophet in the Catholic Bible, might not have recognized Christ if he had seen him and may have missed John the Baptist as the Elijah who comes before the great and terrible day to restore all things for the coming of the Lord, though he prophesied about both. We must read carefully for prophetic utterances in the Christian Bible and in Joyce's comic novel written in the same allegorical manner.

The ending of the episode brings Stephen and Bloom into close physical proximity to one another in such a way as to suggest the possibilities for their later relationship. As Stephen is about to leave the library with Mulligan, he senses someone behind him, so he moves to one side to allow that figure to pass. As he does so, he thinks, "Part. The moment is now" (9.1199). Stephen will use Bloom's passing between him and Mulligan as a way to part from Mulligan; in this way we are allowed to say that Bloom is the one who will allow Stephen to break from the hold Mulligan has on him and leave behind the mockery of his culture. As Bloom passes between the two, Stephen remembers the dream he had the night before: "Here I watched the birds for augury. Aengus of the birds. They go, they come. Last night I flew. Easily flew. Men wondered. Street of harlots after. A creamfruit melon he held to me. In. You will see" (9.1206–8). He recalled this same dream earlier in the day, in "Proteus": "Open hallway. Street of harlots. Remember. Haroun al Raschid. I am almosting it. That man led me, spoke. I was not afraid. The melon he had he held against my face. Smiled: creamfruit smell. That was the rule, said. In. Come. Red carpet spread. You will see who" (3.365–69). Bloom reminds him of "that man" in the dream, which is prophetic in many ways. They will spend some time in the street of harlots. Bloom will invite Stephen into his house, making such a fuss over him that the cliché about "spreading the red carpet" will be apt. The person whom Stephen will see inside is Molly, whose "melons" Bloom holds against Stephen's face in the dream and whose picture Bloom will use in "Eumaeus" to lure Stephen to 7 Eccles street. The most important part of the dream for this point in the text, however, is the detail he did not recall in "Proteus" but does remember this time, that in the presence of this man he flew, "easily flew." It is this father who will enable Stephen to fly successfully, so easily that men will wonder at it. Stephen recalls the time from *A Portrait* when he looked from these very steps at the birds in flight for an augury, and he thought he found one that boded well for his trip to Paris. But that trip ended in failure, and he wound up back in Dublin and back under the influence of the gay betrayer. Only unconsciously does he associate Bloom with the man in the dream who enabled him to escape in wonderful flight from the labyrinth that is Dublin, and we are now to watch to see if Stephen can recognize in Bloom the father he prayed to at the end of *A Portrait* to "stand [him] now and ever in good stead," the father who will liberate and empower him.

So there is the promise that Stephen will be able to escape the limitations that have prevented his flight, and that the reader will escape the limitations of a style perfectly suited to Mulligan's mockery but not suited for the kind of movement upward Joyce is intending and patiently establishing as his goal. It is well known that Joyce wrote at the end of the fair copy of "Scylla and Charybdis" the words "End of First part of 'Ulysses'" and the date "New Year's Eve 1918" (see Groden, 17). Therefore, the episode that follows, "Wandering Rocks," can be regarded as pivotal, beginning the second half of the novel. I choose to include it as part of what I am calling the second phase, or the middle episodes, of *Ulysses* because it is written in the same naturalistic style as the first six episodes, although with a significant twist. In fact, what this episode does to that initial style is to render it incapable of serving any further purpose. "Wandering Rocks" is Joyce's rendering of the absolute limit of naturalism.

In this episode Bloom and Stephen are depicted as they were in their opening episodes, except now they must share our attention with other characters depicted in the same scrupulous manner. We witness the activities and thoughts of other Dubliners as if these were as important for our consideration as Bloom's and Stephen's. This is the verge of naturalism's devotion to realistic depiction, to realistic context, for what could be more realistic than to force us to acknowledge that Bloom and Stephen are just two more Dubliners barely getting through their daily business? This is the only episode to lavish the interior monologue method on characters other than Bloom, Stephen, and Molly. We are in Father Conmee's mind as he walks and rides through Dublin, and in Tom Kernan's, and in young Master Dignam's. Here is the risk of naturalism as Joyce would have it—that if pushed too far, it diminishes the stature of any character one may have been hoping to focus on for special attention and reduces that figure to the status of the ordinary, to a very realistic obscurity.

It is relevant that the wandering rocks are a danger that Odysseus does not have to confront; in book 12 of *The Odyssey* he chooses rather to navigate the perilous passage between Scylla and Charybdis than risk the wandering rocks. "Wandering Rocks" is important to our understanding of Joyce's sense of literary history and the place of the novel in relation to the epic, for this tenth episode suggests that a character aspiring to epic status in the twentieth century must face an artistic danger that the ancient hero could ignore: namely, the modern hero must run the risk of being shattered against the rock of naturalism's understanding of realism, of being threatened by the novel's devotion to the ordinary and the plausible. The modern epic must be, in part at least, a novel, not just because the genre exists for Joyce as it did not for Homer (though that is not a reason to sneer at); the modern hero must face all the threats of critical irony and still emerge as someone worthy of epic status. Buck Mulligan opens *Ulysses*, and his spirit haunts—one might go so far as to say dominates—the first nine episodes; "Wandering Rocks" is the spirit of mockery's last chance to deflate Stephen and Bloom.

Bloom in this episode looks like a pathetic figure buying a dirty book for his overlusty wife who is about to cuckold him. While that is an accurate (and therefore "realistic") assessment of his appearance, it is so narrow and restricted that it is misleading. And Stephen in his first appearance in the episode looks like a young man forsaking a promising musical career for an uncertain literary career; in his second appearance he looks like a pathetic figure unable (or, considering the amount of money in his pocket that he is perfectly able to squander on drink for himself and his companions, unwilling) to help his poverty-stricken family. These are not images of heroic men overcoming the constraints and limits of naturalism; rather, they seem small and even petty and nearly lost to our gaze as we are forced—against our will, it seems to me—to follow many other characters, some of whom we have seen in passing in earlier episodes and some who are new to us entirely. We spend more time with father Conmee than we do with either Stephen or Bloom, and Tom Kernan's mind is more actively engaged with the world around him than Bloom's is in this episode. Tom Kernan's presence is particularly disturbing: as a commercial traveler who wanders through Dublin, he could replace Bloom as the main character in a naturalistic version of *Ulysses*. Clive Hart's excellent analysis of "Wandering Rocks" emphasizes how its narrator is always accurate but often misleading, and that is exactly the point. Naturalism is to be rejected, not because it lies but because in its devotion to "reality" it misses the possible significance of what it is narrating.

"Wandering Rocks" challenges any epic pretensions Joyce and his reader may be harboring by raising to acute awareness the consequences of any narrative's mere choice of subject: by choosing to focus on this man and not that one, a narrative already implies that there may be something special about the person about to be described. Though the novel as a genre tends to focus on ordinary people and not on the extraordinary as the epic does, it nonetheless also contains the tendency to elevate its characters to some special status, implied merely by their having been chosen as objects of the novel's discourse. Joyce wrote "Wandering Rocks," it seems to me, to bring this implicit tendency to the surface, to give the naturalist his last best shot at deflating Bloom and Stephen. It is the epitome of plausibility to witness that, despite their having been chosen by this author as the focal points of his interest for nine episodes, Bloom and Stephen may be no more important, no more interesting, no more complex, no more worthy of the attention than any of the other characters populating the novel, or than any of the other Dubliners walking around Dublin on 16 June 1904. The modern allegory must be both novel and epic, the novel pushed to its extreme and then supplemented by the epic. Homer's hero did not have to face the wandering rock of extreme realism, but Joyce's hero must. Bloom and Stephen must go through this humiliating deflation of this most extreme version of naturalism and then reassume their central place in our attention. Can they be special to us again after this?

There is a wandering rock in this episode that complicates matters somewhat. Back in "Lestrygonians," Bloom was handed a "throwaway" that he at first misreads: "Bloo . . . Me? No. Blood of the lamb" (8.8–9). This piece of paper announces the imminent arrival of one Dr John Alexander Dowie, an American preacher who is in town this day, whom we will hear at the end of "Oxen of the Sun" and who apparently identifies himself as Elijah in restoring the Church in Zion, for Bloom reads on the throwaway that "Elijah is coming." This coming of Elijah to restore all things before the great and terrible day of the Lord—we should recall—is what is prophesied by Malachi at the end of that book of prophecy, which is the very end of the Old Testament. After the initial error of seeing his name on the sheet of paper (and thus identifying himself with Elijah, a mistake and an accident quickly rectified in the naturalist's depiction of the event), Bloom throws away the throwaway. This is a complex moment that gathers up several themes that will continue to be developed throughout *Ulysses*. First we have the presence of Malachi's prophecy, which brings the comic prophet Mulligan back into the scene. We have a man—Dr Dowie—arrogant enough to apply that prophecy to himself, and a man—Mr Bloom—who, after mistakenly applying it to himself, rejects the identification, crumples the paper, and throws it to the seagulls (to see if they can be fooled into thinking it is bread; they cannot be fooled, but that this piece of paper may resemble bread is suggestive). Bloom is right to reject the identification of himself with Elijah, especially in an episode still under the watchful eye of the naturalist, but we will have this identification thrust back upon us at the end of "Cyclops." This crumpled piece of paper is noticed three times in "Wandering Rocks" as it makes a procession of its own through Dublin. I want to quote each appearance:

> A skiff, a crumpled throwaway, Elijah is coming, rode lightly down the Liffey, under Loopline bridge, shooting the rapids where water chafed around the bridgepiers, sailing eastward past hulls and

anchorchains, between the Customhouse old dock and George's quay. (10.294–97)

North wall and sir John Rogerson's quay, with hulls and anchorchains, sailing westward, sailed by a skiff, a crumpled throwaway, rocked on the ferrywash, Elijah is coming. (10.752–54)

Elijah, skiff, light crumpled throwaway, sailed eastward by flanks of ships and trawlers, amid an archipelago of corks, beyond new Wapping street past Benson's ferry, and by the threemasted schooner *Rosevean* from Bridgewater with bricks. (10.1096–99)

The crumpled sheet of paper is consistently called a "throwaway," and the words "Elijah is coming," or at least the name "Elijah," is always mentioned to describe it; these facts make sure that the reader connects this piece of paper to Bloom's inadvertent tip, and the connection is made explicit in the crucial passage from "Ithaca" that, as I argued in the introduction, contains Joyce's most overt clue about how to read his work. In "Ithaca" the "throwaway (subsequently thrown away), advertising Elijah, restorer of the church in Zion" is connected to the "current issue of the *Freeman's Journal and National Press* which he had been about to throwaway (subsequently thrown away)" (17.332–33, 336–37). This pair of throwaways is, to the "Ithaca" narrator, a sign of Bloom's prophetic capacity and thus an indication that there may be, after all and when the novel is almost finished, some truth to the identification of Bloom and Elijah. Back in episode 10 this crumpled throwaway is the wandering rock in question, crumpled because its meaning has been rejected not only by Bloom but by the naturalist who gets his last chance in this episode. The possibility for higher meaning, for epic status, for allegory, was rejected in "Lestrygonians" but reappears in "Wandering Rocks" as a sign that the identification is still possible and as something beyond the naturalist's control. He cannot get rid of it, and it keeps coming back into our view to remind us of other possibilities for the novel, of the larger meanings and higher destinies that have so far not been allowed to be developed. The rejected piece of paper becomes the wandering rock on which higher significance will be built: "the stone that the builders rejected has become the cornerstone"—as in Psalm 118 and the Gospels.

The crumpled throwaway's final appearance in the episode brings it on its way to the "threemasted" schooner *Rosevean*, that miraculous ship he saw over his shoulder at the end of "Proteus." The suggestion is that naturalism of the early episodes and now of "Wandering Rocks" may come to ruin on this wandering rock that bears the possibility that Bloom may indeed be associated with Elijah. Even in this most narrowly focused and rigidly naturalistic episode in the entire novel, there is the indication that naturalism is finished and something more elaborate is about to enter the scene.

These middle episodes begin the movement away from naturalism and toward an abstraction that will seek to isolate something permanent and fixed within the flux of time. The reader has been empowered to read certain aspects of the novel's developments for a pattern that the naturalist narrator would not recognize. In each episode the reader begins to free the plot from the naturalist's hold and place the characters in a pattern beyond the limits of space and time, beyond history and beyond humanism. Each episode in this set brings in a way of reassessing the story from a point of view beyond the material and the merely human. The end of naturalism is the end of the merely humanist ethic, and Joyce will be bringing the book increasingly toward a spiritual reading that never denies history and the body and the human but fulfills them.

Chapter Three

The Novel as Truth
The Problem of Language in *Ulysses*

With "Sirens," Joyce places in the foreground what has been an implicit or underlying problem confronting not only his characters and his narrators but also his own efforts to elevate Bloom to epic status, namely the problem of language. It is nothing new to notice that, for the modernist artist, the material of one's art becomes the subject of a series of experiments, that the material of one's art becomes a problem to be confronted directly and boldly. For the literary artist in this context of modernist experimentation, language becomes not only the medium for the representation of one's artistic intention but also an obstacle to those intentions. Joyce has an acute sense of language—especially of written language—as being used up, as if all of its possibilities have been tried out and there is very little left to do that is original and "modern." In this way Joyce manifests what Meisel calls a sense of belatedness that is the precondition for modernist experiment, of having come late in a tradition of artistic projects. In this Joyce proves himself to be the true heir of Flaubert, as Kenner points out in *The Stoic Comedians*, so keenly conscious of how easily language becomes outdated and phrases become commonplace, how the artist must often resort to wild experimentation or, a last resort, to parody in the effort to express one's own vision in a sincere, fresh, and truthful manner.

The problem of the next episodes, from "Sirens" through "Oxen of the Sun," is whether or not a language can be found capable of presenting Joyce's elevation of Bloom as epic hero and of Stephen as the artist capable of the recognition. In "Aeolus" we caught a glimpse of this theme, as "high falutin" rhetoric is appreciated and, in Bloom and Stephen at least, a danger to be avoided. Stephen's "Parable of the Plums" is, in fact, best approached as a naturalistic puncturing of excessive language that nonetheless implies that vision is still possible, that even in "dear dirty Dublin" one can still catch "A Pisgah Sight of Palestine." In this next stage, in which Joyce makes his most sustained and explicit experiments in what we can call sheer style, he makes language a focus of his attention, making the reader wonder if there is ever to be a halt to the technical pyrotechnics, if there is ever to be found the kind of language that is to be trusted for his purposes. As Dante worries about language in his epic, whether he can find a language capable of bringing his readers to a heaven of absolute justice and truth, so Joyce is careful to show us how language by nature tends toward fraud and how hard it is to find that language of truth. Dante worries about the Ulysses he constructs in canto 26 of *Inferno,* who uses lofty rhetoric to inspire his men to follow him on a journey that ends in destruction. If language can be misleading, or excessive, or outdated, is there one that is capable of presenting the truth? The question for Joyce is: how can the novel present the truth; how can fiction be truthful? The solution is once again to be found only later in "Ithaca," where the most unliterary episode of the novel, perhaps the most unliterary episode in all literature, can present the novel's climax. There is something wrong with literature, with literary language, because there is something wrong with language itself.

In this regard, then, Joyce anticipates the critical preoccupation with language that marks the advances in our thinking made by what we often call poststructuralist theory, which in some of its formulations leads us to doubt the capacity for language to present truth or truths but rather encourages us to notice how all truths are constructed by humans within language and so are no truths at all in an absolute or permanent sense. Joyce is as skeptical about language and its capacity to present truth as any of the skeptical critics Siebers describes, and he is as suspicious of ideals couched in literary language as any of the practitioners of the hermeneutics of suspicion described by Altieri.[1] What marks Joyce's novel as extraordinary is that he presents in the text and within literary language his concerns about language as the very problem to be addressed, as the only medium we have for communicating our ideals yet seriously suspect in its ability to do so. He will try out various kinds of literary language, indicating how none is to be trusted; yet in the series of experiments, each of which is designed to indicate the limits and inherent failings of language as presenter of truth, he nonetheless is able to advance his story and create in the reader a person able to look outside language for the truth.

Joyce's search for a language for truth ultimately goes against the "postmodern" critique that is so tempting to apply to *Ulysses,* though up to a point such a critique does much to explain Joyce's intention. As Lyotard argues, the postmodern culture has given up a search for truth and substituted for it a search for "the set of rules one must accept in order to play the speculative game" (Lyotard, 39). The novelists in particular have so questioned the rules of their art that "those rules must appear to them as a means to deceive, to seduce, and to reassure, which makes it impossible for them to be 'true'" (74–75). And there is no doubt that Joyce has questioned the rules of his genre so extensively that he is worried about the novel's inability to be anything other than deceptive and fraudulent. Kevin Dettmar cites Barthes in a critique of literary art that has become so self-conscious that it can only show the artificiality of all discourse and cannot work in support of a pursuit of truth (Dettmar, 39). From this perspective, the postmodern artist can only deconstruct forms and accelerate our recognition of their obsolescence (Dettmar, 38). Joyce indeed shares this dissatisfaction with inherited forms and shows his reader how inadequate they are to the service of truth, but that does not mean that he has given up on the pursuit of truth in *Ulysses*. In these "language" episodes Joyce develops a critique of literary language and of the novel in particular that clears the ground of previous efforts to represent truth and prepares for his innovation in the later episodes.

At this point I want to recall the insight of Paul de Man in his landmark essay "Criticism and Crisis," in which he demonstrates that one of the great advances in criticism has been to resist the mystifications literary artists are able to perpetuate in their skillful manipulation of language; yet he warns the same critics to beware lest they, in their eagerness to demystify literary texts, fall prey to another and perhaps greater form of mystification, a belief in their autonomy and superiority to the texts they are reading against and showing up. Joyce is creating a reader who is learning to be wary of literary language, who is learning to demystify the kind of romantic language used for the representation of ideals; but he is also careful to create a reader who is not becoming arrogant in this power to read against literature but is still looking for truth, for the ideal, for the noble and high despite the fact that literary language is failing in this quest of presentation. It will be no surprise after these episodes that the truth can only be conveyed by the most unliterary language possible, the catechistic style of "Ithaca."

"Sirens"

With "Sirens" the reader is jolted into a section of *Ulysses* that challenges the ordinary expectations one brings to reading a novel, especially the minimal expectation that one should be able to follow the action of the plot as it affects the characters one has become interested in. "Sirens" still has plenty of plot and character, but one cannot pretend that the manner of presentation of this eleventh episode is not startling and loudly calling for our attention, over and above the kind of attention the novel has been demanding of us. It is almost as if we are being asked to split the novel in two, as if style and content are separate aspects of the art before us. This is suggested by the first sixty-three lines, the "overture" that Joyce begins with; when first read, these lines defy not only understanding—they never become a "meaningful" sequence of words and phrases—but even recognition as a unit of any sort whatsoever. When we learn that the episode is musical and that these opening lines constitute an overture of sorts, at least we gain some measure of comfort when approaching it, and some readers, myself included, have claimed to derive pleasure from the arrangement. But the function of these lines still remains to be explained, and it is my contention that they signal a problem to come that will, from this point on in the novel, be a constant temptation—namely, the temptation to separate the style as pure extravagance and focus on the simpler and still present plot.

One can put this readerly problem this way: one struggles to read through the style to follow Bloom's thoughts and actions at this pivotal hour of the day, and such a "reading through" is still possible and in this episode quite manageable. But we must question if we are intended to "read through" or simply just read. We must determine an important point for this novel and for modernist literature in general: whether the language of this and the following episodes is something that we must struggle to get through in order to arrive on the other side of style and reach what really matters, that is, Bloom's thoughts and actions as four o'clock approaches; or if the language is there to be relished for its own sake and enjoyed, not to be cleared up and made more "readerly."

If I were forced to choose one of these admittedly extreme alternatives, I must choose, as does Stanley Sultan in his *Eliot, Joyce, and Company*, not to lose plot and character. Sultan's presentation of this particular critical crux seems worth reviewing at this point in my argument, for I think no one has processed the problem more gracefully nor taken a position as clear and unequivocal in pursuing its solution. Sultan understands that perhaps the thorniest problem facing Joyce scholarship in the past two decades has been to tackle this issue, whether we are to emphasize story or telling, plot and character on the one hand or style and technical innovations on the other. Sultan recognizes that one possible solution is to try to reconcile these apparent contraries, but he is not at all sanguine that this is possible: even when the critics think and claim to be doing so, they always come down on one side or the other of this issue. The critics Sultan sees on the side of telling are Brook Thomas and Karen Lawrence, and on the side of style he places Hugh Kenner and James Maddox; these are the critics whose work provides the context in which I too wish to place my argument. For Sultan, the notion of story—he calls it "storyness"—is always what Joyce is most interested in, even when his innovations in what we call style and technique are most extreme and provocative; and I agree. The stylistic changes that dominate from "Sirens" onward serve to advance Joyce's intentions about the characters he has been constructing thoroughly for many episodes. I think we must ask for each episode a version of this question: What does this particular stylistic innovation or technical experiment accomplish in bringing Bloom closer to the status of becoming the epic hero the title of the novel suggests he is or is to become?

When we turn from the most narrowly naturalistic episode in all *Ulysses* to the opening of "Sirens," which upon first reading defies any effort at assigning meaning or even function to the words presented, we are jolted from a style obsessed by character and plot to one that, for sixty-three lines at least, seems to have no interest in those parts of telling. I think that is the function of the overture, to force the reader to consider the possibility that style might indeed be suddenly more important than plot, that telling may suddenly replace story as the focus of our readerly attention. When we return to language that does produce meaning in line 64, perhaps the reaction is relief and a renewed comfort in being able to return to character and plot. Even though this style will challenge, it is no longer an opaque screen defying penetration to the plot it contains but rather is translucent enough that, if we work hard and well, we can feel perfectly confident that we know how Bloom feels and what he is doing. The overture ironically has the effect of restoring our desire to penetrate the style, to read through the language to something on the other side that is true. By today's critical standards, such belief in style "containing" plot or in the status of language as a series of signs that point to objects in the world seems naive and old-fashioned; but it is just this model of reading that Joyce is constructing as necessary for his novel. He makes us aware of words as objects in themselves and then brings us back to words as vehicle for representation.

I think that it is important to note that the major stylistic innovations begin just as the novel is approaching one of its plot climaxes, at least as Bloom would see it. It is no coincidence that the technical pyrotechnics begin as Bloom watches the clock move slowly and inexorably toward the hour of Molly's assignation with Blazes Boylan. Making the plot even more tense is the presence of Boylan just out of Bloom's visual path, though certainly within hearing distance. Readers brought up on "readerly novels"[2] are eager to follow Bloom's thoughts and to see what he is thinking and what course of action he will be taking, but they find themselves suddenly within a novel that looks increasingly like a "writerly novel" in which style is more important than character and experiment more important than plot. So our first question for "Sirens" is: why now? Why does Joyce choose just this moment to begin the radical play of styles?

For me the answer lies in Joyce's intention to elevate Bloom to heroic status by the end of the novel. What Bloom is doing at four o'clock at the Ormond Hotel bar—actually, what he is not doing, because he is doing nothing to stop Boylan—does not seem heroic, and Joyce must begin to use extravagant style to render Bloom's inaction in some way noble, his passivity in some way heroic. This elevation of a character flaw into a heroic virtue justifies and explains the stylistic innovations. The style of these later episodes can be said to place the action—or more precisely, Bloom's nonaction—in a context quite different than the one a naturalistic account would offer, a context that can lead us to an appreciation of Bloom's strengths.

The language that is the subject of "Sirens" can be said to be the language of music in general, or more precisely, the language of sentimental song. The songs sung at the Ormond are all about love and loss, and as such they are perfectly suited to encourage Bloom's participation in their sentiment, as he is about to lose his wife's love to "jingle jaunty" Boylan. Having followed Boylan into the Ormond (to take action?), he hides himself from his rival's sight, hears him go off without doing anything to stop him, and stays behind to listen to the love songs, which have the capacity to proffer some rest and comfort from the agitation of his painful thoughts. As he listens to Simon Dedalus sing, he feels "that flow endearing flow over skin limbs human heart soul spine" (11.668–69). Both he and Richie Goulding, we are told, felt that it was "good, good to hear: sorrow from them each seemed to from both depart when first they heard" (11.677–78). Joyce emphasizes the power of music to make "flow": "Flood of warm jamjam lickitup secretness flowed to flow in music out, in desire, dark to lick flow invading. . . . To pour o'er sluices pouring gushes. Flood, gush, flow, joygush, tupthrob. Now! Language of love" (11.705–9). Joyce's language here is an attempt to present the effects of love songs on their hearers, as syntactical clarity and rigor become loose and confused, as nouns flow into one another without logical connection or meaning, as the emotional state of the auditor is described in terms suggesting deliquescence. Music is called here "the language of love" because it blurs distinct emotions into a warm, sweet, gushy confusion, imitating the effects of sentimental love. The pain of loss, which is what the songs being sung in this episode sweetly celebrate, is blurred as various emotions flow into one another and form the "jamjam lickitup secretness" that feels no sorrow because it feels nothing distinctly.

Instead of taking action against Boylan, Bloom remains sitting quietly doing nothing. And when the music stops for a moment, he wishes for more song to distract him from the pain of remembering what is going on, which is regularly brought into the reader's consciousness (because it is regularly recurring in Bloom's) by the contrapuntal repetition of Boylan's "jingle jaunty" procession to 7 Eccles street: "Car near there now. Talk. Talk. Pat! Doesn't. Settling those napkins. Lots of ground he must cover in the day. Paint face behind on him and then he'd be two. Wish they'd sing more. Keep my mind off" (11.912–14). More song is desired because of its capacity to blur emotions until one can forget, but memory is going to be important once again—to this episode and to the novel as a whole. It is important to note that, while he wishes to indulge in the lulling comforts music provides, he is eventually aware of its effects on the rational powers and the will: "What do they think when they hear music? Way to catch rattlesnakes" (11.1049); "Hypnotised, listening" (1059); and his most pointed reflection on music's power, "Cowley, he stuns himself with it: kind of drunkenness. Better to give way only half way the way of a man with a maid. Instance enthusiasts. All ears. Not lose a demisemiquiver. Eyes shut. Head nodding in time. Dotty. You daren't budge. Thinking strictly prohibited" (1191–94).

In a novel that has already, in "Aeolus," shown us the importance of vision over sound, we are prepared to be suspicious of music's effects when those in the piano bar close their eyes and become "all ears," when they lose themselves in the enthusiasm of the moment and become incapacitated from thought itself. The language of music makes them paralyzed, just as Odysseus is lashed to the mast and unable to move in the Homeric original. And this is exactly what Bloom wants to avoid. As in "Lotus Eaters," he does not want to be lulled into the false ease brought on by the language of sentimental love songs. Bloom's challenge in this episode is to resist the soothing power of this language and to think through the charm of music back to his own painful situation. He must will to remember. His challenge, then, is just like that facing the reader: not to become lost in the pleasure of the writerly text but to read through and beyond its charm back to the plot we had been reading fairly clearly and relatively easily through the first ten episodes.

It is instructive to watch how Bloom responds to a song that Richie Goulding calls the "most beautiful tenor air ever written," an aria from the opera *Sonnabula—The Sleepwalker*—an appropriate opera for this episode:

—Which air is that? asked Leopold Bloom.
—*All is lost now.*

Richie cocked his lips apout. A low incipient note sweet banshee murmured: all. A thrush. A throstle. His breath, birdsweet, good teeth he's proud of, fluted with plaintive woe. Is lost. Rich sound. Two notes in one there. Blackbird I heard in the hawthorn valley. Taking my motives he twined and turned them. All most too new call is lost in all. Echo. How sweet the answer. How is that done? All lost now. Mournful he whistled. Fall, surrender, lost.

Bloom bent leopold ear, turning a fringe of doyley down under the vase. Order. Yes, I remember. Lovely air. In sleep she went to him. Innocence in the moon. Brave. Don't know their danger. Still hold her back. Call name. Touch water. Jingle jaunty. Too late. She longed to go. That's why. Woman. As easy stop the sea. Yes: all is lost.

—A beautiful air, said Bloom lost Leopold. I know it well. (11.629–42)

Bloom almost gives into the seductive beauty of the song as he feels his motives "twined and turned." At this hour, as four o'clock is approaching, it is reasonable to suspect that Bloom is motivated by jealousy and the desire for revenge, and the song is able to transform them into something else, some jumble of confused emotions. The next sentence suggests that he is indeed losing the clarity of his thought: "All most too new call is lost in all." He marvels then that the answer to this mournful call is sweet: "How is that done?" Good question: how does music make the sorrowful seem sweet, the painful beautiful? Bloom is about to lose himself in the song: "Fall, surrender, lost." In the second long paragraph quoted, however, he recalls the details of the opera in an effort to reassert the claims of logic and rationality. He pulls himself out of the sweet morass of forgetfulness by saying to himself, "Order. Yes, I remember." He appreciates the order of logic and thought, and this allows for him to remember, in this case merely the plot of the opera in which the aria is sung, but suggestively we see how memory leads to order, how by remembering we can impose some design. Memory is what enables us to reconstruct plot, to achieve "retrospective arrangement." By the power of memory he struggles to return to plot, rather than be seduced by the charms of the sounds, just as the reader of "Sirens" must do with the episode itself. Instead of forgetting his own situation, he weaves it into the plot of the opera: "Jingle jaunty" is the sound of Boylan's procession, and "Yes: all is lost" seems his reluctant but certain verdict that all is about to be lost between him and Molly. He does indeed know the song well, because he is living a similar kind of loss and suffering the same kind of pain. He refuses the solace of music and struggles to regain the powers of orderly thought and thus the power of memory as he recalls his own suffering.

Clearly the style of the episode is meant to render Bloom's behavior larger and more potentially heroic than he would appear if we were still within a naturalistic, interior monologue style. Bloom is not just sitting quietly doing nothing, but actively freeing himself from this language of music and willing to feel the suffering that is his lot. In this insistence on feeling pain Bloom can be seen as a purgatorial figure who intuitively embraces his pain in the hope of overcoming it. As T. S. Eliot observes about Dante's *Purgatorio,* "the torment of flame is deliberately accepted by the penitent. . . . The souls in purgatory suffer because they *wish* to suffer, for purgation" (Eliot, *Selected Essays,* 217). Indeed, one can establish a parallel between "Sirens" and canto 2 of *Purgatorio,* where the newly arrived souls on the island of Purgatory, including Dante and Virgil, wish to be allowed to rest as they listen to one of Dante's love songs sung by the musician Casella. But they are not permitted this indulgence. Instead, Cato, the guardian of the shores of Mount Purgatory, rebukes them, "What is this, laggard spirits? What negligence, what delay is this? Haste to the mountain to strip you of the slough that allows not God to be manifest to you" (lines 121-23). For Dante as well as Joyce, the language of love song renders one weak, slothful, easy; one must assert one's will, against the charms of music, to recall and then relive one's pain if one is to reach the noble goal in store at the end of the process. The other Dubliners indulge in song and so find yet another way to be paralyzed, but Bloom is able to rescue himself from this dangerous sloth and rouse himself to suffer.

What might be regarded from one perspective as a tendency toward masochism is understood from another as an intuitively willed decision to undergo the pain of a purgative process. It is another sign of Joyce's ingenuity that he is able to provide enough grist for either mill—that we can, with much good reason, choose to see Bloom as a man with a psychic disorder or as a man willing to use his suffering as a cleansing experience, as a process preparing him for some higher status. Joyce makes Bloom walk the fine line between a serious personality disorder and the rigorous discipline of a purgative process. Christine Froula tries to explain Bloom's passivity in regard to Molly's infidelity as a symptom of a perversion best explained through psychoanalytic theory (see especially 185ff.), and such an account makes good sense. Bloom is always open to the treacherous irony Joyce establishes through Buck Mulligan as one of the poles of his novel that, in this case, threatens to turn purgation into perversion, heroic effort into farce. One of the central motives behind the comic nightmare of "Circe" is to purge the text of such ironic possibilities.

What "Sirens" accomplishes is to open up the possibility that a certain form of passivity may indeed be heroic, that inaction may indeed be the result of some vigorous inner struggles. With the music of the episode as our temptation, the reader shares in Bloom's dilemma, and some of us may choose to lose the vigor of storyness in favor of a delight in Joyce's technical ingenuity. I would like to think that I enjoy the style of this episode as much as one can, yet I am not going to give up the struggle, now shared by the character in the episode, to return to the bold outline of character and plot. Bloom's very status as a person with a clear and distinct identity is at question in "Sirens," and like him I choose to read beyond the charm of Joyce's language to the "truth" of the character and his plot. The first time we see him in this episode he is referred to as "Bloowho" (11.86), and just a little later he is "Bloowhose" (149). He is also referred to as "Greaseabloom" (180), "Old Bloom. Blue Bloom" (230), "Wise Bloom" (299), "Bloominwhom" and "Bloo" (309), and "prince Bloom" (608). When Simon Dedalus reaches the climactic high note of his song, the narrator conflates the names of Simon the singer, Leopold the hearer, and Lionel the character in the opera into one name, "Siopold" (752). Some moments in "Sirens" explicitly present the problem of identity as the style becomes increasingly interesting in its own right and more powerful in compelling our attention away from character to itself: "The voice of Lionel returned, weaker but unwearied. It sang again to Richie Poldy Lydia Lidwell also sang to Pat open mouth ear waiting to wait. How first he saw that form endearing, how sorrow seemed to part, how look, form, word charmed him Gould Lidwell, won Pat Bloom's heart" (11.717–20). As each auditor becomes absorbed in the musical performance, the sharp contours of personality dissolve and identities blur, losses that serve to comfort those in pain. What is at work in "Sirens" is the power of music to dissolve one's identity, and so one might be tempted to agree with Phillip Herring's thesis that Joyce writes a book undermining our traditional notions of a stable ego and that he understands the "indeterminacies of identity" (see chapter 5 of Herring's *Joyce's Uncertainty Principle*). But once again Joyce's ultimate point is not to deconstruct identity but rather to show the great effort required to reestablish it. Bloom does not take long to rouse himself from the ease of an indeterminate identity by an act of memory: "First night when I saw her at Mat Dillon's in Terenure, black lace she wore. Musical chairs. We two the last" (11.726–27). Once again an image of Molly called up from memory serves him well, even if this happy image of their first meeting is only to lead him to recall as well what she is about to do. This memory of Molly rouses him from this ease and recalls for him—and for us—the plot of his life. That the memory-image is of their playing at musical chairs allows for there to be another use for music, one that furthers plot action rather than deters from it. On the next page in the novel the syntax breaks down as identities continue to blur:

> Goulding, a flush struggling in his pale, told Mr. Bloom, face of the night, Si in Ned Lambert's, Dedalus house, sang 'Twas rank and fame.

> He, Mr. Bloom, listened while he, Richie Goulding, told him, Mr. Bloom, of the night he, Richie, heard him, Si Dedalus, sing *'Twas rank and fame* in his, Ned Lambert's, house. (11.784–88)

The second paragraph is a sober and determined recuperation of the syntax and grammar that establish identity in a text, excessively identifying the person to whom the personal pronouns refer, as if someone a bit tipsy overcompensates for the delirium and with excess of prudence makes the identities clear. The first sentence quoted here is from Richie Goulding's agency, and it is slurred and blurred; the second has Bloom as agent, and it is the one with excessive clarity. In this way Joyce presents Bloom's conscious and deliberate effort of will to overcome the temptation to let his own peculiar situation blend into a confused and enervating vagueness, an indeterminacy of identity that allows escape from his painful plot. Like Bloom, the reader must work against the style of the episode and reassert the logical order of clear syntax; the reader must, like Bloom, rewrite the episode, reading through the blurring of meaning that music accomplishes, and insist on following plot and character, insist on reasserting the novel's storyness.

We should remember that Bloom, like his creator, is attracted to music and its charms. We may regard the following demystification of music as his attempt to control his response to what he finds so seductive: "Numbers it is. All music when you come to think. Two multiplied by two divided by half is twice one. Vibrations: chords those are. One plus two plus six is seven. Do anything you like with figures juggling. Always find this equal to that. Symmetry under a cemetery wall. He doesn't see my mourning. Callous: all for his own gut. Musemathematics. And you think you're listening to the ethereal" (11.830–35). Both of Bloom's arithmetical examples are wrongly computed, but it seems he knows that, for the point is that music can make eight equal two and nine equal seven; you can "do anything you like with figures juggling," as music can make sorrow into sweetness, pain into pleasure. But music really cannot transform these emotions; it can only give the illusion of doing so. Just as one plus two plus six does not equal seven, so sorrow is not sweet and pain is not pleasure, and to say so is wrong and a lie. We are beginning to see Joyce's critique of rhetoric, of style, of artful language: it may be pretty; it may provide a sweet illusion; but it cannot contain, present, or indicate the truth. Joyce wants a language that is adequate for the most lofty purpose of all, to present the truth.

The search for a language adequate to the presentation of truth is precisely what is denied by what we call poststructuralist theory, and Lyotard pointedly declares that the postmodern spirit has given up on this search and instead has sought to understand the rules by which the language game is played. Postmodern critics of *Ulysses* wish to emphasize Joyce's mastery of such rules and his resultant playfulness, a play without telos and so a pure play. I do not want my analysis to lose sight of the Joycean spirit of play, but I do want to insist that the joy in this book is not aimless but rather is quite purposeful: Joyce is playing with language, learning and mastering its rules, in order to discover a language that may be able to indicate "truth." Joyce is a master of language who does not trust language, who is acutely aware that most language, especially the lofty language called poetry, is not capable of presenting truth; in fact, as Joyce shows in these "language" episodes, any effort to present truth will fail and, somewhat more problematically, will lie about its success, perhaps even to itself. As he learned from Dante, language is fundamentally fraudulent, and Dante's Ulysses and Joyce's *Ulysses* register this deep distrust of poetry.

Such recognition does not have to lead to despair. In his analysis of modernism, Lyotard explains that a text cannot hope for the invocation of the sublime if it does not recognize first that such sublimity cannot be presented and can only be invoked by its absence, by a nostalgic acknowledgment that it is not presentable.[3] This helps explain Joyce's extraordinary indirection. He is seeking a style capable not of direct presentation, or clear representation, but oblique indication of truth or sublimity. In these "language" episodes he shows how lofty language cannot represent the truth but can only lie about its ability to do so. In "Sirens" musical language is shown to be untruthful and inadequate. He eliminates the various styles—in "Oxen of the Sun" he eliminates almost every style that has ever been tried out—in order to set the stage for "Ithaca," that unliterary episode that will succeed in invoking what other styles find unpresentable through an unusual kind of absence.

So when Bloom is demystifying the language of music, he provides a model for the reader's behavior, to enjoy and indulge in but not be captivated by the technical virtuosity of the author. Those who remain so in love with artful words for their own sake and not for what they present are like Richie Goulding, so absorbed in the musical performances that he does not notice that Bloom is wearing black and so might be in mourning for someone close. Bloom thinks Goulding "callous," and we are meant to see the dangers of becoming so in love with the play of signifiers that we do not insist that the play at some point be halted and some object be made sensible through language. Joyce has anticipated such a critical view of language and gives us enough "play" that we can enjoy language in its own right and for its own sake as an endless dance of signifiers; yet he also offers a warning about those who do not pull themselves out of such indulgence: they become callous, indifferent to sorrow, indifferent to story and human plot. While in "Nestor," Joyce showed an awareness of the dangers of totalitarian thinking, here he demonstrates an awareness of the dangers, less often cited, of indulging in "pure play" of "aimless joy": such indulgence keeps one from engagement with the world that demands our active sympathy. Joyce makes this point quietly but plainly when Bloom finally leaves the Ormond and notes a sign of Dublin's general and pervasive meanness: "Twentyfour solicitors in that one house. Counted them. Litigation: love one another. Piles of parchment. Messrs Pick and Pocket have power of attorney. Goulding, Collis, Ward" (11.1224–27). While the songs of love seem to indicate that the Dubliners "love one another," Bloom skeptically uses the house of litigation as the basis for debunking this ideal. A professed lover of music, Richie Goulding is a member of a profession here associated with common thievery. It is highly ironic to recall how the music seemed to arouse compassion in its hearers: "Thrilled she listened, bending in sympathy to hear" (11.1085); "All lost in pity for croppy" (1113); "And deepmoved all, Simon trumping compassion from a foghorn nose" (1156). The power of music allows its hearers the illusion that they indeed do love one another, that they can feel sympathy for one another's pain. But this language of music renders this sympathy too easily, and without the clear and sober acceptance of one's own pain, no genuine compassion is possible. Whereas those who indulge in music litigate against one another, the man who is able to move beyond music demonstrates kindness, generosity, and compassion throughout the day.

I have been working to show the justice of this remark by Ellmann, made about this episode but in a different context: "Joyce intended Bloom to see through music, or hear beyond it" (Ellmann, *Liffey*, 104). Bloom's challenge is precisely that of the reader: the first of the truly innovative episodes is written in a manner we are to see through; again, the primacy of vision over hearing is asserted. We are meant to see through the seduction of musical language and hold fast to the characters whom we had the illusion of having come to know so well through the first ten episodes. In this indirect way, by making us struggle to see through the style to story, Joyce makes the characters and plot seem even more real and substantial, for they are assumed to be "there," on the other side of style, if you will. Of course we are meant to delight in the inventive and charming language of the episode, but we are also meant to insist on holding to the clear outline of Bloom we bring to the episode from the others, an outline made clearer by our very effort to see it still despite the obfuscating style. This is the beginning of Joyce's greatest achievement in *Ulysses*, the ability to continue to develop the illusion of the solidity of Bloom and Stephen even as the styles become more "abstract," more challenging, and so more demanding of our critical attention. It is Joyce's "esthetic of indirection," that the characters, once firmly established in the first ten episodes, only grow in substance and boldness of outline as the styles become more indirect in presenting them. Lyotard gives us the language for this achievement, that Joyce can invoke their presence by making us feel their absence.

I go back to Ellmann's analysis for a final point. As penetrating as Ellmann is about "Sirens" in *Ulysses on the Liffey*, he misses a crucial aspect of its significance in understanding the character of Bloom. Ellmann follows almost entirely the logic of the Homeric parallel: "Figuratively, Bloom is lashed to the mast" (Ellmann, 103). Odysseus was able to hear the sirens' song and sail beyond them safely only because of his clever ruse in anticipation of being absorbed in their song. But Bloom must be more like Dante in *Purgatorio* than Odysseus, rousing himself to continue on his way, to continue on his journey by feeling his pain that is his lot this day. Bloom's passivity begins to take on a new look: though he does nothing to stop Boylan or prevent the affair, we begin to appreciate how active his will is in allowing their freedom. He works hard to do nothing; he exerts his will to be passive. He is, we can begin to say, heroically passive.

"Cyclops"

While "Sirens" certainly marks the beginning of wilder stylistic experimentation, the reader is still largely within Bloom's consciousness, even if that consciousness is distorted by the powers of music from which he, and we, escape at the end. So the eleventh episode marks another bridge of sorts, between the early naturalistic episodes and the later, more fully abstract episodes that begin with "Cyclops." This is the significance of the unlikely coincidence or accident that Bloom's watch stops at the precise moment "Sirens" is said (by Hart and confirmed by Kenner) to end, at half past four. This may or may not be the exact hour and minute of Molly's tryst with Boylan, but at the end of "Sirens" we can say that this coincidence signifies that time in some way stops with the eleventh episode and that from this point onward, from "Cyclops" onward, we are somehow out of time. "Cyclops" is unique, up to this point in the novel at least, in that it is the first time in *Ulysses* that we are kept entirely out of Bloom's consciousness. This decision to move outside of the two characters' consciousness and, with the exception of the second half of "Nausicaa," remain outside is an important one for us to consider. The man we have come to know so well from the inside will only be seen from the outside, and moments that we would love to have narrated for us in the lucid manner of the early episodes will for now on be given to us only through difficult and often almost opaque screens of narration. The experience of teaching *Ulysses* has been instructive to me on this point.

Undergraduate readers of this novel, less sophisticated than the academicians teaching them and so more direct and earnest in their demands on Joyce, are often bitterly frustrated by the narration of these episodes that are bringing us to the most important part of Bloom's day. In "Cyclops" we miss the chance of knowing what Bloom is thinking to himself as he delivers his defense of charity; in "Oxen of the Sun" we miss the chance of knowing what Bloom thinks about Stephen and Stephen about Bloom as their paths finally intersect; and most frustrating of all is "Ithaca," where the two main plots are brought to a climax without our being on the inside for any of the important scenes. I want to suggest that we ignore the readerly demands of our students to our peril: their frustration must be in part what Joyce intends by these narrative devices, and we would do well to think about what Joyce gains by these increasingly indirect modes of representation.

While there are still some important events occurring within these narrations, what dominates these episodes is language and in the case of "Cyclops" the alternation of parody and mean-spirited naturalistic narration. The plot of "Cyclops" is simple: Bloom will defend himself, against a hostile antagonist, in a hostile environment, and within a narration that is equally hostile to him; for the nameless "I" who narrates the action of "Cyclops" hates Bloom. But as Groden informs us, "Joyce created the parodies first, the barroom scene came soon after, and the narrative voice developed last" (Groden, 124). If this is correct, then it suggests that Joyce's intentions in "Cyclops" began with the idea of parody, of absurdly inflated rhetoric that he calls in his schema "gigantism." The action—Bloom's preaching against violence and his advocacy of love—which came soon after the parodies, is juxtaposed to rhetoric so inflated and so excessive that no one can take anything it might say seriously. When Joyce developed the "I" who gets to tell of Bloom's defense of love, the episode is complete: it alternates between the excesses of the most inflated language and of the most debased, between the idealism of the loftiest rhetoric imaginable and the meanness of the most cynical narrator. Between the two extremes may lie something we can call "truth."

What is cyclopean in "Cyclops" is the narration, the two opposite excesses that are both one-eyed and thus partial, invalid, and ultimately false. The monster threatening Joyce's hero-to-be is the manner in which he is to be presented, the mode of narration that is to be used to describe his behavior and action. When we think back to *The Odyssey*, we may be struck by just how pivotal an episode Odysseus's encounter with Polyphemus is for the plot of that epic. It is Poseidon's son, after all, who invokes the sea god to oppose the return of Odysseus to Ithaca. But we may forget one aspect of this adventure that may shed light on Joyce's retelling. After the clever ruse that allows his escape, Odysseus makes it safely to his ship and has already sailed some distance from shore when he feels compelled to taunt Polyphemus. The blinded monster judges the location of the ship by the sound of Odysseus's voice and hurls a boulder that almost brings the ship back to shore. As if this were not foolish enough, Odysseus continues to taunt Polyphemus and even tells him his true identity: "Kyklops, if ever mortal man inquire how you were put to shame and blinded, tell him Odysseus, raider of cities, took your eye: Laertes' son, whose home's on Ithaka" (Fitzgerald's translation, book 9, 549–52). This is precisely the information the monster needs to call upon his father to take vengeance on this enemy. If Odysseus had remained "noman," a man without name or identity, humble and anonymous, he would have made it back home safely and easily, with all of his men and with all of his ships.

How do we apply this aspect of the Homeric original to Joyce's version? It allows us to raise the question of identity as central to both epics, both the ancient and the modern. In "Cyclops" the possibility is advanced that Bloom may be elevated to the status of possible prophet (Elijah), or as apostle to the Gentiles (Saint Paul), or even to an identification with Christ. Can Bloom become someone more heroic than he has been so far this day? Can his identity change from being a noman, an ordinary fellow worthy of no more attention than anyone else on 16 June 1904, as "Wandering Rocks" would suggest as his very human limitation? The parodies, which we must recall were devised first, threaten to make any participation of Bloom in some heroic paradigm seem absurd, sentimental, ridiculous. The silly excess of heroic or inflated language renders Bloom's elevation suspect. Once again we can invoke Herring's study of the "indeterminacies of identity" as a warning about making such easy identifications. From this point of view the episode seems designed to deflate any attempt to fashion a heroic identity for Bloom; he may be doomed to remain always a noman.

Let us return to Groden's sequencing of the creation of the episode. Next comes the barroom scene, in which Bloom defends himself and expresses his values. It is essential to notice just how uncharacteristic it is for Bloom to do such things; he usually remains reticent about such matters, reserving his view of things for the silent expression of interior monologue. But at five o'clock at Barney Kiernan's he speaks up, boldly and energetically. It seems plausible to attribute such behavior on Bloom's part to the provocation of the citizen, but still we must insist on noting how unusual it is for Bloom to be provoked by anyone into revealing what he does not want to reveal. As it was for Odysseus, who asserted himself and his identity against Polyphemus, assertiveness may be a dangerous thing for Bloom. This is one of the few times in the novel that Bloom has been provoked to do anything out of character, and his response to the citizen does indeed land him in danger, as the virulent Irish nationalist threatens to attack Bloom and even throws a biscuit tin at him. Homer's hero gave into his "glorying spirit" in needing to taunt the Kyklops, and Bloom lifts himself up to assert a heroic identity by standing up to the citizen. He will even be provoked into making an identification of himself with Christ, and such an identification, established by the man himself, is not something we are prepared for and is something we do not know how to take seriously. The parodies that at times dominate the episode debunk and mock such possibilities.

Had Joyce left the episode with these two components only, we might be forced to conclude that his intentions are like Mulligan's and that perhaps Robert Bell was right after all to think that the novel does seem to approach the witty Buck's perspective. But the third aspect of the episode's structure, and the one that carries the primary burden for narrating its action, complicates the mix and makes Bloom's identity and behavior more difficult to assess: the narrative voice of the barroom scene is as mean, low, and vulgar as any in literature. Indeed, Joyce compares the nameless "I" to Thersites, and the comparison is just. That the narrator has no name and is only an "I" is suggestive: he is one-eyed, the monster of the episode whose blindness to Bloom's character is what we must anticipate and keep in mind in assessing what Bloom is doing , which we know about only through this one-eye's telling. To match the loftiness of the parodies, his view of the world sinks as low as Joyce can bring it. This "I" hates everyone and everything, but he has a special venom for Bloom. So we have two perspectives from which to consider Bloom: one raises him to heights so lofty that they cannot be justified, and the other reduces him to a meanness and vulgarity that we cannot trust because we know too much about Bloom. We doubt both extremes and struggle to "see" Bloom somewhere in between.

This episode then presents the reader with a fairly complex dialectical mode of fictional representation: we move back and forth between extremes of narrative description, all the while watching Bloom perform one of his most strenuous and important actions of the day. On the one hand is the lofty narration of romance, on the other is an extreme of naturalism, and in between the two Bloom expresses his values in his defense of love and advances an identification of himself with Christ. We do not have Bloom's own interior monologue, so we are forced to read through the two kinds of narrative we are given and invent our own.

It is fairly easy to describe the narration of the nameless "I": he is as mean and hostile as any figure in literature; he hates everyone and has compassion for no one. For example, we know Bob Doran from "A Boarding House" and perhaps still feel some sympathy for him. In this episode Bob is off on one of what has apparently become a fairly regular pattern of drinking bouts. Here is what "I" says about him: "The tear is bloody near your eye. Talking through his bloody hat. Fitter for him to go home to the little sleepwalking bitch he married, Mooney, the bumbailiff's daughter, mother kept a kip in Hardwicke street, that used to be a stravaging about the landings Bantam Lyons told me that was stopping there at two in the morning without a stitch on her, exposing her person, open to all comers, fair field and no favour" (12.397–402). From *Dubliners* we know that Mrs. Mooney was looking to get a husband for her daughter by dubious means, but this account is excessive and not to be trusted. There is a grain of truth in much of what the "I" has to say, but his focus is so mean and so low that his judgments are to be rejected. He calls Molly a "fat heap" (503), an assessment we know not to trust, and Bloom "lardy face" (502), a description we are surprised by and know to be false when in "Ithaca" we are given Bloom's height and weight (he is five foot nine and one-half inches tall and weighs 158 pounds, hardly "lardy"). The man is so full of spite that he loses our trust. When he guesses that Blazes is going to have an affair with Molly on the concert tour up north, we are forced to admit that even someone whose views are so scurrilous does lurch into the truth once in a while. But for the most part we are made wary by his excess and cannot trust his assessment of character, though we are forced to rely on his account of the action simply because we have no other.

The other mode of narration, the parodies of lofty rhetoric, are more difficult to assess. These were, according to Groden, the first part of the episode to receive form and so may yield us the deepest intentions the episode had in Joyce's design. When Joyce calls the style "gigantism," we are led to think about the writing of Rabelais, especially in *Gargantua and Pantagruel*. The parodies in "Cyclops" are Joyce's way of bringing Rabelais's critique of language into *Ulysses* and as such occupy an important place in the unfolding of the novel's larger ambitions. When Rabelais was writing his episodic account of his giants' lives, he was supremely self-conscious of his placement in literary history at a turning point in the history of literature and of language in general. He was aware of the extraordinary implications for language the invention of the printing press was to have. Rabelais knew that one of the effects of the sudden ability for mass production of books was for the notion of authority to be questioned. Suddenly words could be printed that did not already have the massive authority of the Catholic Church behind them. Before the printing press, any text in existence had already acquired for itself the authority of the church that then led it to be copied in painstaking fashion by the monks whose job it was to preserve culture and "authorize" the texts that support it. After the invention of the printing press anyone could become an "author" and have his words printed and disseminated and so vie with the "authorized" texts for a position as culture bearer. Rabelais neither laments this nor rejoices in it; he merely uses it as an occasion for humor when he explains how Pantagruel made Gargantua's colors white and blue: "For white signified to him gladness, pleasure, delights, and rejoicing, and blue anything to do with heaven." When Rabelais anticipates the reader's response, that these are quite eccentric assignations of meaning to color, he launches into an attack on the authority of the book:

> Who is exciting you now? Who is pricking you? Who is telling you that white stands for faith and blue for steadfastness? A mouldy book, you say, that is sold by pedlars and ballad-mongers, entitled *The Blason of Colours*. Who made it? Whoever he is he has been prudent in one respect, that he has not put his name to it. For the rest, I don't know which surprises me more, his presumption or his stupidity: his presumption in daring, without reason, cause, or probability, to prescribe by his private authority what things shall be denoted by what colours; which is the custom of tyrants who would have their will take the place of reason, not of the wise and learned, who satisfy their readers with display of evidence; or his stupidity in supposing that without regard to other proofs and valid arguments the world would regulate its practice by his foolish impostures (book 1, chapter 9).

The job of the writer is different after the invention of the printing press: now one must demand of the writer displays of evidence appealing to reason and probability in order to judge the validity of the writer's propositions. No longer is the authority of the book to be assumed; it must be earned by the writer by appealing to the reader's rational judgment in order for the writer to become an author. The written word no longer has a special, almost ontological relation to authority and truth; it must compete with other written words in the court of public opinion for one text to become authority over its rivals.

This has important ramifications on language itself, as Rabelais sees it. One of his ways of suggesting the new status of the written word is to include many lists, some of which go on so long that, by the sheer ingenuity of mind to create so many things to be listed, they elicit our laughter. But it is more than a humorous device; it is a way of suggesting that words have become mere things to be played with, to be added together in no logical order and for no practical purpose. The status of the word, especially the written word, has undergone a shift, and Rabelais suggests that the word has suffered a cheapening, a degradation. There is no mot juste in these lists but rather just the play of mind to find and include as many as possible. The word has fallen from its purity as authority and become an object of consumption. This is why Joyce has so many lists in "Cyclops." One of the first, and longest, is the list of names of Irish heroes, which includes some veritable heroes from Irish history, some names from Irish legend and myth, and some names that do not belong, such as Christopher Columbus, the Rose of Castille, Ben Howth, Adam and Eve, and Guatama Buddha. This list of names does nothing to advance the plot but does much to advance the design of the author in this episode: to make the reader notice the fallen status of the written word. We read these lists and notice that the narrator giving us all these words has no command over them, has lost the control over their meaning, and can only pile them up as if in sheer accumulation of objects there is some authority to be gained.

Joyce brings Rabelais into *Ulysses* to designate the crisis in language that the modern artist feels even more keenly than his Renaissance precursor. Joyce wants to make a hero for his culture out of words but has come to see that the words at his disposal are no longer authorized and have become degraded objects of filth. Joyce follows Rabelais in these parodies in another, but related way, for in making his heroes Rabelais resorts to the wildest exaggerations of their size and intellects. We are meant, I think, to laugh at the "gigantism" but also to question how heroes are to be described now that the criteria of reason and probability have replaced the criteria of romance. Joyce similarly uses exaggeration in his parodic description of the citizen:

> The figure seated on a large boulder at the foot of a round tower was that of a broadshouldered deepchested stronglimbed frankeyed redhaired freelyfreckled shaggybeared widemouthed largenosed longheaded deepvoiced bareknee brawny-handed hairylegged ruddyfaced sinewyarmed hero. From shoulder to shoulder he measured several ells and his rocklike mountainous knees were covered, as was likewise the rest of his body wherever visible, with a strong growth of tawny prickly hair in hue and toughness similar to the mountain gorse (*Ules Europeus*). The widewinged nostrils, from which bristles of the same tawny hue projected, were of such capaciousness that within their cavernous obscurity the fieldlark might easily have lodged her nest. (12.151–61)

The exaggeration is right out of Rabelais, with the same kind of delightful silliness that makes for great humor. Also as in Rabelais, the issues are serious, for what is made suspect here is language itself, and we see clearly that Joyce intends for "Cyclops" to present a crisis in the language of representation, for what is at stake is the possibility for heroic action ever to be presented in literature again.

What Joyce seems to be learning from Rabelais, and including in his own novel, is that the written word underwent in the Renaissance a challenge to its authority, its ability to be trusted, its ability to tell the truth, from which it has never recovered and which has only become more vexed in the modern period. One result of the printing press was the eventual creation of a new genre capable of representing ordinary human life, and Joyce is bringing his novel and the entire genre back to its origins by returning to Rabelais. Joyce wants to resurrect the possibility of representing heroic behavior, and to do so he chooses to confront in "Cyclops" the origin and the end of the novel: the parodic mockery of a Rabelaisian narrator that sets off the chain of events that lead to the novel and the virulent and mean naturalism of the nameless "I" that is the dead end of the novel. The novel begins and ends with the problem of telling the truth. We must turn the action of the episode to see what kind of heroism Joyce is still hoping to establish in Bloom.

In *Gargantua and Pantagruel,* Rabelais does not mock the gospels or those who are good preachers of the gospels. It is as if written language is so debased now that anything and everything is subject to mockery except the Word of God and those who are skilled at making it fresh and vital to contemporary humanity. In "Cyclops," Bloom is made to look as if he is a preacher of Christ's message of love, though a tongue-tied preacher who can barely get his words out of his mouth. In fact, he is very much like Saint Paul preaching love to a hostile audience, for Saint Paul is writing to a divided and divisive Church in Corinth when he presents his famous definition of love: "Love is patient and kind; love is not jealous or boastful; it is not arrogant or rude. Love does not insist on its own way; it is not irritable or resentful; it does not rejoice at wrong, but rejoices in the right. Love bears all things, believes all things, hopes all things, endures all things. Love never ends" (1 Cor. 13.4–8). What prompts Paul to offer this definition is the contentiousness and deep division in the Church established at Corinth; what prompts Bloom to make his far less articulate definition is the hostility he encounters in Barney Kiernan's, hostility that is seen both in the characters in the bar and in the narrator. Joyce's genius in this episode is to assign a possible identification of Bloom with Saint Paul and even with Christ through the screen of a narration that hates him.

He responds with unusual energy to the virulent nationalism of those in the bar, especially the citizen's, whose one-eyed understanding of Irish greatness blinds him to his own venomous attitudes. Bloom interrupts the mean-spirited nationalism with a broader perspective: "Persecution, says he, all the history of the world is full of it. Perpetuating national hatred among nations" (12.1417–18). His audience's response to this is to find in Bloom's more tolerant view a sign of his Jewishness: the words "But do you know what a nation is" (1419) are almost a code for anti-Semitism, for Jews apparently live in a nation and enjoy all the benefits of citizenship while remaining outsiders, culturally alien and loyal to no one but themselves. So in his defense of tolerance and love Bloom becomes increasingly identified as a Jew in the eyes of those in the bar and in the eye of the narrator. Bloom is quick to notice their anti-Jewish sentiments, as he does something he is not accustomed to doing at any other point in the day, which is to identify himself as a Jew: "And I belong to a race too, says Bloom, that is hated and persecuted. Also now. This very moment. This very instant" (1467–68). When he is told to "stand up to it then with force like men" (1475), he responds in a way that is worth quoting in its full context:

>   —But it's no use, says he. Force, hatred, history, all that. That's not life for men and women, insult and hatred. And everybody knows that it's the very opposite of that that is really life.
>   —What? says Alf.
>   —Love, says Bloom. I mean the opposite of hatred. I must go now, says he to John Wyse. Just round to the court a moment to see if Martin is there. If he comes just say I'll be back in a second. Just a moment.
>   Who's hindering you? And off he pops like greased lightning.
>   —A new apostle to the gentiles, says the citizen. Universal love.
>   —Well, says John Wyse. Isn't that what we're told. Love your neighbour.
>   —That chap? says the citizen. Beggar my neighbor is his motto. Love, moya! He's a nice pattern of a Romeo and Juliet.
>   Love loves to love love. Nurse loves the new chemist. Constable 14A loves Mary Kelly. Gerty MacDowell loves the boy that has the bicycle. M. B. loves a fair gentleman. Li Chan Han lovey up kissy Cha Pu Chow. Jumbo, the elephant, loves Alice, the elephant. . . . And this person loves that other person because everybody loves somebody but God loves everybody. (12.1481–1501)

This is perhaps one of the highlights of Bloom's day, as he will repeat this story in some detail to Stephen later in "Eumaus." Bloom's definition is almost mute—after all, is there anything less precise than calling love "the opposite of hatred"? Yet there is a certain nobility to his espousing love as a response to these nationalist hatreds and a certain courage to opposing them audibly. There is no moment in the day, at least no moment we get to see, when Bloom acts more bravely, more heroically, in risking the anger of his audience and standing up to them like a man. Perhaps the only action he feels not useless (and he does say, even here, that force, hatred, and history are of "no use") is to defend the love that supports his tolerance, the love that empowers his passivity.

The responses to his definition are noteworthy. The citizen mockingly calls him "a new apostle to the gentiles," which is, of course, the title reserved for Saint Paul. This is an instructive example of Joyce's irony, that an identification of Bloom with Paul is made by the character we are most inclined to dislike and distrust. John Wyse Nolan reluctantly admits that all Bloom is doing is speaking as Christ would have it, calling us to love one another. The citizen's response to that is to demean Bloom's character by saying that Bloom's motto is "beggar my neighbor," which we know not to be true. As a matter of fact, the reason that Bloom is at Barney Kiernan's at five o'clock in the first place is to wait for Martin Cunningham to take him to the house of the widow Dignam so he can explain the loophole that will allow the widow to collect on the insurance policy even though Paddy had mortgaged it over to a moneylender. We must be aware of the odd gap in the novel, as we will not see Bloom at the house of mourning but will only pick him up later on the strand in "Nausicaa" three hours later. Joyce omits what might be the high point of Bloom's day, saving the widow Dignam from sure and immediate penury, an omission that is even odder once we agree to look for signs of Bloom's ability to be heroic. Not only is Bloom not out to beggar his neighbor, but the reader knows that Bloom in fact was one of the few people not only to pledge money in "Hades" but to put down five shillings on the spot. All this must be said by the reader so that we are able to reject forcefully the citizen's claims. The reader must amass all these details because the hostile narrator surely will not do any such thing even if he knew these facts; and the reader must do this work because we are not in Bloom's consciousness at all in the episode and so must rely on our memory and our ingenuity to be in a position of certainty about the opinions being expressed. So Bloom's barely articulate definition of love is made valid not by any thoughts of Bloom's, nor by any opinions of the characters of the scene, nor by the narrator, but by the reader who "knows" Bloom better than any other figure in "Cyclops" does or could possibly know him. We are making judgments about him and perhaps can even assent to a parallel between him and Paul, even though no one in the episode—not even Bloom—would do so.

Not even the language that ends the quoted material above is trustworthy, for it makes a mockery of the language of love and ends with the most clichéd expression of universal love, "God loves everybody." The citizen can only think of the adolescent (and tragically violent) love of Romeo and Juliet in thinking about this word. Bloom's inept definition perhaps becomes more striking when we read this debased language of love; in a world in which this is what love means, or how we use the word, what can be said but "love is the opposite of hatred"? Joyce has elevated Bloom's inarticulate performance by placing it in a context that is debased on both sides, by the meanness of the characters and narrator on the one hand and by the excess of easy language of love on the other.

The plot of the episode develops significantly when Bloom runs off to see if Martin has indeed shown up yet, for in his absence the patrons of the bar learn from Lenehan that Bloom has won perhaps as much as one hundred shillings on the horse race. We know that this is a mistake on Lenehan's part that he must have learned from Bantam Lyons, who had earlier in the day mistakenly heard Bloom give a tip about the Gold Cup race: "I was just going to throw it away" (5.534). In "Lestrygonians," Bloom made the mistake of seeing his name on a "throwaway" advertising the preaching of Alexander J. Dowie, a throwaway that he threw away, only for it to come back to the reader's field of perception in "Wandering Rocks." This throwaway keeps coming back into the novel and makes its appearance here through Lenehan. The mistake is taking on larger meaning and here fuels their already virulent anti-Semitism: now Bloom can be the caricature of the cheap Jew, as he has won a large sum of money and does not buy a round of drinks to celebrate: "Courthouse my eye and your pockets hanging down with gold and silver. Mean bloody scut. Stand us a drink itself. Devil a sweet fear. There's a jew for you! All for number one. Cute as a shithouse rat. Hundred to five" (12.1759–61). The citizen can barely be restrained from attacking Bloom, who hears the slurs against the Jews and continues to identify himself as a Jew:

> —Mendelssohn was a jew and Karl Marx and Mercadante and Spinoza. And the saviour was a jew and his father was a jew. Your God.
> —He had no father, says Martin. That'll do now. Drive ahead.
> —Whose God? says the citizen.
> —Well, his uncle was a jew, says he. Your God was a jew. Christ was a jew like me. (12.1904–9)

We laugh at Martin's theological error, that Christ had no father, especially in light of Stephen's thinking about the relation of God the Father and God the Son. But perhaps we are meant to see that even the decent Martin Cunningham is not willing to hear Bloom the Jew say that Christ was a Jew. In the heat of the moment Bloom makes the identification of himself with Christ. This is obviously an important moment for my thesis, but we must be careful not to take this as an authorial identification nor allow it to function as a pivot for meaning.

The episode ends as the citizen, enraged by Bloom's words, throws a biscuit tin at him, and Bloom ascends to heaven as Elijah: "When, lo, there came about them all a great brightness and they beheld the chariot wherein he stood ascend to heaven. And they beheld Him in the chariot, clothed in the glory of the brightness, having the raiment of the sun, fair as the moon and terrible that for awe they durst not look upon Him. And there came a voice out of heaven, calling: *Elijah! Elijah!* And he answered with a main cry: *Abba! Adonai!* And they beheld Him even Him, ben Bloom Elijah, amid clouds of angels ascend to the glory of the brightness at an angle of fortyfive degrees over Donohoe's in Little Green street like a shot off a shovel" (12.1910–18). In this passage Bloom is called Elijah, but the language is such that we see him as Christ as well, for he is described as Christ is at the Transfiguration, and only Christ called God "Abba." So the association of Bloom with Saint Paul, Elijah, and Christ all comes to a head as the episode ends. James Maddox notes, "In ["Cyclops"] Joyce fleshes out the Christ parallel and gives substance to the Citizen's sneer that Bloom is 'a new apostle to the gentiles'" (Maddox, 87). But the ending seems to be so excessive in its language, so parodic, that we must pause and proceed carefully. The ending asks the reader to allow that Bloom is indeed rising heavenward as an Elijah taken up from an evil world to the safety and glory of heaven, but we are not prepared to give our assent to this. We can say that some symbolic association here is being established, that Bloom is indeed an "advertising Elijah" who as the episode ends is given a larger identity due to his strenuous defense of Christian love in a hostile environment. Even that, though, may be punctured by the last phrase describing the ascent of the heavenly chariot, moving "at an angle of fortyfive degrees over Donohoe's in Little Green street like a shot off a shovel." We cannot take seriously the identification yet; the language for this identification has not been found yet.

Bloom has acted in a way that allows the reader to begin to consider such identifications, and we are prepared for that throwaway to keep coming back until the right language has been discovered. We cannot trust the mean naturalistic "I" nor the lofty parodic narrator, but in between the two of them we have watched Bloom act bravely in defense of Christian love. That cannot be taken away, even if the styles that presented this to us are not trustworthy. If the novel ended here, I feel that we would be compelled to say that Joyce has intended to debunk such associations even while presenting Bloom as a good man with the proper values. But obviously the novel does not end here, and if we look at "Cyclops" from the point of view of "Ithaca," we see that it is preparatory in establishing the possibility of such identifications and also in getting us outside Bloom's consciousness in doing so. The truth about Bloom is not to be found within his mind, but in our ability to see in him an exponent of permanent and perhaps even absolute values. "Ithaca" will also avoid the direct representation of Bloom's mind as it brings us to a final consideration of these possibilities. The truth is not inside our minds, but in our behavior.

This is where Dorrit Cohn's study is once again useful, for Joyce's novel is not important for its turn back inward, as all the clichés about modernist fiction would have it; *Ulysses* is significant in the history of the novel in its perfecting that ability for fiction to be a transparent window into the mind and then abandoning it. Joyce develops that aspect of the novel to its most transparent and intimate, only to show it up as limited, partial, misleading. From within Bloom's mind can be found only partial truths, humanly colored truths; in finding a position outside these minds the reader can perhaps approach truth. Humanism cannot tolerate discussions of truth in an absolute sense, and so humanism comes close to sanctioning the lie as plausible fiction. Joyce is working to abstract Bloom from the naturalistic context of humanism and to withdraw our attention from the inner workings of his mind, for the truth of Bloom's character is not found inside his mind but outside. The truth is out there, and that is what we will have to learn to see.

"Nausicaa"

The episodes of *Ulysses* seem to be designed to be a series of lessons about the nature of fictional representation and the act of reading. This approach is that of Karen Lawrence in *The Odyssey of Styles in* Ulysses and of Daniel Schwarz in *Reading Joyce's* Ulysses, two major studies of how Joyce experiments with style in order to shape the reader's responses. I am happy to place my study in this company, with the distinction that my project watches more closely for an evolving and progressive movement toward "Ithaca," where a new way of writing, modernist allegory, is finally realized. Lawrence recognizes that the changes in style in the later episodes "reflect the shedding of an artistic belief no longer sufficient to his vision" (Lawrence, 54), but she does not recognize that Joyce's experiments with style have a telos, that the "odyssey of style" has an "Ithaca." We are not simply witnessing the virtuosity of a great literary artist but of a man harnessing those talents in an effort to include the history of the genre he has inherited and to complete it by writing the last novel, the novel as epic, the novel as allegory.

"Nausicaa" will reinforce and expand the lesson of "Cyclops" that it is not important any longer to be within Bloom's consciousness, that to be restricted to Bloom's consciousness is actually a liability and an obstacle in our pursuit of meaning, that Bloom's own opinions of himself are far less important than the ones the reader is able to devise about him, for these approach the status of "truth" in a way that Bloom's own thoughts about himself could never do. We would not like him as much if he thought of himself in the way we are starting to think of him, as an epic hero like Odysseus or a model of Christian virtue; such high valuations of himself from himself would strike us as arrogant and pretentious, if not absurd, and we would reject them. Perhaps in "Cyclops," if we were still bound to a naturalistic depiction of his inner life, we would have to bear with Bloom indulging in some flattering illusions about himself; perhaps, having come up with the loophole that allows the widow Dignam to collect on the insurance policy, Bloom thinks of himself as a clever fellow and the hero of the situation. This might help explain why, as he waits for Martin Cunningham to pick him up and take him to the house of mourning, Bloom is so uncharacteristically assertive and active, why he speaks up so clearly and so boldly. It is not like Bloom to make a claim such as "Christ was a jew like me," which actually has the relationship backward, for Bloom, at his best and highest, could only be a Jew like Christ, not the other way around. Perhaps he is a bit puffed up to be able to announce that a man as well respected as Martin Cunningham is coming to pick him up and he feels proud to have risen in Martin's estimation, when earlier in the day in "Hades," Martin was prepared to be civil to Bloom but nothing more. Bloom might, like Odysseus facing Polyphemus, be glorying in his newfound status, but Joyce has devised a narration that keeps us from any such thoughts. Outside Bloom's consciousness we are not distracted by any pride, or any subsequent puncturing of that pride, that Bloom is most likely experiencing. We are not bound to see the episode from his alternating experiences of confidence and diffidence, from strength to weakness, up and down as his early episodes presented him to us; we can see for ourselves, beyond the limitation of his mind, and make judgments that we are being empowered to make.

Before turning to the way "Nausicaa" advances our instruction about how to read this novel, let us recall once again that we have a gap between "Cyclops" and "Nausicaa," between five forty-five and eight o'clock, the time Bloom spends going to, being at, and coming from the house of mourning. Only Kenner has made a critical point of asking why Joyce leaves such a gap in his narration that has, up to this point, been fairly scrupulous in following Bloom and Stephen carefully. Kenner's guess is that Joyce does not want to bring us to a scene where Bloom feels like a stage Jew, where he is so clever about financial matters that he defrauds the Jewish moneylender (Kenner, *Ulysses*, 102–3). As usual, Kenner's offer is tempting. However, it seems more likely that we are being kept from the one moment in the day when Bloom would probably look like a big man, like a hero, to the Dignam family at any rate. It is not difficult to imagine a scene in which the widow with grateful emotion thanks Bloom for saving her family from penury; how the other men in the scene, especially Martin, feel pleased with Bloom and speak well of him; how an awkward Bloom accepts the thanks and deflects attention from himself. I see back-slapping and handshaking all around, and this we miss! Do we not all like Bloom enough that we would love to see a scene where he looks this good among his fellow Dubliners? Apparently Joyce wants us to miss just this kind of scene. In fact, when Bloom does reflect on his appearance at the house of mourning, he does not call to consciousness any details from the scene there, an indication perhaps of his great humility in not taking his good deed seriously. In any event, we are not to see Bloom's heroism in any public scene, but rather in a much more private and secret way of "Ithaca."

The novel picks up with "Nausicaa," which presents an even more remote view of Bloom than "Cyclops" gave us as we wade through the gush of Gerty MacDowell's narration. Bloom enters her perceptual field and soon comes to dominate her thoughts, which climax with Bloom's climax. We see Bloom as a figure in a sentimental romance written, as it were, by a young Irish woman; he is a figure in a bad book, in a way analogous to the way Emma Bovary "writes" her own story in *Madame Bovary*. The story that she is telling, and that someone is transcribing for us, places Bloom in a world of clichés and conventions so excessive that we cannot take seriously anything narrated. Just as Emma offers a view of the world that is so bookish, so based on sentimental romance that we cannot trust the story as narrated, so we do not trust what occurs in the first half of "Nausicaa." Gerty's view of Bloom is so sentimental and so derivative that Joyce brings us back to Bloom's consciousness through the interior monologue method one last time, as if to puncture that kind of sentimental idealism once and for all. But the way the two halves of this episode—Gerty's half and Bloom's half—interact is more complex than this merely negative lesson on the fatuousness and falsity of sentimental rhetoric.

"Nausicaa" continues the exposure of the bankruptcy of romantic language, here pushed to its most sentimental form. It furthers the exposure begun in "Aeolus" and continued in "Cyclops" of the failure of idealistic language to describe and present heroic action and character. Gerty's sweetly sentimental rendering of Bloom, borrowed from cheap romances and stories from women's magazines, elevates Bloom, without any cause or grounding in what we can still call reality, to the heights of heroic idealism. He is, in her romantic language, "her dreamhusband" (13.431). Her naive idealism, which is constantly juxtaposed with the adoration of the Blessed Virgin Mary (the ideal lady in popular Catholic tradition), is made highly suspect, and the episode is designed to fold neatly in two, as her language gives way to Bloom's thoughts for the last time in the novel.

Richard McKeon's study of the English novel provides the historical analysis of the development of the novel that can help us appreciate what Joyce is enacting in "Nausicaa," in his own critique of the history of the novel. In *The Origins of the English Novel*, McKeon scrupulously documents the ways in which what he calls "romance idealism" is "challenged and refuted" by "naive empiricism," which in turn is met with a countercritique—"extreme skepticism"—that doubts the absolute or universal validity of empiricism and reinstitutes certain elements of romance (21). This scheme, which as McKeon is quick to emphasize is dialectical in nature, provides a useful tool for analyzing not only "Nausicaa" but the novel as a whole. As we have seen, *Ulysses* begins with an exponent of what McKeon calls "naive empiricism" in the medical student Mulligan, whose scientific and materialist perspective causes him to doubt any reality other than the merely physical. McKeon demonstrates that science stands behind the critique of romance idealism, puncturing its claims to truthful narration with apparently devastating ironies (53). The question that McKeon makes central to the study of the history of the novel is central to my examination of *Ulysses:* how to tell the truth in narrative, how to present the truth in language. Buck Mulligan makes the truths of romance idealism seem untenable, and so do the inner thoughts of Bloom as we meet him in "Calypso," where he punctures any flights of idealism of his own romanticism. In Mulligan and in Bloom, but most important in the naturalistic narrator of the early episodes, Joyce builds what seems a solid foundation of a "naive empiricism" capable of doubting any claim of idealism.

For my purposes, the most useful part of McKeon's analysis is his contention that what he calls "extreme skepticism" constitutes a critique of the claims of scientific materialism of Mulligan, of the naive empiricism that sees through the ideals of romance.[4] Both naive empiricism and extreme skepticism are opposed to the falsifications of romance invention, but "the earnest energy of the naive empiricist critique of falsehood renders it vulnerable to the countercritique of extreme skepticism" (48). In its eagerness to debunk the ideals of romance invention, naive empiricism fails to recognize its own limitations and so is open to attack from a more extreme form of skepticism that doubts the doubts of this empiricism. Mulligan is thus "naive" from this point of view, all too quick to dismiss the claims of romance and all too eager to reduce all reality to the lowest forms of physical materiality. Even more pointedly, McKeon claims that "extreme skepticism levels the charge of stealthy romancing even at the style of naive empiricism" (50). McKeon's study of the novel's origins is similar to Siebers's study of contemporary literary theory in that both critics look to go beyond mere skepticism to something more complex. And as Siebers led us to say, so McKeon's analysis allows us to regard Mulligan as, in his naive empiricism, open to the charges of romantic idealism, which is precisely what Stephen understands when he sends the cryptic telegram to his friend: *"The sentimentalist is he who would enjoy without incurring the immense debtorship for a thing done"* (9.550–51). Mulligan is as sentimental as Gerty MacDowell: that is a proposition worth pursuing! The extreme skeptic can see that the supposed plainness of naive empiricism is as stylized as anything, that the claim of naive empiricism to be without rhetoric is as rhetorical as anything in romance convention. Extreme skepticism questions the limits of what naive empiricism claims is universal and absolute objectivity.

This is not to say that naive empiricism does not accomplish anything worthwhile. It clears out the more easily recognizable falsehoods of romantic conventions and lays the ground for more serious claims for truth-telling in narrative. In this light "Cyclops" can be seen as a preliminary clearing of the more obvious lies and distortions of excessive romantic rhetoric. But the mean-spirited "I" who narrates the barroom scene is a figure of rhetoric too, a recognition pressing us beyond his one-eyed point of view to seek a way of narrating truth that sees more than just the lowest terms of existence. "Nausicaa" continues and, I think, deepens this critique, taking the sweetly sentimental rhetoric of Gerty's romantic idealism and exposing it to the withering critique of Bloom's naive empiricism. But his view is not the final one. The initial style is brought back into the novel, for this last time, in order to suggest for one last time its limitations, now as merely another form, though a disguised one, of sentimentality. Mediating the two halves of this episode is a third point of view, an implicit construction of what McKeon calls "extreme skepticism" that is best seen as "the negative midpoint between these two opposed positions, in constant danger of becoming each of them by turns" (McKeon, 119). Joyce manages to construct a third point of view by placing these opposed positions—Gerty's romance idealism and Bloom's naive empiricism—next to one another, and by viewing the episode from this "negative midpoint" the reader is able to see the usefulness of the language in each of the opposed positions and still avoid the temptation to give in to either as a valid way of expressing the truth of the situation. The third position, that of "extreme skepticism," is difficult to maintain, for it always is in danger of turning back to one of the positions it is mediating; the reader must remain focused beyond what is narrated in "Nausicaa," allowing each of the opposed positions to provide us with useful language while remaining in control of how that language is to be used in constructing a "true" version of the story.

It is my contention that the main lesson of "Nausicaa" in the unfolding of the reader's education about how to read the novel is that neither what we can now call romance idealism nor naive empiricism can be allowed to tell the rest of the story. Neither language—neither Gerty's easily recognized excess nor Bloom's more subtle excess—can tell the truth about who Bloom is and what the novel is trying to do with him. Gerty's language is so obviously excessive that it may seem unnecessary to offer an analysis of it from this point of point. However, some of its features do deserve our attention, for what she tries to present in such a lame fashion (an awful pun, I know, but one I think Joyce wants us to make) is to be taken seriously later in the novel in the very different kind of language and style of "Ithaca." Her sentimental idealism presents Bloom as a figure from romance, a man of heroic sensibility with a mysterious destiny. And while we do not trust her way of telling this story, this is exactly what Joyce wants to present. Joyce parodies the romance idealism that has failed to sustain its vision against the rigors of naive empiricism, not only to debunk romance but in a shrewd and indirect way to express his own desires. We can see how loaded with patently false idealism her language is in this sampling from her depiction of Bloom: "Yes, it was her he was looking at, and there was meaning in his look. His eyes burned into her as though they would search her through and through, read her very soul" (13.411–13). Besides the incorrect grammar ("it was her he was looking at"), we have good reason to dismiss her language as false, for while he is looking intently at her, it is not to read her soul. She indulges in such rhetorically driven flights of fancy that she distorts the truth of the scene: "He was in deep mourning, she could see that, and the story of a haunting sorrow was written on his face" (421–22). We know how light his mourning really is, though we can make claims that his wearing black, on a symbolic or allegorical level, is indeed a sign of deep-seated and lengthy mourning over the loss of his son eleven years ago and the gradual loss of Molly since that time and rupturing on this very day. But that is not why he is wearing black on this day, nor is his face at this moment dominated by haunting sorrow. While we dismiss Gerty's understanding of his mourning, we might be prompted by her sentimental speculations to make more meaningful guesses of our own, and we will be encouraged to do so quite fully in "Eumaus" and "Ithaca." Gerty continues, "The very heart of the girlwoman went out to him, her dreamhusband, because she knew on the instant it was him" (430–31). We simply cannot allow any credence to a narrator who talks like this, and we are meant, I think, to delight in Joyce's ability to provide such a parody. Yet in his cunning manner Joyce uses Gerty to express his highest desire as a writer, to represent the ideal. There is a level on which we may apply such words to Bloom, as a "dreamhusband," for in "Penelope," Molly will be falling asleep and recalling her younger days with her husband-to-be, and she will say "yes" to him in that dreamlike state. We will learn to reapply such language to Bloom in later episodes. A poem Gerty has copied from a newspaper called *Art thou real, my ideal?* provides the key for our reading of her narration: her ideal has been kept safe from any contact with reality by virtue of the language she has acquired from her girlish culture.

Joyce also imbues her narration with (from Gerty's point of view at least) unconscious associations with the traditional iconography surrounding the Blessed Virgin Mary and with associations with the end of Dante's *Paradiso,* where Mary is the figure to whom Dante must appeal in order to receive the final vision that confers full beatitude upon him. These are in addition to the sounds of the men's temperance retreat from the nearby church where the men recite the litany of "Our Lady of Loreto." All of these are intended to add to Gerty's presentation of herself as the ideal lady in association with Mary, the ideal lady of the Catholic Church. We will have to return to this point in "Eumaus," where Bloom shows Stephen a picture of a more realistic ideal lady, Molly, as a lure to get him to make the journey back to 7 Eccles street, and in "Penelope," where Molly is more fully offered, this time to the reader, as the more realistic version of the ideal lady, who ends her monologue imagining herself "swimming in roses," Joyce's version of Dante's final cantos of *Paradiso.* Gerty anticipates Molly, as the falsely sentimental version of the ideal lady, and "Nausicaa" introduces the reader to the need for a woman to aspire to this role.

In the middle of the episode sentimental excess is punctured by Bloom's gravity, and the rest of "Nausicaa" is written in the style of the early episodes. We must ask why Joyce has made this decision to return to naturalistic depiction at this point in the novel, to be abandoned for good until Bloom has fallen asleep at the end of "Ithaca," after which Molly gets to "think" for us. Of course, one thing a return to Bloom's consciousness does is to reduce the pretensions of Gerty's sentimental romance. We know with the authority of Bloom's thoughts what he was thinking about her as she was elevating him, all too easily and without any grounding at all in reality, to the heights of romance heroism. But it seems to me that her language was so patently false that we really do not need this return to Bloom-thoughts in order to doubt and debunk her narration. Borrowing McKeon's terminology and schema once again, we are in position to see a dialectical relation between Gerty's style and Bloom's style that exposes the early style as merely rhetorical, as no more realistic than any other narrative screen. No longer does the depiction of the interior consciousness seem innocent and objective, but just another writerly device for representation and just as open to skepticism. We cannot help but be aware of what the first and second halves of "Nausicaa" share: the need to represent consciousness through language. No longer do we marvel at the lucidity of the transparent window onto Bloom's mind; now we wonder if such representation is as neutral as we were prepared to believe before "Sirens," "Cyclops," and the first half of "Nausicaa." Joyce has presented the dialectical relationship between romance idealism and naive empiricism, suggesting the more sophisticated position that the reader can now occupy, that of an extreme skepticism that can doubt Bloom's ability to speak the truth about the world as much as it can doubt Gerty's.

This point may be expressed in the following way: as false as Gerty's language is, at least she is on the lookout for the ideal, which the naturalist depicting Bloom's consciousness has apparently abandoned entirely. As limited as Gerty is in one important way, so is the naturalist in another, equally important regard. For instance, Gerty sees herself as "a radiant little vision, in sooth, almost maddening in its sweetness. . . . Her woman's instinct told her that she raised the devil in him and at the thought a burning scarlet swept from throat to brow till the lovely colour of her face became a glorious rose" (13.511–12, 517–20). This recalls the ending of *Paradiso,* where Dante has a "radiant little vision" that is "almost maddening in its sweetness" in the form of a "glorious rose." It is humorous to consider that Dante's reaching the highest heaven may indeed have been like "raising the devil in him." Gerty wishes to appear to Bloom as a vision of a glorious rose, but Bloom, and the naturalist who presents him to us, will have none of that. In his half of the episode Bloom tries to identify the kind of perfume Gerty was wearing: "Heliotrope? No. Hyacinth? Hm. Roses, I think. She'd like that kind of scent. Sweet and cheap: soon sour. Why Molly likes opoponax" (1009–10). This is a wonderfully devastating debunking of sentimental excess: it is cheap in that it is easy and takes so little work; it is sweet to the point of noxiousness, turning sour soon. But when Bloom thinks that Molly would reject roses, while he might be right about her taste in perfume, we become aware that he has not read "Penelope," as we have, that he has not witnessed her expressed wish to be "swimming in roses" as she brings the novel to its close. While we reject Gerty's too facile elevation, we also reject Bloom's equally easy rejection of it.

The way Joyce chooses to end this episode reveals to us precisely the nature of the limitation of the initial style now being used to present Bloom to us for the last time in the novel. When Bloom decides to leave a message in the sand for Gerty to read the next day if she were to pass that way again, he can only write "I AM A." The efforts to decide what he would have written if he had not decided it was "useless" and "hopeless" to write in the sand seem to me seriously mistaken from the start. The word "useless," which we identified earlier as this Ulysses' special word, is perhaps now to be associated with the kind of narration that has been presenting Bloom's thoughts again. The point is that such depiction cannot fill in this blank to reveal Bloom's identity or description. If the naturalist has such easy and total access to Bloom's mind, then we can say that not even Bloom knows how to fill in this blank, for we do not see him think anything at all about this. If this novel is about the raising of Bloom's identity to the level of allegory, then this style and this man can do no more than present the unfinished sentence "I AM A." If the novel ended here, we would have to agree with Herring's position that identity in *Ulysses* is indeterminate. But obviously the novel does not end here. It is up to the rest of the novel to fill in the blank. "Nausicaa" leads us to this unfinished sentence that alerts us to the purpose of the last episodes, which is to tell us who Bloom is.

"Oxen of the Sun"

Joyce makes explicit in "Oxen of the Sun" what had been implicit in the previous two episodes, that *Ulysses* is enacting the history of the novel in order to arrive at a form and a method that can provide the legitimate process from the world of naturalism on the one hand to the world of symbolic depiction of the ideal on the other. In the previous three episodes we have seen an attempt to expand the dimensions of Bloom's character through the negation of certain ways of telling, bringing us to their limit while at the same time suggesting that something larger is going in with Bloom than can yet be adequately told. "Oxen of the Sun" is the logical conclusion to this process, for in this episode Joyce parodies as many styles and variations of narrative forms in English prose history as he can devise. It is as if he tries out, in order to reject, each and every prose style that has yet been constructed in the history of prose fiction, before even the rise of the novel.

The question that we have learned to ask in the present study is: why does Joyce invent just this style at just this moment for the continuation of Bloom's story? We ought to be fully aware that this approach places premium value upon plot and character over style and technique, that we have decided to subordinate modernist experiment to traditional novelistic concern for story, as Sultan convincingly argues. This is therefore a place of contention as I argue about basic models of interpretation for *Ulysses*, that I am placing value on the technical extravagances as they advance meaning and not as ends in themselves. More recent critics, such as Fritz Senn and Brook Thomas and even Karen Lawrence, have taken the other path and argued that style becomes the motive behind the development of these later episodes, that our enjoyment of Joyce's technical prowess becomes an end in itself. Such a conclusion is a result of the misappropriation of recent theoretical developments. We have gladly chosen to replace the intention of our literary authors for the wills of our theorists, to give up on learning the difficult lessons of our literary artists and replacing them with the lessons of an innovative yet limited set of language theorists. We have, as Charles Altieri argues, become suspicious of authorial intention while indulging in often uncritical acceptance of a powerful theorist. I choose to read for authorial intention and the author's lesson for me as a careful reader. I choose in this present case to read the lessons about reading that Joyce lays out before us as readers of his novel.

With "Sirens" we were able to say that the musical style was invented in order to present Bloom's choice of active participation in suffering over a sentimental resignation to the effects of time, even though it could have been argued in the earlier episodes that Bloom was melodramatically resigned to the effects of time as he avoided doing anything to prevent the breach of his marriage. The stylistic and technical innovation of "Sirens" allowed us to notice an expansion of Bloom's character, even though that character had not undergone the change. Here is Joyce's revision of the history of the novel: rather than have the characters change in order to resolve the plot difficulties, Joyce makes the modes of narration undergo the changes that will resolve them. The innovations of "Cyclops" allow for the further expansion of Bloom's character, as we are allowed to begin to make heroic associations of Bloom with Elijah, Saint Paul, and Christ despite the alternating styles that make such association dubious indeed. The reader is being shown how the origin of the novel, in the dialectical relationship of romance idealism and scientific empiricism, makes problematic the presentation of heroism, which is glimpsed anyway by a reader who is positioned beyond their limitations to recognize the importance of Bloom's defense of love to a hostile audience. In "Nausicaa" this lesson is deepened as the reader continues to occupy a privileged "third" position beyond Gerty's romantic excess and Bloom's down-to-earth naturalism, a privileged ground from which the language of idealism can be taken from Gerty and applied to Bloom in a way Bloom could not allow himself. Even though it can be plausibly argued that Bloom looks pathetic in "Nausicaa"—after all, he is a cuckold who has just masturbated in public—the innovations in style and technique have advanced the plot more than the series of events themselves have done, for we are now more able to make claims about Bloom than we were at, say, the end of "Hades." The plot advances because the styles advance.

Now that Bloom has left blank his identity for us at the end of "Nausicaa," we are ready for an episode that might begin filling in that blank. In "Oxen," when Stephen reappears in the novel after a six-hour and three-episode absence, we are in a sense ready for the continuation of plot proper, of a set of events that bring the two men together for whatever purpose the novel will eventually present. One might question the invention of an almost opaque screen of language for this return to the main plot, for "Oxen of the Sun" poses the most serious challenge for following plot and action of any episode in *Ulysses;* as Hayman puts it, "the verbal structure, which impedes rather than facilitates our attempts to follow the action it adorns, hacks away at the very possibility of communication while conveying the simple circumstance through a variety of absurdly dated and variously appropriate literary positions" (Hayman, 100). I agree with this assessment, though challenges to it such as Brook Thomas's are welcome and make us work harder for our points. Thomas does not want us to "assume that the novel has a referential subject prior to its language" (Thomas, 13), and so we should read what is before us—the language—and not what is behind the language. This seems to be taking the fruits of poststructuralism too quickly and easily and making Joyce into something he is not. The early episodes establish the illusion, in and through language of course, of solid and round characters that is meant to persist despite the obfuscating style(s) of "Oxen." As Hayman says, a simple circumstance is conveyed here, namely that Bloom and Stephen are in the same company for the first time this day and that Bloom decides to follow Stephen, to watch out and over him. Quoting Hayman again, "Everything [in "Oxen"] conspires to distract us from the characters' dilemmas, effectively limiting their validity as individuals" (Hayman, 101). We are not within Bloom's consciousness as he makes the decision to follow Stephen; in fact, we strain to see this crucial plot development at all. The individuals we have been calling Stephen and Bloom still exist—and, I will add and risk the contempt of the ideologues, with the illusion of being outside language—but the stylistic extravagance focuses our attention on the more essential action, Bloom's decision to follow and protect Stephen. The abstracting of the two from the naturalistic contexts of the early episodes has not invalidated those episodes; rather, this process of abstraction has been so successful that it has given us a way to focus on what is permanent and valuable. In these "language" episodes of *Ulysses,* and especially in "Oxen," language has been placed in the foreground of our readerly attention as the problem to be confronted by the modern writer who wishes to elevate a human to some sort of epic status. That there is no adequate language available is suggested by the parodies of the various styles used by prose writers in English from the inception of the language. It is as if the language is all used up, and the writer must experiment more boldly than ever just to get a simple point across, to get a simple plot event made significant.

So as the plot thickens (I use the cliché to make the point as boldly as I can), so does the style. We have almost lost sight of Bloom and Stephen as individuals, each with his own peculiar and eccentric way of moving about in the world; instead we strain to see the broad outline of their novelistic fates, which is simply that they are together and will remain in each other's company for most of the rest of the novel. Once again I would like to turn to the responses of my students, who have often complained that they would love to know what Bloom is thinking about as he makes this decision, and what Stephen is thinking about as Bloom watches and follows him. As typical responses of readers brought up on readerly novels, such expectations are just the point. We are meant precisely *not* to have this information, for it would detract from the essential and permanent. It would at the least render their emerging union idiosyncratic and odd, and at the worst deflate and puncture its significance, the way Bloom's consciousness punctured Gerty's rhetoric. As readers of "Oxen" we are only permitted to make broad, sweeping statements about the development of the plot, or more specifically, that Bloom the father has finally joined the company of Stephen the son.

This brings us to further complications about the point of the prose parodies in "Oxen." These are designed to lead us to reflect on the history of prose fiction in English and some of its most dominant plots, the construction of a family through language and the discovery of an orphan's true identity. One way of viewing the origin of the novel is to acknowledge how a new genre is required in order to provide the discourse or the language that can help stabilize newly emerging social and legal institutions, especially the social and legal formations of the bourgeois family unit. The relations of fathers and sons must be newly codified, and so the novel is constructed to make such relations important and plausible. The subplot of the foundling is relevant, as the orphan without clear social identity and without legal rights learns through the course of his story of his true parentage and so is brought suddenly back into the security of the family unit. McKeon provides a thorough background for these points, as he documents how the rise of the novel coincides with the destabilization of social categories in early modern England. As the laws of inheritance underwent change, England saw "the accelerated mobilization of social, intellectual, legal, and institutional fictions whose increasingly ostentatious use signaled their incapacity to serve the ideological ends for which they were designed." These "legal fictions" are meant to provide a stable and legitimate set of laws establishing a line of inheritance. According to McKeon, "the novel emerged in early modern England as a new literary fiction designed to engage the social and ethical problems the established literary fictions could no longer mediate" (McKeon, 153). Joyce is not mediating the same complex of issues that went into the emergence of the novel in eighteenth-century England, but McKeon's analysis provides a carefully documented background against which we can read "Oxen of the Sun." Joyce parodies the history of the novel in the very episode in which Bloom and Stephen are brought together with the potential for the one to become the father of the other. Joyce seems to know about the novel exactly what McKeon discovers, that it is a genre originated in questions of family, of fathers being established as "legal fictions" so that the sons can inherit the fathers' goods. Bloom and Stephen come together in a maternity hospital—where else should a son be born to a father?—and are presented to the reader through a thick screen of language based on the history of the genre invented for just such a purpose.

The episode begins with a series of utterances that announce the birth of a baby boy: "Hoopsa boyaboy hoopsa! Hoopsa boyaboy hoopsa! Hoopsa boyaboy hoopsa!" (14.5–6). Our frame for reading the episode is to watch for the development of what had been introduced to the reader only through the reductive mockery of Mulligan, that Stephen is "Japhet in search of a father" (1.561). The reader is in a position to recall the earlier episodes that have made Stephen's relation to his father problematic and how Bloom may be the one to replace him in Stephen's sense of himself. We recall that in "Hades," Bloom sees Stephen in the process of walking out to the strand to think the thoughts we already read in "Proteus," and though he points him out to Simon, the biological father misses him. We recall also that, right after seeing Stephen, Bloom's thoughts turn to Rudy in a tender speculation of a father who desires a son. We recall Stephen's words in "Scylla and Charybdis" that allow us to think of fatherhood as a legal fiction, as a relationship established through the discourse of fiction. With all this in mind, we read the history of the novel in "Oxen" as Joyce's effort to write the language that allows for the possibility of Bloom's adoption of Stephen as his heir.

Years of critical attention have made us aware that the episode is loaded with emphases on the process of birth, from contraception to conception to labor to the delivery of a newborn son to Mina Purefoy. The episode is so difficult that we can say, with proper respect for motherhood, that reading is analogous to labor. But the episode ends, not with the birth of a new Purefoy (that happens about three-quarters of the way through "Oxen"), but with the outflinging of the drinking party onto the streets of Dublin to continue their debauch. Following the young men is the "johnny in the black duds," Bloom keeping pace with them so as to keep a fatherly eye on Stephen. From the point of view of the reader of "Oxen," one can say that the labor of reading this episode results in the "birth" of Stephen as the object of Bloom's care, as the process of "adoption" is begun and to be continued. The reader is giving birth to this possibility.

This process of reading and birthing is paramount in "Oxen." As Bloom joins the company of the already inebriated young men, the conversation turns to issues of conception and birth, and the classic Catholic dilemma: if a difficult labor places both mother and child in jeopardy, which one should be sacrificed in order to save the other? The students "all cried with one acclaim nay, by our Virgin Mother, the wife should live and the babe to die" (14.214–15). Their opinion goes directly against the teachings of the Catholic Church and so also against the claims of fatherhood. As Stephen explained in "Scylla and Charybdis," the Church is founded upon the mystery of fatherhood and not motherhood, and so it is only a logical extension of that principle that in the act of delivery the rights of the father should supersede the rights of the husband; that is, the child should live and the wife die. As this irreverent talk continues, Stephen and Bloom begin to emerge from the noise as distinct from the others at the table: "Thereat laughed they all right jocundly only young Stephen and sir Leopold which never durst laugh too open by reason of a strange humour" (237–38). This is hardly enough to allow the reader to make claims about a father-and-son relation for the two, but it is the beginning of their emergence from the dense background of noise and from the dense language of representation that the episode throws at us. The students continue the discussion and turn to the only married man present, Bloom, to give his opinion on the case: "A wariness of mind he would answer as fitted all and, laying his hand to jaw, he said dissembling, as his wont was, that as it was informed him, who had even loved the art of physic as might a layman, and agreeing also with experience of so seldomseen an accident it was good for that mother church belike at one blow had birth and death pence and in such sort deliverly he scaped their questions" (253–59). This is a happy moment for Bloom that earns him the praise of those who want him to exhibit an Odysseus-like quick wit. But it is noteworthy that, in his jest, he has pronounced for the father and against the mother. Upon hearing Bloom's bon mot, "young Stephen was a marvellous glad man" (260), happy, I imagine, to hear someone defend fatherhood as well as to hear such agile wit. The reader is straining to see a growing admiration of Bloom in Stephen. A few lines later we are given a stronger indication of what is going on in Bloom's mind as he looks at Stephen: "now sir Leopold that had of his body no manchild for an heir looked upon his friend's son and was shut up in sorrow for his forepassed happiness and as sad he was that him failed a son of such gentle courage" (271). It is the reader's job to extricate such moments from the density of this text and evaluate them as the significant action of the plot.

This brings us back to a thorny question about texts and our efforts to read them. We must return to the lesson of "Cyclops" that the "truth" is not to be found within the mind of any character, no matter how lucidly drawn and depicted, nor in any language at all, for Bloom's defense of love is almost mute and we are forced to intuit the truth of love and Bloom's capacity for that virtue beyond the text. Joyce has been pushing us to the limits of language, from "Sirens" to "Oxen," so that we were led to conclude that, for Joyce at any rate, the "truth" exists on the other side of language, outside of language, and that we are to read through and beyond the language of these stylistically experimental and language-dense episodes to a perception that can only be hinted at in language but that is fully outside of and before any effort to express it in words. Joyce chose to establish these characters in the early, naturalistic episodes with the strongest illusion of their roundness and solidity so that when we reach these "language" episodes, we do not forget those early episodes but rely on them to pass beyond language and recover the characters, to read through the language to their "actual" existence. These "language" episodes are meant to show us the limit of the medium that must be used to present—and not represent—truth.

For instance, when we learn from one of the many narrative voices of "Oxen" that Bloom "bore fast friendship to sir Simon and to this his son young Stephen" 198–99), are we meant now to disregard what we witnessed through the lucid and accurate narrative lens of the early episodes (in this case, "Hades") and now believe that Bloom and Simon Dedalus are fast friends? Or are we to take with us what we learned from that episode, as if it were reality, and apply that knowledge to this episode, using the early episode as the bedrock of reality from which we can sort through and determine what is so and what is not in these later episodes? If we affirm the latter, then we are placed in a precarious position in the later episodes, not being able to rely on these narrators to tell the truth. But if we grant equal validity to both, we are in a more precarious position, now doubting the veracity of the early episodes as much as the later, and the novel teeters on the brink of meaninglessness. I choose the former, even if only because the other option would threaten our ability to read *Ulysses* to its ending, and Joyce does find a way in "Ithaca" to write in a way that is valid for both the early and late episodes.

Here is another angle on this same problem. When we read that the eating utensils on the table are "frightful swords and knives that are made in a great cavern by swinking demons out of white flames" (14.143–45), we could pretend, in what seems an absurd reading strategy, to believe this narration and that we are, as long as this narrative voice is in place, in the world of magical possibilities of Malory; or we can make the more sensible claim that forks are still forks and knives are still knives and this narrative voice must be read through to arrive at the truth of the situation. But there is yet one more twist and turn to make in thinking this problem through. The possibility of magical transformation by style, in and by the proper language, while to be rejected here, is to be taken seriously regarding the relation of Bloom and Stephen, for Joyce is still searching for the style and language that would allow us to agree that Bloom is becoming father to Stephen.

In "Oxen" a moment of memory is crucial to the beginning of this transformation, and memory will be crucial to this transformation through "Eumaus" and "Ithaca" to its ending in the last words of "Penelope." We are told that Bloom becomes lost in a moment of "retrospective arrangement" (14.1044), a phrase that should by now alert us to the capacity for transformation made possible by a rereading of past events held in memory. The allegory of theologians is analogous to the process of memory and perhaps is even dependent upon it, for memory rereads a moment taken from the past and explores its meaning from a present perspective. Memory in *Ulysses* is understood as a transformative agency and no mere receptacle or storehouse of images from the past; using Rickard's terms and analysis, memory is activist, not passivist, for Joyce. As such, memory is much like the kind of allegory I have alluded to as the shaping principle of the novel, and so we might begin to see how "Penelope" will function as the conclusion to this day, when Molly remembers—or now we can say "rereads"—a moment from her past with Bloom. Both memory and the allegory of theologians are ways of rereading, and as such Dante understands them in *Vita Nuova* and his *Divina Commedia*, as we will see again in "Eumaus."[5] Having come into contact with a young man he would like as a son, Bloom reviews (let us agree to call this process "rereading") his past to see if it can be "retrospectively arranged" to fit this present. He returns to his own youth, seeing himself as he was at roughly Stephen's age, and when he comes back to the present, we are made to contemplate the possibility that one of these young men might be his son: "Now he is himself paternal and these about him might be his sons. Who can say?"

(1062–63). But this possibility is too easily won, and the text almost immediately takes it way: "No, Leopold. Name and memory solace thee not. That youthful illusion of thy strength was taken from thee—and in vain. No son of thy loins is by thee. There is none to be for Leopold, what Leopold was for Rudolph" (1074–77). At this juncture memory is only a receptacle and not an esemplastic power, and so the possibility that Bloom can claim one of these young men as his son is only an illusion.

Stephen makes an important contribution to the reader's ability to understand the role of memory in this episode, and for the novel as a whole, when he is reminded of figures from his past: "You have spoken of the past and its phantoms, Stephen said. Why think of them? If I call them into life across the waters of Lethe will not the poor ghosts troop to my call? Who supposes it? I, Bous Stephanoumenos, bullockbefriending bard, am lord and giver of their life" (14.1112–16). It is no accident that we are brought back to the epithet Stephen gave to himself (in anticipation of Mulligan's mockery) at the end of "Nestor," for it was in that episode that Stephen elaborated, silently, his dissatisfaction with Blake's radical theory of imagination, which we recall rejected the claims of memory altogether. Here Stephen claims for himself power over memory, the power to bring images from the past back to life. The artist, the lord and master over the ghosts from the past, has this power over memory, to make it more than a mere storehouse of images but an active agency capable of transforming the present.

Stephen's reflection on his artistic powers is immediately undercut by Lynch: "That answer and those leaves, Vincent said to him, will adorn you more fitly when something more, and greatly more, than a capful of light odes can call your genius father" (14.1117–19). While we must agree with Lynch that Stephen has not yet earned the powers he claims for himself, are we, as empowered readers, able to extract this moment from the context and apply it as an interpretative principle? It seems to set up for consideration as climax of the episode an image from Bloom's past that features Stephen, Stephen's mother, Molly, and himself. It is important enough to quote in full:

> A scene disengages itself in the observer's memory, evoked, it would seem, by a word of so natural a homeliness as if those days were really present (as some thought) with their immediate pleasures. A shaven space of lawn one soft May evening, the wellremember-ed grove of lilacs at Roundtown, purple and white, fragrant slender spectators of the game but with much real interest in the pellets as they run slowly over the sward or collide and stop, one with its fellow, with a brief alert shock. And yonder about the grey urn where the water moves at times in thoughtful irrigation you saw another as fragrant sisterhood, Floey, Atty, Tiny and their darker

friend with I know not what of arresting in her pose then, Our Lady of the Cherries, a comely brace of them pendant from an ear, bringing out the foreign warmth of the skin so daintily against the cool ardent fruit. A lad of four or five in linseywoolsey (blossomtime but there will be cheer in the kindly hearth when ere long the bowls are gathered and hutched) is standing on the urn secured by that circle of girlish fond hands. He frowns a little just as this young man does now with perhaps too conscious enjoyment of the danger but must needs glance at whiles towards where his mother watches from the *piazzetta* giving upon the flowerclose with a faint shadow of remoteness or of reproach (*alles Vergangliche*) in her glad look.

Mark this further and remember. The end comes suddenly. (14.1359-79)

Bloom arrives at an image from his memory that will prove crucial for the resolution of the novel's plot. Rickard notes that Joyce calls this passage: rendered in "the grave beauty" of Newman's prose style is the "fulcrum" that "hold[s] up the rest" of the episode (Rickard, 126). This "involuntary memory" called up by chance association is the center of "Oxen" because it brings Stephen into a possible filial relation to Bloom. The frown upon Stephen's face at present conjures up an image from the past when Stephen was only four or five and wearing the same frown. The scene disentangled from memory seems so real, it is as if "those days were really present there (as some thought)." Scenes from memory can have the illusion of being so real that they seem present, and some thinkers have advanced as much about memory; this will be useful language for arguing in "Penelope" about the way that memory scene functions as the close of the novel. But this scene in "Oxen" brings Bloom back to that "wellremembered" lilac grove at Mat Dillon's where he first met Molly, the scene that he has already recalled several times this day and that Kenner wants us to consider an image of Eden for Bloom. This time the scene has expanded, for Bloom now remembers, for the first time, that Stephen was there and that the young Dillon sisters and Molly were encircling him. Molly is referred to as "Our Lady of the Cherries," an allusion to the iconography of the Blessed Virgin Mary as queen of heaven and its delights. And Stephen's mother is there, looking upon the little boy with pleasure and encouragement. Bloom and Stephen, Molly and Stephen's mother: Stephen is now an orphan haunted by that mother and searching for a father and perhaps new mother, and this memory scene allows for the "family romance" aspect of the novel's history to be enacted in *Ulysses*. We will see in "Eumaus" how Bloom will entice Stephen back to 7 Eccles street with a picture of Molly and how the text allows us to imagine Molly's role in this romance. This crucial memory scene in "Oxen" is in a way the pivot of this plot, encouraging Bloom to see in Stephen the son he has been missing. It is an extraordinary coincidence that Bloom's first encounter with Stephen was on the same evening in the same Edenic setting as his first glimpse of Molly. We know now that there are no coincidences in this novel, only accidents that eventually fall into place as part of a subtle and complex design. So Bloom now can take this image from memory and use it as the basis for his need for Stephen, to be able to return to that Eden where all three were once present.

It is fitting that this scene be rendered in the style of Cardinal Newman, whom Joyce regarded as the "greatest of English prose writers" and who, in an episode of parodies, "alone is rendered pure" (Rickard, 126). Newman's great text is about memory, about his ability to understand moments from his past that may have seemed inconsequential at the time as, in retrospective arrangement, crucial and pivotal in marking his life's course. Bloom had often thought of this first evening with Molly but had never, until this moment, recalled that Stephen was present in the manner just depicted. What he had not recalled at all because of its apparent meaninglessness is now rendered central to his life, the "fulcrum" of the episode and of this family romance.

There is a passing allusion to the end of Goethe's *Faust,* part 2, when Faust's eternal spirit is welcomed into heaven and all that remains in the devil's hands is his temporal parts (*alles Vergangliche,* all that is transitory). That dramatic poem ends with a prayer to the Blessed Virgin Mary, who, as the "eternal-feminine," draws the penitent souls upward to heaven. Joyce is able to suggest with this allusion to *Faust* that "all that is transitory" about Bloom and Stephen is unimportant and about to pass away, and that in this memory scene we are approaching the permanent and absolute, the truth of the plot of *Ulysses.* In an episode that abounds with images of motherhood, we are drawing upward to the permanent and absolute by the power of Molly—the "eternal-feminine"—in Bloom's memory. It is the power of memory, which for Bloom is under the spell of Molly as "Our Lady of the Cherries," that makes "all that is transitory" wither away, and what is left behind is the "truth" of Bloom's life, that scene with Molly and Stephen in the lilac garden. The temporal parts of the plot have become trivial, and we have approached the permanent and true. What was promised at the beginning of "Aeolus"—the process of abstraction that would move us away from the merely human to the realm of the permanent and true—has come to be.

When the memory scene vanishes, someone says, "Mark this farther and remember." This can be Bloom speaking to himself, as he calls attention to the image from his past while deciding on what course of action and what role to start playing regarding Stephen. But it can also be the voice of the author, and not merely one of his narrators, a voice of authority telling us that this scene from Bloom's memory is special and important and the truth that we must use and follow to the end of the novel. It is an authorial and authorized voice telling us what to accept and remember as we puzzle over the mystery of the novel, for the end will come suddenly: the end of "Oxen" bursts upon us almost immediately, as Stephen "outflings" the suggestion that they all continue their drinking binge at Burke's. The end of the novel will come suddenly as well, and without this memory scene and without the proper focus on the role of memory, it will come and go without understanding. Stephen is born in Bloom's mind through the agency of memory as a possible substitute for Rudy.

Immediately upon these directions from the author the narrator of the moment, who sounds like Ruskin, goes on to connect this birth in Bloom's mind to Christ's nativity. Once again a long citation is necessary:

> Mark this farther and remember. The end comes suddenly. Enter that antechamber of birth where the studious are assembled and note their faces. Nothing, as it seems, there of rash or violent. Quietude of custody, rather, befitting their station in that house, the vigilant watch of shepherds and of angels about a crib in Bethlehem of Juda long ago. But as before the lightning the serried stormclouds, heavy with preponderant excess of moisture, in swollen masses turgidly distended, compass the earth and sky in one vast slumber, impending above parched field and drowsy oxen and blighted growth of shrub and verdure till in an instant a flash rives their centers and with reverberation of the thunder the cloudburst pours its torrent, so and not otherwise was the transformation, violent and instantaneous, upon the utterance of the word.
> Burke's! outflings my lord Stephen. . . . (14.1379–91)

We are invited to enter the stable and join with the studious who are assembled to witness the manifestation of the Incarnation of God in an infant in a crib. The birth of Stephen in Bloom's mind is thus made to be associated with the Incarnation, which is the manifestation of God in a violent and sudden and instantaneous manner, analogous to a thunderclap and lightning. We are brought back to Stephen's witty rejoinder to Mr. Deasy in "Nestor," where God is defined as a shout in the street. Not gradual and part of a human process, but sudden and violent is this manifestation. Stephen has been transformed, violently and instantaneously, into a child who might become the son of Bloom.

This episode ends with a mad dash to Nighttown, where Bloom will follow Stephen with paternal solicitude. The last paragraph of "Oxen" is significant to my argument, for in it are snatches from the preaching of

Alexander J. Dowie, whose sermon was announced in the throwaway Bloom threw away at the opening of "Lestrygonians." That throwaway has returned once again, with its promise of the coming of Elijah once more asserted: "Elijah is coming! Washed in the Blood of the Lamb" (14.1580). Amid the apocalyptic warnings of this preacher, Bloom follows Stephen, now as the father overseeing the doings of a prodigal son. The preparation for this relation is now nearing its end, and so Elijah has appeared and accomplished what Malachi said he would: he has turned the hearts of the fathers toward their children. And perhaps even more is to be accomplished still: as Alexander J. Dowie insists, the restoration of the Church is the matter in hand. And Joyce's allegory will bring about this possibility as well.

This grouping of episodes, from "Sirens" to "Oxen of the Sun," presents language as a problem confronting the modern literary artist in his attempt to elevate human behavior and character to the status of the ideal, to the epic level of nobility. In each of these "language" episodes Joyce manages to suggest that language is the necessary medium through which ideals may be communicated, though the ideal itself is outside of language. He suggests this by making us read *through* the screens of narration to the *other side* of language where character and plot exist. The screens of narration in these episodes have all proven to be unreliable, leading us to conclude that language is used more easily for lying than for truth-telling, for the truth is not within language but outside it. The language in these narrative screens often seems outdated, as if language has been used up, exhausted, no longer to be trusted to perform the important task of representing values. Joyce calls upon his extraordinary skill with words to present these various narrative screens that the reader is forced to read through, see through, to the other side where the truth of Bloom and Stephen lies. The truth is not inside Bloom's or Stephen's consciousness, nor is it inside language itself. It is "out there" in a world of ideals that exist independently of human consciousness and independently of human language that nonetheless must be used to present these ideals from one consciousness to another. That conviction—that the truth can be so communicated—makes these episodes important in their experiments with language. Now that the "true plot" of *Ulysses* has been abstracted from the naturalist's hands and presented to the reader's consciousness, we are ready to watch Bloom prepare for the epic role of father to Stephen's role as son and on another level altogether, a level of meaning I call allegory, to watch for the restoration of the Church in Zion. To continue the naturalistic narration and advance these two symbolic levels all at the same time requires Joyce's use of the "allegory of theologians." We are now ready to watch Joyce's modernist allegory.

Chapter Four

The Novel as *Nostos*
Family Romance Becomes Epic

"Oxen of the Sun" begins for *Ulysses* the "plot" that will now occupy the last episodes, the relation of Bloom the father and Stephen the son. The traditional plot of the English bourgeois novel finally becomes the main action of this modernist novel, as the "orphan" is about to discover his true identity and as the son will now begin a relation with a man who will become his father; and perhaps, on taking him home, Bloom will introduce Stephen to Molly, who then can become the mother. The plot of *Ulysses* can be described as a traditional family romance, as the discourse of this novel prepares for the foundation of a family for the reckless orphan.

The groundwork for this plot was gradually established throughout the earlier episodes, from Mulligan's flippant description of Stephen as "Japhet in search of a father," through Bloom's musings upon Rudy, and most tellingly through Stephen's *Hamlet* theory and its attendant claims about fatherhood. But in "Oxen" this plot bursts forth with thunder and lightning and the madcap ending as father follows son into Nighttown. Joyce's purpose in *Ulysses* is not merely to write a more oblique and complex family romance, but to raise this plot to epic status, to make of this father, mother, and son relation a return to an original kind of family configuration to be renewed by this novel that is straining to become an epic. Since the present culture no longer recognizes this original family and in fact has repressed it from our cultural consciousness, it can be achieved only by the greatest effort and daring. The family romance becomes a plot worthy of the epic.

Joyce noticed that *The Odyssey* is in some ways novelistic in plot in that the great warrior hero Odysseus has domestic goals, merely the wish to return home to wife and son, father and people. This ancient epic poem has a domestic plot, and in this it is the perfect model on which to write a modernist novel with epic design. It is worth noting that the ancient story is about alienation, about not feeling at home in the world, about the brave and even heroic effort to return to a condition from which history (the Trojan War) has separated humanity. In *The Odyssey* only the great man can overcome the various obstacles on the way back home, safely return to his island and enter his house, and face the suitors and kill all one hundred or so with only the help of a couple of aged servants and his son. The lesson from the ancient epic is that it is heroic to bridge the gap between ourselves and the world and feel at home in the world again. Only an epic hero, it can be said, is capable of ending his wandering in a state of exile and return to the home that was ours before the fall.

So by writing a novel based on the ancient epic with this domestic plot, Joyce intends to raise the traditional plot of family romance to epic heights by making the return to the original family configuration his version of the return home. The establishment of the original family moves away from novelistic plot to epic grandeur and heroic achievement. By giving his novel the title *Ulysses,* Joyce indicates not his belatedness from the original story, as Perry Meisel would have it, but his effort to write a version of that story for his time, a modern version of the heroic overcoming of alienation. It is the nature of the epic to provide new values for its culture: whereas *The Odyssey* is read as an epic establishment of a domestic goal for a culture emerging from warrior-dominated barbarism, *Ulysses* is an epic that is offering what seems a new kind of family for a modern culture. But the newness is only a seeming, for it is a lost original family, an ancient family, that is renewed by this text. We are going to watch how in "Circe," Joyce continues the family plot of his novel and begins to place it in a larger context with more public and universal weight; and in "Eumaus" and "Ithaca" how he infuses the novelistic plot with epic design. In his *Nostos,* Joyce will place his novel in a great tradition of epic returns, especially the great Ulysses tradition of Homer and Dante.

"Circe"

The history of the novel, as Dorrit Cohn suggests, tells the story of a turn inward as the interior consciousness of human beings engaged in conducting the ordinary business of their lives becomes increasingly the focus of the novelist's art. Joyce's response to this history of the genre in which he has chosen to work is to culminate it in the extraordinary "transparent minds" that are presented through the interior monologue style of the first six episodes. He brings that history to a close, suggesting that within the mind we can never approach the truth of a situation or condition but only the "human" aspect of the truth. In the episodes that follow the initial style we have watched how Joyce moves away from naturalism and the interior monologue and so also away from humanism and toward abstraction, toward a layer of experience we call the permanent or the absolute. Truth is not found within our minds, not in Bloom's mind, but "out there" in the world of action and observation. Yet "Circe" is famous for its extravagant presentation of the unconscious mind, and so we must account for the return of focus to the interior of the mind, in this case to the recesses of the mind unknown to the characters themselves.

The critic of this episode must never lose sight of its comic nature: the presentation of repressed psychic material is, for the most part, funny and not at all alarming, at least when it is Bloom's unconscious that is presented. (Stephen's, as we shall see, is another, very different matter, and that will be an important critical point.) As Ellmann puts it, "the suppressed desires of Bloom and Stephen [are depicted] in vaudeville form, psychoanalysis turned into a vehicle of comedy" (Ellmann, *James Joyce*, 495). Though the scenes in Bloom's hallucinations can be painful and discomforting for us to read, they never seem to pose a serious threat to Bloom and his conscious sense of an integrated personality. They never seem to leave the part of the mind beneath consciousness and become conscious; that is, they are successfully repressed, kept from entering the conscious state, where the repressed material might indeed render Bloom susceptible to its power and threaten his sense of identity and personality. Bloom's successful repression sustains and advances our estimate of him as a man of reason and poise, equanimity and balance.

We witness in "Circe" a series of hallucinated scenes in which Bloom's repressed thoughts confront, not the character, but the reader. Hugh Kenner suggests that "Circe" presents "a course of psychic purgation" (Hart and Hayman, 356), a remark that requires a small but important adjustment: the reader, not Bloom, is undergoing the "course of purgation"; the reader is in effect suffering the hallucinations and must purge from his consciousness certain attitudes we might be entertaining toward Bloom. There is a trait or a tendency in Bloom's character with which we are familiar and that may indeed be an obstacle to our consideration of Bloom as hero: his extreme passivity. "Circe" presents this passivity in its worst light, as a form of masochistic perversion that enjoys suffering. The hallucinations of "Circe" seem more of a challenge to the reader than to Bloom, especially to the reader who hopes to continue efforts of following Bloom to a heroic conclusion. While Bloom is hardly disturbed by the series of violent scenes of psychic conflict, the reader must confront the worst thoughts we can have about Bloom: that he is sexually guilty, that he has a deep-seated perversion rendering him unable to act in any way that might prevent suffering, that he has actually cooperated with Molly and Blazes to facilitate their affair so that he might enjoy the strange pleasure of being a cuckold. It is my contention that Joyce presents a comic nightmare of such hallucinations about this aspect of Bloom's character so that we can purge from our consciousness the doubt that Bloom is not heroically passive in Christ's way but merely a pathetic cuckold suffering from a degrading perversion. "Circe" is the reader's purgation, not Bloom's.[1]

I want to note that Stephen's hallucination is different from Bloom's in one important respect: he is conscious of his hallucination and acts out a response to what he witnesses—namely, the ghostly mother that haunts him. Stephen must face what is haunting him, unlike Bloom who passes unscathed through a more lengthy series of hallucinations. Stephen is placed in the same position as the reader, forced to admit the thoughts that one would rather repress but that must be confronted if we are to move on. The reader and Stephen are thus brought together as readers being prepared for an allegorical conclusion.

In the same essay Kenner offers another important comment for understanding "Circe": "To change one must only (only!) change one's role. As the episode ends, Bloom is *playing* Stephen's father" (Kenner, 360). For Kenner, the purpose of "Circe" is to allow us to assent to what we have been anticipating and hoping for, which is that Bloom can be said now to be playing the role of Stephen's father. And at the end of the episode, in the one hallucination that may be conscious for Bloom and therefore affecting his sense of identity, Bloom sees hovering over the prostrate Stephen a vision of Rudy as he would appear at age eleven, the age he would be if he had lived. Indeed, it seems right to say that at the end of "Circe" and because of "Circe," Bloom can now play this role. Kenner makes the further point, and one that complicates matters and helps us establish the proper attitude toward this and the last episodes, that a character in *Ulysses* can consciously play a role that the author has not endorsed and that the character's "true" role is something only the reader will know. Kenner makes this point in his discussion of Stephen, who thinks he is playing Hamlet while he is "really" playing Telemachus. We can make a similar point about Bloom at the end of the episode: he thinks he is playing Stephen's father, and indeed the novel seems to demand that he does; but in "reality" he will be playing the role of Christ, a role that he assumed in "Cyclops" under pressure but will play out in "Eumaus" and "Ithaca" unbeknownst to him. One plot of *Ulysses*—the plot of the novelistic *Ulysses*—demands this fatherly role for Bloom, but if Stephen refuses to play son, that plot is, if not negated, at least made suspect and weakened. It is Stephen's job as artist and ours as empowered readers to see beyond the novelistic climax of a father-and-son reunion and observe the allegorical climax of the Incarnation.

I want to sketch the "plot" of Bloom's hallucinations in order to be able to present with some force the nature of the purgation the reader is being forced to undergo. I see five major hallucinated scenes, four of which are directly related to the issue of Bloom's sexual guilt and the utter passivity that characterizes his response to Molly's infidelity. In the first, which begins at 15.248, we witness a series of figures who, in various ways and degrees, scold Bloom for his behavior. This initial series begins with his father and mother, who then give way to a sequence of "substitute" love objects in Bloom's life, beginning with Molly (who appears as, and insists on being called, "Mrs Marion" here, for it is her association with Boylan that matters to Bloom and to us and that will be slowly emerging as the main point of the hallucinations). Following Molly is a bawd offering a fifteen-year-old virgin to Bloom, which raises the possibility of incest; then Bridie Kelly, Bloom's first girlfriend; then Gerty; and then Mrs. Breen. These are the various "love objects" Bloom has had in his life who have tried to substitute for the initial love object, the mother who is denied Bloom by the first figure in the sequence, the father. Obviously this sequence is grist for a Freudian mill, and the result of that kind of analysis would be to suggest Bloom's guilt for having loved his mother and the various failed attempts to replace that love. The first hallucination, then, suggests that we must consider Bloom as a guilty and forlorn man who has lost his ability to keep his love object, his wife Molly, and that by giving her to Boylan he is reenacting that initial loss and the initial suffering attendant to that loss.

In the second major hallucination we witness a court proceeding against Bloom (15.859ff.), which quite forcefully advances the issue of Bloom's "guilt" regarding his sexual desires and behavior. On trial, he is accused of having unseemly sexual fantasies, he appears masochistic (he likes "the spanking idea," for which he positions himself and waits expectantly), and he is called a "well-known cuckold" (1117). This second sequence advances the first, in which Bloom's general sexual guilt is deepened by his perverse enjoyment of being cuckolded. One might go so far as to say that he responds to his general guilt by punishing himself by allowing Molly's affair, a punishment that, satisfying an unconsciousness call for justice, gives him pleasure.

The fourth major hallucination further humiliates Bloom in the reader's consciousness, as he must undergo a pathetic relationship with the madam of the brothel, Bella Cohen. Bella becomes Bello, and Bloom transforms into a cowering and pathetic figure dominated by a manly mistress. Bloom's guilt and shame become increasingly clear and painful for us to be witnessing when Bello says to him, "I wouldn't hurt your feelings for the world but there's a man of brawn in possession there" (15.3134–35). Scene by scene the reader's worst thoughts are presented in this nightmarish episode, exaggerated to grotesque caricature and so made comic by the excess. The reader's worst suspicions about Bloom are not to be repressed any longer but made part of the text, as we see these thoughts made into comic caricature and laugh at our worst suspicions through Joyce's buffoonery. What might have festered if not expressed we have seen and smiled at.

Indeed, Joyce shows an uncanny grasp of the nature of sexual perversion in the way these hallucinated scenes work together. Christine Froula cites Louise J. Kaplan's sociocultural analysis of perversions and claims that "perverse scenarios involve parodies of gender that are, at their most extreme, not playful and freely chosen but compulsive, desperate and fixed. They are fueled by rage against those originary authorities, the victim's parents, who, by laying down the law of gender, cut the child off from the full range of human feeling and imagination, driving into unconscious the 'cross-gender' longings which that law constructs as such and forbids" (Froula, 185). The hallucinated scenes do indeed begin with Bloom's father and mother and work out the "law of gender" that first deprives Bloom of pleasure and then drives Bloom to take pleasure in his wife's infidelity. Bloom's perversion—his willingness to be a cuckold and the pleasure derived from that status—is depicted in these hallucinated scenes, and one may draw the conclusion that Joyce is finally defining Bloom as perverse in this episode. I think quite otherwise. The comedy of the scenes renders them harmless, showing us a potential for perversion that Bloom happily avoids. To allow "Circe" to define Bloom as clinically perverse would be to miss the point of the episode's great humor, which is to show us our own worst thoughts about Bloom and purge them.

Even in the hallucinations Bloom often comes off well, and in this fourth hallucination Bloom shows some of his typical resilience. When the goddess from the photograph above his bed scolds him and makes Bloom confess his guilt (in Italian, *Peccavi*, to force the association with Dante and the process of purgation in *Purgatorio*), Bloom at first cringes and obeys but then regains the strength to defend himself and exposes the ethereal goddess as a fraud. Bloom had earlier in the day wondered about the nature of goddesses, whether their bodies were as vulgar as the human body. He planned to inspect the statues in the museum to see if they had orifices for defecation, an experiment Mulligan apparently caught Bloom carrying out between "Lestrygonians" and "Scylla and Charybdis." The revulsion we may feel at inhabiting these human bodies is forced upon us by an unnaturally cold attitude that pretends perfection as it scolds us. The "nymph," as she is referred to in the stage directions, calls for "no more desire" but "only the ethereal" (15.3435–36) and tells Bloom he is "not fit to touch the garment of a pure woman" (3458). Bloom allows the nymph to accuse him and to make him feel the full depth of his perversion, prompting the Dantesque confession. But he rebounds from self-deprecation and exposes the goddess as vulgar in her own being and thus fraudulent. Bloom defends the human body against this stone-cold and pure goddess, even as he is warding off repressed thoughts of a perversion that the body has brought him perilously close to. Being in the flesh and so being creatures of desire leads us to the possibility of perversion, but Bloom does not allow himself ultimately to fall victim to the degrading accusations of these impossibly high standards. Confronting our worst fears about Bloom's character and overcoming them by the comedy of the episode, we also see once again Bloom's strength and may even admire him in the midst of what could have been overwhelmingly degrading.

In the fifth and final hallucination for Bloom he witnesses the act of sexual intercourse between Molly and Blazes. In this last and most humiliating fantasy Bloom opens the door for Boylan, who "hangs his hat smartly on a peg of Bloom's antlered head" (15.3763–64); Bloom asks permission to bring "two men chums to witness the deed and take a snapshot" (3791–92); and we watch as he watches his wife and lover make love on his bed. It is perhaps painful for the reader to watch this scene, but it seems more comic than painful, more prone to make me laugh than cry. And that is the point: the reader has had his hidden thoughts made manifest in the text and comically purged. We can think of nothing worse of Bloom than to suspect that he has been complicit in the affair and that he would actually enjoy watching it in some form of masochistic punishment. Here is the thought made textual and comic and in the process purged from the book. The book has gotten rid of its nagging doubts about Bloom, and the reader has seen his suspicions about Bloom's character exposed; to use some Freudian language about dream-work, they have been made manifest and rendered silly. We can follow Bloom on his way toward heroism.

In tracing this "plot" I skipped the hallucination in the middle of the series in which the reader watches Bloom play out a fantasy of heroism. This is central to the "plot" of the hallucinations, because what we are being prepared for is precisely the possibility that this potentially pathetic man is actually a hero. The novel has presented us with a plot that hinges on Bloom's decision to do nothing about the act of adultery he knows Molly is planning to commit and by this hour has most likely committed. We have, in fragments strewn throughout the episodes in which we are in Bloom's mind, watched how this act has been the pivot of his thoughts and how he has worked strenuously to do nothing. In "Circe," through the hallucinations I have just sketched, this passivity has been purged of its possible associations with perversion and pathos. The central hallucination, in which Bloom is called variously "the world's greatest reformer," "emperor-president and king chairman," and even "the Messiah," presents the reader with the opposite error, that this man with a quiet and passive nature may indeed be some sort of hero, may be roused to do something that will uplift him in the reader's estimation and allow us to call him a hero. This too must be purged from the reader's consciousness, not to eliminate the possibility that Bloom may be elevated to heroism, but to eliminate a certain kind of heroism from our consideration.

The kind of greatness in this fantasy is public and political, and easily turned awry and debunked. The fantasy the reader may have about heroism is that it will operate clearly and directly in the world of public affairs and move the world closer to justice and decency. The modernists all long to revivify heroism, and Pound's understanding of the heroic model, up through *The Pisan Cantos* at any rate, is limited to the political and economic.[2] Bloom in this hallucination is a comic savior pledging to redeem the world: "My beloved subjects, a new era is about to dawn. I, Bloom, tell you verily it is even now at hand. Yea, on the word of a Bloom, ye shall ere long enter into the golden city which is to be, the new Bloomusalem in the Nova Hibernia of the future" (15.1542–45). As soon as this hope is allowed to enter the text, a sign of trouble appears as well, as the mysterious man in the mackintosh from "Hades" tries to expose Bloom as a fraud. But Bloom is at this point so beloved by the crowd that the new era is ushered in by a new way of dating our lives in time, for this is now "year 1 of the Paradisical Era" (1632). As our lives in time were reevaluated after Christ, so now they are reevaluated after Bloom. The crowd does turn against him finally and irrevocably when Alexander J. Dowie denounces Bloom as the beast from the Book of Revelation. The reader's longing for nobility and heroism is the subject of this central hallucination. Our desire for Bloom to be a hero is allowed to enter the text, and it is made to look ridiculous; this kind of heroism, public and political, is made to look naive and childish as the response to our longing for the noble. This does not mean that heroism and nobility are to be denied to us, but this kind is expunged from the reader's set of expectations.

The two distinct kinds of hallucinations—the four sexually motivated hallucinations and this heroic fantasy—are brought together as this central one comes to its close, for Bloom is rejected by the crowd when he is exposed as "a finished example of a womanly man" (15.1798-99); that is, he is exposed as effeminate and weak, just as the other hallucinated scenes present him. He is not a strong man in a traditional heroic mode but passive and gentle, womanly in comparison to the panoply of epic heroes from the literary tradition of the West. At this point, after Bloom gives birth to "eight male yellow and white children," "a voice" asks, "Bloom, are you the Messiah ben Joseph or ben David?" to which Bloom responds, with Christlike ambiguity, "You have said it" (1833–36). We will soon read a mock genealogy of Bloom, ending with a direct quotation from the Vulgate, "et vocabitur nomen eius Emmanuel" (1868–69). The hallucination ends with Bloom, humiliated and reduced to a clownish figure, speaking as Christ on the Way of the Cross, "Weep not for me, O daughters of Erin" (1935). The traditional manly valor and exploits of epic heroism give way to a passive, effeminate kind of figure who suffers and is associated with Christ in his suffering. The reader has been freed from looking for a public and political kind of heroism—manly, epic heroism—and can now look for a gentle man who makes passivity and suffering into heroic virtues, as Christ did. Bloom's passivity, freed from its associations with perversion and pathology, is also freed from a manly model of heroism.

Stephen's single hallucination is different from those experienced by Bloom in that Stephen is conscious of his nightmare and responds to it in the action of the plot; in this Stephen is like us, having to witness and respond to his hallucination in order for the novel to be able to advance to the Nostos of the final three episodes. It is quite plausible for Stephen to suffer a psychotic episode, for he has been drinking heavily throughout the day, has not eaten anything, has had a number of trying emotional experiences, and most important and established as one of the first "facts" about him in "Telemachus," he is prone to musing about his mother in fairly melodramatic terms. The reader's hallucinations about Bloom are prelude to the action of "Circe," which begins with Stephen's hallucination, leading him to the encounter with the British soldiers from which Bloom rescues him; fully four-fifths of the episode is devoted to the reader's purgation, and then the "plot" of "Circe" comes quickly and develops furiously. We are ready to watch how Stephen's repressed nightmare becomes visible, not just to us but to Stephen as well. We see how images from the morning rise up and oppose him. First Mulligan, dressed as a court jester, appears and repeats the offensive words: "She's beastly dead. The pity of it. Mulligan meets the afflicted mother" (15.4170); it is Mulligan's mockery that introduces the mother to Stephen's reeling consciousness, and the ironic identification of himself with Christ on the Way of the Cross provides some depth to the scene to come. The Mother (for that is the stage-direction name Joyce provides for her) calls on Stephen to repent, and as he refuses she becomes increasingly sinister and ghastly. He refuses to serve (*Non serviam*), recalling his lengthy discussion with Cranly in *A Portrait* about his refusal to perform his Easter duty for his mother's sake. The

Mother, who represents the body and so represents history in this novel (as opposed to the father who represents the Spirit and the realm of the permanent), prays to God for her son in terms that make her the Blessed Mother: "Have mercy on Stephen, Lord, for my sake! Inexpressible was my anguish when expiring with love, grief and agony on Mount Calvary" (4238–40). She is transformed into the Blessed Mother, but with a twist: it is the Mother who died—with love, grief, and agony—on Calvary. The Mother suffered and died for Stephen, yet he refuses to repent and strikes out against her with his "ashplant." Joyce has made Stephen's mother into the Mother, with the extreme and even heretical language of Mariolatry, to infuse Stephen's situation with the larger dynamics of symbolic significance. Since early in the novel the mother was associated with the body and with history, it is legitimate to begin saying that Stephen is freeing himself from the powerful forces of the Roman Catholic Church in its secular office of oppressor of the people.

To ensure that we get the point, Joyce includes as a stage direction to this moment from "Circe" parts of Stephen's musings on Blake and history from "Nestor": "He lifts his ashplant high with both hands and smashes the chandelier. Time's livid final flame leaps and, in the following darkness, ruin of all space, shattered glass and toppling masonry" (4243–45). For Stephen, striking the mother is his effort to annihilate history, and as he rushes out we may be tempted to say that he has freed himself from history and has entered a world of new and unfettered possibilities. But history is not so easily escaped, as he himself noted in "Nestor," for out on the street he just happens to encounter two British soldiers, whom he insults and one of whom knocks Stephen to the ground. Having tried to free himself from history, he runs right into two of its more obvious representatives. He has rejected church but runs into state; as he tells the soldiers, "But in here it is I must kill the priest and the king" (4436–37). Bloom the father-to-be settles accounts with Bella Cohen and rushes out to protect and save Stephen from these tokens of the power of history. Freed from the Mother and so from the oppression of the church over our lives in the body, Stephen is not yet freed from history, as the representatives of imperial power confront and eventually lay him low. It takes the man who is about to become his father to save him from these forces of history and bring about an alternative way to take on one's identity within the inescapable matrices of historical forces.

Before his hallucination Stephen recalled the dream he had already brought to his consciousness in "Proteus" and, with more detail, at the end of "Scylla and Charybdis," when Bloom departed from the library between Stephen and Mulligan. Bloom's presence calls the dream back to

Stephen's mind in "Circe." First Stephen "extends his arms" and recalls, "It was here. Street of harlots. In Serpentine avenue Beelzebub showed me her, the fubsy widow. Where's the red carpet spread?" (3930–31). When Bloom approaches Stephen, saying to him, "Look," Stephen responds, "No, I flew. My foes beneath me. And ever shall be. World without end. (*he cries*) *Pater*! Free!" Bloom persists in asking Stephen to look ("I say, look"), which is exactly what Stephen will do in "Ithaca" when he does look and sees that Bloom is the "traditional figure of hypostasis." But it is too early for that kind of looking. Stephen feels that this man approaching is one of those who wants to "break [his] spirit," not the man who gave him the ability to fly so that men wondered. That Simon appears next, to begin Stephen's ghastly hallucination, signals that despite his own theorizing about fatherhood, Stephen has not yet freed himself from biology and from history, and so he cannot recognize the spiritual father that his dream prophesied for him. The red carpet will be spread for him at 7 Eccles street, not Serpentine avenue. First he must confront the mother, denying her and so history, before he can see the spiritual father.

The "plot" of "Circe," then, is quite simple. Having followed Stephen on the hunch that he might need some help, Bloom becomes his protector and watches over the prostrate young man; and as the episode ends, Bloom has one more hallucination, seeing Rudy at age eleven hovering over Stephen. It is difficult to determine with certainty whether Bloom is conscious of this hallucination or not; Kenner thinks he is, and I happen to agree, but the novel does not demand that Bloom be self-consciously playing Stephen's father as much as it demands the reader's assent to this role for Bloom. Stephen has been haunted all day by mother and finds a father; Bloom has been haunted all day by wife and finds a son. The action of "Circe" enables the reader to follow a "new" plot, as the mother-haunted son gets what he needed but did not know he needed and the wife-haunted father gets a son he did not think was possible. The two characters may be blind to this plot, and we are perhaps imposing a design on their lives of which they are completely unaware. Both have moved away from the women who haunted him throughout this day, the women who tie them to the body and to history, and now can move in a freer space allowing the spiritual relationship of father and son. Bloom the father is bringing Stephen the son away from history and back home, where a new relation to history can be fashioned under this father's influence. This different kind of father will bring the son home to a different kind of mother, and from this return to an original condition a new way of being in history is made possible. What has been merely family romance is taking on larger significance as the family to be constructed in this novel is an original family attained by making a heroic return home. We are now ready for the Nostos, for the return of the father and son to the home so long deferred.

"Eumaus"

"Eumaus" begins the Nostos, the return home after a period of exile, wandering, and alienation. One is wise to reflect on the modernist use of the *Ulysses* theme as the great myth of alienation, as a way of grounding a modern awareness of the need to overcome alienation in one of the most venerable and most ancient of all texts. W. B. Stanford, in his classic study *The Ulysses Theme,* establishes the history of the *Ulysses* theme in the western literary tradition and in his last chapter describes the works of Joyce and Nikos Kazantzakis as the most comprehensive versions of *Ulysses* since Homer. My earlier book, *Pound's Epic Ambition,* documents how fully Pound relies on Homer's version of the wanderer in enacting his modern epic poem. It is reasonable to conclude that the modernist artist is attracted to Homer's epic mainly for its domestic theme, for its epic version of the family romance wherein the great man is able to overcome alienation caused by history and return to his original condition in which he—and we all—felt at home in the world. That *The Odyssey* is so frequently invoked by the modernist artist suggests the modernist desire to locate alienation, not as a peculiarly modern or new condition caused by the onset of new economic and political systems (i.e., capitalism), but as a permanent and unchanging condition, perhaps the very condition that inspires us to write. Wallace Stevens says as much: "From this the poem springs: that we live in a place / That is not our own and, much more, not ourselves / And hard it is in spite of blazoned days." We write because of the need to tell stories that allow us the illusion of having overcome alienation, the fiction that the world is a home in which we feel we belong. Stevens implies that all great literature has this root and this ambition, to bring us on an imaginative journey back home.[3]

As Joyce begins the last part of *Ulysses* he invents a narrator who, in his tired and cliché-ridden language, is able, without his knowing it, to invest the simple circumstance of Bloom bringing Stephen back to 7 Eccles street with language indicating what Stanford calls "the Ulysses theme," most particularly the aspects of this theme identified by Stanford as its two major tendencies: the centripetal journey of Homer's Odysseus and the centrifugal journey of Dante's Ulysses as depicted in canto 26 of *Inferno* (see Stanford's last chapter, "The Re-Integrated Hero"). Homer's story is mediated by Dante's. As I argue in the preface to this study, Joyce owes more to Dante's example than he does to Homer's, especially in Dante's Ulysses who stands for the figure of a poet who can inspire men to embark on a dangerous journey with beautiful but fraudulent language. To avoid this danger Joyce invents a narrator who hides the great tradition of Nostos. The language of "Eumaus" is hardly lofty or inspiring; it is rather tired and riddled with clichés and conventions that disguise more than reveal the great tradition in which this return is to be placed. The reader must pierce the disguise of this language and recover the tradition in which Bloom's and Stephen's journeys are to take on their significance.

Homer's story is presented to the reader quite often through the language used to describe the life and character of the enigmatic sailor D. B. Murphy, a man of the sea who has wandered through the world and so looks superficially more like Odysseus than Bloom does—though this kind of identification, on the most basic and literal level of similarity, is obviously not the right one for us to make. So the reader, by noting the sailor's function as a false Odysseus, is learning to be wary of reading on the most literal level or the most obvious level. The literal level of meaning will not bring us to the hero who will bridge the gap between us and the world that makes us alienated. But this false Odysseus is the one who brings the issue of Nostos into *Ulysses,* as Murphy claims to be making his way back home: "That's where I hails from. My little woman's down there. She's waiting for me, I know. *For England, home and beauty.* She's my own true wife I haven't seen for seven years now, sailing about" (16.419–21). Bloom, the true *Ulysses,* responds quietly in a way quite complex: "Mr Bloom could easily picture his advent on this scene, the homecoming to the mariner's roadside shieling after having diddled Davy Jones, a rainy night with a blind moon. Across the world for a wife. Quite a number of stories there were on that particular Alice ben Bolt topic, Enoch Arden and Rip Van Winkle and does anybody remember Caoc O'Leary. . . . Never about the runaway wife coming back, however much devoted to the absentee. The face at the window! Judge of his astonishment when he finally did breast the tape and the awful truth dawned on him anent his better half, wrecked in his affections" (16.422–32). Bloom could easily picture Murphy's return because such returns have so often been the topic, in the instances Bloom can recall, of popular and sentimental literature. Bloom's reference to these stories calls attention to the tradition of the return, though the one that Joyce is using—Homer and Dante—is conspicuous by its absence from Bloom's list. The greater tradition of homecoming is implied by the tired, conventional language of the narrator, even though the conscious references of the character and his narrator are limited to popular and sentimental literature. We have seen, especially in "Nausicaa," that Joyce is able to employ sentimental language derived from popular texts to register the need for the noble and the ideal, and in "Eumaus" the tired, cliché-ridden narrator is unconsciously pointing to a greater tradition of Nostos underlying the popular legends. This also explains why Joyce has devised the sleepy, worn-out narrator: not because the characters are sleepy and worn (though that is true and works as an explanation in a mechanical way), but because the stories of return are now, by the time we reach the twentieth century, old and conventional and merely the stuff of trite and sentimental legend. Nothing indicates the degree to which Joyce feels what Perry Meisel calls "a sense of belatedness" than the way this episode presents its theme. The idea of Nostos is old—it is our first and therefore our oldest story, in both our Hebrew tradition (Genesis, Eden, and the Fall of Man) and in our Hellenic tradition (*The Odyssey*). Accordingly, the language of return is old and borrowed and conventional, and Joyce's genius in "Eumaus" is to rely on a tired and worn narrative voice that hides, disguises, a more energetic tradition. Rather than try to invent a new language with which to present this theme—for by the time we get to this era all language has been used up and all styles are exhausted—Joyce decides to invent an absurdly conventional narrator who can only show us how tired and worn the theme is. Beneath this sleepy narration confined to popular and sentimental tales, however, lurks a tradition that seems ever new and vigorous. Genesis and *The Odyssey* are not old texts, but young ones, the ones that felt the problem of alienation without tradition and without precursor but expressed its sensibility of desire for home in ways that were new and fresh if only because unprecedented. The legends of the recent past are old and worn, and underneath these tired texts lie the freshness and originality of Genesis, Homer, and Dante.

In the Homeric original Eumaus is the loyal swineherd who is the first person Odysseus meets on his return to Ithaca, but Odysseus does not feel able to trust this man and so remains concealed behind an elaborate disguise. So we can say that the conventional language of Joyce's "Eumaus," which is about the right theme, cannot be trusted and that the real tradition must be hidden, disguised. In the passage quoted above, Bloom further reflects that the stories of Nostos are never about a runaway wife returning home or about a wife who stayed at home but who was not patiently awaiting her husband's return. Bloom imagines a story in which there is "no chair for father" by the fire and in which "uncle Chubb or Tomkin" has usurped the husband's place and sits "eating rumpsteak and onions," and the wife holds "her brandnew arrival . . . on her knee, *postmortem* child" (16.434–37). Through Murphy, the evident but false Odysseus, we are introduced to the ancient theme of homecoming and then watch as Bloom imagines his own story as a different version of the homecoming, the husband returning to the unfaithful wife. Through the false Odysseus Murphy the disguised Odysseus Bloom is able to place his own story as a variation upon the great tradition of homecomings. Beneath the surface that presents the theme (Nostos) and the hero (Murphy) in ways that are not trustworthy, the reader can find traces of the greater tradition of return and the genuine hero enacting a new version of that theme in Bloom. The reader has been empowered through earlier episodes to read beyond false styles, and now—finally, as we make the return home—there is something on the other side of the style, a great classical tradition of epic homecomings in which Bloom's story will finally be told and finished.

It is through the sailor Murphy, who dominates the talk at the cab shelter, that Joyce is able to register most of the most blatant references to sea wanderings that in turn establish *The Odyssey* as one of the bases of the episode. For instance, Murphy claims with false modesty to have "circumnavigated a bit" and then describes, at the keeper's request, some of the queer sights he has seen in his years at sea. We also have a series of references to a pivotal moment in Homer's story, where Odysseus reveals his true identity to the suitors when he is able to string the great crossbow. In "Eumaus" this reference is made obliquely: Bloom, doubting Murphy's stories, understands the sailor's penchant for tall stories as a temptation for "any ancient mariner who sailed the ocean to draw the long bow" (16.844); Murphy, leaving the shelter for a moment to urinate, nudges a sleeping companion, "Let me cross your bows mate" (920); and, most tellingly and most indirectly, Bloom invites Stephen to try the stale bun again with "Have a shot at it now" (807). In *The Odyssey,* Telemachus tries to string the bow and almost succeeds in doing so after much effort, Homer's way of suggesting that the son is rising in status and almost meeting the heroic father; these "hidden" references to Homer's story are there to suggest that the episode is about the revelation of identity, as the process of raising Bloom to heroic status is finally begun by placing his story in this "hidden" tradition.

It is an extraordinary coincidence that the sailor Murphy is from the mystery ship that ended "Proteus": "We come up this morning eleven o'clock. The threemaster *Rosevean* from bridgewater with bricks" (16.450–51). Murphy brings this ship back into the play of meaning of *Ulysses* as the brick-laden ship that defied natural law matches what these last episodes are to do to Bloom, raising the flesh-and-blood man against the natural law of gravity to some epic status. But Murphy is not all that he claims to be, and Bloom's skepticism about his identity leads him to ask a question about one of the few places Bloom has some knowledge of, Gibraltar, a place that Murphy is uncomfortable in being asked to describe:

"I'm tired of all them rocks in the sea, he said, and boats and ships" (622). This question silences Murphy, but it inspires the narrator to describe Bloom's thoughts, which describe the sea and the seafaring life in ways that call to our minds, though not to Bloom's or the narrator's, Ulysses from canto 26 of *Inferno*. In the course of a sustained reflection on such a life, Bloom thinks about how he has several times seen an old sailor staring out at the sea "dreaming of fresh woods and pastures new, as someone somewhere sings" (632–33); that "the sea was there in all its glory and in the natural course of things somebody or other had to sail on it and fly in the face of providence" (638–40); and that the sea is dangerous, for a ship is "liable to capsize any moment, rounding which he once with his daughter had experienced some remarkably choppy, not to say stormy, weather" (650–52). Succinctly Joyce has managed to outline the story of Ulysses from canto 26 of *Inferno*, which is so important to the *Ulysses* theme and to Joyce's own conception of it. Dreaming of going to a place unknown to man, a place that has never before been seen and so is new and fresh and original, Ulysses seduces his men to follow him beyond the pillars of Hercules, one of which is Gibraltar. For Dante and the medieval mind in general, the pillars of Hercules represent the limit of our knowing and our experience, and so Ulysses stands for the poet, obsessed with the desire for new experience, who uses his gift of rhetoric to lead man beyond what God intends; he "flies in the face of providence" to find these "fresh woods and pastures new as someone somewhere sings." And having broken God's command, he is doomed to die in sight of the island of Purgatory, a "wreck off Daunt's rock" (16.906). Dante's Ulysses functions here to register the need to renew the quest for home, that the return home could be as boring and anticlimactic as Tennyson thought it would be in his "Ulysses." But this desire for the new is also indicted, for if the one leads to boredom and triviality, the other leads to destruction.

Homer's hero enacts a centrifugal journey back toward the home he once enjoyed and can still remember, while Dante's Ulysses enacts a centrifugal journey away from home, beyond the limits of experience allowed by our culture and toward new experience. Stanford sees these two opposed tendencies reconciled by Joyce, and so do I, but not in the mechanical way described by Stanford, for whom Stephen is the centrifugal wanderer and Bloom the centripetal figure. His solution works up to a point, but the two apparently opposite tendencies in the *Ulysses* tradition are reconciled as the desire for the new and unprecedented brings us, surprisingly, back to an original home that seems new only because it has been forgotten in our cultural memory. The only way to get to the truly original is to leave what seems like home in search of the new, for the new is really the ancient, the primordial, the original. Joyce is going to enact a variation on the family romance so odd and apparently so perverse that it seems like a journey away from the known and allowed and toward the new and the mad; but it is this new family configuration that will once again renew the possibility that the world can be our home.

Through the action of "Circe," Bloom began to function in the plot of the novel as Stephen's father, and now in "Eumaus" he is taking the son back home. If 7 Eccles street is to function in this family romance as home, then Molly must be the new mother replacing the nightmarish mother Stephen shattered back in "Circe." We are forced to admit a bit of discomfort in applying this thesis to the episode when Bloom shows Stephen a picture of Molly:

> —Do you consider, by the by, he said, thoughtfully selecting a faded photo which he laid on the table, that a Spanish type?
> Stephen, obviously addressed, looked down on the photo showing a large sized lady with her fleshy charms on evidence in an open fashion as she was in the full bloom of womanhood in evening dress cut ostentatiously low for the occasion to give a liberal display of bosom, with more than vision of breasts, her full lips parted and some perfect teeth, standing near, ostensibly with gravity, a piano on the rest of which was *In Old Madrid*, a ballad, pretty in its way, which was then all the vogue. (16.1425–33)

Molly is a replacement vision for Stephen, substituting for the mother who had been haunting him all day long and against whom he struck out toward the end of "Circe." Having freed himself from the mother who was trying to intimidate and confine him, Stephen was saved from the forces of history (the British soldiers) by a substitute father who now seems to be offering him a substitute mother; the orphan is finding his true parents, as the most traditional of novelistic plots is coming to fruition. But this mother is not a pious figure representing a frigid religiosity but a woman of fleshy charms who delights in sexuality and who even, in her monologue in "Penelope," imagines having sex with Stephen. In his study on *The Tradition of Return*, which I will describe more fully later, Jeffrey Perl describes Molly's role as the mother in a new Trinity in ways that are quite sound, not as "Holy Ghost" but as flesh-and-blood woman of sexual desire and sexual delight (see Perl, 214–16). But rather than see only this as a new Trinity in a new theology, I want to remain satisfied, for the time being at least, with the terms of the family romance and see her as the mother provided by the father to replace the nightmarish mother. As such, this moment in the text is startling and potentially perverse. This "mother" of sexual appetite and sexual pleasure is offered by the "father," certainly a new and different kind of father than the one we are accustomed to contemplating, the one we think of in Freudian terms as the father of the law, the father who says no, the father who prevents the child's continued relation to the mother. This father gives the child over to a mother who allows desire: "I can teach him the other part Ill make him feel all over him till he half faints under me then hell write about me" (18.1363–65). Rather than have desire shut up into a narrow range of sanctioned outlets, this mother allows for a free flow of desire so that the child can "feel all over him," all parts of the body now allowed pleasure. If this is a novel about an orphan finding his true parentage, and up to a point it is, then the father is a new kind of father and the mother a new kind of mother. Symbolically, this father gives to the child the mother he so desires; this father allows the child to remain close to the ground of desire, the source of desire.

The Oedipal family so epitomized by *Hamlet* is replaced by this anti-Oedipal family, one in which desire is not repressed and shut up into narrow zones that become often violent and aggressive. In using these terms I mean to invoke the extraordinary study of the oppressive culture of capitalism by Gilles Deleuze and Félix Guattari called *Anti-Oedipus: Capitalism and Schizophrenia*.[4] Without now embarking on a full application of this study to *Ulysses*, I still want to employ some of its main features to underscore the potential that this new anti-Oedipal family has for the restoration of freedom and desire in the modern capitalistic world. As Deleuze and Guattari seek to free us from the fascism of a culture that is based on "the twofold law of structure and lack" (Deleuze and Guattari, xiii), so too Joyce wants to free us from a family that is structured upon lack, upon the father's saying "No" to the child who wants the mother, upon which negativity a culture of loss is founded. Upon the Oedipal father's "No," a culture of narrowly confined desire leading to aggression is constructed. In this return to the founding moment of a new family, Joyce has created a father who is extraordinary for his passivity and who is not afraid to allow the sexual pleasure of the women he normally, under the Oedipal culture, should be controlling: his wife and daughter. What has been a puzzle, that he does nothing to prevent Molly's affair, now takes on a strange and lucid logic: he was working hard to be passive so as to become a new father giving a new law, a law based on "Yes" ("Yes I said I will Yes") and the free flow of desire. When he runs away from Boylan at the end of "Lestrygonians," at that point we might have been so much a part of the Oedipal culture that we could only see that action as cowardly and perverse; now we have a way of seeing that act as one of genuine and difficult bravery worthy of an epic hero, who will overcome the constraints and dictates of his culture and emerge as a new father. This is the hallmark of the epic hero, that he can rise above historical conditions, above the degraded but conventional values of his culture, and give a new law to that culture. Only a hero can rise above his cultural norms and free himself from the petty jealousy that makes of the father a tyrant.

Bloom's strange passivity becomes the founding virtue in this symbolic family, as he is now a man so secure and loving that he does not have to prohibit the son from loving the mother but can introduce the son to the mother and give him over to her. The key to the establishment of this anti-Oedipal family is the father's ability not to be aggressive, not to assert himself and his rights and privileges, not to demand and control, but rather to be passive and permissive. What was so odd in Bloom's character—his extreme and apparently cowardly passivity—was gradually elevated through the experimental episodes to something more serious and noble and here becomes the essential foundation of a new family configuration, one in which desire is allowed to flow freely and in which such desire can be love. We saw Bloom work so hard at being passive throughout this day, a day on which his capacity for such passive permissiveness is most sorely tried, in order for us to see him as this new father who makes this new family possible. We finally understand why Bloom is so poised against force and violence and hatred, and sees in all manifestations of these only a useless expenditure of energy. What is "useless" to this *Ulysses* is any kind of action based on a different kind of family, the kind of action that *Hamlet* endorses: vengeance, aggression, and violence.

"Penelope" establishes Molly's sexuality as her most dominant personality trait, and beyond the feminist debate about the implications of her monologue lies the fact that Joyce has made the mother in his family romance sexually preoccupied. We can even trace in her monologue the movement from guilt about her sexual nature toward a freedom and openness that allows her to act on her needs. At one point early on she blames Bloom for "trying to make a whore of me" (18.97), and later in the episode she absolves herself from any such guilt and anxiety about appearances. As I already indicated, this mother is able to imagine a sexual encounter with her son: "if I can only get in with a handsome young poet at my age I'll throw them the 1st thing in the morning till I see if the wishcard comes out or Ill try pairing the lady herself and see if he comes out Ill read and study all I can find or learn a bit by heart if I knew who he likes so he wont think me stupid if he thinks all women are the same I can teach him the other part Ill make him feel all over till he half faints under me then hell write about me lover and mistress" (18.1358–65). This "mother" imagines herself lover and mistress teaching the young son "the other half," making him "feel all over him." Desire is unlocked by this new family configuration, in which the father gives this sexually powerful mother to the son; the son can now feel all over him, not confined into narrow and restricted zones, but a body free from oppression and capable of full pleasure. The body that has been in mourning for its loss of joy and pleasure is capable of being redeemed by this new family configuration. Bloom and Stephen have worn black this day for reasons capable of being explained on the literal level of meaning but also capable of symbolic meaning as the mourning of our loss of contact with the world. The body has not been denied by this epic return home but fully reconciled with being in the world. Alienation can be overcome by the heroism of the father who founds this new and original family.

This now helps us understand the dream that Stephen was recalling bits of throughout the day, the one in which a man held a melon to his face and bid him enter his house to see someone waiting for him. We know now that the man is Bloom, the melon is a symbol of Molly's sexuality, and the house Stephen will enter is 7 Eccles street. The detail from "Scylla and Charybdis" that Stephen was able to recall only when Bloom brushed past him is most telling: "Last night I flew. Easily flew. Men wondered. Street of harlots after. A creamfruit melon he held to me. In. You will see" (9.1207–8). In the presence of this father and this mother Stephen can fly. He will find the liberation that was so elusive throughout *A Portrait of the Artist as a Young Man,* the ability to fly as he escapes from the labyrinth of Dublin, the maze of modern culture that traps us, paralyzes us. This liberation of Stephen is made quite clear in "Ithaca" when Bloom leads Stephen out of the house and into his garden, and this ordinary moment—after all, Stephen is merely saying good-bye to Bloom and going on his way—is given the solemnity and significance of the Exodus story, in which the people of Israel leave the bondage of Egypt in order to be free in the desert of exile. I will return to this moment in my next chapter, but at this point it must be said that the heroic father has been able to free the son from the confines of the paralytic culture of Ireland, oppressed by church and state, and provide for the son the opportunity to wander in exile and find the garden of promise. The family romance is about a new family configuration capable of liberating the son so that he can escape from the oppression of the modern capitalistic society.

This family romance, so intimately tied to the novel and its rise as a genre that it may well be its essential plot characteristic, is elevated by Joyce to epic heights through Bloom's extraordinary passivity. Joyce requires of his hero an act of passive acceptance that is beyond the capacity of most men and certainly not in Joyce's own character, for as Ellmann documents so fully, Joyce's most serious flaw as a man may well have been his obsessive jealousy regarding Nora. In fact, Joyce had in earlier works already presented the theme of jealousy and tried out ways of coping with it. In "The Dead," Gabriel Conway is forced to deal with the recognition that he is not the only man in his beloved wife's consciousness and learns a powerful lesson in humility in trying to come to a way of acceptance of Michael Furey's place in Gretta's life. The self-abnegation forced upon Gabriel is a lesson already learned by Bloom, though Gabriel's source of jealousy—a passionate but unfulfilled love affair years before he ever met Gretta—is much less severe than what Bloom has faced on this most momentous of days for his peace of mind. In *Exiles,* Joyce presents the theme of jealousy, though once again the source of the jealous rage and its way of being handled by the hero are not at all like Bloom's. It is as if Joyce had been preparing for this plot all his life, to create a character capable of doing what Joyce himself found impossible, not only to permit but to look upon the act of betrayal and then accept the beloved as if nothing had happened. This act of passive acceptance, which I will document more fully from "Ithaca" in explicating this same act in terms of allegory, is Bloom's great epic achievement, the extraordinary act of a great man that is, in strict conformity to the novel's rules, plausible and, in strict conformity to the epic's rules, rare and beyond a normal man's abilities.

We are finally beginning to understand why Joyce has chosen to make Molly commit an act of adultery for the first time on this day, 16 June 1904. If the history of the novel is closely linked to the social need for a stable family unit based upon the father's legal rights, then adultery, as Tony Tanner has brilliantly demonstrated, is the act that most seriously threatens the establishment of this new domestic order.[5] If we are watching in *Ulysses* the establishment of a new kind of father, then the act of adultery is the event that creates the space for the emergence of this father. Without her transgressive act, to use Tanner's terms, the old social unit is intact and, as we have seen, that old order is oppressive and paralyzing. Molly's transgression of the marriage contract breaks that old order and creates the space for Bloom to work to create a new family unit based on a new kind of fatherhood. He returns, not to the old order, but to a broken home—the furniture in 7 Eccles street has been rearranged by the adulteress and her lover—a disrupted home that he is to set right, by doing nothing. He lies down next to her as if nothing had happened, talks to her about his day as if nothing were wrong, kisses her in the usual way, and falls asleep. The act of transgression creates the opening for Bloom's heroic passivity to rise to epic heights and create a new kind of father and thus a new kind of family.

But if the history of the novel is also closely linked to the rise of a new ideal of domesticity and female authority, as Nancy Armstrong has convincingly argued,[6] then Molly should be more than just this transgressor who opens up possibility for the male epic hero. In true novelistic fashion, in the way Armstrong demonstrates for the eighteenth-century novel, it is up to the woman to establish this new order, to "authorize" it with her writing; that is why Molly gets the last word, the last episode written in Joyce's imitation of Nora's ungrammatical writing. Joyce told Budgen that "Penelope" is "the indispensable countersign to Bloom's passport to eternity" (*Letters* 1, 160). So if "Ithaca" is Bloom's passport to eternity, the document that allows him to travel from time to some permanent order as epic hero, then that document is not valid until Molly countersigns. Whatever one might want to say about other effects of Joyce's effort to counterfeit a woman's signature, this much is now apparent: that for the new family to be created, the mother must sign off on it. The male hero may still be the center of our attention and occupy the main action of the epic, but the founding of the new family is not valid until the woman's writing appears next to the male's, until the woman is authorized to have the last and ratifying word. Of course, we all know that that last word is "Yes." She endorses the new family configuration that Bloom created in his heroic passivity.

As Tanner points out, this theme of adultery and its reparation is also the theme of the Homeric epics, as the action of the *Iliad* is occasioned by the abduction of Helen by Paris and the action of the *Odyssey* is about a return to domestic values as the heroic male wanderer returns to the faithful Penelope (Tanner, 23). It is this domestic theme of the *Odyssey* that must have inspired the comments by Samuel Butler and T. E. Lawrence that Perl records in his argument about the epic aspect of *Ulysses*, "that the *Odyssey* was the first novel of Europe" (Perl, 175). In this regard Joyce has made the novel take on epic heights as a complement to Homer's having made the epic turn on a domestic theme. Just as Homer's epic established a sense of home for his culture, so Joyce is establishing in his epic a new sense of home based on a new family configuration for his modern culture. The novel has taken on an epic theme, establishing a way for us to feel at home in the world.

We see that *Ulysses* is evolving in the complexity of its design and intention. What began has a purposeless depiction of reality has become a highly purposeful articulation of the traditional novelistic theme that is now reaching epic proportions. Bloom is not consciously working to become a new kind of father nor consciously giving Molly to Stephen as a new kind of mother; on the most literal level, on the most reductive level, there is only the cuckold Bloom bringing Stephen home and perversely pandering to him. *Ulysses* has at least three levels to its unfolding of meaning, and the first level is the level of irony, of history, what Dante calls the literal, in which we reject symbolic meaning and insist on the most naturalistic meaning. On this level Bloom is returning to an adulterous wife who might continue her adulterous behavior next week on the concert tour in Dublin. This level is well established and never effaced, as the allegory of theologians has it. But the reader has been empowered to read the book on another level at the same time, a level of meaning in which these characters take on significance through a tradition of the novel and in "Eumaus" in a tradition of the epic poem. The reader has been watching "real" life (first established through the naturalism of the early episodes) take on the design of a novelistic plot (which is gradually presented through the "language" episodes and climaxes in "Oxen"), and now the novelistic plot is taking on the design of the epic Nostos. The book is slowly gathering weight, as the naturalistic lives of the characters continue to unfold but layer after layer of meaning is being added. From real life to novel to epic: that is the progress of *Ulysses* up to this point.

The novelistic aspect of *Ulysses* has been given symbolic weight by the epic tradition in which the return to 7 Eccles street has been placed, as the epic Nostos is a movement to what seems a new kind of family but is in fact the original family based on love and liberty, so what seems new is really a return. Dante's Ulysses seeking the new has dared to travel to where no man has ever traveled, and has found not unprecedented experience but ancient experience renewed, our first experience renewed. *Ulysses* as novel is not merely about an orphan finding his family but is an epic concerned with establishing a new kind of family that in turn has the capacity to make the world our home once more.

Chapter Five

The Novel as Allegory
Bloom as Christian Hero

As we have just seen, the final episodes of *Ulysses* bring the reader to a position of finding traces of a great epic tradition that can provide higher meaning for and more universal application of Joyce's novelistic plot. But in these same episodes Joyce indicates the shortcomings of this aspect of his plot and brings his novel one step higher, to a final perspective that is absolutely fixed and stable, permanent and true. "Ithaca" and "Penelope" will offer a fixed point from which to review the entire process of the novel, a fixed point that allows the naturalistic novel to continue and remain valid and the epic to conclude, while also offering a level of signification that is higher, nobler, and in an absolute sense true.

Joyce anticipates and includes the modern anxiety about language and truth by placing in the foreground of his novel the very issue of presenting something outside language through language, the issue of the capacity for language to indicate the presence of a transcendental signified that is itself outside language and that can ground the play of signification and halt what would otherwise be an endless and restless deferral of meaning. In what I called the "language" episodes, Joyce has tried out various kinds of discourse, indicating in episode after episode that the reader must read through and beyond the language offered to reach a truth outside of language that is valid and permanent. The most important of the episodes for this purpose is "Cyclops," in which the truth of "love" is suggested through Bloom's inability to define and explain it. Joyce has created an aesthetic of extreme indirection in which we must infer the presence of something outside the text that can in turn ground the meaning of the novel as we review it. But in these "language" episodes we see only the failure of language and must read through the failure and guess at the presence of a grounding truth on the other side of language. Finally in "Ithaca," the most unliterary and oblique episode of all, we are given directly and unequivocally but at the same time secretly and mysteriously this moment of grounding, the point in the text where the transcendental signified is indicated, when Stephen the artist sees in Bloom "the traditional figure of hypostasis."

In finding a way to write a multilevel ending to his novel in which each level is equally valid and true while some are more important than others, Joyce is following Dante's practice in his *Divina Commedia,* which in turn is following the kind of biblical exegesis outlined by Saint Paul. For Paul, Dante, and Joyce the Incarnation is the only event that can ground the otherwise endlessly deferred process of signification. For these writers of allegory the Incarnation is the mystery of the Church that solves all problems of interpretation and allows for a belief in the literal as well as in various levels of symbolic meaning. Joyce's genius is in seeing that only this event can answer the anxieties about language that modern language theories stemming from structural linguistics and poststructuralism have intensified and institutionalized. Joyce returns, through Dante, to biblical exegesis as a resolution to this problem of language and truth.

So there are four levels to Joyce's novel as there are four levels to Dante's "allegory of theologians," though I want to change the terms in describing Joyce's modernist allegory. First there is Joyce's naturalism, his scrupulous imitation of real life so literal that it can only end in reduction and death. On this level Bloom is merely a decent man who manages to return home to an adulterous wife, but the marriage is still in jeopardy and, despite the great affirmation, he remains a cuckold. As such Buck Mulligan would see him, and as far as this way of seeing the world is valid, that verdict is valid. There is then the novelistic level of meaning, as Bloom slowly but surely is being abstracted from this reductive, literal level of meaning and elevated to be a figure in some design. This begins with "Aeolus," the abstraction from his naturalistic context of Bloom as a "real" man and the imposition of a design upon his life. This is the paradox of every novel, for the genre is proud of being more "realistic" on the one hand and yet a commitment to that realism without the imposition of artistic design that would render the work a meaningless and rambling depiction of our lives until death. Bloom is made a figure in a novel as he becomes a possible father for Stephen. We just finished watching how this family romance becomes a more heroic story of establishing a new kind of family as the center for a revitalized culture based on pleasure and love: this is the epic level of significance. There is one further level of meaning that I will call allegory even though, most accurately, allegory describes the method that allows for the full range of all these meanings.[1] This last level makes of Bloom more than an epic hero: on this level of meaning he is a Christian hero establishing a new Church based on permanent values of an absolute nature. While all four levels are valid, these last two levels are higher in meaning and more universal in significance, and this last one goes outside human culture and reaches for a truth that is eternally and absolutely valid. Beyond Bloom as epic hero, which is valid and important in the context of modern western culture, is Bloom the Christian hero, which is valid and important in terms that are eternal and true in an absolute sense.

It seems at first glance that the application of the analogy of painterly abstraction to Joyce's intentions in *Ulysses* may suffice to bring us to the climax of the novel's actions, for as we moved away from the naturalistic depiction of realistic characters we began to see what Hulme saw in abstract painting, which is the tendency to dissolve the human and present the permanent. Certainly, one may plausibly but misleadingly claim, the lucid surface of naturalistic representation of plot and character gives way in *Ulysses* to the ever thicker and at times almost opaque surfaces of the later episodes, enabling the elemental features of Bloom's character to take on more prominence and importance than his quirks and idiosyncrasies, which naturalism was so adept at portraying. As naturalism recedes and abstraction advances, the trivial and ordinary that define actual human existence diminish in importance as the permanent and universal become dominant. But Joyce's use of the allegory of theologians allows him a more complex and satisfying resolution than the one just described. As I indicated in my second chapter, the analogy to abstract painting, at least as understood by Hulme, is only partially successful in explaining Joyce's intentions, and the application of this kind of allegory will be more successful.

Joyce never abandons realism even if he abandons the one way of representing reality called naturalism. In "Ithaca," Joyce presents a great deal of information about his characters meant to continue and develop the illusion that they are indeed "real." The allegory of theologians allows Joyce the possibility to maintain a commitment to what Dante calls the literal level of signification and what we have been calling the naturalistic level of reality, while at the same time he expands the meaning and significance of his characters and plot, expanding them beyond one level of reality to be meaningful on the novelistic, epic, and allegorical levels of signification. As Joyce develops these different levels he never abandons that first one, the one introduced by Buck Mulligan in the opening lines, the one that cannot move beyond material reality. Joyce wants not to deny or escape from the material confines of our lives in the body but to explore ways of finding meaning within these confines. The allegory of theologians, based as it is on the mystery of the Incarnation, never loses sight of the body[2] and its life within space and time even as it explores larger meanings, even a level of meaning that is outside time itself.

Up to this point in Joyce scholarship no one has done better than Stanley Sultan to explain the two different and apparently opposed options that a critic must choose between when trying to reconcile Joyce the naturalist and Joyce the symbolist. Sultan makes a strong case that we should pursue plot and character over style and technique by understanding that Joyce intends his stylistic innovations and technical experiments to be advancing a plot and not to suffice as objects of attention in themselves. While my own approach seems to agree that style is subordinate to plot, I think that the allegory of theologians provides an original way of resolving these apparently opposed approaches. We know Wilson's and Goldberg's objections, that Joyce erred in failing to maintain his focus on plot and character, and also the more historically challenging view of Georg Lukacs that Joyce's aestheticism is an abandonment of the artist's commitment to present our lives in history and ways of coping with forces of oppression. But critics who so desire have found ways to discuss character and plot in the last episodes because Joyce still wants the literal, naturalistic dimension of his novel to be developing in the Nostos, right up to the very last words of "Penelope." Daniel Schwarz, an astute reader of the naturalistic aspects of *Ulysses,* makes his position clear: "I shall argue that Joyce always returns from his fascination with stylistic innovation to focus on his characters" (Schwarz, 59). Joyce's language suggests that the "fascination with stylistic innovation" is something of an extravagance, if not an outright error, to "return from." At the other extreme is Brook Thomas, an equally good reader whose "post-structuralist" perspective leads him to say this: "The point remains that there is no action independent of the book's styles. Joyce's supreme achievement is creating the illusion of a subject matter that does not exist" (Thomas, 126). Thomas never wants to be misled that there is anything but style; Schwarz never wants to lose plot and character because of mere style—these are the opposite poles of criticism that the allegory of theologians just may be able to reconcile.

I want to look briefly at the approach James Maddox takes in *Joyce's* Ulysses *and the Assault on Character,* for it seems to me that he comes the closest to resolving the problems I have been addressing. Early in his book he makes this important and promising observation: "Style and narrative perspective gradually diminish the individual importance of character in *Ulysses,* but there is an underground current—the reader's own interest—running counter to this diminishment" (Maddox, 17). We remain interested in Bloom as a character through all the experimental episodes mainly because the early naturalistic episodes did such a thorough job of establishing the illusion of his reality. But Maddox is unable to sustain the double focus he suggests is possible. If we glance at some of the conclusions he draws about "Ithaca," we see quite readily that he follows those who see the Nostos as abstract. Of "Ithaca" he says, "The style loses sight of the human significance of the question and becomes absorbed in a purely mathematical calculation" (188). Maddox takes a phrase from Joyce's crucial letter to Frank Budgen and misapplies its intention: the form of "Ithaca" is a mathematical calculation, but the content is exhaustively "human." The letter says that the reader will "know everything" about what Bloom and Stephen are doing, and this "everything" as content is as worthy of our attention as the formal "mathematical calculation" is. Maddox makes the claim that "this style does have one supreme virtue: its very qualities of abstractness and (when it can find the right subject) lucidity allow for an intense and depersonalized vision of the book's most elemental patterns" (189–90). The depersonalized pattern, the disembodied design, is what I object to in this account: Bloom is still very much a person and still has very much a body! Maddox writes: "Perhaps the most uncanny and memorable effect of the chapter is its placement of the characters—especially Bloom—beneath the infinitude of the heavens. 'The cold of interstellar space' and 'the apathy of the stars' rule over the chapter and at times render Bloom and his problems completely insignificant" (197). I have quoted Maddox at length because he sees as well as any critic of *Ulysses* the "abstraction" of "Ithaca" and its powerful effects on elevating Bloom to the starry heights (though for what he is so elevated Maddox seems quite uncertain). Maddox's emphasis, on the loss of the human and of the personal, seems a serious error that can be corrected without losing what his analysis has gained for us.

We saw in "Cyclops" the ridiculous effort to make Bloom a figure of Elijah-Christ, as the parodic narrator of lofty prose tried to force the very human Bloom to ascend, against gravity, heavenward and become a symbol of some kind of divine testimony about the eternal value of love. We saw in that episode what Joyce's goal was and his recognition that lofty language is not capable of this movement against gravity of a fully human character. "Ithaca" is going to try the trick again, but not by abandoning the human, the bodily, the personal aspects of Bloom. If Bloom is to ascend and become a starry symbol of Christian virtue, it will be as a man with a body and a human destiny that remains as valid as his symbolic identity.

The problem with the theory of abstraction that Maddox applies fruitfully but ultimately shortsightedly is that it introduces what may be a false dilemma. In attacking "humanism" Hulme arrives at a recognition of what we now call "aporia": "The whole subject has been confused by the failure to recognise the *gap* between the regions of the vital and human things, and that of the *absolute* values of ethics and religion. We introduce into human things the *Perfection* that properly belongs only to divine things by not clearly separating them" (Hulme, 32–33). Abstraction, as Hulme presents it and as Maddox applies it, forces upon us a gap, an abyss, between realms that apparently are irreconcilable, between the human on the one hand and the divine on the other, between the vital and the perfect, between the time-bound and the timeless. While this gap is unbridgeable in any merely human aesthetic or ethic, it is resolved in Christian theology in the mystery of the Incarnation, the belief that Jesus Christ is both divine and human at the same time. In Jesus, in the Incarnation, the realms of the timeless and the time-bound are found in a single person, reconciling them and making the gap no longer unbridgeable. In Jesus, the man bound by time also has full knowledge of things eternal and absolute. The youthful Joyce was seeking a principle capable of allowing a legitimate process from the world of the human to the world of the ideal, and what he discovers is that Dante had already discovered this artistic principle in the allegory of theologians, based as it is on this theological mystery.

In discussing this kind of allegory John Freccero makes the distinction between the pilgrim who experiences the events of the poem's plot and the poet who understands the full significance of the narrated events: "The pilgrim's view is much like our own view of history and ourselves: partial, perhaps confused, still in the making. But the poet's view is far different, for it is global and comprehensive, the total view of a man who looks at the world, his neighbourhood, and indeed himself with all the detachment of a cultural anthropologist. The process of the poem, which is to say the process of the pilgrim, is the transformation of the problematic and humanistic into the certain and the transcendent, from novelistic involvement to epic detachment" (Freccero, 25). Freccero understands that the *Divina Commedia* describes a process in which the poet moves from being time-bound toward the achievement of a more complex state, still in time but also detached from it and so able to view the temporal order from the vantage point of eternity; that he uses a formulation similar to mine, from the novelistic to the epic, is confirmation on the deepest level that Joyce is an extraordinarily astute reader of Dante and is working at an application of Dante's method of writing that is not at all superficial but subtle and deep. Discussing Cacciaguida's prediction of Dante's exile, to occur two years after the date of the vision, Freccero says, "This 'now' of the blessed, like a geometric *figura*, enables Cacciaguida to prophesy Dante's future without ambiguity. It provides the place to stand from which the pilgrim comes ultimately to see himself and the world around him under the aspect of eternity" (26). This goal, for a purely and merely human figure to move toward a fixed and permanent position from which to view himself and the world as understood timelessly, is what unites Joyce's *Ulysses* and Dante's *Divina Commedia*. I will demonstrate that, having prepared for it gradually throughout the entire unfolding of the novel, *Ulysses* arrives at just this kind of eternal and absolute perspective in "Ithaca." We have seen the hints of such a destination strewn throughout the novel, most boldly in the identification of Bloom with Elijah, who must come before the great and terrible day of the Lord. Finally, having arrived "home" at last, we come to a position as readers from which we can review the earlier events of the novel in a "retrospective arrangement" and understand them now in a certain and transcendent way. What Freccero says about the *Divina Commedia* I will show about *Ulysses*—that the "synthesis of eternity and time is the goal of the entire journey: the vision of the Incarnation" (27).

Before turning to "Ithaca" we must return briefly to "Eumaus" and see how Joyce has already indicated, in the manner in which Bloom was "offering" Molly to Stephen, that we are watching the development of Joyce's modernist version of Dante's medieval allegory. Bloom described Molly to Stephen before showing him her picture: "My wife is, so to speak, Spanish, half that is. Point of fact she could actually claim Spanish nationality if she wanted, having been born in (technically) Spain, i.e. Gibraltar. She has the Spanish type. Quite dark, regular brunette, black" (16.876–79). Stephen responds, "Then, Stephen said staring and rambling on to himself or some unknown listener somewhere, we have the impetuosity of Dante and the isosceles triangle miss Portinari he fell in love with" (885–87). Stephen is saying this either "to himself or some unknown listener somewhere," but not to Bloom; it seems quite likely that the unknown listener so indicated is the reader, who is quite literally and completely unknown to Stephen, yet who is being addressed anyway to make sense of the introduction of Dante and Beatrice into the text. It is probable that Stephen's description of Beatrice as an isosceles triangle owes something to Hulme's description of abstract art as geometric and therefore permanent and absolute, and so we see that Stephen attributes to Dante a tendency toward abstraction in his elevation of Beatrice toward the almost transcendent status she enjoys in *Vita Nuova* and *Divina Commedia*. But Stephen, and not Joyce, is mistaken in this, for Beatrice in *Vita Nuova* is not a geometric figure beyond humanity but a flesh-and-blood woman whom Dante encountered on the streets of Florence and for whom Dante felt a passion that begins as sexual desire.[3] Dante tells the story of the transformation of this erotic desire into a higher love, a transformation through memory of sexual passion into something ultimately so lofty that Beatrice becomes almost Christlike in significance, described in one poem in terms that are always reserved for Christ, in terms of the

Incarnation of the Word made flesh. *Vita Nuova* is Dante's "Book of Memory," describing how what was once purely sexual is transformed into the divine by the process of reviewing the emotions in memory. We will see the application of this understanding of memory when we turn to "Penelope"; the point here so far is that Stephen introduces Beatrice into the text in a way that shows his lack of understanding and also that signals the author's intentions to make the Incarnation a significant part of the ending of his novel.

Beatrice is not Christ, but Dante is able to transform her into "the ideal lady of my mind" who, at the end of *Vita Nuova*, brings him the vision that becomes the *Divina Commedia,* the ideal lady who brings him his vision of Christ. Back in "Nausicaa" we saw the false rhetoric of a sham ideal lady in Gerty MacDowell, who denies her eroticism and presents a false sense of noble love. Gerty functions in the text as a false ideal, as a version of idealism not grounded in healthy sexual passion. When Bloom tries to interest Stephen in Molly by showing him the sexy picture of her, Joyce indicates his own understanding of Beatrice as an ideal lady of the mind who is also a vigorously sexual woman. Molly is this story's Beatrice, voluptuous and desiring. On one level Molly is the mother whom the father is offering to the son; but on the next level of signification she is also Stephen's Beatrice, a woman who leads him back to the straight way and who inspires his vision of transcendence. Stephen needs no sexual relation, or any other kind of relation, to Molly for this relation to hold, for Beatrice had no relation to Dante, beyond a nodding acquaintance, in the ordinary Florentine reality. Molly is Bloom's lure to bring Stephen back home to 7 Eccles street; we recall Stephen's dream, in which a strange man opened the door and spread the red carpet and bade him enter to see someone special.[4] Stephen will not see Molly directly, but he will see Christ in Bloom, and so a version of *Vita Nuova* is being established in "Eumaus" as Stephen is being given a vision (in Bloom's photo) of a beautiful woman who will bring him back to Christ.

On the literal level of significance it is unlikely that Stephen is following Bloom home because of the faded photograph of Molly, but on the level of allegory it is the source of his movement back home, the inspiration that pushes him to begin the journey; this is like Dante being encouraged by Virgil to begin the journey through hell by that poet's description of Beatrice's solicitude. In "Ithaca," Joyce continues their journey and quickly takes them inside 7 Eccles street, where the climaxes of the novel/epic/allegory take place. Having begun their Nostos in "Eumaus," Joyce develops a mode of representation that is quite unliterary and therefore surprising as the choice of style for the climax of the action. But after all the flights of rhetoric that we saw being debunked and exposed as bankrupt throughout the novel, it makes some sense to couch the climax in a style that has no pretensions to be literary in any way. The "cold, bald" style of this episode is based on the Catholic catechism and, as Walton Litz tells us, on nineteenth-century textbooks, such as Richmal Mangall's *Historical and Miscellaneous Questions* (Litz, 394). The sciences behind "Ithaca," according to Joyce's scheme, are astronomy and geology, the sciences of vast space and vast time; these are the sciences that come closest to an eternal perspective, though still bound by human limitation, and so correspond well to the implicit perspective of the catechist, who seems to know what God knows. The style of "Ithaca," then, presumes a vantage point on the action of the world that is as close to the eternal as humanity can achieve. The narrator of "Ithaca" merely states the facts that are known with absolute certainty from a position of lofty detachment.

From this high and detached point of view, Bloom and Stephen and eventually Molly might appear quite small and insignificant. We can return to Hulme's ideas about the tendency of modern abstract art to record only shapes and patterns that stand as geometric figures of stillness and perfection, and to Maddox's argument that in "Ithaca" the characters appear merely as "images" and, placed as they are under the infinitude of the stars, their problems appear petty and insignificant. There is validity to these conclusions, as the vastness of the narrative perspective might indeed lead us to sneer at any emotions at all, no matter how strong and even important they could appear in other contexts. This failure to consider the human aspects of the story is a loss that all the critics who emphasize style and technique share; only Walton Litz has been able to present the paradox of "Ithaca" properly: "The notesheets provide overwhelming evidence that the 'dry rock pages of *Ithaca*' are supersaturated with Bloom's humanity, a humanity that is enhanced if anything by the impersonality of the prose. As any viewer of the recent film will remember, 'Ithaca' yielded scenes of far more warmth and feeling than those provided by such 'dramatic' episodes as 'Hades' and 'Nausicaa.' Once again, in the contrast between the apparent coldness of the episode's form and its actual human effects, we are confronted with a paradox to be solved" (Litz, 393). The paradox is that the most abstract episode is also the most human, but this is no paradox if we apply the allegory of theologians to this episode and thus to the novel as a whole, for it is essential to this kind of allegory that the literal level of reality never be effaced or abandoned as the symbolic dimension takes shape and becomes dominant. This need to maintain the literal or human dimension in the most abstract episode explains what Kenner has called "the aesthetic of delay," a phrase he invents to describe the way in which *Ulysses* comes to its climax: "The last two episodes, 'Ithaca' and 'Penelope,' supply missing facts for so many suspended patterns, momentous and trivial, that a reader who should work carefully through them sentence by sentence, equipped with perfect knowledge of the rest of the book, would experience bewilderment from the very profusion of small elements dropping into place" (Kenner, *Ulysses*, 79). We learn more facts about Bloom in the last two episodes than we do in the previous sixteen combined, and this "filling in" of Bloom's life serves to maintain and even enhance the illusion of his solidity at the very time the abstraction is attempting to elevate him to allegorical status. It is only when the novel is almost over that we are given a description of Bloom: "height 5 ft 9 ½ inches, full build, olive complexion" (17.2002–3). We learn what is in his desk drawers and what is on his bookshelves, even the precise details of his financial status, information we normally never gain about our closest friends in what we call "real life." The illusion that Bloom exists on the naturalistic level of reality is never abandoned, even if the mode of narration that usually presents such naturalism ends with "Wandering Rocks." We were led to see the limitations of naturalism but now are forced to recognize that this kind of view is still developing in "Ithaca" and "Penelope." As Bloom is to be elevated to the stars, he is also remaining a flesh-and-blood man.

In fact, there is so much sheer information in "Ithaca" that we are tempted to agree with Umberto Eco's view that "if you take away the transcendent God from the symbolic world of the Middle Ages, you have the world of Joyce" (Eco, 7); that is, you have the delight in the multiplicity of the created world and all its objects without the center that allows for the complex but rigorous order. Instead of an orderly cosmos, we are left with chaos, and "Ithaca" is so filled with information, some pertinent to our interests and some seemingly irrelevant to the characters we had become interested in, that it might seem this chaos is without a center, a sheer accumulation of information without center, purpose, or system. Eco understands Joyce's fascination with lists as a sign of Joyce's wish to accumulate so much material that the medieval system that once explained it all crumbles under the sheer weight (9–10). According to Eco, Joyce is an artist wishing to "dissolve the ordered Cosmos into the polyvalent form of the Chaosmos" (11). This is a tempting offer, for it does justice to Joyce's efforts to include much material, especially in "Ithaca," that seems to lack an organizing principle. This episode is written in what appears an arbitrary manner, question following question whose answers supply an enormous amount of information and defy any structure that might hold them in an ordered way.

Eco allows us to see the tension in "Ithaca" well, and I agree with him that if there were no center to be discovered providing this order, then

Ulysses would be well described as "chaosmos." The abundance of information in "Ithaca" with no apparent relevance to Bloom or Stephen or Molly might cause us to give up looking for the transcendent order that would allow for the "retrospective arrangement" I have been calling for. But the reader who has been empowered throughout the course of the novel is capable of finding such a center, a transcendental signified that is the fixed point toward which the novel has been moving and from which the novel receives a complex but cohesive ordering. This reader can and must sift through the accumulation of material and read for plot, and when the reader makes the decision that there is relevant and irrelevant information and can find the human plot in the midst of the chaos, then the center is found and the novel can proceed to its allegorical conclusion.

The key to the discovery of the novel's center is not Stephen the son, but Stephen the artist—the young artist shunned and neglected by the Dublin literati but whose integrity and devotion are beyond question; the artist who delivered "The Parable of the Plums," which insisted on the priority of vision over sound. We have been exposed to so much interesting noise, lofty rhetoric, and stylistic experimentation that we may be suspicious of literature and its propensity for delivering sounds and voices; we now are seeking to go beyond sound toward vision, as Stephen was trying to do in "Aeolus," beyond music toward clear sight, as Bloom was trying to do in "Sirens." We as readers have been learning, often on our own but also through Stephen, and now we must watch what Stephen the artist does and sees in "Ithaca."

Four stories are being concluded in "Ithaca" and "Penelope": the realistic story of the cuckold Bloom returning to an adulterous wife; the novelistic story of Bloom the father bringing Stephen home to 7 Eccles street as a possible son, offering him asylum for the night and perhaps for the future; the epic story of Bloom the symbolic father beginning a new kind of family for the reinstitution of a loving family based on pleasure and freedom; and the allegorical story of Bloom the figure of Christ founding a new Church for the modern age. Stephen sees in Bloom a hidden identity, that Bloom is a Jew like Christ. I will now follow this story up to its conclusion, while also showing how the other three are also brought to their respective endings.

"Ithaca" begins with two questions and answers that introduce us to the apparent tension between the lofty, abstract form and the human content. The question "What parallel courses did Bloom and Stephen follow returning?" is detached and distant, and it elicits pertinent information: they started walking "united both at normal walking pace"; "then, at reduced pace with interruptions of halt"; and finally, "disparate, at relaxed walking pace." The answer is given with scientific accuracy and impersonality, and we are asked to read through this style to catch the "human" or "novelistic" content. They begin walking "united" because Stephen needs help walking; then they walk "at reduced pace with interruptions of halt" as they stop, I am presuming, to talk; finally they walk at "relaxed pace" and are disparate as they approach Bloom's home, from which we can infer that Stephen is able to walk on his own and that they are in no hurry to get anywhere, perhaps because they are enjoying their conversation. This last conjecture is confirmed by the answer to the second question: "Of what did the duumvirate deliberate during their itinerary?," upon which follows a long list of topics. Their walk is not silent or strained, but relaxed and friendly. The narrator is not capable of such a human description with clear focus and judgment; this narrator can only give the facts, and plenty of them. It is the reader's job to sift through the information and discern the human scene, invent the human context and significance. We are supplied with plenty of information with which we, the empowered readers, must conclude the novel. The reader makes the meaning.

Not always is the information given with such scrupulosity so easily made to be relevant or meaningful. After Bloom boils some water for their cocoa, we must read these two questions: "For what personal purpose could Bloom have applied the water so boiled?" and, after we learn that one such purpose is night shaving, "What advantage attended by shaving by night?" Bloom has no intention of shaving at this point, nor does the information about the advantages of night shaving help us (in any way I can see, at least) in following the "action" of the episode's plot. Such irrelevant or meaningless information is quite frequent and I think intended to suggest that the view from the cosmic height is often unfocused. From such height we may be able to detach ourselves from the pressures and strains of being time- and space-bound, but such distance loses focus and meaning.[5] Such information makes us aware of the process of signification, that meaning is a human construct made by people within the confines of space and time. The reader makes the meaning with the information that the almost absolutely omniscient but unfocused narrator provides. I think we are meant to make meaning, not give up on it, to ignore the irrelevant (after enjoying the often comic and sometimes beautiful images) and determine the essential. This process comes to its climax with Stephen's piercing recognition of Bloom's hidden identity.

Because many of the details in "Ithaca" are not in any way relevant or meaningful to the various plots one may construct for *Ulysses*, we are allowed to say, along with the best postmodern critics, that this text has elements of pure play, of images or details that are not to be brought into any pattern of meaning whatsoever but permitted to remain discrete and random and free. We look back from this privileged episode to the rest of the novel and can apply this principle to many of its details: they are not to be brought into a totalizing pattern that assigns meaning to each and every aspect of the text. In "Ithaca" in particular the lofty narrator accumulates an enormous amount of details that escape any placement within a plot, but this does not mean that the text resists all pattern and all plot. The reader, following Stephen, must learn to see the center of the text and assign meaning to a good number but certainly not all of the details the episode accumulates. We can delight in pure play and at the same time find meaning and order; that is what modernist allegory permits, for this episode and the novel as a whole. While the postmodern critics have taught us to value the playful aspect, the text remains "modernist" in its achievement of a center for meaning and order.

The reader can enjoy the playfulness of the episode but not be deterred from finding the transcendental signified that grounds the meaning of some of the details. The reader is in the position to read allegorically: lofty and distant and so freed from the pressures of history, yet still time-bound and space-bound and so still able to read for human meaning. After several less than relevant questions the narrator asks what is on the shelves of the Blooms' kitchen dresser. Amid the objects listed in what we can assume is an exhaustive list are these: "an empty pot of Plumtree's potted meat, an oval wicker basket bedded with fibre and containing one Jersey pear, a halfempty bottle of William Gilbey and Co's white invalid port, half disrobed of its swathe of pink tissue paper" (17.304–7). These are, of course, signs of Boylan's earlier visit, presented in language that is quite sexually charged (the basket is bedded; there is one pear; the bottle is half disrobed) to our ears but not to those of the narrator, who only gives us the facts in neutral description. We are aware of the sexually charged situation, not the narrator who only sees the objects so described. If we were in an early episode, we would be inside Bloom's mind watching him make mental adjustments to take in these objects; here we are given only the things themselves without human meaning. We supply that meaning and create the plot for the episode's unfolding based on the information so delivered.

While we are distant and lofty we are also human and passionate: that is the position of Incarnation, eternal and temporal, divine and human. If Bloom is to be raised to the starry heights, it will be as a flesh-and-blood man and not as a symbol. That is precisely what is implied by a detail supplied in the course of narrating Bloom's stratagem in getting into his locked house without his key. He climbs over the area railings and lowers "his body gradually by its length of five feet nine and a half [thus we know his height] to within two feet ten inches of the area pavement," from which position he prepares to fall. "Did he fall?" may seem a silly question, and it is meant to be comic, but it also underscores the episode's purpose, which is to raise Bloom to the stars. Yes, we are told, he did fall "by his body's known weight of eleven stone and four pounds in avoirdupois measure, as certified by the graduated machine for periodical selfweighing in the premises of Francis Froedman, pharmaceutical chemist of 19 Frederick street, north, on the last feast of the Ascension" (17.86–87, 90–94). He falls according to his weight, which is the measure of the gravitational pull exerted by the earth on his body's mass; that is, he falls because of gravity, the tendency to bring objects down to earth that must be overcome if Bloom is to reach the starry heights. By having his narrator mention the fact of the date on which Bloom last weighed himself—the feast of the Ascension, when Christ, who is a flesh-and-blood creature as well as the divine, overcame the force of gravity and rose to heaven—Joyce implies that such an elevation may occur. The importance of this moment in the novel's overall design is even more certain when we recall Mulligan's "Ballad of Joking Jesus," which mocks, among other aspects of Christ's divinity, his Ascension ("Olivet's breezy—Goodbye, now, goodbye!"). Mulligan is the prophet who, in his mockery, announces one of the book's goals, to defy this kind of reductive mockery and assert a belief in an ideal that is lofty and divine and capable of defying gravity.

It is in this context that we are reminded of Bloom's inadvertent prediction of the winner of the Gold Cup, which in "Ithaca" is called prophecy. The elevation of Bloom to the status of an Elijah, a Saint Paul, or even Christ that was attempted so explicitly in "Cyclops" did not succeed; the rhetoric that attempted to raise Bloom as Elijah and as Christ (the two are conflated, or perhaps confused, by that "Cyclops" narrator) was not able to remain free of the mockery that punctures ideals in the modern age. The elevation of Bloom that is to take place must be indirect and subtle, even secret and hidden, and thus kept safe from the mocker's irony. Here is where the thesis of Frank Kermode's brilliant study of narrative enters my argument, for Kermode argues that in reading or interpreting there is always an inside and an outside, spiritual readers on the inside who can see and recognize and carnal readers on the outside who fail to see beyond the material fact. This is at the heart of Jesus' parables, to keep the message of the kingdom of heaven from those on the outside.[6] Joyce has worked in this episode to present the ideal in such a way that the Mulligans of the world cannot even see it around them, for the Mulligans would delight in the random detail and the apparent display of meaninglessness and recognize Stephen's vision for what it is. These Mulligans can still read this novel with great interest in and deriving pleasure from the humor and reductive irony that is always at work, but their eyes are blind to the truth presented. The veil has not been lifted from their eyes.

Stephen's role is becoming clearer. He is the one, after all, who told a parable in this novel, and we may doubt whether anyone understood its spiritual meaning (though when Stephen tells it to Bloom in "Ithaca," Bloom expresses admiration for it); Stephen is the artist who, as spiritual reader, can recognize in Bloom what we have been led to believe is there, the presence of Christ. Stephen left the mocker's company and joined Bloom's, and we must follow Stephen to see if he can see in Bloom signs of something higher, an allegorical dimension. We recall his retort to Mr. Deasy in "Nestor" that God is a shout in the street. As we noted then, Stephen understands God as a sudden eruption into time, but he is misremembering Isaiah, who said that the servant of God will not make his voice heard in the street nor quench a burning wick nor bruise a reed. His retort was an improvement on Deasy's misunderstanding of history, but can he see the Incarnation in someone unassuming, humble, apparently quite ordinary?

I will put it plainly: as was the case in "Aeolus" and "Scylla and Charybdis," but on a higher level now, the reader is learning to read the ending of the novel by watching Stephen's reading of Bloom. Among the first things we learn in "Ithaca" is that Stephen is talking to Bloom and may in fact be quite talkative. He had not been slow to be rude to anyone throughout this day and even to Bloom earlier, especially in the first half of "Eumaus," and the mere fact that he is following Bloom home suggests that something different is happening within Stephen in this Nostos. We recall the famous moment from "Eumaus" when Bloom "passed his left arm in Stephen's right and led him on accordingly. / —Yes, Stephen said uncertainly because he thought he felt a strange kind of flesh of a different man approach him, sinewless and wobbly and all that" (16.1721–23). Stephen has not met a man like Bloom before, and his approach has evidently disturbed him. His uncertain "Yes" is proleptic of Molly's ringing affirmative. When Bloom finally gets into his house, he takes off his hat, gets a candle, lights it at the stove, and walks to the front door. The obsessively precise narrator tells us that this all takes four minutes, and Stephen is still there at the front door, patiently waiting. The narrator cannot make the human point but has given us enough information so we can conclude that Stephen must really want to enter Bloom's home. What makes him so eager? That is not at all clear, and perhaps we are better off not knowing the inner workings of Stephen's mind. All we know is that he is willing to wait four minutes for Bloom to unlock the front door and bid him enter. The question that follows even more certainly and tellingly indicates a new attitude in Stephen: "Did Stephen obey his sign? Yes." Obedience is, after all, what a son owes a father.

Stephen the son is becoming Stephen the artist, as one level of meaning is giving way to the next and ultimate level. The relation between these two higher levels is prepared for throughout the novel by the presence of the Elijah motif, which opens the novel in the figure of Malachi Mulligan, the ironic prophet who calls for the coming of Elijah. Malachi's prophecy reads, "Lo, I will send you Elijah the prophet, before the day of the Lord comes, the great and terrible day, to turn the hearts of the fathers toward their children, and the hearts of the children toward their fathers, lest I come and strike the land with doom" (Mal. 3.23–24). We are never allowed to forget this prophecy as the events of *Ulysses* unfold, as the throwaway that is thrown away keeps coming back, and back, in various forms. Finally, as the father-and-son plot has been fulfilled in that Stephen's heart is turned toward Bloom (Bloom's was already turned toward Stephen), the next stage can arrive: Stephen the son who now obeys his father and enters will now get the vision of "the great and terrible day of the Lord"—only it will be quiet and humble, as Christ was.

What is it, then, that Stephen will see in Bloom? We recall again from "Eumaus" something that Stephen probably said flippantly but now becomes quite serious: "*Ex quibus,* Stephen said in a noncommittal accent, their two or four eyes conversing, *Christus* or Bloom his name is or after all any other, *secundum carnem*" (16.1091–93). Stephen says this as his eyes converse with Bloom's; he is looking at him carefully, trying to figure out who this strange man is. In the ninth chapter of his letter to the Romans, in describing God's plan of salvation through the people of Israel, Saint Paul says, "Theirs the patriarchs, and from them, according to the flesh, is the Messiah" (Rom. 9.5). Apparently Stephen is responding to Bloom's Jewish identity and makes a quip that from the Jews comes the Christ, whose name may just as well be Bloom. In an odd description the narrator tells us that Stephen says this "in a noncommittal accent," as if Stephen is not yet committing himself to this identification. What was said in jest in "Eumaus" is told again, with the authority of the omniscient narrator of "Ithaca":

> What were Stephen's and Bloom's quasisimultaneous volitional quasisensations of concealed identities?
>
> Visually, Stephen's: The traditional figure of hypostasis, depicted by Johannes Damascenus, Lentulus Romanus and Epiphanius Monachus as leucodermic, sesquipedalian with winedark hair.
> Auditively, Bloom's: The traditional accent of the ecstasy of catastrophe. (17.781–86)

The names mentioned here as describing the "traditional figure of hypostasis" are writers—two of the church doctors and one the fictional governor of Judea before Pontius Pilate—who described the physical appearance of Jesus. What Stephen sees in a man who does not look at all like Jesus—Bloom is not six feet tall, is not light-skinned, and does not have auburn hair—is nevertheless "the traditional figure of hypostasis," that is, the joining of the divine and human natures in Christ. This is Bloom's "concealed identity," at least as Stephen sees it. The sentence Bloom was trying to write in the sand has been completed by the young artist who is seeking a visionary experience grounded in time. Stephen sees in Bloom the Incarnation of Christ, the way Dante saw that same miracle in Beatrice. He sees it presumably because Bloom, for no apparent motive other than a desire to do good, took care of him when he needed care, "in orthodox Samaritan fashion." But no matter what the reason, Stephen has a vision of the Incarnation, of the mystery that reconciles the eternal and the temporal realms, the divine and the human orders. It is not a shout in the street but something quiet and humble, the vision of God in man because of spontaneous desire to do good and to love.

We recall Stephen's error back in "Telemachus" where he puzzled over the term "hypostasis" and mistakenly thought it was used to describe the Eucharist, with which it nevertheless has certain affinities; the Eucharist is the ritual sacrifice that brings the divine into something ordinary for our partaking in the Incarnation. What is mocked at the beginning of *Ulysses* by Buck Mulligan returns, as we quite seriously consider the possibility of the human and the divine intersecting in our lives. The time-bound has, for an instant, been opened up to the timeless; as time continues, while still bound to time by the body he inhabits, Stephen recognizes in Bloom's kindness the silent eruption of the divine into the human world.

When Stephen refuses Bloom's offer to stay the night or live at 7 Eccles street, we are not forced to conclude that this meeting has been uneventful but quite the contrary: it is not everyday that one witnesses the Incarnation! Stephen's refusal does not in any way disrupt the allegorical level of significance, though it may damage the novelistic (for the family romance to conclude, Stephen ought to live with them and maybe even marry Molly) and may disturb some of the force of the epic level (for the new family may require at least some way of confirming their new relationship, even if only symbolically). The novel fails, and the epic replaces it as cultural document advancing a new ethical order, but the allegory succeeds most fully as representing a truth outside culture, outside history, outside language itself. That truth is "Love. I mean the opposite of hatred." Stephen takes pains not to hurt Bloom's feelings when he declines the offer of hospitality: "Promptly, inexplicably, with amicability, gratefully it was declined" (17.955). Counterproposals are "advanced, accepted, modified, declined, restated in other terms, reaccepted, ratified, reconfirmed" (960–61), which holds out some slender hope that their relation may continue. But for Stephen his vision is enough, as the miracle promised by the appearance of the *Rosevean* has been fulfilled.

Joyce indicates quite clearly that we are to read the conclusion of his novel as a modernist version of the allegory of theologians, for he loads their leave-taking with references that point to Dante's plan for writing his *Divina Commedia:*

> In what order of precedence, with what attendant ceremony was the exodus from the house of bondage to the wilderness of inhabitation effected?
>
>
>
> Lighted Candle in Stick
> borne by
> BLOOM
> Diaconal Hat on Ashplant
> borne by
> STEPHEN
>
>
>
> With what intonation *secreto* of what commemorative psalm?
>
> The 113th, *modus peregrinus: In exitu Israel de Egypto: domus Jacob populo barbaro.* (17.1021–31)

The language used to describe what Bloom and Stephen are doing (going out of the house into the garden) is as ceremonious as the "attendant ceremony" they actually perform. We are not allowed to know what is in their minds as they perform this ritual, nor do we know whose idea it was, why they do it, or with what attitude they do it. It is probably just a comic way of leaving the house, a sign of the good fellowship and high spirits they feel in one another's company. But we are blocked from the naturalistic viewpoint that would render the scene with irony and reduce its importance, perhaps even puncture it. From our lofty vantage point we see a ceremony performed, one that reenacts the Exodus of the people of Israel out of the bondage of Egypt into the freedom of the desert, where they are free to pursue their goal of reaching the promised land. As a little joke between the two men, they make a ceremony out of going to the garden to urinate under the stars, but from the detached point of view of this omniscient narrator they are leaving the bondage and beginning (only beginning, after all these pages) a wandering toward a promised land.

The "intonation *secreto*" of the 113th Psalm is used not merely to underscore the parallel between Bloom and Stephen on the one hand and the house of Jacob on the other; it is used also to bring us to Dante,[7] who uses precisely this psalm in the second canto of *Purgatorio* and then cites it again in the famous letter to Can Grande in which he elaborates for his patron the method of allegory he uses in his great poem. As Charles Singleton was the first to note, by using an example from Holy Scriptures to explain how to read his poem, Dante was implying that the *Divina Commedia* must be read using the allegory of theologians (see Singleton, 66–75).

According to this kind of allegory, the exodus of the house of Jacob from the slavery of Egypt to the freedom of the desert is a historical event that actually took place but whose real or full significance arrives only with Christ, who redeems us from the slavery of sin and allows us the freedom to choose that may result in our entering blessedness. According to Singleton, this is the clue to the meaning of the entire *Divina Commedia,* so it is quite perceptive of Joyce to have noted what Singleton was to establish as the major principle in the interpretation of Dante. Someone is intoning this psalm silently (what is an intonation *secreto,* anyway?) as Stephen and Bloom enact their ritual. It cannot be Bloom, who would not know the psalm nor its musical accompaniment; it might be Stephen, who would know such things; it might be the background music for this crucial scene provided by the narrator. To my mind it does not much matter, for what is important is that we are given, through this scene, a clear signal from Joyce about how to read his novel, that we are to read *Ulysses* with the allegory of theologians. Stephen's recognition of Christ in Bloom will allow Stephen to escape from the maze of Dublin and to fly safely in the middle way, still a human body but aloft in the sky with confidence and ease. This recognition of Stephen's is the "center," the "transcendental signified," that orders the rest of the novel.

When they leave the house, they look up and see "the heaventree of stars hung with humid nightblue fruit" (17.1039). The suddenness of this line is extraordinary: it is an eruption of poetry into the "cold bald" style of "Ithaca," and as such it stands out from the rest of the episode. It is Joyce's homage to Dante, in the way each of the three sections of the *Divina Commedia* ends with Dante's visionary experience of the stars. This lovely burst of poetry places Stephen and Bloom with a cosmic perspective, seen from the perspective of these Dantesque stars. The prose then goes on to place them in the vastness of space in geologic terms and the vastness of time in astronomical terms in the episode's more usual scientific style. So here they are, finally having become what Joyce in his letter to Budgen said the style of "Ithaca" would make of them, "heavenly bodies, wanderers like the stars at which they gaze" (*Letters* 1, 160).

What has occurred with Stephen's recognition and this ritual enacted silently, without the intrusive mockery of Mulligan anywhere to be found, is the founding of a new Church, an apostolic order based on eyewitness accounts of Christ's life. Stephen has seen Christ and is performing this ritual of a new Church as he values the freedom he has just won by his recognition of the Incarnation. It is Joyce's intention to indicate that a new Church is founded at 7 Eccles street, for it is no coincidence that "Eccles" is the root for the Greek word we translate as "church," *ecclesia.* In bringing this young man home to 7 Eccles street where "they drank in jocoserious silence Epps's massproduct, the creature cocoa" (17.369–70), Bloom did not know he was doing anything so important for the modern world, but Joyce is writing an allegory about the founding of a new Church for a secular age based on eyewitness testimony of a man acting with the genuine love and charity of Christ. Joyce is famous for basing his text on "real" events and places and people, so it is no surprise that there really is an Eccles Street in Dublin. What is more astonishing is that on 16 June 1904 it was unlet, allowing us to say that Joyce invented occupants for an unlet house, not wishing to disturb any of the other figures in Dublin for his novelistic purposes. His genius lies, after all that, in allowing the possibilities in the street name to become ever more important until we are led to see that Bloom and Stephen have just performed a ritual of a Church being remade in this very house.

As they look heavenward and admire the stars, Bloom notices and draws Stephen's attention to "the light of a paraffin oil lamp with oblique shade projected on a screen" (17.1173–74). Watching over them and shedding light on them is Molly: she is one of the stars too. Having noticed this, Bloom invites Stephen to urinate alongside him under her influence, as they fertilize the garden that earlier in "Calypso" Bloom had noticed was in need of fertilizing. Maddox notices the triangular figure of the three figures, with Stephen and Bloom on the ground and Molly behind the window shade as the apex of the triangle (194–95). As Hulme argues, in modern abstract painting the depiction of geometric shapes is a way to move away from the human and accidental and time-bound toward the divine and essential and timeless, and this triangle at this moment in the text is Joyce's way of suggesting that the union of these three is a perfect and timeless union, the founding of the universal Church. On the literal level this is an easy scene to laugh at, and so we should; but the laughter should not be reductive and does not take away from our ability to read the scene symbolically, as the fertilizing of the garden by the new Church.

Their leave-taking is accompanied by signs that indicate some cosmic approval of the proceedings, signs that the narrator notes in his usual tone of cold detachment. As the two men urinate in the garden, a star shoots across the sky "from Vega in the Lyre . . . towards the zodiacal sign of Leo" (17.1211–13), from a constellation associated with Stephen the artist toward a constellation associated with a man named Leopold. Schwarz sees this as an indication of Stephen moving toward Bloom (Schwarz, 244), and surely the artist-son has made this movement. At the very moment of leave-taking, as Bloom and Stephen shake hands, they hear the peal of the bells in the church of St. George, a sign indicating the joyful response of the new Church of Eccles to the union of the two men.

Boyle notices that both men hear in these bells the echo of bells from early that morning, when the sound led to depressing thoughts: for Stephen, thoughts of his mother's deathbed; for Bloom, thoughts of "poor Dignam" (Boyle, 13–14). The bells in "Ithaca" signal joy, and so this episode finishes the shift in focus that transforms sadness and loss into joy and unity. Finally, as Stephen walks away Bloom, now alone, hears "the double reverberation of retreating feet on the heavenborn earth, the double vibration of a jew's harp in the resonant lane" (17.1242–44). Critics have puzzled over this "jew's harp," but I think Boyle has hit on the right reference, which is to David's harp that accompanies the singing of the psalms (Boyle, 14–15). As their exodus from the house to the garden was accompanied by a psalm, their leave-taking is also given the sound of holy music. The earth on which Stephen walks is now "heavenborn," not a lonely sphere but one connected to holy and high things. What Stephen has seen and recognized in Bloom is given cosmic approval.

This is Joyce's attempt to maintain the permanent and eternal values of Christianity—mercy and love—without any of the trappings of the Church that has become so obnoxious in his eyes. This is no paralyzing ritual or mind-numbing dogma, but a new Church based on clear vision of Christlike behavior, like that Stephen has seen in Bloom; the only ceremony is spontaneous and joyful, simple and happy, as are Stephen and Bloom's exodus into the garden and their urinating under Molly's light once there. Joyce's new ecclesia is playful and simple, and in response to a decent man's spontaneous act of charity.

But Bloom's day is not done, and his greatest act is for us, not Stephen, to see, though we must see Bloom as Stephen came to see him. Once alone and finally on his way to the destination he has been deferring all day long, which is Molly's bed, Bloom is described in terms that cannot relate to a human being but only to some object in the depths of space:

> Alone, what did Bloom feel?
>
> The cold of interstellar space, thousands of degrees below freezing point or absolute zero of Fahrenheit, Centigrade, or Reamur. (17.1246–47)

Only a heavenly body can feel this kind of cold; the answer is meant, I think, to suggest the state of mind Bloom is trying to feel as he makes the return to Molly. To be able to lie next to his adulterous wife is going to take an extraordinarily cold mind! That Bloom's hobby is astronomy and there are several astronomy texts on his bookshelves (we found this out on the pages following this description, underscoring the point that the man who has become a star still has bookshelves and a personality reflected on those shelves) is becoming increasingly relevant to our understanding of his achievement and the style that is used to describe it. Bloom's greatest challenge of the day is just now coming to pass as he tries to achieve the detachment to himself and his problems that the style of "Ithaca" imitates. Feeling the cold of interstellar space, he begins his journey back to Molly, and the first thing that occurs must test the cool detachment he has tried to conjure: he bangs his head against the newly rearranged furniture. Boylan, at Molly's instigation, has rearranged the domestic order of Bloom's life, an accurate assessment on both the literal and symbolic levels. The chairs that have been rearranged have various significances attached to them by Bloom, including "circumstantial evidence." Having achieved the "cold of interstellar space," he must try now to maintain that detachment as he confronts various signs of Boylan's earlier presence.

Bloom had been putting off coming home all day long, deferring the inevitable encounter with a now-unfaithful wife. We may still regret that we do not have the naturalistic narrator's lucid depiction of Bloom's consciousness as he makes his way upstairs, into the bedroom, and finally into bed; instead, we are given a scrupulously "objective" account of his entering the bed, one so externally precise that it almost ignores any sense of tension or drama:

> Bloom's acts?
>
> He deposited the articles of clothing on a chair, removed his remaining articles of clothing, took from beneath the bolster at the head of the bed a folded long nightshirt, removed a pillow from the head to the foot of the bed, prepared the bedlinen accordingly and entered the bed. (17.2108–13)

We are not allowed into the workings of his mind as he enters the bed, surely one of the climactic moments in a novel based upon *The Odyssey*. The perspective of the "Ithaca" narrator is almost inhuman in its detachment, beyond the human passions that would dominate a naturalistic telling. Rather than perceive the intense range of emotion that must be coursing through his mind—anger, shame, hurt, guilt—we are allowed only to see the action itself. His sorest challenge occurs as he enters the bed:

> What did his limbs, when gradually extended, encounter?
>
> New, clean bedlinen, additional odours, the presence of a human form, female, hers, the imprint of a human form, male, not his, some crumbs, some flakes of potted meat, which he removed." (2122–25)

This is Bloom's extraordinary act, that he is able to remove the flakes of potted meat from the bed, lie down next to Molly, and kiss her good night in his usual way. His passivity, which earlier in the day may have seemed a sign of weakness if not perversion, has been elevated to epic proportions, as I argued in my last chapter. But here the achievement is seen as substantiation, and development, of Stephen's great insight. For what manner of man is this who can be so humble, so forgiving, and so loving as to brush from his bed the adulterer's crumbs and then engage in the usual relationship with the wife who was callous enough to leave them there? This is Bloom's triumphant act of Christian behavior, to forgive and love those who hurt us.

The telling is almost inhuman, which may be Joyce's way of indicting a humanistic ethic that, concentrating on passion and intricate psychology, would not be able to reach any higher way of being. But *inhuman* may be the wrong word, for perhaps Bloom's act of love and forgiveness is a higher form of humanity, so high and noble that it can ignore petty "human" passions and act with genuine love. We are given the outline of Bloom's emotional responses, as the narrator tells us that Bloom passed through a series of psychological states: starting from envy, the most damaging emotion, in that it seeks to harm the other who has what one covets; to jealousy, in which one still wants what the other has without the malice of envy; to abnegation, the diminishing of the importance of one's self as a way of coping with loss (Bloom's hobby, astronomy, is an aid in this, as one's problems look pretty small from a cosmic vantage point); and ending with equanimity, the calm and peace of mind that enable Bloom to brush away the crumbs and kiss Molly good night. He was able to perform this extraordinary act of charity and forgiveness by reflecting on "the futility of triumph or protest or vindication: the inanity of extolled virtue: the lethargy of nescient matter: the apathy of the stars" (17.2224–26). For a man capable of such sublime indifference to earthly affairs it is futile to protest or seek vengeance, and it is inane to preach or act self-righteously. Bloom is passive to an extraordinary degree, to the point that he is compared to the "lethargy of nescient matter." But his passivity, which in "Calypso" was a weakness keeping him bound, is now a virtue shining brilliantly, for it is the result of the "apathy of the stars." Such is sublime apathy, lofty apathy. He is able to forgive an adulterous wife who was so callous as to leave signs of her infidelity all over the house, and even in bed, because he has indeed been elevated to a starry height, as a "light to the gentiles" (as he jokingly describes himself to Stephen early in "Ithaca"), a shining example of Christian forgiveness and love for us to behold and marvel at.

We are brought back to "Cyclops," where the identification of Bloom with Elijah, Saint Paul, and Christ was tried out, only to be rejected at that point because of the inadequacy of the styles available there. But what is not taken away by any of the debunking that occurs in that episode, even the last image of Bloom with Elijah taking off like a shot off a shovel, is Bloom's vigorous if clumsy defense of love and his definition of it:

> —But it's no use, says he. Force, hatred, history, all that. That's not life for men and women, insult and hatred. And everybody knows that it's the very opposite of that that is really life.
> —What? says Alf.
> —Love, says Bloom. I mean the opposite of hatred.
> (12.1481–85)

What might have seemed clumsy and inarticulate now seems more pointedly expressed, for we have learned that "love" is not just a word that exists within a complex web of language but an action, a kind of behavior that "everybody knows." It does not need defining any longer; it needs doing. It does not require fancy rhetoric or lofty poetry; it requires action. Love is outside of language. And when Bloom for no apparent reason came to Stephen's rescue and treated him with kindness and concern, that was an act of Christian love. That is why Stephen sees—not hears, but sees—in Bloom the traditional figure of hypostasis, for Stephen saw love in action and recognized Christ in this unassuming man. And that is why the unliterary language of "Ithaca" is the proper style for the presentation of this mystery, for we are not meant to be wooed by language to come to this event but to see plainly and starkly—Joyce says baldly and coldly—love in action, the Incarnation of Christ in Bloom.

That he forgives an act of adultery brings us back to the theme of a new Church, for God in the Old Testament promises in prophet after prophet, but especially in Jeremiah and Hosea, to forgive his adulterous people. Bloom is the Incarnation of Christian love who forgives his people, Molly coming now to represent the Church, which is apt, for she shares the same first name and birthday with Mary, the Blessed Mother, who is the patron of the Church on earth. It was part of the prophetic mission to remind the people of their covenant with God to which they, the people of Israel, have been unfaithful, an infidelity that was quite often called adultery. Hosea is called upon to marry a harlot so that the act of reconciliation that God ultimately intends can be made manifest in the children born of this union. So there is a final, ultimate reason for making the plot of *Ulysses* turn upon the theme of adultery, for it is Joyce's way of suggesting that the entire culture of the modern western world has fallen away from the promise it once made with God—fallen away mainly because of the reduction of ideals due to the rise of materialism and the philosophies of materialism, such as Darwinism, Marxism, and psychoanalysis. Joyce makes Molly an adulterer to stand for a Church—a people of God—who have turned away from the revealed ideals of Christ and have followed more "modern" ethics. As Bloom forgives Molly her adultery, so Christ is forgiving the Christian world its adultery: now it is up to Molly, and us, to say "Yes" to this act of forgiveness and love.

This is why Molly must have the last word: the novel hinges upon her ability to accept this act of love from Bloom. As Joyce wrote to Budgen, "The last word (human, all too human) is left to Penelope. This is the indispensable countersign to Bloom's passport to eternity. I mean the last episode *Penelope*" (*Letters* 1, 160). For the allegorical level, the last word is left to the representative of humanity, still in the flesh and fresh from the act of adultery that now marks our possible divorce from our God. But I want to offer a brief reading of "Penelope" that allows us to bring the novel to its various conclusions, and before doing so I want to review how *Ulysses* has developed as a carefully orchestrated modernist version of Dantesque allegory, operating on various levels of signification—successfully, happily, completely—without any one canceling out the other.

The application of this notion of "modernist allegory" as Joyce's version of the allegory of theologians allows readers of *Ulysses* to assert that Joyce's great novel is not monolithic in meaning, which would be to reduce its richness and diversity to something too simple and too inflexible, and yet not a chaos or "chaosmos," in which we are to delight only in the play and virtuosity of this master-maker without the concerns of plot and character. Following Dante in his letter to Can Grande, we can say that *Ulysses* is polysemous, having not an infinite variety of possible meanings but a certain limited yet still enriching number of meanings, all equally valid though some of higher consequence and worth. This is why *Ulysses* has been able to please readers in so many different ways, as if Joyce wrote a novel that was able to give satisfaction to a variety of readerly needs. It is, at its first and most naturalistic level, an extraordinarily rich account of three characters caught within the modern Irish state trying to find fulfillment, if not escape. On this level there is room for disagreement regarding the degree of success the three characters have met. Negatively, one might say that Stephen is still a failed artist, unknown and unencouraged by any one of the literary circles of 1904 Dublin, who now has no place to call home; Molly is an adulteress with the prospect of being eventually sent out on her own by Bloom; and Bloom is still a cuckold who endures this bitter new family arrangement. One might want to press here for some happier prospects, but that would bring us to a reader confronting their lives less as "real life" on this most literal level and more as characters within a familiar design of the traditional English novel. On this "novelistic" level there is some hope for reconciliation between Bloom and Molly, for after all she ends her monologue with a "Yes." But this affirmation is subject to ironic deflation, for the "Yes" is to a memory sixteen years ago, and she more than likely will continue to have her affair with Boylan when they go on the concert tour the next week. Stephen was shown some warmth from an unexpected source, and this image of a father might help propel him toward a finer sense of himself and the possibilities of good things occurring in ordinary circumstances, certainly fine material for a fledgling artist. And Bloom, having come back home and shown his wife his continuing love for her, may have won our respect as a good man getting through a difficult day with a glimmer of hope that that famous "Yes" will mean more than breakfast in bed tomorrow morning.

But even on the novelistic level the prospects for great things are slim, which is why those who enjoy the stylistic pyrotechnics so much may want to dismiss plot and character, for the plot and character of the novelistic *Ulysses* do not afford the kind of affirmation of joy and happiness that the experience of reading the book provides. There appears a great gap between the joy of this text and its plot, at least on these two levels. But as I have been showing all along, these two levels, valid and accurate as far as they go, do not exhaust the plots for these characters. On the epic level Molly's monologue is crucial in allowing us to see what kind of symbolic mother she may be and what this kind of new family may mean as a replacement for the kind of culture that Joyce has so scrupulously documented from *Dubliners,* through *A Portrait,* and even in the naturalistic episodes of *Ulysses.* That culture, now identified with the ghastly mother of pious Christian culture, is smashed and replaced by a new father bringing the son to a new mother. On this level the plot seems more satisfying, as offering something hopeful to be established through this work of art. And the stylistic innovations do not seem mere play and ornament, but now essential to the enlarging of the novel's plot into epic dimensions. On this epic level of signification Molly's monologue is climactic, for she must acknowledge the power of the passive Bloom and agree that this kind of passive hero is better than the merely virulent but otherwise inferior Boylan. Her slow and gradual and reluctant acknowledgment of Bloom's superiority, climaxed in the "yes I said yes I will Yes," is crucial to the establishment of the new family as a symbolic replacement of the old culture based on fear and guilt by a new culture of freedom and joy. She, as the ground on which the family rests, as the woman whose control over the domestic is now acknowledged and revered, must be a willing and eager partner to this new father and the son they wish to liberate. This happier reading, on the epic level, even spills back to the novelistic: maybe her "Yes" even means on that level that she recognizes, in the gentle and loving husband who treated her with respect and love despite her act of transgression, the superiority of Bloom over Boylan. As we read from the higher level back to the lower, even their possibilities for something greater seems to be enhanced.

On the highest level of the text, the allegorical, where Bloom is the Incarnation recognized by Stephen and by the reader at the end of "Ithaca," Molly's monologue is even more poignant and more final. She has recognized her true husband's kindness and steadfast love as virtues far superior to the pleasures she enjoyed with Boylan. While she at first remembers her sexual pleasure from that afternoon, she gradually begins to recall more and more instances of his rude and degrading treatment; for example, she recalls early in the monologue the "determined vicious look in his eyes" (18.153). After recalling many instances of Bloom's decency and the love they have shared, she makes what seems a final determination: "no thats no way for him has he no manners nor no refinement nor no nothing in his nature[8] slapping us behind like that on my bottom because I didnt call him Hugh the ignoramus he doesnt know poetry from a cabbage" (18.1368–71). It had seemed that Bloom had forgotten her needs, and he allowed her the absolute liberty to choose her own way, which she did, and it seems perhaps she regrets it. One may look back on some details about this day with fresh eyes. Perhaps she wanted Bloom to do something about this affair. After all, she left the slip of Boylan's letter for him to see back in "Calypso," just enough not hidden under the pillow as to attract his attention, get him to inquire, and then get him to make a scene. But he does not wish to do anything to prevent her; and when he returns home after the act, with the house rearranged and the crumbs in the bed, even then he says nothing. It is this passivity that haunts her; it is this ability to love her still that causes her ruminations. Without his doing anything at all but loving, she decides to turn back. That is Joyce's allegorical climax: that she, as Church, turns back to the loving, passive God who wants us to be one with him.

For *Ulysses*, "yes I said yes I will Yes" is a carefully constructed last phrase. The first "yes" is followed by "I said": she remembers having said "yes" sixteen years ago on Howth. Bloom had remembered the very same back in "Lestrygonians," when we were still in a naturalistic novel and when memory of happy days gone by could only aggravate and depress one's present mood. But memory has been liberated by all the experiments in style, especially by "Ithaca," with its great distance and detachment. For memory is more than a receptacle for images from the past; it is an agent of transformation, as Dante knew in *Vita Nuova,* that book about how an ordinary woman became the ideal lady of my mind. In "Penelope," another book of memory, another ordinary woman is transformed, as Molly changes from Calypso to Penelope, from adulteress to faithful lover. As I have said all along, with Rickard and Yates as aids to this understanding, memory is not just a box from which we pull out images from the past, but rather an agent of the mind that, in the medieval world, came the closest to God's way of looking at human events, for in memory temporal distinctions count less, time is flattened out into space, and events from sixteen years ago are no further off than events from 4:30 this afternoon. If "Ithaca" approaches God's way of viewing human events by its great detachment and indifference, then "Penelope" imitates that eternal perspective through its reliance on memory. That is why the image that depressed Bloom at lunchtime can be recalled as the final image for the entire work, for from memory's vantage point, sixteen years ago on Howth is every bit as real and "now" as her lovemaking just hours earlier. And by saying "yes I said," she recalls and ratifies that initial decision to say "yes" to Bloom.

In the words "yes I said yes I will Yes" she recalls the first promise as if it were ever present (and it is) and then makes another promise, a renewal of vows, if you will. "yes I said yes I will Yes": I remember our first covenant, and I fell; I renew it now and promise again to be faithful, from this point on, forever. And if I fail again, I know that this Incarnated God will be as gentle and loving and merciful, again and again. The new Church, founded at 7 Eccles street, is renewed, based not on dogma and law but on freedom and love and forgiveness. The seedcake that Bloom and Molly share is the Eucharist in this text, passed from mouth to mouth in the act of ever new love. *Ulysses* began with a mockery of the Eucharist, and so it is appropriate that it ends with this sexually charged scene of a love meal where the bride and the bridegroom are always young, always loving, and always free. The image that ends the book is the image of a new order, a new Church founded by Stephen's vision and made open to us all by Molly's renewal of her nuptial vows.

Joyce's highest ambition in *Ulysses* has been to find a way to present his timeless truth: that love and mercy are the values that exist outside space and time and outside language itself, and that they can be the basis of a permanent order, or of a Church at 7 Eccles street to which the few of us who care to do so may belong. If Molly is still unfaithful on the literal level, and if Stephen never crosses paths with Bloom on the novelistic level, and even if the new epic family proves to be just another culturally relative configuration becoming fascistic, the love and mercy of Christ as seen in Bloom—first by Stephen, then by the reader, and then by Molly—are eternal.

Conclusion
Allegory and High Modernism

What Joyce discovered in thinking through the history of the novel, three great modernist poets—Ezra Pound, T. S. Eliot, and Wallace Stevens—discovered twenty years later as they wrote under the pressure of the events of World War II. There is a thesis hidden in that sentence, that the novel must be seen as inadequate, requiring the supplement of the epic poet's ambition; and that ambition, under the pressures of history, leads the poet to discover allegory as the only viable solution to the dilemma that history has forced upon his desire for ideals and heroism. The purpose of this conclusion is to demonstrate briefly that the poems these three modernist poets wrote during the war move toward allegory in the way Joyce first discovered, and that from this demonstration began a definition of high modernism as inherently allegorical in the sense I have been describing in Joyce's *Ulysses*. High modernism may be defined as a kind of literary writing that seeks to reconcile the demands of being in history with the equally pressing desire for the ideal or noble. It is a development of a romantic desire for the ethereal that has confronted history and found within space and time evidence of the high and noble.

While Eliot's response to *Ulysses* is justly famous, it has more to do with self-definition than with an objective critical assessment of Joyce's novel. Yet it is worth noting that in his response Eliot announces that the novel is ended as a literary form: "No one else has built a novel upon such a foundation before: it has never before been necessary. I am not begging the question in calling *Ulysses* a 'novel'; and if you call it an epic it will not matter. If it is not a novel, that is simply because the novel is a form which will no longer serve; it is because the novel, instead of being a form, was simply the expression of an age which had not sufficiently lost all form to feel the need for something stricter. . . . The novel ended with Flaubert and with James" (Eliot, "'Ulysses,' Order, and Myth," in *Selected Prose*, 177). Eliot assumes that the novel is no longer a form that serves the purposes of modernity, in that it can only set forth the limitations of humanity and not present its higher possibilities. The novel as a genre ended with the scrupulous attention to the intricacies of thought and character presented by Flaubert and Henry James. It is a realist tradition that Eliot assumes to have developed and to have recently ended. Eliot's review goes on to its more famous articulation of the mythic method, as a "way of controlling, of ordering, of giving a shape and a significance to the immense panorama of futility and anarchy which is contemporary history" (177). He sees that something is going on in *Ulysses* beyond the depiction of our lives in time that is the ordinary purpose of the novel, and though this sentence describes *The Waste Land* better than it does *Ulysses*, it serves to inform us that Eliot saw in Joyce's work a model for his own poetic projects. Having ended the novel and created modernist epic and modernist allegory, Joyce brings to the great modernist poets inspiration and direction.

Pound also meditates upon the relation of his epic project to the history of the novel. In preparing a place in literary history for the epic poem, Pound early on made claims that the novel was intimately bound with humanism and with the failure of humanity to see its relation to the divine or noble or ideal worlds: "After the Trecento we get Humanism. . . . Man is concerned with man and forgets the whole and the flowing. And we have in sequence, first the age of drama, and then the age of prose" (Pound, *Spirit of Romance*, 93). Unlike Lukacs, who sees in the development of the realistic novel an advance in literary art, for Pound literary history witnesses a decline from an epic art that registered ideals and visions of beauty to a prosaic art that documents human nature.[1] As we saw implicit in Joyce's text, Pound advances a critique against "Humanism" that is tied intimately to artistic representation, in that an art bound to the merely human will only register values that are relative and ultimately corrupt. This "fall" in literary art reflects a fall in mankind itself, no longer seeing and so no longer recording the higher aspects of life. Like his friend Eliot, Pound sees a line of great prose art from Flaubert through James to Joyce, where the "diagnosis" (Pound, *Literary Essays*, 97) of the ills of humanity has been made, and that particular literary job has been completed. Their rigor and precision have prepared the room for his own project, the discovery—it is really a rediscovery, a renewal—of beauty and nobility in the modern world. Canto 7 presents an interesting scene: a version of literary history beginning with Homer and running through Ovid, Bertrans de Born, and Dante, finishing up with the prose tradition of Flaubert and James, after which he presents himself making his own "ghostly visits" seeking "buried beauty." The modern poet, embarking on his epic project, first articulates his relation to a finished prose tradition that he will now supplement in his epic poem, by renewing the beauty and nobility that have fallen from our field of perception.

These ideas mark Pound's affinity with Joyce's much more scrupulous and comprehensive account of the novel's inadequacy for the needs of literary artists seeking to oppose the reductionist tendencies of the modern world. The genre that was born to meet the emerging needs of eighteenth-century society has done what it could and has now reached its point of exhaustion, having diagnosed (to use Pound's terms) but not able to provide a cure. Pound's emerging epic project is shaped by his sense of the novel's ultimate shortcomings, and it is no coincidence that the three poets whose greatest achievements I shall now describe see themselves as poets writing in the epic strain. To write a "long poem containing history" is the challenge each of these poets feels compelled to undertake, as the novel gives way to the epic and the epic, under the strain of history, moves toward allegory.

Four Quartets

I begin with Eliot's attempt at the great long poem for several reasons: first, it was begun earliest, with *Burnt Norton* finished in 1935; second, his use of the model of the Incarnation in his writing is most explicit; and third, his poem has an interesting and instructive history. *Burnt Norton* is written as a complete and comprehensive poem, having (he seems to claim) found the way to a still point outside of time that is safe from its ravages and from which one can discern the pattern amidst the apparent chaos of our lives in time. But when World War II began, this resolution seemed far too facile, and he had to rework the poem to meet the pressures of time and history more successfully; in doing so he came to the mystery of the Incarnation as the organizing principle of the long poem. Under the pressures of history, and perhaps with *Ulysses* in his mind, Eliot came to write his version of modernist allegory.

Burnt Norton is a most interesting poem to consider in trying to map the arc of Eliot's poetic career, for it occupies a middle ground between *The Waste Land* and the "Ariel" poems, and the poems he wrote after the war began that make up the rest of the *Four Quartets*. *The Waste Land* brings the reader on a fragmented and torturous journey to a primordial place where one wishes to hear the voice of God speaking through the thunder. The anxious and almost desperate conclusion to the poem is fraught with images that make us wonder if the figure in the poem is actually hearing the thunder speak or is instead hallucinating, hearing what he so desperately wants to hear, which is moral instruction from the other world. Especially interesting is the use of the journey to Emmaus: in Luke's gospel an unknown traveler turns out to be the resurrected Jesus, revealing himself in the breaking of the bread at supper; in Eliot's version one is not sure if Christ is present or not. Eliot confuses matters even more in his notes to the poem where he says that his passage based on Luke's story was inspired by a report of an Antarctic expedition, in which the travelers kept having the illusion that someone else was present along with them. So faith in the Christ event may be mere delusion, or it may be truth. The thunder may just be noise, or it may be God's moral imperatives giving shape and order to our lives. *The Waste Land* is a religious poem presenting the agony of the crisis of doubt, unresolved but hopeful at its end. "The Journey of the Magi" brings us further toward certainty, as one of the magicians remembers the manifestation of God in the child Jesus many years ago now. Yet this poem also offers itself as a poem of acute religious need, as the speaker wishes for another such experience—"it was, you may say, satisfactory"—in the present, to renew that wondrous feeling of having seen the divine in the world. In this poem the speaker has had the experience, but the memory of it is not enough; he needs another such experience, and we may presume another, and another.

Burnt Norton continues this theme and makes claims to have finished it for Eliot. The argument of this poem is that there are "special moments" we have access to in our lives in time, and these moments stand for something that may well be outside time. The "what might have been" moment in the rose garden that opens the poem is the standard by which all other such moments—and images of other such moments will accumulate throughout the four poems—are measured, as moments of childish innocence in which all seems well. *Burnt Norton* seems to make a fairly simple resolution: we have these moments; we can recall them through the power of memory whenever we will; and if we purify ourselves from contamination from the ordinary "twittering world" through a descent to darkness, we can escape from time and reach the stillness that these moments promise. The last lines of the poem seem to promise us fulfillment through such moments:

> Sudden in a shaft of sunlight
> Even while the dust moves
> There rises the hidden laughter
> Of children in the foliage
> Quick now, here, now, always—
> Ridiculous the waste sad time
> Stretching before and after.
> (*Burnt Norton*, 5)

These special moments make the rest of time seem waste and sad; there are moments that are full and happy, and these bring us out of the world into the pattern that reaches the stillness. The moment of fulfillment so hoped for in *The Waste Land* and whose repetition is so longed for in "The Journey of the Magi" is now recovered, as we look out for such random moments of higher consciousness and recall them as we need to in making from them a pattern that rises out of time.

If this seems all too easy—and I admit I may have made it seem more facile than the poem suggests—Eliot thought so too and decided to use *Burnt Norton* as a base poem from which he could elaborate this same theme and make its resolution more complex, more satisfying. Five years later, when the war had begun and the pressures of history became obvious and overwhelming, he began to publish a quartet a year, coming eventually to the same fundamental position arrived at in *Burnt Norton* but in a way that calls for the presence of the Christ event. It is not possible to escape from history, from time, and into the timeless as easily as the first quartet so blithely claims, and so a more rigorous solution must be found, one that allows for transcendence while still respecting the forces of history, a solution that respects the random and discrete while still allowing the possibility of a return to unity and wholeness. That solution is the Incarnation, and it leads to Eliot's version of modernist allegory.

The second quartet, *East Coker*, ruthlessly challenges the first poem's easy transcendence by insisting on time as a destroyer, time as something that may indeed hold in store a handful of these special moments but that moves inexorably toward death. To put it simply, these moments, as wonderful as they may be, do not stop time; they do not ward off death; they do not cure our temporal dilemma. *East Coker* begins with language reminiscent of the Book of Ecclesiastes, in which anything we build is destroyed in time. Even the special moments we experience are now subject to the rigors of being in time: "the pattern is new in every moment / And every moment is a new and shocking / Valuation of all we have been" (*East Coker*, 2). Nothing is stable or permanent in *East Coker*, and the moments that were the source of so much hope in the first quartet now are called "echoed ecstasy / Not lost, but requiring, pointing to the agony / Of death and birth" (*EC*, 3). These moments are not lost, because memory still operates and can bring them back to consciousness, but only as echoes of the real thing, as muted versions of the happiness they were. Memory as understood in *East Coker*, under the sway of time and change, is like memory in the early episodes of *Ulysses*, as in "Lestrygonians," where Bloom could use memory only to make the present seem diminished from a happier and fuller past. These moments are not lost but now actually point to and require the "agony of death and birth." If we hear the faintest allusion to Christ's agony in the garden, that would help explain why the agony is of "death and birth," for Christ's agony in the garden and death are what lead to the birth as resurrected body. The point is made clear in the fourth part of *East Coker*, where we are told our only health is the disease of our body and that our only drink is the dripping blood and our only food the bloody flesh: "In spite of which we like to think / That we are sound, substantial flesh and blood— / Again, in spite of that, we call this Friday good" (*EC*, 4). Even though *East Coker* rather ruthlessly insists on time as destroyer of our flesh and blood, it turns softly to the hope that Christ, in accepting death for us, gave us the possibility of resurrection and of nourishment in the Eucharist. The power of time is ignored in *Burnt Norton* and given prominence in *East Coker,* and this new focus on time as inescapable brings Eliot to the Christ event as the one event in human history that may solve his problem with time.

The Dry Salvages does not allow time to recede as a problem, but it does bring a clearer focus on these moments that are in time yet promise something out of time. As he continues to think about these moments—and there has been a gradual accumulation of images suggesting the variety of forms these moments may take on—they become increasingly meaningful:

> The moments of happiness—not the sense of well-being,
> Fruition, fulfillment, security or affection,
> Or even a very good dinner, but the sudden illumination—
> We had the experience but missed the meaning,
> And approach to the meaning restores the experience
> In a different form, beyond any meaning
> We can assign to happiness.
>
> (*Dry Salvages*, 2)

The moments that were in *East Coker* merely leading to the agony of our death here are recuperated by assigning meaning to them. As we remember these moments, they take on a deeper, fuller meaning and begin to shine with the light of illumination. As we saw with Joyce, memory is no longer understood as a mere receptacle of images but as a transformative agent capable of restoring the experience. In this, as with Joyce, Eliot has arrived at the medieval understanding of memory and its powers as described by Frances Yates in her classic study *The Art of Memory*,[2] in which she documents how a classical system designed for easy recall for the purposes of rhetoric and oratory becomes for the medieval mind a way to work upon images until they become light-filled and indicative of God's presence in the world. Eliot has made a huge claim, that memory can restore to the present a moment from the past and make it more meaningful now than it was then; and with that new meaning that moment becomes light-filled in the special way that illumination suggests: the light of spiritual knowledge. This is not much different than the way Joyce ends *Ulysses* with an image in memory that has been brought to the present as the breathless climax to the novel, as an image that early in the day led to Bloom's depression and at the end of the book is restored as his passport to eternity. The moments in *Four Quartets* have not previously been meaningful in any way but have been recorded to seem unique to the speaker's experience and so to encourage us to accumulate our own special moments as we try to follow the poem's course. The moments have been mere images and now, by the power of memory, have been transformed into something charged with spiritual meaning.

Four Quartets is moving toward the ability to find, and live within, what Eliot calls "the point of intersection of the timeless with time" (*DS*, 5). But since only the saint can really accomplish that full joining of one's life with the Christ event, he tells us what life can be for the rest of us:

> For most of us, there is only the unattended
> Moment, the moment in and out of time,
> The distraction fit, lost in a shaft of sunlight,
> The wild thyme unseen, or the winter lightning
> Or the waterfall, or music heard so deeply
> That it is not heard at all, but you are the music
> While the music lasts. These are only hints and guesses,
> Hints followed by guesses; and the rest
> Is prayer, observance, discipline, thought and action.
> The hint half guessed, the gift half understood, is Incarnation.
>
> (*DS*, 5)

As we make the fateful decision to live for and around these moments, they grow in meaning until we are given the gift of Incarnation. Our lives take on the pattern of Christ's life, as we live more and more fully for these moments that increasingly shine with the brightness of timeless love. Eliot has taken imagism and made it the basis of allegory, as the image, not symbol but mere depiction of some natural event, becomes larger and larger in meaning until it becomes Incarnation.

In *Little Gidding* we are given Eliot's fullest statement about the powers of memory:

>   This is the use of memory:
> For liberation—not less of love but expanding
> Of love beyond desire, and so liberation
> From the future as well as the past. Thus, love of a country
> Begins as attachment to our own field of action
> And comes to find that action of little importance
> Though never indifferent. History may be servitude,
> History may be freedom.
>
> (*Little Gidding*, 3)

Memory is the agency of the mind that can take the discrete moments of special consciousness and work on them until desire becomes love and this love frees us from attachment to the world—from "Attachment to self and to things and to persons." Memory frees us from the mere attachment to the various objects in the world that is desire by expanding love beyond desire. This is quite in keeping with Bloom's kind of love, beyond mere desire for Molly and large enough to allow for mercy and forgiveness. By this use of memory, we are able to engage in the proper attitude toward history: what occurs in the arena of history (and recall that the war is raging and, in early 1942, going quite badly for the British) is of little importance, though we are not indifferent to the events. Still in the body and so in history we care about the events we call historical and yet, freed by memory into timeless love, we see beyond history also and so see the action of little importance. This is the way the Incarnation has us see and feel about history.

History enters *Four Quartets* through the last quartet, *Little Gidding*, in which Eliot presents himself as an air-raid warden walking through a battered London after a German bombing raid. This placement of his own war-time activity on behalf of his nation brings the pressures of history into the poem as something to be met and overcome by his allegory:

> In the uncertain hour before the morning
> > Near the end of interminable night
> > At the recurrent end of the unending
> After the dark dove with the flickering tongue
> > Had passed below the horizon of his homing . . .
> > I met one walking. . . .
>
> (LG, 2)

The scene dissolves into a Dantesque encounter with a "dead master," a "familiar compound ghost" who seems to represent a great tradition of poetry and who will advise Eliot to accept the fire of purgation: "From wrong to wrong the exasperated spirit / Proceeds, unless restored by that refining fire / Where you must move in measure, like a dancer" (LG, 2). What is most fascinating in all this is that the image of the Holy Spirit bringing the fire of purgation is "the dark dove with the flickering tongue," an image of a German dive-bomber with its painted fire-grin along its nose as it drops its load of bombs on London. The forces of history bring not only destruction but also the opportunity for purgation, for liberation. In the fourth section of *Little Gidding*, Eliot again brings this image into the poem:

> The dove descending breaks the air
> With flame of incandescent terror
> Of which the tongues declare
> The one discharge from sin and error.
> The only hope, or else despair

Lies in the choice of pyre of pyre—
To be redeemed from fire by fire.
(LG, 4)

We are born into a world of desire that can burn us; desire is "the intolerable shirt of flame / Which human power cannot remove" in the next stanza. But history provides us with the opportunity to transform the fire of desire, which consumes us, into the fire of purgatory, which cleanses us, and even into the fire of Pentecost, which gives us the fullness of God's spirit. History becomes less important for its political and military outcomes than for its possibilities of spiritual fulfillment.

This is the lesson of the Incarnation: that when we are joined to the mystery of Christ, occupying the "point of intersection of the timeless with time," we are freed to live in history for eternal purpose, within space and time with the intention of reaching our spiritual ideal. What might have begun as a simple effort to halt time and reach another order of existence is rendered more complex and satisfying as Eliot writes a poem based on the Incarnation, based on our ability to meditate on special moments of human consciousness until they shine with the light of God, until we move in the world as Christ moved in the world. Having at first attempted to halt time and escape from history, Eliot comes to write his version of modernist allegory that allows reconciliation of the two orders, of the timeless with time, the divine with the human. With Incarnation providing access to this point of intersection, he can write: "Here the impossible union / Of spheres of existence is actual" (DS, 5). The permanent and timeless have found a way to coincide with the relative and temporal.

Notes toward a Supreme Fiction

Eliot's version of allegory is much more poetic than it is theological; that is, it is firmly based on poetic images that may be interesting and arresting but that are also ultimately meaningless until they are rendered increasingly meaningful by the power of memory with a meaning that is eventually significant of Incarnation. Images that are random and fragmented in our lives—images that could be scattered through the "Waste Land" of the modern world—are meditated upon in memory until they bring us into the pattern of Christ's life. The fragments of imagism are given unity by their becoming whole in the mystery of the Incarnation, as images depicted by poetic power are given meaning by the theological terms.

Without the explicit use of the theological terms, Stevens's version of allegory is quite similar in *Notes toward a Supreme Fiction*. The volume of poems that precedes this long poem, *Parts of a World,* presents an interesting paradox as its underlying theme: Is the world irredeemably broken down into fragments, its constituent "parts," or is there a discernible unity that can unite these discrete parts into a single "world"? Which word do we emphasize, "parts" or "world," fragments or unity? Without venturing into analysis of this volume, we can cite the opening lines from what may be its central poem, "Asides on the Oboe," to indicate the struggle Stevens has chosen to undertake in his poetry:

> The prologues are over. It is a question, now
> Of final belief. So, say that final belief
> Must be in a fiction. It is time to choose.

The world that has been broken down into its constituent parts needs to be given the fiction of unity, requires belief that can once again unite the parts and form a world. Even if we cannot quite muster the requisite belief, at least we can say that we believe, and this saying is enough. *Notes toward a Supreme Fiction*—which as James Longenbach makes clear was written immediately after *Parts of a World* though placed at the end of the next volume, *Transport to Summer*[3]—takes up the task that "Asides on the Oboe" begins, which is to find a way to write a fiction that does not negate the real, the parts, while forging a fragile but satisfying unity.

Stevens was fascinated by the relation of the parts to the whole, of the real to the imagined; it is part of his modernist inheritance, especially from Eliot and Pound, to note that the world is broken down into fragments that the poet's imagination has the job of bringing back into unity. But the economic and political crises of the 1930s and the onset of World War II forced him to think through the relation of the real to the imagination in a way that could allow him to write his "long poem containing history." While *Notes* does not at first glance seem to be about history or the war that is its most visible and pressing manifestation, the coda that ends the poem, addressed to the soldier on whose war the poet's war depends, brings the violence and dangers of history into the poem clearly and pointedly. Longenbach shows how central to Stevens's design this coda was, bringing the war into the poem's deepest intentions. The war makes the real seem more powerful than it might appear during times of relative peace; the horrors of military violence make the real seem much more important and worthy of attention than the fictions of the imagination. Nonetheless, *Notes* is about the imagination and its ability to fashion the supreme fiction that makes our lives in the real seem not only bearable but worthy.

The object of Stevens's great long poem is to find a way for humanity to be reconciled to our lives in time, and to achieve such a reconciliation is, in fact, the act of heroism. As Stevens puts it late in the poem, "Perhaps, / The man-hero is not the exceptional monster, / But he that of repetition is most master." The poem is, then, a culmination of Stevens's lifelong concern to confront and resolve the anxieties and the potential despair inherent in monotony and repetition in our ordinary lives. Yet, written during 1942, this theme acquires a larger urgency and demands a fuller understanding of the powers of the imagination. The poem is a response to the need for the life of the imagination to stand up to the pressures of history as embodied in the extraordinary violence of World War II. The coda that ends the poem makes explicit a theme that runs throughout, which is that there is always a war for the poet, though not always for the soldier; that the war in which the poet is engaged depends on the war that the soldier is called on to fight; that the imagination is always fighting against the pressures of history or reality, trying to give us a way of feeling satisfied in this difficult and at times violent world. The poem is inspired by the actual war abroad to meditate on a more constant war that great poets are always fighting.

This may all sound melodramatic, but under the pressure of the violence of the actual war the literary artist seems to feel the need to rise higher than normally he would and recognize what his words are aiming to accomplish in the reader's sensibility. Again, it seems it requires the unusual pressure of the war for this generation of modernist poets to reassess and develop their thinking about the role of their imaginative play and its relation to the ordinary world. I turn briefly now to a lecture Stevens wrote just weeks before the bombing of Pearl Harbor, "The Noble Rider and the Sound of Words," for in this lecture he offers a theory on the purpose of great poetry that is surely inspired by, and responding to, the news he has been following closely of the war in Europe.

At the heart of this lecture is Stevens's conviction "that the idea of nobility exists in art today only in degenerate forms or in a much diminished state, if, in fact, it exists at all or otherwise than on sufferance; that this is due to failure in the relation between the imagination and reality. I should now like to add that this failure is due, in turn, to the pressure of reality" (Stevens, *Necessary Angel*, 12–13). Late in the essay he repeats the claim, "There is no element more conspicuously absent from contemporary poetry than nobility" (35). Stevens notes that "the spirit of negation has been so active, so confident and so intolerant that the commonplaces about the romantic provoke us to wonder if our salvation, our way out, is not the romantic. All great things have been denied" (17). These statements place Stevens within the model of reading I set up for *Ulysses*, especially the opening episodes in which Stephen is looking still for romance in a world dominated by the mocker Mulligan, who embodies for that novel and for modernism "the spirit of negation." What Stevens most likely means by "the romantic" is the Blakean version of the romantic sensibility that flies high in reaction against this spirit of negation. For Stevens, this spirit of denial is embodied by the work of Freud, whose *Future of an Illusion* was intended "to suggest a surrender to reality" (14). In this text Freud "disagrees with the argument that man cannot do without the consolation of what he calls the religious illusion and that without it he would not endure the cruelty of reality. His conclusion is that man must venture at last into the hostile world and that this may be called education to reality" (15). Freud wants us to grow up and do without this illusion, and this "surrender to reality" negates and denies all the great things Stevens seems to think we need and that poetry is now best capable of providing.

These terms are now quite familiar to us, as we can trace a high modernist theme in the need for the noble and ideal in a world of reduction, negation, and denial. What spurs Stevens's thinking is that the last ten years of American social life have been dominated by "an extraordinary pressure of news—let us say, news incomparably more pretentious than any description of it, news, at first, of the collapse of our system, or, call it, of life; then news of a new world . . . ; and finally news of a war. . . . And for more than ten years, the consciousness of the world has concentrated on events which have made the ordinary movement of life seem to be the movement of people in the intervals of a storm" (*NA*, 20). This pressure of news, coupled by the spirit of negation already prevalent, represents a pressure of reality overcoming the power of the imagination to depict suitable images of the noble and ideal. The "possible poet" must emerge who can lead the imagination back into proper relation to this powerful and new reality. Stevens clearly describes the function of this poet in relation to his readers or his audience, "to make his imagination theirs and that he fulfills himself only as he sees his imagination become the light in the minds of others. His role, in short, is to help people to live their lives" (29). For most of us, the pressure of reality is so great that we lose all sense of the noble and ideal, and the poet's job is to give us back our imagination by giving us his imagination, with which we can project our own ideals onto the world. In the phrase that gives rise to the poem we are about to analyze, the poet "gives to life the supreme fictions without which we are unable to conceive of it" (31).

For Stevens there is something in the poet's use of words that lends nobility to the things described. The poet naturally then seeks the noble despite the fact that the world as presently constituted seems to deny the very thing. "For the sensitive poet, conscious of negations, nothing is more difficult than the affirmations of nobility and yet there is nothing that he requires of himself more persistently, since in them and in their kind, alone, are to be found those sanctions that are the reasons for his being and for that occasional ecstasy, or ecstatic freedom of the mind, which is his special privilege" (*NA*, 35). Though the world is dominated by a modern spirit of negation and at present by a war that opposes the ideal and noble by its gruesome violence, the poet is engaged in a constant war to affirm the noble and the ideal, to give us the illusions that we are at peace and free in a world that is our home. The poet gives us the supreme fictions that we need to make the world appear unified and our lives satisfying.

In *Notes toward a Supreme Fiction,* Stevens suggests that all supreme fictions have the same fundamental plot and same fundamental purpose: to make us feel at home in the world, that familiar plot from the *Odyssey* that Joyce used as the underpinning to his epic story of a return home. For Stevens, all poetry is inspired by this theme:

> From this the poem springs: that we live in a place
> That is not our own, and much more, not ourselves
> And hard it is in spite of blazoned days.

The purpose of poetry is to provide us with the fiction that the world is our home, that we belong here and assume our identity here. This is the illusion that Freud, and all realists, would like to take away from us so we can face the hardships of life directly, like mature and able people. But poetry is able to cast over the world its sound of nobility, transforming the alien earth into a possible home. Our lives begin to take on some shape because of the gift of poetry:

> The poem refreshes life so that we share,
> For a moment, the first idea . . . It satisfies
> Belief in an immaculate beginning
>
> And sends us, winged by an unconscious will,
> To an immaculate end. We move between these points.

No longer lost in the middle of history, no longer confused in the midst of a present with no trace of its origin or sense of its end, we are given a plot by the power of poetry, which is that we began in a pure way, at an immaculate origin, and are moving toward a similarly pure goal. A more realistic approach to human life would deny these points of origin and telos as merely projections or constructions of the human imagination with no validity and with some dangerous consequences. Siebers describes Haydan White's skeptical description of "reality" as "a mere sequence of brute facts"; according to White, any sense of coherence or wholeness that we have made from these brute facts is to be rejected as merely "human constructions" that, out of desire for order, we have imposed on the world of the real" (Siebers, 15–16). As Siebers wishes to teach us how to be skeptical of such standardized skepticism, in this case by wondering why human desire for order is to be so easily and completely rejected as unreal and unnatural, so Stevens wishes us to consider the imagination, which is the source of unity and order, as natural and real as the reality against which and with which it works. Stevens allows the imagination's tendency to posit beginnings and endings to stand as a given of the human mind, as something we are capable of imagining and therefore part of the human world we are constructing.[4] The imagination begins its pressing back against history and the real by insisting on its rights to create the fiction of our origins and goals, to construct a plot—a fiction—that can reconcile us to the hard conditions of life on this planet. In Stevens's formulation is the conviction that the great poet has replaced the novelist in being the literary artist capable of giving us these necessary fictions. The novel has become too bound to the real without the light of imagination, while the poet can bring the imagination into intimate relation with the real. Stevens refuses to surrender to the realists and insists that the human imagination is a force capable of making certain adjustments in our attitudes so that we can feel less alienated and less purposeless.

In order to feel as if we are acting out our own nostos in an alien world, Stevens thinks that we need an image of heroism, an abstract image to inspire and by which we can measure our heroic efforts. Stevens offers an image of what he calls "major man," what he calls the "exponent" of man, "abler in the abstract than in his singular, / More fecund as principle than particle." Major man raises our capacities to a higher power, as the mathematical exponent can raise the value of a number to extraordinary levels merely by being attached to the number. Stevens calls him "this foundling of the infected past," an orphan with no connection to a personal history and so free to emerge in the present clean and pure and as an image of our greatness. When Stevens gives him a description in the last section of the first part of the poem, he is a man on the outskirts of town in an old coat and slouching pantaloons, "looking for what was, what used to be." The image is clearly that of Charlie Chaplin's little tramp, that carefree vagabond able to escape from various predicaments to wander about freely in a life of searching—in Stevens's poem, searching for something that once was. The hero is he who seems unattached to anything in the world and who lives at the margins of the culture, where one is free enough of the constraints of the real world of history to find that elusive thing that can reconcile us to the world.

This figure must remain abstract and cannot become the rigid statue of General Du Puy, who remains merely a curiosity for lawyers and doctors to study the past; and the fictions we devise must similarly be open to change so that they can keep from becoming just another old story with no relation to the present. Stevens laments "that poetry is a cemetery of nobilities" (*NA*, 35), once offering fresh ideals and fictions but now merely offering memorials. There must be constant renewal of the relation of the real and the imagination, for these things of opposite natures "seem to depend on one another," and they "embrace and forth the particulars of rapture come." The imagination is the permanent of the two in this dialectical pair, compared by the poet to Latin as an unchanging language of high culture in comparison to the vulgate and the lingua franca of the real. The imagination must always work to be near the real, to be in union with the real, to be engaged with the ever-changing and at times frightening conditions of the real, and from their intimate relation rapture comes.

The poet wants to give us his imagination, his ability to light up the world with nobility and the fiction of the nostos. And by having this pure and potent imagination, we approach more closely to the real that is our goal. Ironically, the realist without imagination is the one who has chosen to remain locked up in a darkness where the real is estranged, and the poet's imagination is the agency that brings us close to an intimate relation with the real:

> To find the real,
> To be stripped of every fiction except one,
>
> The fiction of an absolute—Angel,
> Be silent in your luminous cloud and hear
> The luminous melody of proper sound.

The supreme fiction, the one that we are not to strip from us, is the fiction of an absolute, of an order timeless and permanent. Without this fiction we do not find the real; it remains alien to us in a confused array of discrete particulars. This fiction is the "necessary angel" that brings us back the world we have lost. As a later poem, "Angel Surrounded by Paysans," puts it:

> Yet I am the necessary angel of earth,
> Since, in my sight, you see the earth again,
>
> Cleared of its stiff and stubborn, man-locked set,
> And in my hearing, you hear its tragic drone
>
> Rise liquidly in liquid lingerings,
> Like watery words awash. . . .

This necessary angel is appearing to peasants in a new nativity scene in which what is born is the possibility of our being at home in the world, seeing it without all the clutter of human categories. It is still a human perspective, for it is our seeing and our hearing that are cleansed by this angel so that we see and hear the earth again. We see and hear as an angel would, in space and time but perceiving the absolute. The earth has been cleared of its corruption by this angel, this figure of the powerful and absolute imagination, who gives its way of perceiving the world to us and so gives us the world again.

The imagination is of an order that is absolute, or at least that is the supreme fiction we must never abandon. It is unchanging in its power and capacity to transform the world into a higher, nobler, and more satisfying place in which to live our lives. That Stevens calls it an angel, and more pointedly the necessary angel of earth, indicates that it is near to God, near to holiness, near to the eternal and permanent world of the divine. In fact, in a late poem, "Final Soliloquy of the Interior Paramour," he says,

> We say God and the imagination are one . . .
> How high that highest candle lights the dark
>
> Out of this same light, out of the central mind,
> We make a dwelling in the evening air,
> In which being there together is enough.

The imagination may not be God, but when "we say" that they are one—when we posit that fiction—the darkness of the world is broken by "that highest candle," a candle that gives a high and holy light to the world. This light allows us to make a dwelling, a home, where we can experience what it feels like to have enough, to be enough. The supreme fiction is that we have an imagination that is God-like and that can light the world with a loftiness and nobility that makes our individual lives worth living and that makes the world our home.

This is Stevens's version of Incarnation: that each of us lives in a world that is inescapable and to which we are bound by our bodies and sense, and yet each of us has access to an imagination that is angelic and even God-like, transforming that world into something higher and nobler and capable of being our home. Stevens calls for the imagination to be in constant and complex relation to the real, never allowing the real to be so strong that we lose the angelic influence and never losing contact with the real and think, along with poets such as Blake, that we are approaching some pure realm of ideals. We are given the illusion that we belong in this world by the influence of the necessary angel. There is in this relation of two orders of being—the timeless and the temporal, the angelic and the human, the imagination and the real—the only way for us to be reconciled to our lives in time.

The Pisan Cantos

When Ezra Pound was placed in the Detention Training Center (D.T.C.) in Pisa in 1944, not only was his life put in jeopardy, as a man to be brought back to the United States to stand trial for treason, but his epic project was also placed in great risk. He had, most directly and explicitly, been engaged in writing a long poem containing history, and much of his effort was devoted to finding and recording examples of good political action in the past in the hope that political leaders of the present may be inspired and guided by a tradition of nobility. Pound opened his poem of history to the present in a unique and compelling way when he hopefully made the discovery that Mussolini was the man of the present hour who was acting in the great tradition Pound had been forging in *The Cantos*. As Peter Makin claims, Pound "had put all his credit as a writer behind Mussolini" (Makin, 233), and with Mussolini's fall and his own arrest and internment, Pound's life and project were in jeopardy. If Mussolini had failed to usher in a new age of economic justice for Italy that could spread, largely through the poet's efforts, to America and the West in general, then what direction would the epic poem take now, with Mussolini dead and disgraced and his poet on trial for treason by the nation he thought he was working for?

Having placed his political and poetic hopes in Mussolini, Pound began *The Pisan Cantos* with the poignant expression of tragedy: "The enormous tragedy of the dream in the peasant's bent shoulders" (canto 74, p. 424). The epic has given way to tragedy, as the project of hopeful possibility becomes a project of lamentation and despair at the failure of the dream of economic justice. But the epic hopes would be asserted once again when Pound found a way to elevate himself, in his condition as great poet, as the heroic survivor of the debacle. Bereft almost totally of any books or resources with which to continue his writing, he was forced to rely upon memory; and as he meditated upon the power of memory, he began to understand its powers in a way already discovered by Joyce and Eliot, as an agency of the human mind capable of discovering a layer of experience best called allegory.

In Pisa, which for someone immersed in Dante could easily be regarded as a place of treacherous fraud (and he does refer occasionally to Ugolino's tower), Pound may have felt that the Ugolino story was perilously close to his own. Ugolino narrates a story that is so heart-wrenching that we may be led to forget that, if he also is confined to the icy depths where treacherous fraud is punished, he must have acted treacherously himself. The reader might indeed be tempted to apply this model to Pound's situation; for while we may be led to sympathize with the sixty-year-old poet placed in an outdoor cage for several weeks exposed to the elements, we might wish to recall, as Dante insists we do for Ugolino, that the man we feel pity for may indeed be a traitor. So one "plot" for *The Pisan Cantos* is to watch how Pound attempts to exonerate himself from the charge of treachery and find a way of continuing his epic project despite the tragedy of the fall of the Fascist state.

On the first page of the Pisan sequence he indicates that he will no longer keep himself out of his poem, as for the most part he has done in the preceding cantos. We read on this page, "No Man, No Man? Odysseus / the name of my family" (425). He will not hide behind the relative anonymity of being "the poet"; he will not claim to be the "no man" who wrote the verses of the Seven Lakes Canto ("by no man these verses"), which presented the goal of political action as "a people of leisure" free from political or economic oppression and living in harmony with natural processes. To be "the poet" of the dream, a disembodied "no man," was a comfortable mask, but it may also have been a ruse, even a lie, and for now on there will be no lies. It is as if he is saying, "I'm a man with a name and a personal history." It seems to indicate that he is going to accept responsibility for his words and actions that led him to his predicament and not hide behind a mask of being a poet merely writing irresponsible fictions. This act of taking responsibility for his words might remind him of the axiom of Fascist thought that he repeated often and includes in canto 78: "wherein is no responsible having a front name, a hind name and an address" (479). The cleverness of Odysseus that helps him escape from Polyphemus's cave will no longer be used by Pound as he comes to terms with his imprisonment in a cage. He will present himself to us as a man with a name and address, as a man with a personal past based on a personal identity retained in memory. In short, he will not forget who he is in these cantos, nor will he allow us to forget where his actions have led him.

Other moments from the opening canto secure this point. Still on the first page Pound addresses his reader as "You who have passed the pillars and outward from Herakles" (425). That aspect of the Ulysses theme was important to Pound early in *The Cantos*, the wanderer who will not return to Ithaca but who instead bravely, recklessly, sails beyond the Pillars of Hercules to find new wisdom and new experience. But now he distances himself from that figure who eschews nostalgia—"*You* who have passed the pillars." Later, in the midst of an important declaration of his faith in the possibility of the city whose terraces are the color of stars, he includes a word from the opening of canto 8 of *Purgatorio*—"ch'intenerisce": "at sunset / ch'intenerisce / a sinistra la Torre / seen thru a pair of breeches" (431). The sunset Pound sees from his cage is like the sunset as described by Dante in Purgatory, "turning back the longing of seafarers and melting their heart the day they have bidden dear friends farewell." Pound includes the tower of Ugolino, the place where he suffered, "seen thru a pair of breeches," to remind the reader of the scene of the experience of this particular sunset and the odd vantage point Pound has of it; but he uses canto 8 of *Purgatorio* against Dante, for Dante's pilgrim must eschew the natural longing for home while Pound will indulge in memories of the past. With little but memory to solace him, Pound prepares for its use and begins to contemplate its powers. Just a couple of pages earlier he writes lines that echo the opening of the eighth canto of *Purgatorio:* "el triste pensier si volge / ad Ussel. A Ventadour / va il concire, el tempo rivolge / and at Limoges the young salesman / bowed with such french politeness" (428). "The sad thought turns back" to places special to Pound from his personal experience in a happier past, and he indulges himself in recalling such memories. He is not going to follow Dante in this regard and avoid this kind of nostalgia that evokes the merely personal; this point is made especially clear and compelling with the last phrase of canto 74: "we who have passed over Lethe" (449). We know that Dante is immersed in Lethe at the top of Mount Purgatory after his painful itinerary has been completed by his personal confession to Beatrice; and that immersion takes from him all memory of sin. Pound will not immerse himself in this river, not yet at any rate: he crosses over the river of forgetfulness, for he needs to remember all he has said and all he has done.

A cursory glance at the Pisan sequence is enough to convince anyone that personal memories are included often enough that they must be important to the structure and meaning of these poems. But Pound also remembers his positions on economic policy, his advocacy of Italian fascism, along with many other cultural fragments stored in his memory. What is new in this sequence is that the personal dimension of the poet's life is now laid alongside the public side; these poems offer, I think, a reconciliation of the private man with his public mission. In this regard, a passage from canto 78 becomes particularly important. In a little more than a page Pound includes fragments that suggest his trip from Rome to Gais to see his daughter Mary, a passage from Gawin Douglas's translation of *The Aeneid,* images from his present predicament, and phrases from Fascist rhetoric. His inclusion of his painful journey from Rome to visit Mary brings his personal life into the poem in a radically new way: never before in the poem do we have a sense of the man with a complicated personal life. The purpose of this visit was to set things right between himself and Mary; to tell her the truth about himself and her mother, Olga Rudge; and to reveal the existence of Dorothy Pound and her half brother Omar. As I argue in my book on Pound, I read its inclusion here as a penitential journey, as personal confession. But what is so fascinating about this passage is how the confession moves directly into the Scottish translation of Virgil's epic. Aeneas is able to begin the process that will culminate in the great empire by denying his personal life and living out only his public destiny. Aeneas has little trouble denying himself the happiness of living with Dido in a great city already well under construction; he leaves her quickly and easily when Mercury reminds him of his higher destiny, to found Rome. The juxtaposition of Pound's personal life with Aeneas's destiny suggests that Pound is putting his personal life in some kind of order through confession, allowing himself now to follow his public destiny in a way analogous to Aeneas's strong-willed devotion. It is a wonderful juxtaposition of Christian confession and classical epic. And after a brief depiction of the D.T.C. he assembles a few phrases from the rhetoric of Italian fascism, concluding now that "those words still stand uncancelled" (479). His mission is to rise above mere personality to be the prophet of the dream of the ideal city, whose latest effort was just destroyed by the Allied Powers but whose words "still stand uncancelled" by this defeat. Pound writes these Fascist slogans for the future, for men and women inspired by this dream to use and implement. He hopes that his record of the dream is written on something more durable than gelatine: "but if the gelatine be effaced whereon is the record?" (479). What we have here is a fascinating juxtaposition of the most personal moment in all *The Cantos* with his ambition to be the Aeneas-like prophet keeping the dream of the ideal city alive for the future to act upon.

Pound has insisted that he will not forget his personal past; he has insisted that the Pisan sequence will be a record of what he finds as he remembers his past. So what has he discovered on his memory voyage? Here is where we see the similarity with the way Joyce and Eliot came to understand the powers of memory. What he discovers in this journey of memory is that he has an affinity with the great Hebrew prophets, and with Christ. He discovers that this old man confined to a cage by his own people is in fact in the tradition of great prophets from the Old Testament. He discovers that his life has fallen into a pattern based on the prophetic tradition of the Bible fulfilled by Christ.

This process of discovery begins with a wonderful mistake found by Rouse, the translator of Homer with whom Pound had correspondence: "and Rouse found they spoke of Elias / in telling tales of Odysseus" (426). When Rouse first let Pound know this, it must have seemed an interesting accident that had little relevance to his own interest in Homer and the whole tradition of wanderers in literary history. But now, as he lies in a cage incarcerated by the very people he had meant to be serving, might not the fate of the Hebrew prophet, to be castigated by his own people for the words he has pronounced against them, seem surprisingly his own? That it is probably an error, to mistake Elijah for Odysseus, is not at all an obstacle to someone who wants to use the mistake as a revealing prophecy of his own identity, for as we saw with Joyce and the accidental prophecy of "throwaway" throughout *Ulysses*, the prophecies are often not understood by the very people who utter them and the application may be revealed only much later. Can this mistake have been related to Pound so that he could, when he needed it, recall it and apply it to his own predicament? The wanderer theme has been predominant in *The Cantos* from its first page, and now—suddenly and surprisingly—Pound finds that the mistake is prophetically true, that Pound's wanderer, now closely identified with himself, does have a component of the Hebrew prophet in him.

I want to recall here that Pound was almost totally denied access to books for the first and only time in the course of writing his epic, but he was allowed a copy of the Bible. It was his genius to find congenial passages in a book he was not prepared to find congenial to his purposes, passages that allowed him to continue his poem's journey and elevate the destiny of his wandering hero, who is now the poet himself as survivor of the fall of Italian fascism. I imagine him searching through a book he has often castigated and finding passages that, with a shock of unexpected recognition, place him in a tradition of Old Testament prophecy. He begins citing such passages in the opening canto of the Pisan sequence, referring first to Isaiah, who encouraged his hearers "to redeem Zion with justice" (429); these words from the first chapter of Isaiah establish one of the prophet's major themes, which is that his audience is made up of a people fallen from the covenant to whom God has sent this messenger with the command to rebuild the great city. A few pages on we find this phrase from Isaiah repeated, with some pertinent additions: "with justice shall be redeemed / who putteth not his money out on interest / 'in meteyard in weight or measure' / XIXth Leviticus or / First Thessalonians 4, 11" (434). That the redemption of Zion will occur when there is honesty in the measures of wealth used has long been the basis of Pound's economic thinking, now derived from the Torah. And we are sent to Saint Paul to read "Aspire to a tranquil life, to mind your affairs, and to work with your own hands"; this advice is more ambiguous, but I think it is an admonition to the initiates to avoid the turmoil of the war's aftermath and continue their study and effort to build justice. Still in the opening canto of the Pisan sequence, another major prophet is cited:

> and there is also the XIXth Leviticus.
> "Thou shalt purchase the field with money."
> signed Jeremiah
> from the tower of Hananel unto Goah
> unto the horse gate $8.50 in Anatoth
> which is in Benjamin, 8.67 . . .
> From the law, by the law, so build yr/ temple
> with justice in meteyard and measure.
> (440)

Added to Leviticus and Isaiah are moments from Jeremiah in which the prophet is instructed to purchase a certain field for a certain amount of money; this actual field paid for with money earned by actual labor is to become a symbol for the people of Israel that the great city shall be rebuilt when economic practices are sound, when the measures are just. Pound is able to find in the Jewish law and prophets a commitment to build the just city, a city here on earth built by a people called to justice and equity, and by including these references he is adding a new dimension to his wanderer and, more profoundly, discovering his own true identity, as the incarnation of this type of prophet in the present.

I have often been tempted to claim that *The Cantos* is a version of what Sacvan Bercovitch, following Perry Miller, calls "the American jeremiad," an American genre based on biblical prophecies in which the speaker calls on a fallen people to remember the covenant God made with their fathers and return to a way that is just and true. What Bercovitch says about the American jeremiad is true of *The Pisan Cantos*: "For all their catalogues of iniquities, the jeremiads attest to an unswerving faith in the errand" (Bercovitch, 6). In fact, as Bercovitch points out, the writer of the jeremiad feels even more committed to his model and his ideals after the fall than he could have before, for the fall from the way is, in fact, part of the biblical pattern that inspires the writer to speak in the first place. Bercovitch makes a distinction between the American version of the jeremiad and its European model, which is that it does not lament a people's backsliding and despair over their prospects; rather, it celebrates God's correction of the people's errors as the mission or errand is thus validated and to be continued. As Perry Miller noted in his groundbreaking essay on this American genre, for all the bewilderment and chagrin registered in the jeremiad, "there is no surrender" (cited by Bercovitch, 9). Pound in no way distances himself from the economic ideas he had been espousing before his arrest, nor does he recant of his allegiance to Italian fascism and Mussolini. After its defeat he has found a way to be more committed than ever and elevate his own status as survivor of the Fascist goal of justice chosen to continue the dream. He too celebrates that the Fascist dream of justice is "now in the mind indestructible," made a permanent part of Western culture by the fall of the Fascist state and by Pound's heroic effort now to record it. He has discovered a model for himself that allows and even encourages his continued commitment, the role of Hebrew prophet. Never, in fact, does a poet identify himself this closely with the prophets of the Old Testament, as his own predicament mirrors quite neatly the treatment of the prophets by the very people they sought to teach.

There is one line, coming from Micah, that Pound is so fond of that he repeats it, to my count, six times in the Pisan sequence, including on its final page (where its source is finally acknowledged): "each in the name of its god." Why does Pound quote Micah so frequently? We need to see the context from which he pulled this congenial line. It comes from Micah 4, which is concerned (it should not come as a surprise at this point) with the restoration of the just city by the Lord:

> Many nations shall come and say, "Come, let us climb to the mount of the Lord, to the God of the house of Jacob, that he may instruct us in his ways, that we may walk in his paths." For from Zion shall go forth instruction, and the word of the Lord from Jerusalem. He shall judge between many nations; they shall beat their swords into plowshares, and the spears into pruning hooks; one nation shall not raise the sword against another, nor shall they train for war again. Every man shall sit under his own vine or under his own fig tree, undisturbed; for the mouth of the Lord of hosts has spoken. For all the peoples walk *each in the name of its god,* but we shall walk in the name of the lord, our God forever and ever. On that day, says the Lord, I will gather the lame, and I will assemble the outcasts, and those whom I have afflicted. I will make of the lame a remnant, and of those driven far off a strong nation; and the Lord shall be king over them on Mount Zion, from now on forever. (Mic. 4.2–7, my emphasis)

Pound, always or at least still interested in the pagan gods and goddesses, quotes a line that seems to endorse a toleration for polytheism. But in its context we see a more complex set of ideas. Each person can come to Zion in the name of his own particular and perhaps peculiar god; but once there, he will receive instruction from the Lord, who shall be king over all peoples ruling from Mount Zion from now on forever. Those who have been cast off, those who have been afflicted, those made lame and driven far off—these are the remnants of the chosen people who shall become the foundation of a strong nation. I think that this is Pound's cryptic way of moving to Zion to hear the word of a God he had never expected to be serving; he moves in the name of his god—I think it is Aphrodite—and at Zion discovers that the great king to restore the world to justice is the God of the Hebrews, the Messiah, the Christ.

How far do I want to take this? As far as Pound seems to suggest. On the second page of the Pisan sequence he quotes the "R. C. chaplain's field book" (426); one of the few books Pound found at the D.T.C. was this sixteen-page summary of the major elements of the Roman Catholic Mass, from which, he claims in canto 67, Pound "learned what the Mass meant, / how one should / perform it" (467). Back in canto 74 he makes an interesting conflation of the Mass and Christ's last words on the cross: "Est consummatum, ite" (432). Just as Christ expresses on the cross that his sacrifice is the fulfillment of God's complex plan for salvation, so Pound discovers in his Pisan cage that his arrest, internment, and possible execution are the fulfillment of his destiny: to have believed in the dream of the just city, live with the efforts to realize it, and survive its present defeat—survive and now record it as its great prophet, in a line of great Hebrew prophets extended to include even Christ. Pound "learned what the Mass meant" not only from the chaplain's field book but from his own discovery of a sacred, providential dimension to his own life. These poems written in Pisa are his ritual enactment of this discovery, his Mass. If allegory is defined as the discovery of a Christ dimension to one's life, as the gradual realization that one's destiny is taking on the pattern of the Christ event, then *The Pisan Cantos* qualify quite neatly and fully. As in Christ's case, what seems a betrayal and failure is in truth the fulfillment of a destiny. Still in canto 74 he compares his predicament with Christ's : "with Barabbas and the two thieves beside me" (436). Is Pound more like Barabbas, the brutal revolutionary, or Christ, the prophet of the dream? Placed among criminals by the very nation he was intending to serve and save (much as Christ was), he discovers that, as it was for Christ, it was his destiny to be castigated and brutalized by his own people. In the fiction of the poem (and may we not say about *The Cantos* what Singleton says about the *Divina Commedia:* the fiction is that it is not a fiction?) Pound has discovered that he has been brought, against any willing or knowing of his own, to an unexpected place as the fulfillment of a greater, more public destiny. His Mass is over; his destiny has been made sacred and noble despite appearances, and we are dismissed to go on and continue the effort to build "the city of Dioce whose terraces are the colour of stars."

What is extraordinary about Pound's version of modernist allegory is that it is made to join neatly with the political aspirations of his epic poem; it is made to retain fully the public and political aspects of *The Cantos* by placing them in the pattern of the providential design of biblical prophecy. Pound relies more fully on the Hebrew prophets than he does on Christ or the Christian teachings of Paul because he does not want to leave his earthly goals and purposes behind as he pursues a spiritual city. His city is to be made here on earth, as the Hebrew prophets thought Zion would be built with justice in this world.

Having established this aspect of his identity, having reconciled the private man with the public mission, in canto 80 he will finally be freed to undergo that immersion in Lethe denied in the opening canto:

> when the raft broke and the waters went over me,
> Immaculata, Introibo
> for those who drink the bitterness
> Perpetua, Agatha, Anastasia
>   saeculorum . . .

> Les larmes que j'ai crees m'indonent
> Tard, tres tard je t'ai connue, la Tristesse,
> I have been hard as youth sixty years.
> (513)

Plunged into the bitter waters of Lethe, he emerges pure and ready to confess his wrongs: he has been too hard; he has not allowed suffering to soften and heal him. He accepts his suffering now and is softened by his own tears. This is Pound's version of Dante's tearful confession and immersion in Lethe at the top of Mount Purgatory, after his suffering had brought him to the river of forgetfulness.[5] Pound learned "how to perform" the Mass from the chaplain's field book he so fortuitously discovered, and he embellishes this crucial scene of personal confession with the language of the Roman Catholic Mass: its opening phrases, its litany of martyrs, its language of eternity. As an artist he would naturally see the Mass as a performance, as an artistic ritual conferring sacredness to the ordinary. These cantos are his Mass, elevating his person to the dignity of the Hebrew prophets and to the status of Christ. As the Mass is the ritual reenactment of the Incarnation, the joining of the divine and the human in the sacrifice of the cross, these cantos present Pound's elevation as he is sacrificed.

I want to point out how extraordinary it is that during the war these three modernist poets, who had been developing their own ways of trying to ennoble and dignify their culture, came to write their own unique but related versions of modernist allegory, as if it were the pressure of history and the dangers of political violence that forced them to further their understanding of the powers of the imagination, an understanding that can be considered "romantic." It is as if a hundred and more years of romanticism, in the first part of this century dominated by technology and the human sciences, were forced to undergo a serious reevaluation of its understanding of the imagination and its powers, resulting in its diminishment in favor of realism by some or its continued assertion of privilege now brought into closer contact with the historical and the real by others. The four modernists in this study are concerned with maintaining a valued place for the imagination despite the increasing pressures from history, which are not new in kind but certainly in degree as the rate of change and advance make the conditions of history more intimidating to the imagination and its quest for the permanent than ever before. These four modernists seek and in allegory find a way to reconcile the pressures of history with the ideal and the noble, to reconcile our lives in time (which are often and at the moment of their writing—during World War I for Joyce and World War II for the others—violent and brutal) with our sense of the timeless and permanent. Each worked differently and toward different ends, as is natural since their earlier projects were leading them on different trajectories; but all four turned to the Christ event as the model for their greatest achievements as poets, as the modernist allegory allowed them to meet the demands of the real and the historical on the one hand and the permanent and absolute on the other.

Their achievements are all linked to Dante's allegory of the *Divina Commedia*, which similarly synthesizes the demands of our lives in time with the ideal order of God's eternal judgment. Dante's final image of a wheel that revolves around the sun and the other stars is meant to suggest the reconciliation of these two orders (see Freccero, "Dante's Final Image," 245–57). The wheel turns like a circle around God and so achieves the perfect order of eternity, yet the wheel also and at the same time moves forward in a linear fashion as our bodies do in time. Still in time yet united with eternity, our lives patterned on the model of the Christ event both move forward in time and circle God eternally.

How does Joyce fit in with the other three? I want to be careful not to claim his influence over them as they wrote these works twenty years after the publication of *Ulysses*. Yet it is widely known how closely Pound and Eliot, at least, were watching the growth of that book as it went to the *Little Review* during and immediately after the devastation of World War I, and perhaps that education did more than lead to *The Waste Land* and the opening motifs of *The Cantos*. Perhaps they had recourse to Joyce's model as they developed their own attitudes toward history and the eternal. But influence is not what I am interested in establishing as much as a new way to appreciate the greatest achievements of those poets we call the high modernists. They found in allegory their way to be both rigorously historical and idealistic, to be skeptical about our culture and still give it its ideals and values. This ability to reconcile our lives in the real with the values of our imaginings is a lasting gift of this version of literary modernism.

One of the major achievements of high modernism is to provide a sense of unity and order to the culture in which these writers find themselves. Yet the kind of unity achieved in modernist allegory cannot fairly be called totalizing or in any way leading to totalitarian tendencies, for a cardinal principle of Dante's allegory, based as it is on the allegory of the Bible as initiated by Saint Paul, is that not every detail from the Old Testament must be brought into the unity of the Incarnation. Many "historical" or "literal" events from Jewish history bear no further meaning than they appear to, and the rereading occasioned by allegory allows them to remain discrete and unassimilated. The same holds true for these modernist allegories. Not every detail is reducible to the Incarnation, for the Christ event is not a principle of monism that demands all facts or details to become explicable in its light. Rather, the Incarnation unites a distinct and limited series of concrete fragments into an important unity while allowing fragments not brought into this unity their autonomy to belong to other series or to shine alone as interesting and arresting phenomena. This allows these high modernists to respect difference and diversity while still not giving up on the attempt to forge a satisfying unity based on the permanence of the eternal order. It allows the array of details that offer delight—the *jouissance* of the fragment—to continue to do so while bringing a certain series of these fragments into a whole that is outside time.

This is a different view of the modernists than the one offered by postmodernist apologists who want to find in the poetics of high modernism a tendency toward totalitarianism, located especially in the will to take all fragments and force them into a supreme fiction, a unity that controls the meaning of every detail. The politics of the cold war, with the threat of totalitarianism causing many poets and literary critics to view the resistance against unity as heroic, also caused us to give up on the effort to find unity and the order of the ideal. The reaction against totalitarianism in the 1950s, which led us to value the fragmented and the different, became in its own way as totalitarian as what it opposed, for it prohibited the search for unity and the ideal that are the very things that give us identity and meaning. The modernists of the generation, beginning early with Joyce and continuing during World War II with the other three, found in the Incarnation a poetic principle capable of allowing for difference and for unity at the same time, reconciling our forward movement in a linear time without order or meaning with a circular movement around a fixed point that assigns meaning and value. I would like to think that this view of the high modernists may give further momentum to the critical resistance to the powerful forces in literary theory that have blocked our attempt to seek the wholeness of an ideal order. In any event, the greatness of these modernists is their ability to recognize and respect the richness and power of the temporal—that is why history is at the center of their projects—and not surrender to time and give up on the possibility of finding an important and satisfying unity.

These modernists may then have solved a problem that becomes the poetic and critical problem of the 1950s and is only now beginning to be dealt with forcefully, as the recent work of critics such as Altieri and Siebers bears witness—namely, the dilemma of postmodernism, which leads us to forego our desire for unity and order because we fear totalitarianism so deeply. The postmodern poet and the poststructuralist critic fear fascism so deeply that they are willing to give up on all master narratives and all large designs and settle for delight in the local and discrete unit not assimilated to any larger pattern. We do not have to agree with Lyotard that we have lost the nostalgia for the lost narrative (Lyotard, 49). We do not have to agree that nostalgia is an attitude to eschew, an attitude that locks us into backward-looking regret and results in a longing for the imposition of some order into the chaos of our lives. We may legitimately long for a lost narrative that can bring our lives into an order that is not total and thus not ruthless in driving out fragments or details (or persons) that do not fit its pattern. We may legitimately long for a lost narrative that gives meaning to our lives while still allowing us the pleasure of the unattended moment. The modernists, living before the full revelation of the horrors of totalitarian control, already see the dangers of order and the falsity of systems but do not choose to give up on the possibility of a satisfying order or a pattern so elegant and lofty that it reaches the stillness. In the principle of the Incarnation, and so in modernist allegory, the modernists find a point of balance, a position from which we can allow many aspects of our lives to remain unattached and free with the potential for *jouissance,* and from which we can at the same time review a series of fragments and assign them a higher meaning as they take form and become a pattern that brings us a glimpse of the permanent and the absolute. Perhaps this study of these modernist artists will prevent the caricature of modernism as incipient fascism and allow us to consider order and the ideal still viable goals for art and criticism.

It may be argued that this "solution" is too narrow and small, available only to an artist open to the possibility of embracing a Christian mystery as the foundation of an artistic project. As a response to this objection, I would like to recall the pioneering work done by William Lynch on this issue in his book *Christ and Apollo*. He carefully articulates the position that the Christian imagination is best equipped to undertake the difficult task of searching out the infinite within the finite, the ideal within the historical, the permanent within the world of flux. And it is because the figure of Christ shares in both natures that these opposed terms are attempting to describe that the Christian does not fear the messy world of history and fly, like Blake and Apollo, away from it. Rather, the Christian imagination is able to plunge into the world of fact and detail without the fear that it will be overcome by them and wander aimlessly in a world of highly charged fragments without ideal or order. Immersed in history, it has confidence that within that world it will find the ideal incarnated. That Christ lived in history accords history a value that must be respected, and that he lived outside time validates our aspirations for the eternal. These are no longer two distinct orders but are joined in the figure of Christ. And one does not necessarily, according to Lynch, need to believe in Christ to appropriate this principle as the cornerstone of the artistic project. The Christ event becomes the model on which we can base our efforts to discover the point of intersection between the timeless and time, the space where the temporal and the permanent may indeed coincide. The Incarnation need not be a matter for faith alone but, as we have seen, can function as a ground for a way of reading and a way of writing. Christ becomes the model of the genuine artistic project as he has been the center of a theology, and in the work of these four high modernists we see the Christian imagination establishing a model for our lives in time. In the model for reading that I have suggested may lie a hope that we can read for the ideal and the permanently valuable in the texts we have come to cherish as part of our cultural heritage.

Notes

Introduction

1. The phrase comes from the title of Karen Lawrence's important study *The Odyssey of Styles in Joyce's* Ulysses, which has an approach that I find quite inspiring, namely, to watch for the way the reader is made to move through a series of stylistic innovations and technical extravagances that render the reader the "hero" of the novel, as he emulates the voyage of Odysseus and avoids the various dangers along the way. My reading of the reader's journey is quite different from Lawrence's, for she does not find in the novel a place for the reader to call home, a style that is final and secure and from which the reader can, with the safety and certainty of having become grounded in a home, review the novel's course and offer a final expression of the meaning and importance of the journey. With Lawrence it is a journey with no definite end, whereas I think the novel brings the reader to "Ithaca," to the home, and leads the successful reader to a vision of something permanent and full. The reader's reading comes to a conclusion in my study.

Schwarz's book is also important to my study in his focus on the various ways Joyce is teaching his reader how to read his novel. Indeed, I make the same claim and use Schwarz's language for the claim. However, as with Lawrence, Schwarz offers various "lessons" that do not proceed toward an end, whereas my study emphasizes how *Ulysses* is a progressive series of lessons that prepare us for "Ithaca."

With these differences made clear, I want to place my study alongside theirs as another effort to follow the authorial signs that Joyce is careful to place within his text as so many exegetical clues about how to return home.

2. Implicit in my argument is my conviction that the high modernists who figure in this study—Joyce, Pound, Eliot, and Stevens—anticipate the responses to poststructuralism that we have been watching slowly develop momentum in the academy during the past decade. Theorists such as Charles Altieri and Tobin Siebers are in a position regarding poststructuralism and cultural materialism that is strikingly similar to the position in which the modernists found themselves during the early part of the century as they tried to find a language and a style

capable of representing something absolute and permanent in an intellectual climate that had been learning to reduce and doubt the ideal.

The way I would sketch the arc of literary theory relevant to my study, structuralism, in its effort to locate deep structures in a synchronic view of human institutions, gave rise almost immediately and quite powerfully to what is now labeled "poststructuralism," in that this later was keenly focused not on the structures themselves in isolation from history but on the various historical forces that gave rise to these structures, the complex and often dirty process of construction whose description becomes Derridean deconstruction and Foucauldian archaeology. The original attempt to locate stable structures outside history only made the question of history more prominent and more powerfully focused than ever before. The theorists who come after poststructuralism, those who want to describe the possibilities of the existence of ideals and of their expression in language, must respond to the rigors of thinkers such as Jacques Derrida and Michel Foucault. One cannot ignore history but must place the investigation of the ideal within rigorous historical matrices. My argument about the high modernists is that they are doing just that as they respond to the various attacks on the permanent and the absolute made by the powerful thinkers of the nineteenth century, especially Charles Darwin, Karl Marx, Friedrich Nietzsche, and Sigmund Freud. And the mystery of the incarnation, which is the ideal entering the body and so entering history, will be at the center of the projects of representing the ideal.

3. Stephen uses a phrase from canto 31 in *Purgatorio*, where Dante confesses to Beatrice that he fell too much in love with "present things" (*le presenti cosi*) and failed to follow "the ideal lady of his mind" toward heaven: "Present things with their false pleasure turned my steps as soon as your face was hid" (lines 34–36). Joyce has Stephen make the claim that the artist's aim is to work upon "present things" so that the "quick intelligence" may go beyond them and reach toward the ideal.

It is instructive to note Dante's place in this important passage from *Stephen Hero*. First, it shows just how early on and how thoroughly Joyce is reading Dante with an eye toward allegory. Second, in Dante these "present things" are the occasion and cause of Dante losing his way, and at the end of the purgatorial experience he recognizes that the things of the world are dangerous to follow. Dante confesses that he was too narrowly focused on these natural things and required the extraordinary grace of having seen hell and undergone purgatory to move beyond them and back to Beatrice. Joyce is warning himself not to become narrowly bound to nature and naturalism and to work upon the present things until they bring us upward toward the ideal.

4. In *Cosmopolis: The Hidden Agenda of Modernity*, Stephen Toulmin makes the argument that the scientific developments arising out of the philosophical ration-

alism of the sixteenth and seventeenth centuries have had the unfortunate result of narrowing the horizon of expectations and limiting the kinds of questions that can be asked about our meaning and significance. He argues that we need a return to the more flexible tolerance of the premodern humanists (by this he means Desiderius Erasmus, Michel Montaigne, François Rabelais, and William Shakespeare, among others) whose humanism was able to elude dogmatic position-taking that the scientific method and the Enlightenment actually hardened and made even more confining than the most dogmatic religious mind of the sixteenth century had been able to accomplish. It is this "modernity" of rationality and intellect, whose eminence is achieved at the expense of imagination and intuition, that the high modernists are opposing.

5. Mockery is a major theme in *Ulysses* and in modernist literature in general, a reflection perhaps of Christ's warning that the one unforgivable sin is mockery of the holy spirit. Mockery is a theme given exquisite expression by W. B. Yeats in a short lyric of his long poem *Nineteen Hundred and Nineteen*. After three stanzas in which we are asked to mock the efforts of the good, the wise, and the great, we are asked in the final stanza to turn the mockery back on itself in the way that Siebers, Altieri, and Paul de Man ask us to turn skepticism and suspicion back against themselves:

> Mock mockers after that
> That would not lift a hand maybe
> To help good, wise or great
> To bar that foul storm out, for we
> But traffic in mockery.

Mockery is an attitude that not only debunks ideals but also does no good in the world, attempts no building, and achieves nothing worthwhile.

6. Kermode erects a principle for the interpretation of narrative from Jesus' explanation, which is derived from Isaiah, of the reason he speaks in parables: "He described them as stories *told to them without*—to outsiders—with the express purpose of concealing a mystery that was to be understood only by insiders. So Mark tells us: speaking to the Twelve, Jesus said, 'To you has been given the secret of the kingdom of God, but for those outside everything is in parables; so that they may indeed see but not perceive, and may indeed hear but not understand; lest they should turn again, and be forgive'" (Kermode, 2). The parables he tells, then, are designed to speak only to those already on the inside, who already in some way know the truth; those not so privileged will only be able to see the manifest content but not penetrate to the secret inside.

This "secrecy" is a principle of much narrative fiction, in Kermode's argument, but the terms and the spirit of the secrecy are quite in keeping with the method of allegory, especially as Saint Paul describes it; for those who can only read the manifest content, the letter or literal level, are condemned to an ignorance that is quite dangerous spiritually, while those who can read the letter and the spirit, who can read allegorically, are to be saved. Joyce has a deliberately obscure and indirect narrative designed to conceal (yet at the same time to reveal, to insiders) a secret, the identity of Bloom as a figure of Christ. We can place Kermode's study alongside Umberto Eco's in order to provide a way to think about a kind of obscurity that is meant not to imitate a chaos but to conceal within an apparent chaos a satisfying order. Kenner makes the comment that "Joyce is a great concealer of climaxes" (Kenner, "Circe," 352), and what Joyce is accomplishing in "Ithaca" is the simultaneous concealing and revealing of his great climax, concealing it from those outside and revealing it to those inside.

7. This book by Lynch was published in 1960 and deals with texts very different from the ones of this study, while using language very different from my own. Yet it is an important book that ought to receive some attention in the present climate of debate in which we want to find a way to describe the search for ideals that allows for a rigorous sense of time and space as the conditions for idealization. For Lynch works with great care to describe a Christian imagination that is best suited to resolve the need for ideals on the one hand and respect for history and the conditions of "reality" on the other. My study of these modernist writers is another attempt, as it turns out, to describe a Christian imagination and its ability to resolve this perpetual problem for art.

Chapter One

1. Ian Watt's still-important contribution to the study of the novel, *The Rise of the Novel,* is right to identify the development of the criterion of plausibility as the definitive characteristic of the novel, that events and motives detailed in the novels must be represented as seem most plausible by the standards of the culture in which they arise. Watt notes that, in the eighteenth century with the rise of the middle class and its values, this often turns out to mean the reduction of motive to sexual desire and economic gain. Michael McKeon, in his more complex study *The Origin of the English Novel,* sees this as a crucial phase as prose fiction developed from a romance idealism into a naive empiricism that sought to debunk the stories of romance by being more empirical, that is, by doubting the ideal and insisting on reducing high motives to something lower. McKeon's study is useful to a study of *Ulysses* because this novel will recapitulate the history of the novel, from romance idealism to naive empiricism, and seek a resolution in what McKeon calls an extreme skepticism, in which we doubt the doubting of the empiricists. Mulligan is the exponent of Watt's "formal realism" and McKeon's "naive empiricism," debunking all values and reducing them to their lowest terms.

2. I will turn to Stevens's lecture in the conclusion where I describe briefly how *Notes toward a Supreme Fiction* can be read as an example of modernist allegory. But it is useful to note here that Stevens is very clear about how he views his age and

the writer's role in it when he says, "There is no element more conspicuously absent from contemporary poetry than nobility. There is no element that poets have sought after, more curiously and more piously, certain of its obscure existence" (*NA*, 35). This statement expresses Joyce's project and in a way may be one of the statements best able to express the goals of high modernism.

3. I have already quoted the final stanza to this lyric in note 5 to the introduction. It is again worth noting, and repeating, that this modernist project, of turning mockery and skepticism and suspicion against themselves, is shared by another important poet who did not evolve the strategy of modernist allegory but who nonetheless expresses the modernist desire for presentation of, and reverence for, the ideal. The Incarnation will provide Joyce with the most satisfying resolution of the problem of history and the ideal.

4. Joyce seems to be aware of the theory of history behind anti-Semitism, that it implies a totalizing view of history, in that a force is posited as trying to gain global domination (in this case, the Jews) against whom one must fight by taking total control of one's own culture. Hannah Arendt described the totalitarian states as first having to posit a totalizing force already at work against whom they oppose their own totalizing efforts. For Arendt, anti-Semitism is not merely anti-Jewish sentiment but a way of thinking that places the Jews at the center of a conspiracy against the health and well-being of western culture. In order to justify their own totalitarian agenda, the Nazis had first to posit a global conspiracy to fight against, a prior totalizing force that their own totalizing efforts would be aimed at thwarting.

Within naturalism, history is the arena in which good forces must compete against bad forces and work to bring about the great end of the process of history, the manifestation of God in Deasy's terms. Joyce wants to think outside this kind of history bounded by purely human intentions and human efforts, in which the sudden introduction of the ideal from above can profoundly alter the course of history and keep it from degenerating into the nightmare of totalitarian states squaring off against one another, which is exactly what happened in the decades after Joyce finished this novel.

5. It is worth recalling that Joyce decided to retain the word "crosstree" even after Budgen, who was a sailor, informed him that the proper word was "yard." Joyce wanted "crosstree," it seems reasonable to assume, for the suggestion of Christ's death on a tree made into a cross. The ship that defies nature at the end of "Proteus" is meant to suggest the Christ event, which also defies nature.

6. This is a crucial point already stated in the introduction and to be developed in my treatment of the "Ithaca" episode—that modernist allegory does not seek to totalize while it accomplishes its unification of discrete moments into a pattern that provides climax and satisfaction. Not every moment from the Old Testament is figurative of the Christ event, and not every moment from the early episodes must be brought into the pattern of the Incarnation that I will be estab-

lishing in "Ithaca." Indeed, "Ithaca" is littered with delightful moments that are absolutely without any relevance to any aspect of the novel's meaning. So we do not have to forego the pleasure of the text while finding the unity of the Christ event in this novel. We can gain all the satisfaction of a high significance without losing the delight in the moment.

7. I do not want to make this kind of autobiographical detail essential to my reading of the novel, but it is interesting to read the letters Joyce wrote to Nora while he was away from Trieste for some months in 1909. At that time "Cranly" hinted that Nora had known other young men and been intimate with them before Joyce first went walking with her on 16 June 1904. This information, which turned out to be false, caused Joyce great grief and led him to write some distraught and mean letters back to Trieste. His jealously about Nora's fidelity, which these letters demonstrate as extreme and even excessive, might help to underscore the role of fidelity in *Ulysses* as the most important aspect of our relationships with one another and with God. That the novel's plot turns on Molly's infidelity and Bloom's struggle to accept it seems more urgent in considering Joyce's own character.

8. In *Finnegans Wake,* Joyce describes *Ulysses* as "his usylessly unreadable Blue Book of Eccles," a description that emphasizes the destination (7 Eccles street) as well as the way there, a meditation of the "uselessness" of so much of our activity. In his book of puns this pun unites the title with the theme of uselessness.

9. In "Penelope," Molly recalls some of Bloom's letters to her in which he expressed his admiration for her body: "his mad crazy letters my Precious one everything connected with your glorious Body everything underlined that comes from it is a thing of beauty and of joy for ever" (17.1176–78). Bloom's reverence for her "glorious Body" is important in a book that is never to forget the place of the body in our lives, that will not seek to escape the body but attempt rather to make it rise against gravity and ascend heavenward. Molly's "glorious Body" can be associated with Christ's resurrected body, glorious and eternal.

Chapter Two

1. This is how Wyndham Lewis in *Time and Western Man* characterizes the style of the entire novel, as "telling from the inside" and therefore "psychological" (Lewis, 107); for Lewis, *Ulysses* is written under "the intensive dictatorship of Space-time" (100). While only the opening episodes are accurately described in these terms, Lewis nonetheless provides us with the proper terms and perspective from which to view the working of the later episodes, as reacting against the tyrant of naturalism, Space-time (and in a way that Lewis would have endorsed, if he had recognized it!) and establishing something more permanent and stable out of the flux.

2. Levenson is the first literary historian I know of to worry about "dating Hulme" (which is the title of his first of two chapters on Hulme). The ideas Hulme

advanced in 1908 differ significantly from the ones advocated in 1914. "In five years," Levenson argues, "he has renounced virtually every major proposition to which he had given assent" (Levenson, 97). From an early advocacy of Henri Bergson's philosophy and a belief that modern poetry ought to imitate impressionist painting, Hulme becomes a vigorous exponent of abstraction in art and hopes that the tendency toward abstraction seen in painters signals a return to the quest for permanence and absolute values that dominated the Middle Ages and that the Renaissance (as Quinones also argues) gave up on.

3. It is quite extraordinary that Joyce develops, in isolation from the kinds of intellectual movements and the societies that helped them share positions, a similar attitude toward his art as Hulme was describing in London during the same years. Stephen in *A Portrait* is arguing for an art that is static and in which "the mind is arrested and raised above desire and loathing" (205). Such static art is opposed to kinetic art that seeks to arouse desire or loathing, desire to possess and therefore to move toward a thing or loathing to abandon and therefore move away from a thing. The art Stephen and, I think, Joyce are aiming at is one that is not about the things in the world but above the world, where we contemplate the permanent and eternal. Art is not to imitate our lives in the world, which are kinetic, but to raise us above the world, where we are free to consider another order of being.

4. Toward the end of "Structure, Sign and Play in the Discourse of the Human Sciences," Derrida makes the point that structuralism may have a deep tendency toward despair: "Turned towards the lost or impossible presence of the absent origin, this structuralism thematic of broken immediacy is therefore the saddened, *negative,* nostalgic, guilty Rousseauistic side of the thinking of play whose other side would be the Nietzschean *affirmation*" (Derrida, *Writing and Difference,* 292). Bloom turns toward the lost origin of his love, and, within naturalism at any rate, the result is a despairing nostalgia. Joyce will not make the Derridean turn toward the Nietzschean affirmation of play without center, however; he will instead work to make the center approachable and recoverable, through memory of a higher order than naturalism allows.

The work of Derrida, in this essay and elsewhere, serves to highlight the acute consciousness that Joyce brings to the issue of memory, of lost homes and the possibility of recovery: he is not in any way naive about such a backward-looking stance leading to guilt and despair, but he does not despair of such a return: that is the postdeconstructive argument of my study—that Joyce sees all that poststructuralism sees and moves us beyond it before we even knew it existed.

5. I have relied on John Rickard's work on Joyce's understanding of memory and its various powers, but at this point I want to indicate the important earlier work of Frances Yates in *The Art of Memory,* in which she describes what she calls "the medieval transformation of the classical art of memory" (Yates, 55). Classical treatises on rhetoric taught that one can improve one's ability to remember by

associating a thought with an image and that the more striking the image the better we would remember its associated thought. Medieval theologians, especially Albertus Magnus and Thomas Aquinas, extended the powers of memory so that it becomes more than a repository of images and associated thoughts. Memory for them becomes what Samuel Taylor Coleridge would call an esemplastic power, capable of transforming these images and ideas until they become signs of eternal truths and spiritual realities. Memory becomes an agency of the human mind capable of leading to God.

I used Yates's study to describe how Eliot understands memory in *Four Quartets* (see "In Dante's Wake: T. S. Eliot's 'Art of Memory'" in *Crosscurrents* 38, no. 4 [winter 1988–89]), and I will allude to this set of ideas in my conclusion when I treat *Four Quartets* as modernist allegory. But I want to point out here that Joyce, like Eliot a student of Dante all his life, sees in memory more than a receptacle for images from the past whose consideration leads to despair, though in "Lestrygonians" that is all memory is and all it can do is lead to despair. Later in the novel we will have moved well passed naturalism and memory will become much more "medieval" in its application.

6. Joyce begins this possible theme for Stephen in "Telemachus" when the mocker Mulligan refers to Stephen as "Japhet in search of a father" (1.561), which is the title of a sentimental novel of the early nineteenth century by Frederick Marryat about a foundling with an obsession to find his father. Mulligan makes this comment after having described to Haines the gist of Stephen's Hamlet theory, and so this theory and Stephen's obsession with fathers and the tradition of sentimental novels about orphans and fathers is prophetically announced by the mocker Malachi. I will make much of this theme of the novel in my third and fourth chapters.

7. Once again I want to underscore how keenly Joyce anticipates the major themes of Derridean deconstruction. Joyce recognizes and celebrates that the Church, and his novel, is founded on a void, on the mystery of the father that is merely a construct without grounding or reference to any transcendent signified. But Joyce's conclusions are not Derrida's, for Joyce will not give up on the possibility of filling this void with a center. While in episode 9 Bloom is a ghostly absence, in "Ithaca" he will be seen by Stephen as the incarnation of Christ and so function as a presence outside language upon whom the edifice of a new church can rest securely.

8. This description of Bloom anticipates the later identification in "Cyclops" of Bloom with Saint Paul, a Jew who brings the message of Christ to the Greek world. Paul, a highly educated man who knew Greek culture well, is also a fervent and strict Pharisee deeply learned in Jewish law and committed to the preservation of Jewish ritual. Bloom is like Saint Paul in that, as a Jew (at least in the eyes of Mulligan here and of the pub patrons in "Cyclops"), he will bear the message of Christ, and in fact embody it, to a Gentile world; and Stephen will recognize it.

In *Allegory in Dante's Commedia,* Robert Hollander claims that Saint Paul is one of the most influential men in western cultural history in his ability to bring the Hebrew emphasis on linear history into clear and meaningful relation to the Greek emphasis on an eternal realm of ideals. The relation of Jewish and Greek cultures is a theme in *Ulysses,* where jewgreek will meet greekjew, where history and the timeless are reconciled.

Chapter Three

1. I want to repeat, and by repeating underscore, the correspondence between Joyce's skepticism and the kind of skepticism recently made central to our literary debates by the various strands of poststructuralist theory. Joyce writes a novel in which he demonstrates how he has seen through the various languages that have been used before to present ideals. He works with great vigor and famous ingenuity to demonstrate that he is not fooled by any language, especially by any "high" language that seeks to impress us with its nobility and power. Yet Joyce is not, because of this skepticism about language, skeptical about ideals. He has not given up on the possibility of suggesting, through language, a realm of ideal attainable by human beings. In this Joyce offers a valuable lesson for those of us impressed by the skeptical hermeneutics of poststructuralism but not willing to surrender the possibility of idealism. Indeed, Joyce and the other modernists of this study provide a hope that language can be used, if not to present ideals or even represent them, at least to indicate their possibility.

2. Of course, I am using the terms made famous by Roland Barthes, especially in *S/Z.* Joyce's novel is unique because it begins as one kind of novel and develops into the other, as the reader must become increasingly the maker of the novel's meaning. Barthes asks a question that might be the one Joyce is asking: "Why is the writerly our value? Because the goal of literary work (of literature as work) is to make the reader no longer a consumer, but a producer of the text" (Barthes, 4). In the "readerly" novel the reader becomes idle and passive: "he is left with no more than the poor freedom either to accept or reject the text: reading is nothing more than a *referendum*" (4). Joyce begins *Ulysses* with a "classic" example of the readerly in which the reader can do no more than follow; from "Sirens" onward the reader is led to make decisions and provide meaning in a way that is quite empowering. Yet the reader is not left in a state of total freedom but is being carefully led by a powerful author to come to a way of reading that is fulfilled in "Ithaca."

3. In an essay called "What Is Postmodernism?" Jean-François Lyotard makes a statement that fits nicely within my argument about Joyce's self-conscious anticipation, and rejection, of the ways of thinking that are currently in place in the academy and that we call either poststructuralism or postmodernism: "Joyce makes us discern the unpresentable in the writing itself, in the signifier. A whole range of accepted narrative and even stylistic operators is brought into play with

no concern for the unity of the whole, and experiments are conducted with new operators. The grammar and vocabulary of literary language are no longer taken for granted; instead they appear as academicisms, rituals born of a piety (as Nietzsche might call it) that does not alter the invocation of the unpresentable" (Lyotard, 80–81). Joyce indeed makes us aware, in these "language episodes" I am analyzing, of the grammar and vocabulary of literary language, and in true "postmodern" spirit he shows up such language as incapable of presenting truth or the absolute. But Joyce does have a concern for unity and is bringing us beyond these various negative lessons about literary language toward a language that can indicate the unpresentable truth. Joyce is not postmodern in having given up on unity or truth, but his way of reconciling us to such terms is so complex that it may indeed reconcile our respect for the skepticism of postmodernism with our need for truth and ideals. This reconciliation is the triumph of medieval and modernist allegory, to be described in chapter 5 and the conclusion of the present study.

4. It is worth noting that the structure of McKeon's thesis regarding the history of the novel is similar to the one developed by Tobin Siebers regarding recent critical theory. As Siebers seeks to identify valid responses to the skepticism of poststructuralist thought, so McKeon sees in the development of the novel a skeptical response to the skepticism of "naive empiricism." McKeon's "extreme skepticism" turns the skepticism of science against itself and provides legitimate space for the construction of ideals in the same way that Siebers asks us to turn the skepticism of poststructuralism against itself.

5. This is the first moment in the novel where memory seems to be functioning in a larger way than the "naturalistic" manner we saw earlier in "Lestrygonians," where the recalling of happier days only serves to make Bloom depressed. The phrase "retrospective arrangement" is used to signal the kind of reviewing of the past that rearranges events into new patterns and so "rereads" them for new meaning. Memory is about to become a more powerful agent of the mind, as Dante understands it in *Vita Nuova*, which he calls his "Book of memory" and in which he rereads the experience of Beatrice in light of a later vision that allows him to understand his past, and the kind of poems he wrote in that past, in a new and more satisfying way.

Chapter Four

1. As we saw in "Sirens," Joyce presents the temptation to see Bloom as psychologically disturbed, as a masochist who wishes to suffer. That view is poised against a higher view of Bloom's character, one in which we say that he is a purgatorial figure embracing his suffering as a way to purge his own sinfulness and reach a purer and more disciplined state of being. The "Freudian" reading of Bloom as masochist is poised against a reading of Bloom as purgatorial, and Joyce indicates the reductiveness and ultimate emptiness of the former reading. Again,

now in "Circe," there seems grist for the Freudian mill to debunk Bloom as perverse and pathetic. But Joyce never chooses to allow the Freudian reading any privilege, because it is always reductive and depressing. Joyce is bringing the reader's own doubts about Bloom, which derive from psychology and are given scientific rigor by Freudian psychoanalysis, to become manifest and become purged. In "Sirens," Bloom is purged; in "Circe" the reader is. In other and fewer words, "Circe" does to the reader what "Sirens" did to Bloom: to bring a Freudian view into the text in order to reject it.

2. One of the most important aspects of Joyce's epic is that the ordinary becomes the heroic. Joyce's model allows us to avoid the emphasis Pound will make in his epic, where the public and the political is the arena for heroic action. Joyce understands this temptation and brings the reader's need for this kind of heroism into the text, only to reject it soundly as ludicrous. The modernist project aims at a renewal of heroism and nobility, and Pound will be the only one of the four to seek the political and public as the space in which heroism works out its ambitions. The modernists are for the most part private and personal in their vision of heroic destiny, and this too comes in great part, and for Joyce directly, from the Incarnation as model. Even Pound learns this, in Pisa. It is only in "Circe" that we see this kind of heroism as a possibility for Bloom, and its absurdity is Joyce's comment on the prospect of a political hero for the modern world. If only Pound had understood this, before Pisa.

3. The epic in general is about "home" and the possibility of a return home. As such it is highly nostalgic and seems to be a genre unfit for a progressive view of the world that looks to the future with hope and energy; it is the genre that Nietzsche and Derrida would condemn as most backward-looking and guilty. But in making "home" the goal of a heroic enterprise, the modernists recognize that it is not easily available nor a mere wish to be stated, but a project.

Odysseus seeks to return home after a war, Aeneas's mission is to find his true home, Dante risks the descent to hell in order to return to Eden and thence to his heavenly home, Adam and Eve are cast out of home in order to begin the process of return—the great epic tradition is about having fallen from home and the tremendous desire and heroic effort required to begin the work of return. That the epic has this "domestic" theme prepares us for the gradual development of the epic into the novel, and the novel (in Joyce's hands at least) back into the epic.

4. *Anti-Oedipus* describes a general tendency toward totalization in modern western culture that seeks to impose total control over the body and its avenues for experiencing pleasure. Deleuze and Guattari's emphasis is on the body as victim of a capitalist culture that creates a split between mind and body. This split allows the mind the illusion of freedom at the expense of the body, whose relation to experience is made distant and detached and therefore "schizophrenic." Joyce's new family configuration seeks to create a culture of joy and pleasure in

which the body can feel all over, in which the subject is so constructed to feel a fuller range of pleasure in and through the body.

5. Tanner's study provides the hint that allows us to solve one of the more prominent puzzles of *Ulysses:* why the plot of adultery. With Tanner's study, we go beyond playing armchair psychologist and wondering about Joyce's own private obsessions, and return to a study of the genre in which Joyce is writing, or at least the genre Joyce begins in. For the theme of adultery opens up the space for the end of the novel and beginning of the epic. Adultery threatens the stability of the domestic unit so new to modern society and so important to its establishment; female power is most threatening and must be contained. Molly's desire is what threatens the stability of the family, and her act threatens to break it up; indeed, the novelistic family is broken in order for the epic family to be configured.

6. Nancy Armstrong's study also emphasizes the role of women in establishing the family and again provides the background for *Ulysses,* whose plot is set in motion by a woman and finished when a woman says yes to the male hero. In a very real way Molly is the authority who establishes this new family. Molly brings about the breakdown of the traditional bourgeois family with her act of adultery and authorizes the inauguration of the new family with her rousing acceptance of Bloom at the end of "Penelope." As Armstrong's work makes clear, the novel is the genre that brings about a new possibility for female authority, and Joyce recognizes that aspect of the novel's history and pays homage to it in his last episode.

But what Joyce is doing here is bringing the novel's tendency to inscribe female authority into relation to the epic's surprisingly similar attitude toward women. For in *The Odyssey* and the *Divina Commedia,* which are the two most important epics underlying Joyce's text, female characters play crucial roles in bringing the male heroes "back home." Penelope tricks Odysseus into revealing his identity and allows him the emotional release that brings him back home; Beatrice is the lure Virgil uses to arouse the desire in Dante to make his journey through hell and up the mountain of Purgatory, on top of which he enters Eden and is reunited with Beatrice. These female characters function as pivots in the plots of these epics, and Joyce recognizes that what characterizes the novel's novelty in regard to women and authority was already present in the epic. Their desire for these women leads the male heroes to make the return, but the last word is given to the female characters in the epic and in the novel. Penelope allows for the renewal of Odysseus's identity, Beatrice for the rebirth of Dante as a self capable of entering heaven. Molly is Bloom's passport to eternity, the female authority who on the epic level of significance in this text establishes Bloom as father of a new kind of family.

Chapter Five

1. It is worth quoting at some length from Dante's famous letter to his patron Can Grande: "It is to be understood that the meaning of the work [the *Divina*

Commedia] is not simple, but rather it is polysemous, that is, having many meanings. For the first meaning is that which one derives from the letter, another is that which one derives from the things signified by the letter. The first is called 'literal' and the second 'allegorical,' or 'mystical'" (cited in Musa, 37).

So all "mystical" meanings are allegorical, but Dante then lays out three kinds of allegorical meanings: the moral sense, the allegorical sense, and the anagogical sense. Joyce develops four layers of meaning: the real or the literal, the novelistic, the epic, and the allegorical. All four levels are equally valid, but not all are equally important. For Dante, the salvation of the soul is more important than the journey of the people of Israel from bondage into the wilderness, but both are equally valid and the one is ground for the other. So for Joyce, Bloom's passivity on the literal level may signify weakness, but on the epic and allegorical levels it acquires dignity and significance. This achievement, of four distinct yet related levels of meaning, is Joyce's most significant debt to Dante's example.

2. The body plays a crucial role in Christian theology, in Dante's *Divina Commedia*, and in *Ulysses*. The central mystery of Christianity is the Incarnation, the act of God in which he takes on flesh and lives a fully human life. When Jesus, who is both God and man, who is (in Eliot's phrase) "the point of intersection of the timeless with time," dies and is resurrected, it is the human body that dies and it is in bodily form that he is resurrected. As the author of the letter to the Hebrews helps us understand, it is because of the Incarnation of God that we have a compassionate judge, one who fully shared in our weakness and so can announce an eternal judgment that is both human and divine.

In Dante's poem he consistently makes us aware of his body. In *Inferno* he is drawing down toward the center of all gravity, as if the body must descend to hell and belongs. In *Purgatorio*, however, where all the shades marvel at Dante's presence as a bodily creature among them, we watch how he at first struggles to climb the mountain but as each sin is erased from his forehead how he climbs as easily as we go downhill. In *Paradiso* he ascends through the heavens as a bodily creature, and Beatrice explains (in canto 2) that it is indeed the nature of the human body, once purged and perfected, to rise.

This is the theological and poetic context for Joyce's emphasis on Bloom's body—his defecation, his sexual lusts, his eating habits, and his dwelling on the formula for falling bodies. The body cannot be escaped, as history cannot be escaped and as the literal level of our lives cannot be escaped. But it is the body that is redeemed, as is history, in the miracle of the resurrection. As we will see, the feast of the Ascension plays a role in "Ithaca," for that is the feat on which we celebrate Christ's overcoming of the law of gravity and of falling bodies, which is the hope of the resurrection.

3. From the very start of the *Divina Commedia*, as early as canto 2 of *Inferno*, Beatrice is used by Virgil as the lure to inspire Dante to enact the journey through hell and up Mount Purgatory. Virgil describes her intervention on Dante's behalf,

a story that arouses Dante's desire for the dark and dangerous journey. Singleton describes this aspect of Beatrice's role in his book *Journey to Beatrice*, in a chapter called "Goal at the Summit." Throughout this book Singleton demonstrates the way in which Beatrice is figured as a substitute for Christ, as a sort of minor incarnation sent to Dante in 1300 as his own personal, private representation of Christ, the genuine Incarnation. Molly functions in a similar way in *Ulysses*, as a lure bringing Stephen to 7 Eccles street, where Stephen will see the manifestation of Christ in Bloom, which is Stephen's private showing of a minor incarnation, a gift from God for Stephen's nurturing. Another chapter in the same book, "Justification in History," is a useful gloss on this aspect of Beatrice's role, as Dante's own private gift from God so he can write his vision.

4. This is an important feature of Joyce's novel—the way in which dreams come true, the way in which the accidental becomes necessary, the way the apparently fortuitous becomes part of a design. Stephen's dream of being led into a stranger's home, where the red carpet is spread out to welcome him in as a cherished guest, does indeed come true. In something called real life, or on the literal level of meaning, this is just an accident, a coincidence, something that could happen by fortune (just as Bloom's inadvertent tip about "throwaway," by sheer coincidence, is fulfilled). But Joyce loves to play with the accidental and the coincidental, because there is a fine line between accident and necessity, between coincidence and design. Fiction is a kind of writing in which the random is meditated upon until it seems to be part of a design. The novelist as designer stands in analogical relation to God as providence. These dreams come true, these accidents as design, are Joyce's way of suggesting God's hand in the lives of his characters.

Dante may be the source of this meditation in *Ulysses* also. For in canto 7 of *Inferno*, Fortuna is described as controlling all material wealth and being in a manner that is purely random, wholly accidental; there is no controlling, or predicting, or forestalling the operations of fortune because they are wildly random. That's human life on earth. But in canto 7 of *Paradiso*, the corresponding heavenly canto to *Inferno*'s canto 7, Beatrice explains the divine plan in which God becomes man for all human salvation. Both chance and providence are at work in our lives, and coincidence is the point at which the one becomes the other.

5. There is in "Ithaca" so much nonrelevant information that we might want to call it Joyce's "schizophrenic" episode. One feature of the working of the schizophrenic mind (and unfortunately Joyce had too much acquaintance with these workings through Lucia) is its inability to distinguish the essential from the nonessential, the foreground from the background, the useful from the useless. To the schizophrenic mind, all information is equally meaningful, or more properly, all information is equally without meaning, without relation to any principle at the center which can order and assign meaning. Joyce in "Ithaca" makes the reader work against this kind of chaos and find a center, and the center is in Stephen's visionary experience of Bloom. Joyce imitates chaos and forces the

reader to live either in a random universe with no privileged center or in a world of much confusion but with a stable center governing the meaning of certain information rendered significant. The ability to assign meaning from a privileged center is redemptive from what can be regarded as schizophrenic chaos and meaninglessness.

6. As I discussed in note 6 of the introduction, Kermode provides us with a model for narrative fiction that places a need for secrecy at the heart of all story. Some will get it, some will not—that is how all stories go. Joyce has taken that principle as far as it can go in fiction: all readers of *Ulysses* have read that Stephen sees in Bloom the traditional figure of hypostasis, yet few have ventured to emphasize that recognition as the center of the book's meaning. Joyce has with great care made the simple declarative statement of this miracle something easy to ignore, overlook, reduce, explain away. And he has written a book that is polysemous so that readers who do not get it will still enjoy reading the text, will in fact write about their joy in reading that may indeed blind them to the discovery of this secret identification.

7. Earlier in the episode we learn that Bloom and Stephen met twice before: "the first in the lilacgarden of Matthew Dillon's house" (17.467), with Stephen's mother and Molly both present; the second time in the coffee room of the Breslin hotel in the company of Simon Dedalus and Stephen's Uncle Charles, at which time Stephen invited Bloom to dinner, an invitation that Bloom was wise enough to decline with the same kind of grateful appreciation that Stephen uses to decline Bloom's offer of asylum on 16 June 1904. But we discover "a third connecting link between them" (17.477–78)—that they both knew Mrs. Riordan, the Dante of *A Portrait*. This fact allows us to say that Stephen and Bloom have Dante as a connecting link, a little joke that establishes the possibility that Dante's method of allegory is what links the two together in a pattern that unites them in a manner far higher than the novelistic level can recognize.

8. While it may be dangerous to attempt to elevate the remark "nor no nothing in his nature" into a principle for reading the novel's ending, with all that has gone on before, this remark seems wonderful confirmation that naturalism can bring us nowhere, for there is "nothing in nature" when all is said and done. As Molly is about to bring the novel to its rousing finish, it will not be by thinking of Boylan with this "nothing in his nature" but by thinking of Bloom who can rise, still in nature, to the starry heights.

Conclusion

1. Lukacs works with precision and rigor to make an important distinction between realism and naturalism, in which the latter is drawn toward depiction of weakness and pathology while the former is poised to depict the individual working to resist the conditions of nature and impose his will on them. Lukacs is also concerned with the question of allegory in modernism, which he declares to be

preoccupied with a description of our alienation from objective reality. So my study in effect is positioned between these two poles, the naturalism that reduces human will to impotence and allegory that seeks to escape from the real from which it is alienated.

Modernist allegory is, as I have been arguing, a special kind of allegory capable of resolving these twin excesses. Pound's comment is a sign of his own desire to reduce the novel to a genre that has done whatever it could—diagnose the conditions of reality—and must be supplanted by a genre capable of discovering greater possibilities—Pound thinks that genre is the epic when he writes the words I have quoted, but he will be writing "modernist allegory" in Pisa. The novel is over and must be supplemented by the epic, which becomes allegory.

2. I used Yates's study in an essay about *Four Quartets* that describes closely Dante's place in the poem but fails to see how Eliot was discovering, in memory, the allegorical dimension of our lives in time. Eliot is the clearest of the four modernists in this study in claiming that memory brings about a meaning in the discrete moments of our lives that increase in significance until these moments signify the various aspects of the Christ event—Annunciation, Incarnation, Pentecost. Eliot develops the medieval understanding of memory that Yates describes and assigns to it the power to write allegory. Memory is central to Joyce's conclusion, to Pound's poem as he writes it in Pisa, as well as to Eliot's poem (Stevens does not fit this paradigm as nicely); Yates provides the context for Eliot's poem, and Eliot then makes of memory the agency that writes allegory. And this, after all, brings us back, as always, to Dante.

3. Longenbach makes this point in his chapter on Stevens called "It Must Be Humdrum," pages 271ff. It is a point I want to make briefly because, though the poem was written during the war and in response to it, it nevertheless is the solution to his entire life's work as a poet and is to be read as the climax of a volume of poems of peacetime.

Longenbach's chapter devoted to *Notes* is the best analysis of the poem that I have read and anticipates the description of it I am making here as "modernist allegory." He notes the failure of humanism to provide a way to reconcile our lives in time with our needs for permanence (259), and he sees Stevens's poem as reaching "toward a condition that could be embodied only by a Wittgensteinian silence or Dante's multifoliate rose" (261). In a very real sense my own brief analysis of Stevens's greatest poem is meant to develop Longenbach's superb analysis merely by placing the poem in the context of these other "modernist allegories" and seeking to apply that term to it.

4. Stevens's understanding of the imagination is therefore quite like Blake's, in that both poets see the imagination as containing images that are not found in nature but nonetheless are real and, more than that, true in the highest sense. In this radical appreciation of the imagination's power, Stevens is like Saint

Anselm of Canterbury, whose *Proslogion* is based on the proposition that whatever the mind is capable of imagining must exist, or the mind could not contain it. Images of a perfect home are not mere fancy but signs of an eternal truth.

5. In an essay called "Bestial Sign and Bread of Angels" in his collection *Poetics of Conversion,* John Freccero describes *Inferno*'s canto 33 in a light that makes the parallel between Ugolino's predicament and Pound's quite striking, all the more so when one considers how Pound is aware that he is imprisoned in the same city as Ugolino and even makes claim to see Ugolino's tower. Ugolino was being offered, by his sons, the opportunity to repent of his own sinfulness, for his sons are offering themselves to be eaten by their father in a way that could have prompted his recognition of Christ's offering of himself to his Father and our ability to partake of that sacrifice in the Eucharist. But Ugolino refuses to break down and soften into repentance; he tells us that he turns to stone rather than let his sons see his pain. Pound does repent of his hardness and breaks down and weeps, which lifts him from hell up to the top of Purgatory, where he finally can be immersed into Lethe because of his confession. Pound's proximity to Ugolino's tower most likely prompts the poet's meditation on the potential within himself to be hard and cold like Ugolino.

Works Cited

———. *The Divine Comedy*. Translated by Charles S. Singleton. London: Routledge, 1971.

———. *Letter to Can Grande. Essays on Dante*. Edited by Mark Musa. Bloomington: Indiana University Press, 1964.

———. *Vita Nuova*. Translated by Mark Musa. New York: Oxford University Press, 2000.

Altieri, Charles. *Postmodernisms Now: Essays on Contemporaneity in the Arts*. University Park: Pennsylvania State University Press, 1998.

Arendt, Hannah. *The Origins of Totalitarianism*. New York: Harcourt, Brace and World, 1966.

Armstrong, Nancy. *Desire and Domestic Fiction: A Political History of the Novel*. New York: Oxford University Press, 1995

Barthes Roland. *S/Z*. Translated by Richard Miller. New York: Hill and Wang, 1974.

Bercovitch, Sacvan. *The American Jeremiad*. Madison: University of Wisconsin Press, 1978.

Blake, William. *The Poetry and Prose of William Blake*. Edited by David V. Erdman. Garden City, N.Y.: Doubleday, 1970.

van Boheemen, Christine. *Joyce, Derrida, Lacan, and the Trauma of History: Reading, Narrative and Postcolonialism*. Cambridge: Cambridge University Press, 1999.

Boyle, Robert. *James Joyce's Pauline Vision: A Catholic Exposition*. Carbondale: Southern Illinois University Press, 1978.

Brown, Dennis. *The Modernist Self in Twentieth-Century English Literature: A Study in Self-Fragmentation*. New York: St. Martin's, 1989.

Cohn, Dorrit. *Transparent Minds: Narrative Modes for Presenting Consciousness in Fiction*. Princeton: Princeton University Press, 1978.

Dante, Alighieri. *The Divine Comedy of Dante Alighieri*. Translated by John D. Sinclair. New York: Oxford University Press, 1961.

Deleuze, Gilles, and Felix Guattari. *Anti-Oedipus: Capitalism and Schizophrenia*. Translated by Robert Hurley, Mark Seem, and Helen R. Lane. Minneapolis: University of Minnesota Press, 1983.

De Man, Paul. *Blindness and Insight: Essays in the Rhetoric of Contemporary Criticism*. Minneapolis: University of Minnesota Press, 1983.

Derrida, Jacques. *Writing and Difference*. Translated by Alan Bass. Chicago: University of Chicago Press, 1978.
Dettmar, Kevin J. H. *The Illicit Joyce of Postmodernism: Reading against the Grain*. Madison: University of Wisconsin Press, 1996.
Eco, Umberto. *The Open Work*. Translated by Anna Cancogni. London: Radius, 1989.
Eliot, T. S. *Four Quartets*. New York: Harcourt Brace, 1974.
———. *Selected Prose of T. S. Eliot*. Edited by Frank Kermode. New York: Harcourt Brace, 1975.
———. *Waste Land and Other Poems*. New York: Harcourt Brace, 1955.
Ellmann, Richard. *James Joyce,* rev. ed. New York: Oxford University Press, 1982.
———. *Ulysses on the Liffey*. New York: Oxford University Press, 1972.
Freccero, John. *Dante: The Poetics of Conversion*. Edited by Rachel Jacoff. Cambridge: Harvard University Press, 1986.
Froula, Christine. *Modernism's Body: Sex, Culture, and Joyce*. New York: Columbia University Press, 1996.
Groden, Michael. *Ulysses in Progress*. Princeton: Princeton University Press, 1977.
Hart, Clive, and David Hayman, eds. *James Joyce's* Ulysses: *Critical Essays*. Berkeley and Los Angeles: University of California Press, 1977.
Hasan, Ihab. *The Postmodern Turn: Essays in Postmodern Theory and Culture*. Columbus: Ohio State University Press, 1987.
Herring, Phillip F. *Joyce's Uncertainty Principle*. Princeton: Princeton University Press, 1987.
Hollander, Robert. *Allegory in Dante's* Commedia. Princeton: Princeton University Press, 1969.
Homer. *The Odyssey*. Translated by Robert Fitzgerald. New York: Farrar, Straus andGiroux, 1998.
Hulme, T. E. *Speculations: Essays on Humanism and the Philosophy of Art*. Edited by Herbert Read. London: Routledge and Paul, 1936.
Joyce, James. *Critical Writings*. Edited by Ellsworth Mason and Richard Ellmann. New York: Viking, 1959.
———. *Finnegans Wake*. New York: Penguin, 1982.
———. *Letters of James Joyce*. Vol. 1. Edited by Stuart Gilbert. New York: Viking, 1966.
———. *A Portrait of the Artist as a Young Man*. New York: Bantam Classic and Loveswept, 1992.
———. *Stephen Hero*. New York: Norton, 1969.
———. *Ulysses*. Edited by Hans Gabler. New York: Random House, 1986.
Kenner, Hugh. *The Stoic Comedians: Flaubert, Joyce, and Beckett*. Berkeley and Los Angeles: University of California Press, 1975.
———. *Ulysses*. Baltimore: John Hopkins University Press, 1987.
Kermode, Frank. *The Genesis of Secrecy: On the Interpretation of Narrative*. Cambridge: Harvard University Press, 1979.

Lawrence, Karen. *The Odyssey of Style in* Ulysses. Princeton: Princeton University Press, 1981.

Levenson, Michael H. *A Genealogy of Modernism: A Study of English Literary Doctrine, 1908–1922*. New York: Cambridge University Press, 1984.

Levine, George. *Darwin and the Novelists: Patterns of Science in Victorian Fiction*. Cambridge: Harvard University Press, 1988.

Lewis, Wyndham. *Time and Western Man*. Boston: Beacon Press, 1957.

Litz, Arthur W. *The Art of James Joyce: Method and Design in* Ulysses *and* Finnegans Wake. London: Oxford University Press, 1961.

Lukacs, Georg. *Theory of the Novel: A Historico-Philosophical Essay on the Forms of Great Epic Literature*. Translated by Anne Bostock. Cambridge: MIT Press, 1971.

Lynch, William F. *Christ and Apollo: The Dimensions of the Literary Imagination*. New York: Sheed and Ward, 1960.

Lyotard, Jean-François. *The Postmodern Condition: A Report on Knowledge*. Translated by Geoff Bennington and Brian Massumi. Minneapolis: University of Minnesota Press, 1984.

Maddox, James H., Jr. *Joyce's* Ulysses *and the Assault upon Character*. New Brunswick, N.J.: Rutgers University Press, 1978.

Makin, Peter. *Pound's Cantos*. London: G. Allen and Unwin, 1985.

McKeon, Michael. *The Origins of the English Novel, 1600–1740*. Baltimore: Johns Hopkins University Press, 1987.

Meisel, Perry. *The Myth of the Modern: A Study in British Literature and Criticism after 1850*. New Haven: Yale University Press, 1987.

Musa, Mark, ed. *Essays on Dante*. Bloomington: Indiana University Press, 1964.

Perl, Jeffrey M. *The Tradition of Return: The Implicit History of Modern Literature*. Princeton: Princeton University Press, 1984.

Pound, Ezra. *The Cantos of Ezra Pound*. New York: New Directions, 1970.

———. *Literary Essays*. Edited by T. S. Eliot. Norfolk, Conn.: New Directions, 1954.

———. *The Spirit of Romance*. New York: New Directions, 1968.

Quinones, Ricardo J. *Mapping Literary Modernism: Time and Development*. Princeton, N.J.: Princeton University Press, 1985.

Rabelais, François. *Gargantua and Pantagruel*. Translated by Burton Raffel. New York: Norton, 1990.

Rickard, John S. *Joyce's Book of Memory: The Mnemotechnics of* Ulysses. Durham, N.C.: Duke University Press, 1999.

Schwarz, Daniel R. *Reading Joyce's* Ulysses. New York: St. Martin's, 1987.

Sicari, Stephen. "In Dante's Wake: T. S. Eliot's 'Art of Memory.'" *CrossCurrents* 38 (1988): 413–34.

———. *Pound's Epic Ambition: Dante and the Modern World*. Albany: SUNY Press, 1991.

Siebers, Tobin. *Cold War Criticism and the Politics of Skepticism*. New York: Oxford University Press, 1993.

Singleton, Charles S. "Allegory." In *Essays on Dante,* edited by Mark Musa. Bloomington: Indiana University Press, 1964.

———. *Commedia: Elements of Structure.* Cambridge: Harvard University Press, 1957.

———. *Journey to Beatrice.* Baltimore: Johns Hopkins University Press, 1977; 1958.

Stanford, W. B. *The Ulysses Theme.* 2d ed. Oxford: Blackwell, 1963.

Stevens, Wallace. *The Collected Poems of Wallace Stevens.* New York: Vintage, 1990.

———. *The Necessary Angel.* New York: Random House, 1965.

Sultan, Stanley. *Eliot, Joyce, and Company.* New York: Oxford University Press, 1987.

Tanner, Tony. *Adultery in the Novel: Contract and Transgression.* Baltimore: Johns Hopkins University Press, 1979.

Thomas, Brook. *James Joyce's* Ulysses*: A Book of Many Happy Returns.* Baton Rouge: Louisiana State University Press, 1982.

Thornton, Weldon. *Allusions in* Ulysses*: An Annotated List.* Chapel Hill: University of North Carolina Press, 1968.

Toulmin, Stephen. *Cosmopolis: The Hidden Agenda of Modernity.* New York: Free Press, 1990.

Watt, Ian P. *The Rise of the Novel: Studies in Defoe, Richardson, and Fielding.* Berkeley and Los Angeles: University of California Press, 1957.

Yates, Frances A. *The Art of Memory.* Chicago: University of Chicago Press, 1966.

Yeats, W. B. *Collected Poems of W. B. Yeats.* 2d ed., New York: Simon and Schuster, 1996.

Index

Abraham, 10–11
abstract art, 167, 171, 173, 184, 229n. 2
abstraction, 66–67, 69–70, 77–78, 83–84, 131, 139, 143, 166, 167, 168–70, 173–74, 206, 229n. 2
Adam and Eve, 234n. 3
Adams, Robert, 23
adultery, 148, 163, 188–89, 234nn. 5, 6
Aeneas, 211–12, 234n. 3
Aeneid, The, 211
Aeolus, 166, 179
aesthetic of delay, 173
Aldington, Richard, 24
alienation, 153, 155, 161
allegory, xiv, xv, 1, 10, 126, 128, 141, 145, 162, 166, 172, 174–75, 177, 179, 181, 184, 189, 191, 193–94, 199–200, 209, 216–18, 224n. 3, 226n. 6, 235n. 1, 238nn. 1, 2; dimension of reality, 12; medieval, 171, 218; of poets, 13, 14, 37–38; of theologians, 13, 14–16, 19–21, 24, 27, 30, 38, 48, 56–57, 74, 136, 141, 164, 166–68, 170, 173, 182–83, 189
Altieri, Charles, 5, 17–18, 97, 130, 219, 224n. 2, 225n. 5
"American jeremiad, the" 214
Anselm of Canterbury, Saint, 239n. 4
Anti-Oedipus, 234n. 4
anti-Semitism, 44, 117, 119, 227n. 4
Aphrodite, 215
Apollo, 220
"aporia," 169
Aquinas, Thomas, 230n. 5
Arendt, Hannah, 44, 227n. 4
Armstrong, Nancy, 162–63, 234n. 6

arranger, 70–75, 77–78; effects on naturalism, 70
art, 6, 229n. 3
Ascension, 15, 37, 178, 236n. 2
Augustine, Saint, 6, 21

Barabbas, 216
Barthes, Roland, 25–26, 27, 231–32n. 2
Beatrice, 21, 171–72, 211, 224n. 3, 232–33n. 5, 235n. 6, 236n. 3
Beer, Gillian, 14, 32, 38
Bell, Robert, 31, 36, 59, 112
bells, 184–85
Bercovitch, Sacvan, 214
Bergson, Henri, 229n. 2
Bible, the, 8, 10, 15, 213, 218; Old Testament, 19, 228n. 6
biblical exegesis, 166
birth, 133–35, 140
Blake, William, 5–6, 8, 40–41, 43, 45, 84, 137, 151, 203, 208, 220, 239n. 4; concept of imagination, 41–42, 239n. 4
Bloom, Leopold, 28, 38, 47–51, 53–55, 59–60, 90; and consciousness, 121, 127; consciousness of, 121–22; elevation of, 178; and imagination, 62; love objects of, 146; and Moses, 72–74; and Odysseus, 52, 54, 56, 89, 134; as Christ, 22, 57–58, 83, 130, 140, 145, 150, 166–67, 169, 172, 175, 178–81, 183–85, 187–89, 191, 192, 226n. 6, 236n. 4; as Christian hero, 165–66; as Christian love, xiv; as Elijah, 22, 130, 169, 171, 178, 187–88; as epic hero, 159–60, 166–67; as

246   Index

Bloom, Leopold (*continued*)
    father, 132–34, 136–38, 140–42, 145, 146, 151–52, 158–60, 162, 179–80, 185, 189, 190; as Jewish, 122, 175, 180, 231n. 8; as passive hero, 82–83, 85–86, 89, 101, 109, 118, 123, 144, 148–50, 159–60, 161–62, 163, 187, 189–92, 235n. 6; as Saint Paul, 130, 178, 187, 231n. 8; sexual guilt of, 146; as star, 185, 187, 238n. 8
Bloom, Molly, 48, 50–53, 57, 138, 172; bed, 185–86; body of, 60, 63, 228n. 9; as eternal-feminine, 139; infidelity, 146–48, 162–63, 186–87, 189–90, 228n. 9; and Blessed Virgin Mary, 188; and memory, 190; monologue of ("yes"), 189–92; as mother, 138, 139, 145, 146, 150–51, 152, 158–59, 160, 189, 190; picture of, 171, 172; power of, 189; as representative of Church, 188–89, 191; sexuality of, 158–61; as star, 184
Bloom, Rudy, 133, 137, 140, 142, 145, 152
body, 147–48, 161, 167, 228n. 9, 234n. 4, 235–36n. 2
Boylan, Blazes, 50–51, 61–62, 146, 148, 189, 191, 238n. 8
Boyle, Robert, 28, 30, 185
Brandes, George, 85
Brown, Dennis, 2
Bruno, Giordano, 21–22
Budgen, Frank, 163, 169, 183, 227–28n. 5
Butler, Samuel, 163

Cacciaguida, 170
Calliope, xiii, xiv
Can Grande, 13, 182, 189, 235n. 1
Casey, Edward, 20–21
catastrophes, 45
Catholic Church, 28, 113, 127, 134, 141, 151, 185, 215, 217, 230–31n. 7; catechism of, 173
Catholic Mass, 54–56, 215–17

Cato, xiii
chaosmos, 23, 174–75, 189
Chaplin, Charlie, 206
Christ, 9, 12, 15–16, 19, 27, 36, 46, 48, 122, 145, 149, 170–72, 180–81, 183–84, 196–99, 201, 212, 215–18, 220–21, 225n. 5, 227–28n. 5, 236nn. 2, 3, 238n. 2, 239n. 5
Christian imagination, 28, 220–21, 226n. 7
Christian theology, 170, 235n. 2
Christianity, 9, 185
Church; founding new, 183–85, 188, 192; *see also* Catholic Church
Clifford, Martha, 57
Cohen, Bella, 146, 151
Cohn, Dorrit, 67, 69, 121, 143
Coleridge, Samuel Taylor, 230n. 5
comedy, 144
Conmee, Father, 34, 92
Conway, Gabriel, 162
Crane, Stephen, 32
critical theory. *See* theory, critical
"crosstree," 227–28n. 5
culture, 1, 3
Cunningham, Martin, 122–23

Daniel, Arnaut, xii–xiii
Dante, x–xv, 1, 6, 13–14, 15, 16, 21, 23, 57, 66, 97, 104, 109, 127–28, 136, 143, 147, 148, 153–55, 157, 164, 166–67, 170–72, 182–83, 189, 191, 194, 200, 209–11, 217, 224–25n. 3, 230n. 5, 233–34n. 9, 234nn. 4, 5, 234–35n. 6, 235n. 1, 235–36, 2, 236n. 3, 236–37n. 4, 237–38n. 7, 239n. 2; language as fraud, 97, 107; method of writing allegory, 13, 218; pilgrim, 16, 104
Darwin, Charles, 3–4, 14–15, 32–33, 38, 45–46, 188, 224n. 2
de Born, Bertrans, 194
de Man, Paul, 5, 98, 225n. 5
Dedalus, Simon, 34, 101, 105, 135
Dedalus, Stephen, 30, 34–36, 38, 42, 83, 90; as artist, 137, 145, 175, 179–80, 181, 184, 190; attitude

toward history, 45; and Blake, 41; Hamlet theory, 39, 84–85, 89, 142, 230n. 6; and Moses, 75–76; and mother, 63; and passivity, 86; as son, 132–34, 136–38, 140–42, 145, 151–52, 158–59, 179–80, 185; as Telemachus, 145; *see also Hamlet*
Defoe, Daniel, 6
Deleuze, Gilles, 159, 234n. 4
Derrida, Jacques, 4, 89, 224n. 2, 229–30n. 4, 233n. 3
desire, 200–201
despair, 229–30n. 4
Dettmar, Kevin, 9, 25–27, 84, 98
Dignam, widow, 122
Dillon, Mat, 138, 237n. 7
Divina Commedia, x–xv, 1, 136, 166, 170–71, 182, 216, 218, 234–35n. 6, 236n. 3
domestic, 142–43, 153, 163
Douglas, Gawin, 211
Dowie, Dr. Alexander J., 17, 140–41, 149
"Drama and Life," 7
dreams, 236n. 4
Du Puy, General, 206
Dubliners, xiv, 14, 33–34, 51, 75, 113, 162, 190

Easthope, Anthony, 2
Ecclesiastes, Book of, 197
Eco, Umberto, 22–23, 174–75, 226n. 6
Eden, xii, xiv, 138–39
Elijah, 13, 17, 74–75, 90, 93–95, 120, 140–41, 180, 212
Eliot, George, 32
Eliot, T. S., 5, 9, 24, 29, 104, 193–94, 195–201, 218, 224n. 2, 230n. 5, 235n. 2, 238n. 2; concept of memory, 196–200, 238n. 2; and history, 200–201; mythic method, 194; special moments, 196–97, 199, 201; time as destroyer, 197–98
Ellmann, Richard, 46, 108–9, 144, 161–62
Emmaus story, 195–96

empiricism, 124–25
Enlightenment, 3, 225n. 4
epic, xiv, xv, 91–93, 132, 141, 142, 143, 161–63, 164, 165–66, 181, 187, 193–94, 211–12, 216, 233–34n. 3, 235nn. 6, 1, 238n. 1
epic hero, 122, 143, 149–50, 154, 156, 159–60, 163, 167, 223n. 1
Erasmus, Desiderius, 225n. 4
esthetic of indirection, 108–9
Eucharist, 181, 192, 239n. 5; mockery of, 22
Exiles, 50, 162
Exodus story, 161, 182–83, 185
extreme skepticism, 124–25, 128, 227n. 1, 232n. 4

fall, 194
family, 88, 132–35, 142, 164, 166, 172, 189–92, 234n. 5, 234–35n. 6
family romance, 138–39, 142–43, 152–53, 158, 160–61, 166, 181
father-son relationship, 134–36, 142, 145, 152, 179, 180
fictions, 206–8, 219
Fielding, Henry, 10
Finnegans Wake, 228n. 8
fire, 200–201
Flaubert, Gustave, 32, 194
Fortuna, 236–37n. 4
Foucault, 224n. 2
Four Quartets, 195–201, 230n. 5, 238n. 2
fragments, 219–20
fraud, xi, xii
Freccero, John, 15–16, 20, 170–71, 239n. 5
Freudian philosophy, 3–4, 146, 148, 159, 203–4, 205, 224n. 2, 233n. 1
Froula, Christine, 50–51, 62, 104, 147

Genesis, 155
Gibraltar, 156–57
gigantism, 110, 113, 115
God, 15, 19; as imagination, 208
goddesses, 147–48
Gold Cup, 11, 12, 178
Goldberg, S. L., 14, 168

Gould, Stephen Jay, 45
gravity, 7, 32, 37, 49, 51–53, 83, 127, 156, 178, 235–36n. 2
Greek culture; compared with Jewish culture, 231n. 8
Groden, Michael, 67–69, 76, 83–84, 110–11, 113
Guattari, Felix, 159, 234n. 4
Guinicelli, xii–xiii

hallucinations, 144–52; of Leopold Bloom, 145–50; of Stephen Dedalus, 145, 150–52
Hamlet, 142, 145, 159, 160
Hardy, Thomas, 32
harp image, 185
Harris, Frank, 85
Hart, Clive, 92
Hartman, Geoffrey, 18
Hassen, Ihab, 22–23, 66
Hayman, David, 37, 77, 131
Hebrew tradition, 155
Hellenic tradition, 155
heroism, xiv, xv, 7, 123, 130, 148, 149, 156, 161, 202, 206, 233n. 2
Herring, Philip, 27–28, 105, 111, 129
Hebrew prophets, 212–15, 216–17
historical imagination, 76
history, xiv–xv, 40, 151, 152, 153, 164, 193, 197, 200, 202, 205–6, 208–9, 217–20, 224n. 2, 227n. 4; of the novel, 124, 129, 130, 132, 133, 143, 151, 162–63, 193–95, 227n. 4, 232n. 4; and spirit, 43
Hollander, Robert, 10, 15, 231n. 8
Holy Spirit, the, 200
home, ix, x, 155, 158, 164, 185–87, 205, 223–24n. 1, 233n. 3
Homer, xii, 24–25, 143, 153–57, 163, 194, 212
Horace, xii
Hosea, 188
Howells, William Dean, 32
Hulme, T. E., 29, 64–67, 71, 167, 169–71, 173, 184, 229nn. 2, 3
human vs. divine, 170, 180, 201

humanism, 65, 70, 83, 88, 121, 143, 169, 194, 225n. 4, 239n. 3
hypostasis, 30

ideal, 2, 7, 18, 127, 141, 178, 208, 218, 231n. 8
idealism, 6, 125, 126, 130, 172, 226n. 7
identity, 111–12, 129, 156
Iliad, 163
illusions, 203–5
imagination, 202–7, 217
imagism, 199, 201
Incarnation, xv, 9, 15–16, 28, 30–31, 36–37, 42, 44, 46–47, 140, 145, 166–67, 170–72, 177, 179, 181, 183, 188, 191, 192, 195, 197, 199–201, 208, 214, 217–21, 224n. 2, 227n. 3, 228n. 6, 230–31n. 7, 233n. 2, 235n. 2, 236n. 3, 238n. 2; and women, 63
Inferno, x–xi, xii, xiv, 153, 157, 235–36n. 2, 236–37n. 4, 239n. 5
infidelity, 61, 78–79, 234n. 5
interior consciousness, 128, 143
interior monologue, 8, 91, 103, 111, 123, 143
"intonation *secreto*," 182
Irish nationalism, 73, 75
irony, 5
Isaiah, 179, 213, 225n. 6

James, Henry, 194
jealousy, 162
Jeremiah, 188, 213
Jesus. *See* Christ
John of the Cross, Saint, 6
"Journey of the Magi, The," 196
Joyce, James; letters to Nora, 228n. 7; in relation to Pound, Eliot, and Stevens, 218; and Saint Paul, 68
just city, the, 214–16

Kaplan, Louise J., 147
Kazantzakis, Nikos, 153
Kenner, Hugh, 25, 62, 83, 96, 99, 122, 138, 144–45, 152, 173–74, 226n. 6

Kermode, Frank, 22, 178, 225–26n. 6, 237n. 6
Kernan, Tom, 20

language, x–xv, 2, 5, 18, 25–27, 72, 76, 96, 106–7, 114–16, 118–19, 125, 126, 128, 131–32, 135, 141, 154, 155, 165–66, 169, 231n. 1, 232n. 3; failure of, 123
Lawrence, Karen, 1, 21, 38, 99, 121, 130, 223n. 1
Lawrence, T. E., 163
Lee, Sidney, 85
Lethe, 211, 216–17, 239n. 5
Levenson, Michael, 65, 229n. 2
Levine, George, 14, 32, 38, 45–46
Leviticus, 213
Lewis, Wyndham, 39, 229n. 1
literal dimension of reality, 12
Little Review, 68–69, 76, 218
Litz, Walton, 67–68, 173
Longenbah, James, 202, 238–39n. 3
lotus flower, 53–54
love, 165, 169, 187–88
Lucan, xii
Lukacs, George, 168, 194, 238n. 1
Lynch, William, 28, 42, 137, 220, 226n. 7
Lyons, Bantam, 11
Lyotard, Jean-Françios, 25–26, 47, 97–98, 106–7, 109, 219, 232n. 3

MacDowell, Gerty, 123, 125–30, 132, 172
Madame Bovary, 123
Maddox, James, 99, 120, 168–70, 173, 184
Magnus, Albertus, 230n. 5
Makin, Peter, 209
Malachi, 180, 230n. 6
Malory, 136
Mangall, Richard, 173
Mangan, James Clarence, 6
Marryat, Frederick, 230n. 6
Marx, Karl, 3–4, 189, 224n. 2
Mary, Blessed Virgin, 123–24, 127, 138, 151, 188

materialism, 188–89
McKeon, Richard, 124–25, 127, 132–33, 226–27n. 1, 232n. 4
Meisel, Perry, ix–x, 9, 24–25, 143, 155
memory, 20–22, 54, 62, 79–82, 102–3, 136–40, 157, 171–72, 191–92, 196, 197–200, 209–12, 229–30nn. 4, 5, 232–33n. 5, 238n. 2
Messiah, the, 12
Micah, 214–15
Miller, Perry, 214
mockery, 22, 133, 225n. 5, 227n. 3
modernism, 5, 24, 153, 177, 193, 218–20, 211, 224n. 2, 227nn. 2, 3, 233n. 2, 238n. 1
modernist allegory, xiv, 5, 14–15, 20, 24, 27, 121, 177, 189, 194, 195, 197, 201, 216–18, 220, 227n. 3, 228n. 6, 230n. 5, 232n. 3, 238n. 1, 239n. 3
moments, 197–99, 201
monologue method, 84
Montaigne, Michel, 225n. 4
Moses, 12
mourning, house of, 122–23
Mulligan, Buck, 3, 19–20, 24, 30–31, 36, 42, 54, 59, 89–91, 104, 124, 133, 142, 150, 166, 167, 178, 181, 183, 227n. 1, 230n. 6, 231n. 8
Mulligan, Malachi, 180
Mulligan's Song, 37
Murphy, D. B., 154–57
music, 101–8, 130
Mussolini, 209

"naive empiricism," 124–26, 128, 226–27n. 1, 232n. 4
nameless "I," 110, 112–13, 116, 125
narrative, 178
nativity, 140
naturalism, xiv, xv, 5, 12, 14, 19–20, 32–33, 37, 39–40, 41–42, 45–49, 52, 58, 60, 62, 66, 77, 81, 91, 92, 94–95, 112, 121–22, 127–30, 131, 135, 143, 165–67, 168, 173–74, 227n. 4, 229n. 4, 232n. 5, 238n. 8

Nazism, 227n. 4
necessary angel, 207–8
negative midpoint, 125
New Criticism, 17
Newman, Cardinal, 139
Nietzsche, Friedrich, 3–4, 39, 81, 224n. 2, 229–30n. 4, 232n. 3, 233n. 3
nobility, xiv, 141, 149, 193, 203–4, 217, 227n. 2, 233n. 2
"Noble Rider and the Sound of Words, The," 203–4
Nora, 161, 163, 228n. 7
nostalgia, 25, 81, 107, 219, 233n. 3
Nostos, 153, 155, 164
Notes toward a Supreme Fiction, ix, 201–8, 227n. 2, 239n. 3
novel, xiv, 1, 7, 10, 121, 193–95, 226–27n. 1, 234n. 3; epic theme of, 163–64; history of: *see* history, of the novel

Odysseus (Homer), 53–54, 122, 142, 153, 154–56, 157, 210, 212, 223n. 1, 234n. 3, 234–35n. 6
Odyssey, The, 142–43, 153, 155–56, 163, 186, 205, 234–35n. 6
Oedipal family, 159
Old Testament. *See* Bible, the, Old Testament
openness, 22–23, 28
order, 27, 174–75, 219, 226n. 6
Ovid, xii, 194

parables, 225–26n. 6
Paradiso, xii, xv, 127, 128, 237n. 4
Parts of a World, 201–2
passivity, 50–51, 62, 80, 82, 104, 144, 150, 161–62, 231–32n. 2
Paul, Saint, xv, 8, 10–11, 15, 19, 20, 111, 116, 118, 120, 166, 180, 213, 216, 218, 226n. 6
Penelope, 234–35n. 6
Pentecost, 201
"poet, the," 210
Perl, Jeffery, 8, 9–10, 39, 46, 158–59, 163

personal moments in Pound, 211–12
perversity, 50, 62, 104, 144–50, 158–59
Pisan Cantos, The, 149, 208–18
play, 176–77, 190, 229–30n. 4
plot vs. character, 168
poet vs. pilgrim, 170
Polyphemus, 110–11, 122, 210
Portrait of the Artist as a Young Man, A, 33–34, 65, 77, 90–91, 150, 161, 190, 229n. 3, 237n. 7
postmodernism, 9, 23–27, 45, 81, 176–77, 219, 232n. 3
poststructuralism, 2, 5, 9, 18, 97, 131, 166, 168, 224n. 2, 230n. 4, 231n. 1, 232n. 4
Pound, Ezra, 5, 29, 64, 149, 153, 193–95, 208–17, 218, 224n. 2, 233n. 2, 238n. 1, 239n. 5; and history, 209; and memory, 209–12; and Mussolini, 209, 214; politics in, 209, 216
Pound's Epic Ambition, 153
psychoanalytic perspective, 50, 104
Purgatorio, xii, xiii, xiv, 147, 182, 210–11, 224n. 3, 236n. 2
parody, 110–13, 115, 120, 126–27, 129, 132–33, 138, 169

Quinones, Ricardo, 38, 43, 229n. 2

Rabelais, François, 113–16, 225n. 4
readers, power of, 17–22, 176, 177, 179, 231–32n. 2
reading, act of, 99, 121
realism, 8, 167, 217, 238n. 1
reductionism, 1, 31–32, 37, 204
rereadings, 30, 136, 232–33n. 5
retrospective arrangement, 171, 232–33n. 5
retrospective illumination, 16, 20
return home. *See* home
Revelation, Book of, 149
rhetoric, xi, 125, 172–73, 178
Rickard, John S., ix, 20–21, 136, 138, 192, 230n. 5
Riordan, Mrs., 237n. 7

Roman Catholic Church. *See* Catholic Church
Roman Catholic Mass. *See* Catholic Mass
romance heroism, 127
romance idealism, 124–26, 128, 130, 226–27n. 1
romantic language, 123
romanticism, 6–8, 41–42, 84, 98, 112, 123, 124, 130, 193, 203–4, 217
roses, 128
Rosevean, 156
Rouse, 212
Ruskin, 140

schizophrenia, 237n. 5
"special moments," 196
Schwarz, Daniel, 1, 121, 168, 184, 223n. 1
science, 124, 173
scientific empiricism, 130
sea, 157
secrecy, 226n. 6, 237n. 6
Senn, Fritz, 25, 130
sentimental romance, 123, 127
sentimentalism, 125–28, 154–55
sexual guilt, 146
sexual perversion, 147–48
sexuality, 172
Shakespeare, William, 225n. 4
Siebers, Tobin, 4–5, 9, 23–24, 36, 97, 125, 205, 219, 224n. 2, 225n. 5, 232n. 4
signification, 176, 232n. 3
Singleton, Charles, xiii, 13, 27, 182–83, 216, 236n. 3
skepticism, 125, 128, 205, 227n. 3, 231n. 1, 232n. 4
soldiers, British, 151, 158
Sordello, xii
Stanford, W. B., ix, 153, 157–58
stars, 183, 185–86
Statius, xii
Stephen Hero, 6–7, 30, 33, 41, 66, 224–25n. 3
Stevens, Wallace, ix, 5, 29, 33, 153, 193, 201–8, 224n. 2, 227n. 2, 238–39n. 3; fiction of unity, 202, 205–8; and imagination, 202–8; and nobility, 203–5, 207–8; possible poet, 204
storyness, 99, 104, 106
stream of consciousness, 40, 67, 69
structuralism, 4, 224n. 2, 229n. 4
style, 22, 26, 99–101, 103–4, 106, 121, 129–32, 136, 168–69, 189–90
Sultan, Stanley, 99, 129, 168
sunset, 210
Swedenborg, Emanuel, 6
symbolism, 38–39, 71, 126, 129, 151, 159, 161, 164, 166, 168, 173, 184, 190

Tanner, Toby, 162–63, 234n. 5
Telemachus, 156
telos, 121
Tennyson, 157
theory, critical, 130
Thomas, Brook, 59, 68, 99, 130–31, 168
throwaway, 11, 12, 17, 58, 93–94, 119–20, 140, 180, 212, 236n. 4
time, 130, 197–98, 202; and space, 226n. 7, 229n. 1
Torah, the, 213
totalitarianism, 4, 23–24, 218, 219, 220, 227n. 4, 234n. 4
Toulmin, Stephen, 8, 225n. 4
tradition, 164
tragedy, 209
transcendental signified, 165–66, 175, 177, 183
triangle figure, 184
truth, xi, xii, xiv, xv, 26–27, 122, 124, 125, 126, 134–36, 139, 141, 143, 165–66, 167, 181, 192

Ugolino, 209, 210, 239n. 5
Ulysses (Dante), x, 153, 157, 164
uniformitarianism, 45
unity, 24, 218–19
useless, 129

van Boheemen, Christine, ix

Virgil, xi–xii, 172
Vita Nuova, 21, 136, 171–72, 191–92, 232–33n. 5
Vulgate, 150

wanderer theme, 210–13
Waste Land, The, 24, 195–96, 218
Watt, Ian, 10, 226–27n. 1
wheel image, 218
White, Haydan, 205
widow Dignam. *See* Dignam, widow
Wilson, Edmund, 14, 168
woman, role of, 162–63, 234–35n. 6

Wordsworth, William, 40–41
World War I, 217, 218
World War II, 23, 29, 193, 195, 197, 200, 202–3, 217, 219, 238–39n. 3
Worringer, Wilhelm, 65

Yates, Frances, 21–22, 192, 198, 230n. 5, 238n. 2
Yeats, William Butler, 36, 225n. 5

Zion, 213, 215
Zola, Emile, 32